Translation Performance, Translation Process, and Translation Strategies

Language in Performance **4**

Edited by Werner Hüllen and Rainer Schulze

Wolfgang Lörscher

Translation Performance, Translation Process, and Translation Strategies

A Psycholinguistic Investigation

gnv Gunter Narr Verlag Tübingen

CIP-Titelaufnahme der Deutschen Bibliothek

Lörscher, Wolfgang:
Translation performance, translation process, and translation strategies : a psycholinguistic investigation / Wolfgang Lörscher. – Tübingen : Narr, 1991
(Language in performance ; 4)
ISBN 3-8233-4074-3

NE: GT

Als Habilitationsschrift auf Empfehlung des Fachbereichs 3 (Literatur- und Sprachwissenschaften) der Universität Gesamthochschule Essen publiziert mit Unterstützung der Deutschen Forschungsgemeinschaft.

Gedruckt auf säurefreiem und alterungsbeständigem Werkdruckpapier.

Druck: Müller + Bass, Tübingen
Verarbeitung: Braun + Lamparter, Reutlingen
Printed in Germany

ISBN 3-8233-4074-3

Table of Contents

List of Diagrams

Preface

This study marks the preliminary termination of a research project which I carried out at the University of Essen, Federal Republic of Germany, between 1982 and 1987. The aim of this project was to develop a methodology for investigating the mental translation process and to analyze it in specific ways.

The present monograph is based on my professorial dissertation (*Habilitationsschrift*) which was accepted by the Department of Literature and Linguistics at the University of Essen. The original German manuscript was slightly revised, adapted for publication, and translated into English.

This book would not exist without the assistance of people to whom I owe a debt of gratitude. Students of Essen University as well as pupils from various schools kindly agreed to act as subjects and thus provided the data basis for the investigation. I can only express my sincerest thanks for their cooperation.

Furthermore, I am grateful to Rupprecht S. Baur, Hans W. Dechert, René Dirven, Claus Færch, Juliane House-Edmondson, Gabriele Kasper, Karlfried Knapp, and Hans P. Krings for critical comments and helpful suggestions. Without their expert knowledge and competence, this book would certainly not be quite the same.

I would like to express my special thanks and gratitude to Werner Hüllen on whose suggestion I undertook the study of performance analysis. He read and commented on the various drafts of the manuscript and often made me reflect on and alter parts of both the theoretical background and the practical analysis of this study. In numerous discussions with him I was able to profit a great deal from his vast knowledge and experience of the domain of the investigation as well as of neighbouring disciplines.

Last but not least, I owe great thanks to Richard J. Brunt whose native-speaker competence in English was of immense help to me, and made me re-write and improve parts of the manuscript to make them sound more English.

In spite of all the assistance I received, it goes without saying that any incorrections or deficiencies in this book are the sole responsibility of the author.

This book could not have been written without the constant patience and understanding of my family to whom it is dedicated with gratitude.

The Author.

1 Introduction

Communication across language boundaries has never been more important and necessary than today. The worldwide interdependence in such areas as the economy, culture, politics, and science requires a continuous exchange of information. This is brought about by communication systems which span the world and provide information in spoken or written form. Under these circumstances translation – besides foreign language learning – plays an extremely important role. That society does indeed attach a high value to translation follows from at least four facts (cf. Krings 1986a: 1):

i. In social reality translation is a very widespread form of (interlingual) language use. Every day, a multitude of documents, specialist texts, literary products, letters, instructions, etc. are translated to make communication possible or easier.

ii. For a very long time translation has been an object of academic reflection. This becomes evident from the huge number of publications listed in the relevant bibliographies[1].

iii. For many years the scientific investigation of translation has been an established and institutionalised academic discipline in many countries.

iv. The training of translators takes place in special, institutionally organised societal subsystems (universities, special colleges, or the like). There are specific courses of study and final examinations.

1.1 Object of Investigation and the Relevant Research Discipline

The object of this investigation is translation performance as it is to be found empirically in a corpus of data. Translation performance as part of the comprehensive subject of translation will be investigated with a specific interest and aim. Accordingly, this study ought to be situated within the domain of translation theory. But this discipline, until very recently, has been primarily concerned with two phenomena: with translation as a *product* and with translation *competence*:

---

1 Bausch/Klegraf/Wilss 1970 and 1971; van Hoof 1973; Lehmann 1982.

– Translation as a product, i.e. a written text in a target-language (TL) as the result of a translation process, has traditionally been described and analyzed by a comparison with the respective source-language (SL) text (cf. Harris 1977: 106; Königs 1987: 163; Toury 1980b: 103). The relation between the SL text and the TL text has been dealt with in a large number of different and highly theoretical models of equivalence[2]. By and large, these models have been *prescriptive* rather than *descriptive* (cf. Levý 1967: 1179; Toury 1979; 1980b) and of very limited use to the practical translator.

– Translation theory was mainly competence-oriented and focussed on (professional) translators' internalised knowledge. The models of translation were theoretical and speculative rather than empirical and concentrated on idealizations rather than on actually occurring data. (cf. Toury 1980a: 41).

As a consequence of translation theory being product- and competence-oriented, hardly any attention has been given to the *process* by which a translation is produced, and to translators' actual performance (cf. Reiß/Vermeer 1984: 41; Krings 1986a: 2ff.). This narrowing of the object and the dimensions in which it is investigated have only recently been realized to be a deficit. As a result, the first approaches to a new type of translation-procedural and performance-analytical research are beginning to take shape[3]. The present study can be situated within this newly developing research paradigm. With respect to its object and – as will be shown later – to its epistemological interest and its methodology, it does not fall into the traditional paradigm of translation theory.

1.2 Aim, Epistemological Interest, And Scientific Approach

In view of the state of translation theory, as outlined in section 1.1, the aim of the study is as follows:

> On the basis of a corpus of orally produced translations, the linguistic *performance* of translators will be investigated. This will be done in order to reconstruct translation *strategies*. These underlie translation performance, operate within the (mental) translation *process*, and are thus not open to direct inspection. The translation strategies reconstructed in this way will first be analyzed *qualitatively*. With respect to their internal structures, they will be

2 Cf. van den Broeck 1978; Koller 1978; 1979/[2]1983: 95; Ladmiral 1981: 393; Newman 1980: especially 35ff.; Stolze 1982: 167ff.; Toury 1978; 1979; 1980a; b; 1981; Wilss 1977: 156ff.

3 Cf. Dechert/Sandrock 1986; Feldmann/Stemmer 1987; Gerloff 1986; Hölscher/Möhle 1987; Krings 1986a; b; Lörscher 1986; 1987; Sandrock 1982.

classified into types of strategies and they will be formalised into a model of analysis. As a next stage, the translation strategies will be analyzed *quantitatively*, i.e. with respect to their frequency and distribution in the data corpus.

The translations constituting the data corpus were produced exclusively by non-professional translators, because of the hypothesis that every individual with a command of two or more languages also possesses a rudimentary ability to mediate between these languages (cf. Chapter 4). One aim of this investigation is to furnish proof of this hypothesized basic ability to mediate. My epistemological interest, which combines with the aim of the investigation, is of a primarily psycholinguistic kind. In psycholinguistics it is common practice to investigate linguistic performance in order to gain specific insights into the underlying mental processes (cf. Olson/Clark 1976: 27; Foss/Hakes 1978: 18; Garnham 1985: 1ff.; Prideaux 1985).

My investigation follows the same procedural approach. This study analyzes translation performance as it is to be found in a corpus of data. Thus it takes an empirical approach to its object of investigation, an approach which is usual in performance analysis. Furthermore, it makes use of the method of interpretive reconstruction, a method which is also widely used in that discipline. On the basis of the epistemological interest of this study, its aim, and the hypothetical assumptions made, the mental translation strategies used by the translators will be recorded, described, and analyzed by a specific sense-constitution in the data.

2 Structure of the Study

This study is divided into nine chapters. Following the introduction (Chapter 1) and these remarks on the structure of the study (Chapter 2), it will be shown in Chapter 3 that – and why – the investigation of the translation process is still largely a desideratum. Various models of the translation process will be discussed and critically evaluated with respect to the aim of this investigation.

Chapter 4 deals with the fundamental principles of performance-analytical research into the translation process. The introductory remarks (4.1) are followed by considerations on the empirical investigation of translation performance (4.2). The hypothetical construct of a universal rudimentary ability to mediate, which is considered to be the basis of all translating, will be discussed and critically reflected on in 4.3. Section 4.4 deals with the methodology of performance-analytical investigations in general, and with that of the present one in particular. The chapter is closed by considerations on the notion and on the various concepts of strategy, leading to a specific definition of translation strategy (4.5).

Chapter 5 focusses on the empirical investigation of the translation process. After the introductory remarks (5.1), a model for the strategic analysis of translations will be developed on the basis of actually performed translations (5.2). It consists of translation strategies, of their elements, and of translation versions. The model is applied to four translations and detailed qualitative analyses are made and commented on (5.3).

The essential results yielded by the qualitative analysis are analyzed quantitatively in Chapter 6. The introductory remarks (6.1) are followed by a quantitative analysis of the translation *problems* of the corpus (6.2). The translation *strategies* are analyzed quantitatively according to their structural types as regards their frequency, distribution and success in solving problems (6.3). Select elements of translation strategies are analyzed in the same way. Chapter 6 is terminated by an investigation of individually caused differences in strategy use and by a summarizing comparison of strategies for translation *into* and *from* the mother tongue.

Hypothetical assumptions on the translation process resulting from the qualitative and the quantitative analysis of the data, will be outlined in Chapter 7. Thus translation can be considered a retrospective-prospective process (7.1) which is largely controlled by an expectation structure (7.2) and which ranges between an interlingual exchange of signs and a mediation of sense (7.3).

At the end of this study some concluding remarks are made (Chapter 8) and a bibliography (Chapter 9) and index (Chapter 10) are appended.

3 Investigating the Translation Process

In section 1.1, theses on translation theory were presented and critically evaluated with respect to their relevance for the aim of this study. It was stated that translation theory can by and large be characterized as *prescriptive*, *competence-oriented* and *product-oriented*. Descriptive, performance- and process-oriented approaches to translation are hardly more than a desideratum at the moment. The *empirical* investigation of the translation *process* seems to be especially important for three reasons:

1. As far as the psycholinguistic investigation of translation is concerned, it can be expected that only on the basis of empirical studies of translation performance using a process-analytical approach can hypotheses on what goes on in the translator's head be formed. Thus, light could be shed on translation as a mental process which is still largely unknown and uninvestigated (cf. Smelcer et al. 1980; Koller 1981; Swain et al. 1974; Mininni 1981).

2. As far as psycholinguistic investigation in general is concerned, it can be expected that empirical studies of translation performance will yield general insights into language processing, about aspects of the mental processes of speech reception and speech production and about the mental strategies employed by the language user.

3. As far as the teaching of translation is concerned, it should be possible to make use of knowledge of the translation process for teaching translation. If certain translation strategies turn out to be successful, it might be worth considering teaching these strategies in one way or another[1].

This study mainly focusses on the first of the above-mentioned reasons, since aspects of translation as a mental process are the primary object of the investigatlon.

3.1 Models of the Translation Process

Within the domain of translation theory, reflections have sometimes been made on the translation process and models have been constructed. They try to capture those components of the translation process which the authors consider to be especially relevant in respect of their own specific epistemological

---

1 Cf. Krings 1986a: 500ff.

interest. In the following sections such models of the translation process will be outlined and evaluated on two – partly overlapping – dimensions:

i. on an *internal* dimension; The models will be examined as to their exactness and simplicity[2] and with a view to assessing the quality and coherence of the model components and their assumed interplay.

ii. on an *external* dimension; On the one hand, the models will be examined as to their similarity[3] to their object. The question as to whether these models have any psychological reality is of central importance here. To what extent can the models capture the mental processes which occur in the human translator in real time? On the other hand, the models will be examined as to whether they can be used as a theoretical framework for this study, given its specific aim and epistemological interest.

3.1.1 Diller/Kornelius

The first model of the translation process to be discussed here was developed by Diller and Kornelius (1978: 16f.). The following diagram represents the model graphically:

Diagram 1: Diller and Kornelius' Model

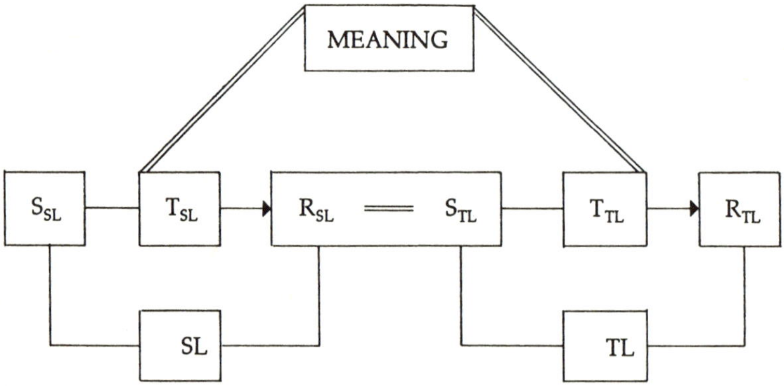

According to this model, a sender (S) produces a text (T) in a source-language (SL). The translator functions both as a source-language receiver (R_{SL}) of the source-language text (T_{SL}) and as a target-language sender (S_{TL}) who produces a target-language text (T_{TL}) for a target-language receiver (R_{TL}). The crucial criteria for the TL text to be a translation of the SL text are a change of the

2 Cf. Stachiowak 1965

3 Cf. Stachowiak 1965.

linguistic code (SL → TL) and the equivalence of meaning of the two texts. Thus, equivalence of meaning functions as the constant factor both inter*lingually* and inter*textually*. According to Diller and Kornelius, meaning comprises seven components (1978: 16):

i. the object a text-segment[4] refers to;
ii. the kind of reference;
iii. the features, qualities, etc. ascribed to the object by a text-segment;
iv. the kind of ascription;
v. the illocutionary force of the text-segment;
vi. the way in which the illocutionary force is realized in the text-segment;
vii. the intended characteristics of the illocutionary act.

The enumeration of these components shows that meaning, according to Diller and Kornelius, comprises much more than semantics. An SL text and a TL text can only be considered to be equivalent in meaning when they are semantically (components i., iii.), pragmatically (component v.) and stylistically (components ii., iv., vi., vii.) equivalent (cf. Diller/Kornelius 1978: 10, 16).

A. *Internal Criticism*

i. Diller and Kornelius' broad and complex concept of meaning leads to serious problems for translating. According to the authors' definition, a translation is considered to be adequate when it has the same reference, the same predication and the same illocution as the original (Diller/Kornelius 1978: 10). Thus, for a translation to be *adequate*, fewer conditions have to be fulfilled than the seven components of meaning listed above. The latter have to be taken into account by the translator during the translation *process*. This leads to contradictions because an inadequate translation resulting from a translation process could nonetheless correspond exactly with the source-language text in all its components of meaning. Diller and Kornelius' definition of a translation implies serious problems, too. According to their definition, two texts such as

1a E pericoloso sporgersi
1b Nicht hinauslehnen

or 2a Keep off the grass
2b Betreten des Rasens verboten

would *not* be considered adequate translations. Although they correspond to each other as regards their illocutions – they are prohibitions – as well as their implicit references, they contain different predications.

---

4 The term 'text-segment' is used to denote a stretch of text of principally variable length, which can only be determined in any particular case. Text-segments can be part of lexemes, lexemes, syntagmas, phrases, clauses, sentences, and (rarely in my data) combinations of sentences.

In contrast to this view, it is a matter of fact that the translations 1b and 2b as well as 1a and 2a are the conventional modes of realization of a specific prohibition in the respective language and culture. To deny texts 1b and 2b the status of adequate translations would mean to exclude texts from the domain of translations which are generally and sensibly considered to belong to it[5].

Diller and Kornelius are probably aware of the problems inherent in their definition of a translation because, in connection with stylistic and text-type conventions, they discuss texts similar to 1b and 2b under the heading of translation. The contradiction to the inadequate definition remains, however. It ignores the fact that the same illocutionary act can be realized in semantically (propositionally) different ways.

ii. A further problem in Diller and Kornelius' approach is the fact that the semantic meaning, which the authors consider to be part of the entire meaning, has the status of an inter*lingual* and inter*textual* constant. According to Catford (1965: 35), however,

> *... the view that SL and TL texts 'have the same meaning' or that 'transference of meaning' occurs in translation is untenable. ... Meaning, in our view, is a property of a language. An SL text has an SL meaning, and a TL text has a TL meaning. ... This is necessarily the case, since, following Firth, we define meaning as the total network of relations entered into by any linguistic form – text, item-in-text, structure, element of structure, class, term in system – or whatever it may be.*

In Catford's view, languages are self-contained systems of meaning because of those different forms, structures, etc. quoted above, which constitute meaning. This is why a full transference of meaning from one language to another (= total translation) is generally not possible. Therefore, the task of a translation must be

> *... to select TL equivalents not with 'the same meaning' as the SL items, but with the greatest possible overlap of situational range.* (Catford 1965: 49)

Or, in other words,

> *... SL and TL texts or items are translation equivalents when they are interchangeable in a given situation.*

---

5 Newmark (1977, 1981, 1982) distinguishes between *communicative* and *semantic* translation. The former type "*attempts to produce on its readers an effet as close as possible to that obtained on the readers of the original.*" (1977: 164). The *meaning* (and form) of the SL text and its elements is subordinate to the main *function* of the translation, i.e. to produce on its readers an effect similar or equal to that which the SL text produced on the SL addressees. "*Semantic translation*", on the other hand, "*attempts to render as closely as the semantic and syntactic structures of the second language allow, the exact contextual meaning of the original*" (1977: 164). The rendering of the meaning (and form) of the SL text in the target-language is the principal aim of the translation, whereas the similarity or sameness of effect of the SL- or TL-text on its addressees only plays a subordinate role. (Cf. also House ^{2}1981: 188ff. who distinguishes between *covert* and *overt translation.*

The view that different languages possess different systems of meaning, and that meaning, therefore, cannot function as a constant in translation, is also taken by Coseriu (1978, 1980: 47ff.). He considers the function of translation to be

> *einen gleichen Textinhalt in verschiedenen Sprachen auszudrücken. Da nun die einzelsprachlichen Inhalte verschieden sind, der 'übersetzte' Inhalt aber 'der gleiche' sein muß, kann dieser Inhalt auch nicht einzelsprachlich, sondern nur übereinzelsprachlich sein.* (Coseriu 1978: 20)

As to the linguistic content (*sprachlicher Inhalt*), Coseriu distinguishes between three main types:

a. meaning (*Bedeutung*); this is the linguistic content which is exclusively given by an individual language, "*die Gesamtheit dessen, was allein ... durch eine bestimmte Sprache verstanden wird ...*" (1980: 47; for a different view cf. Frege 1969b: 41ff.)

b. denotation *(Bezeichnung)*; this is the reference to an extra-linguistic fact, "*... der Bezug auf die außersprachliche 'Sache', auf den außersprachlichen 'Sachverhalt' oder 'Tatbestand', bzw. das außersprachlich Gemeinte selbst. Die Bezeichnung ist zwar nur über sprachliche Bedeutungen erreichbar, sie fällt aber keineswegs mit der Bedeutung zusammen.* (1980: 20; for a different view cf. Frege 1969b: 41ff.)

c. sense *(Sinn)*; this is the special content communicated by a text, "*der besondere Inhalt eines Textes oder einer Texteinheit, soweit dieser Inhalt nicht einfach mit der Bedeutung und mit der Bezeichnung zusammenfällt.* (1978: 21) *... die Gesamtheit dessen, was gerade durch den Text und nur durch den Text verstanden wird ...* (1980: 47; for a different view cf. Frege 1969b: 41)

Thus, sense (as the contents of a text) and denotation (as the reference to extralinguistic facts) are not bound to an individual language. The task of translation must therefore be to convey the same denotation and the same sense into another language by means of the meaning of that language (cf. Coseriu 1978: 21).

By postulating the same sense and denotation for a source-language text and its translation, Coseriu places the century-old question of the theoretical and practical possibilities or impossibilities of translation (cf. Koller 1979: 134ff.; Albrecht 1973: 5ff.; Winter 1961, ^{2}1971) into a new perspective. He rejects the examples put forward in support of the view that translation is generally not possible. Among such examples are the German word *Wald*, which, according to the protagonists of the impossibility of translation, cannot be rendered into Spanish or French. Another example is the German adjective *gemütlich*, which is said to have no translation equivalent at all. Coseriu takes these examples as indicative of a typical and unfortunate confusion of translation theory (cf. 1978: 26). He argues that translation cannot be expected to bring about what language in general cannot achieve. The feelings and associations connected with *Wald* are not evoked by the word *Wald* as such, but rather by the forests themselves as the 'things' the word refers to. The fact that these feelings and associations cannot be communicated is not a shortcoming of translation, but one of its natural limitations; a limitation which also applies to language in general. Or, as Coseriu (1978: 26) puts it:

> *Nicht all das in einem Text G e m e i n t e , sondern ... nur das in einem Text sprachlich G e s a g t e , d.h. das durch die Sprache in ihrer Zeichenfunktion A u s g e d r ü c k t e , das 'Verbalisierte', ist in dieser Hinsicht Gegenstand der Übersetzung und kann grundsätzlich übersetzt werden.* (Cf. Koschmieder 1965a, 1965b)

iii. Diller and Kornelius' postulate that an SL text and a TL text should have the same meaning in all its components and its entirety can only be considered to be utopian[6]. The prescriptive, competence-oriented nature of the model becomes evident here. The authors refer to the concept of *translation equivalence*, a concept whose nature is highly controversial in translation theory[7], and which Diller and Kornelius equate with *equivalence of meaning*, in the allembracing fashion defined above. In order to make the model capture reality better, a twofold reduction of Diller and Kornelius' 'strong' concept of equivalence is necessary:

First, the postulate that an SL text and a TL text should have exactly the same meaning in all its dimensions must be abandoned. Rather, certain aspects of meaning could be concentrated on and expressed in an optimal way, according to the goal(s) of the translation. A model with such a modification would be an approximation to functional translation theories[8]. Equivalence would thus be a hierarchical concept with the different levels of the hierarchy resulting from the goal(s) of the translation[9]. Such a 'weak' concept of equivalence could much more adequately capture the practice of translation than the unrealistic postulate of an entire sameness of meaning. **Second**, the postulate of translation equivalence (in the sense of the 'weak' concept, as outlined above) must also take into account the specifics and requirements of the respective text type[10]. Furthermore, Reiß (1984: 87) points out that, on the different levels of a text, equivalence cannot be realized in the same way,

---

6 Cf. also the criticism outlined in ii. above and Dressler 1972.

7 Cf. Koller 1978, 1979, ^{2}1983: 176–191; Königs 1981: 84ff.; Reiß 1984; Reiß/Vermeer 1984: 124–170; Wilss 1977: 157–191; van den Broeck 1978. There is neither unanimity about what equivalence is, nor how to proceed in order to get to an adequate TL text being the result of a translation process.

8 Cf. Hönig/Kußmaul 1982; Reiß/Vermeer 1984; House ^{2}1981.

9 Cf. Reiß 1984: 86ff.

10 Cf. Reiß 1976, 1984; Reiß/Vermeer 1984.

> ... *daß es Äquivalenz zwischen AT* (Ausgangstext, source-text; W.L.) *und ZT* (Zieltext, target-text; W.L.) *auf verschiedenen Ebenen eines Textes als Kommunikationsmittel gibt. Die einzelnen Elemente auf den verschiedenen Ebenen können aufgrund der Verschiedenheiten der Sprachen und der soziokulturellen Einbettung der Kommunikation in den meisten Fällen nicht invariant und nicht alle zugleich äquivalent gehalten werden.*

B. External Criticism

As to the psychological reality of their process model, Diller and Kornelius (1978: 17) point out:

> *Fig. 1* (i.e. diagram 1; W.L.) *stellt korrekt die Tatsache dar, daß wir es beim Übersetzen immer mit dem Übersetzen bereits vorhandener Texte zu tun haben. Über den eigentlichen Übersetzungsvorgang, der sich im (hier mit $E_{AS} = S_{ZS}$ bezeichneten) Übersetzer vollzieht, sagt sie jedoch nichts, außer daß die Bedeutung des AS-Textes mit der des ZS-Textes identisch zu sein habe.*

Two remarks must be made about this view of the authors:

i. It may well be a fact that professional translators work with texts only and that texts (not sentences or words) are the material for translating. This is far less so with the subjects whom I have investigated and who do not possess an elaborated translation competence but only a rudimentary ability to mediate (cf. section 4.3). As the collected data suggest, the textuality of the material to be translated often plays only a minor role. For non-professional translators, sentences, clauses, phrases, or even single words often represent the units of translation[11] which they try to convey as a whole into the respective target-language.

ii. As the authors admit, their model cannot capture the *mental translation process* which takes place in the translator's brain. So Diller and Kornelius do not say anything about the mental processes of the translator receiving and interpreting a source-language text, of transferring its meaning, or of producing the target-language text[12].

---

11 As to the concept of 'unit of translation' cf. Diller/Kornelius 1978: 21ff.; Kade 1968; Koller 1979, [2]1983: 116ff.; Königs 1981.

12 This enumeration should not suggest that reception, transfer, and production are phases with clear-cut borderlines which occur in a strict temporal sequence. As e.g. Hönig 1976; Hönig/Kußmaul 1982: 94 and Seleskovitch 1976 have pointed out, the translator's reception of the SL text is largely controlled by his/her activity as translator. S/he does not receive and process the SL text in a vacuum, but with a view to translating it. This coincides largely with the findings of psycholinguistics on text reception (cf. van Dijk/Kintsch 1983; Hörmann [2]1977; McDonough 1981: 40ff.; Ballstaedt et al. 1981; Rickheit/Strohner 1985), and on re-telling texts (which presupposes receiving and understanding them(cf. Kintsch 1974; Kintsch/Greene 1978; Hoppe-Graff 1984; Rumelhart 1975; Thorndyke 1977; Wolff 1985, n.d.).

From the remarks made above, it becomes clear that Diller and Kornelius' model cannot keep its claim of being a model of the translation *process*. It only states some of the factors involved in the translation process and shows their interplay as one would theoretically postulate it. However, *what* takes place in the translator's mental system and *how* it takes place there have not been considered.

3.1.2 Nida

Nida's model of the translation process is based on his hypothesis that

> *... a careful analysis of what goes on in the process of translating ... has shown that, instead of going directly from one set of surface structures to another, the competent translator actually goes through a seemingly roundabout process of analysis, transfer, and restructuring.* (Nida 1969: 484)

According to Nida, the phases involved in the translation process – Analysis, Transfer, Restructuring – can be schematically illustrated as follows (cf. Nida 1969: 484):

Diagram 2: Nida's Model

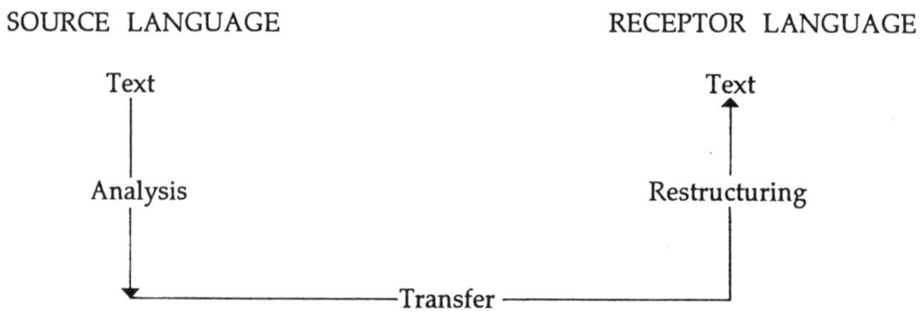

In the first phase, the translator analyzes the message of the source-language "... into its simplest and structurally clearest forms ..." (1969: 484). The analysis of the SL text has three aspects: grammatical, referential-semantic, and connotative.

In the **grammatical** analysis, surface structures are transformed back into kernels[13], following early transformational generative grammar[14]. In other words, complex language structures are transformed into simple ones by the translator. These back-transformations occur intuitively and aim at expressing

13 Although Nida gives no precise definition of what he means by *kernels*, he uses this notion in the sense of "... near-minimal structures at some point between the deep structure and the surface structure." (Nida 1969: 485)

14 Cf. Chomsky's 1957 model, as presented in *Syntactic Structures*.

the (syntactic) relations between the constituents "in the clearest and least ambiguous manner" (Nida 1969: 485).

The **referential-semantic** analysis delimits the potential range of meaning of lexical items, so that their specific meaning in the respective context can be exactly detected. The delimitation of meaning can be brought about in two ways:

First, by an analysis of the syntactic structure. Thus, for example, the lexeme *water* in the sentence "She drank the water" is unambiguously recognizable as a noun, whereas in the sentence "She will water the plants", it clearly functions as a verb. **Second**, by paying attention to the semotactic structure (i.e. collocations of lexemes). Thus, text segments can be semantically disambiguated. For example, when the lexeme *run* collocates with *man* or *dog*, its range of meaning is reduced to one segment, i.e. "pedal action of an animate being, involving relatively fast movements in space." (cf. Nida 1969: 490)

According to Nida, the analysis of the **connotative** component of meaning is primarily a stylistic one and comprises every linguistic unit from the sounds and sound configurations to the entire discourse. Connotative analysis does not, however, comprise "the emotive response to the thematic content of the communication", because "this is something outside the realm of linguistics ..." (Nida 1969: 491). In Nida's view, connotative analysis is problematic because

> *we cannot employ judgments based on binary contrasts of a positive or negative character.* [Therefore, W.L.] ... *the extent of difference in individual evaluation becomes much greater, but this should not be surprising or alarming. This is the very nature of stylistic analysis, namely, the wide differences of judgment by different persons, even trained professional critics.* (Nida 1969: 492)

Transfer is the second phase in the translation process. It operates on the level of the kernels or near-kernels[15], for two reasons:

First, the meanings and the meaning relations of the message to be transferred are more explicit in the simpler structures. **Second**, languages are much less distinct on the level of the kernels or near-kernels than on the structurally more complex levels. As a consequence, the message can be transferred in the exactest way possible on the level of the kernels or near-kernels (Nida 1969: 492).

In the transfer phase, three types of changes systematically occur vis-à-vis the SL text:

1. **complete redistribution**: This primarily concerns idiomatic expressions, such as English: *stowaway*; German: *blinder Passagier*;

15 What constitutes the difference between a *kernel* and a *near-kernel* is nowhere defined by Nida. Cf. also *A. Internal Criticism* later in this section.

2. **analytical redistribution**: This occurs when a single lexeme in the SL corresponds to a combination of lexemes in the TL, such as German: *Geschwister*; English: *brothers and sisters*;

3. **synthesis**: This occurs when a combination of lexemes in the SL corresponds to a single lexeme in TL, such as English: *semi-luxury foods and tobacco* (cf. Pons Globalwörterbuch. Teil 2: Deutsch – Englisch. Stuttgart 1983, 485) German: *Genußmittel*;

In the third and last phase of the translation process (synthesis or restructuring), the kernels transferred into the target-language are transformed into surface structures. This process of synthesis is highly dependent on the structure of the target-language and has both formal and functional dimensions (cf. Nida 1969: 493). Among the formal dimensions are the stylistic level and the text type which the production of the TL text tries to realize. The functional, or dynamic, dimension of the process of synthesis is its orientation towards the addressee of the translation. The kernels transferred into the target-language are processed in such a way that the surface structures of the TL text are optimally directed towards the receptor. Or, as Nida puts it,

> *the role of the receptor is crucial, for a translation can be judged as adequate only if the response of the intended receptor is satisfactory.*

Thus,

> *translating* .. [is, W.L.] *'reproducing in the receptor language the closest natural equivalent of the message of the source language, first in terms of meaning and second in terms of style'*. (Nida 1969: 494 and 495; cf. also Koller [2]1983: 119)

A. *Internal Criticism*

i. The notion of *kernel* as used by Nida is nowhere defined and remains vague. This is deliberate on the part of the author; he argues that "linguists differ as to the precise formulation of these structures..." (Nida 1969: 485). He gives only a working definition, which he thinks is generally accepted. According to this, kernels are "... near-minimal structures at some point between the deep structure and the surface structure" (1969: 485). It remains unclear, however, what is meant by *near-minimal* and by *at some point* between the deep structure and the surface structure. The terminological obscurity is made even greater by his also using the term *near-kernel*, obviously in free variation with *kernel.*

ii. Because of this lack of an exact definition, it is left to the translator's discretion to determine *kernels* and *near-kernels* and to split complex structures into simpler ones. Obviously, this intuition-controlled process reveals many individual differences and can lead to kernels or near-kernels which are specific for an individual translator. Additionally, this may be *one* reason for the fact that the processes of transfer and synthesis, which operate on the elementary structures, lead to different translations among different translators.

iii. The method of back-transformation, which Nida applied to translation, is no longer employed by him, as can be seen in his later publications (cf. also Faiß 1972). Several reasons may account for this, for example the manifold translator-specific differences involved in this method, and the dubious nature of the kernel-concept in transformational generative grammar[16]. In spite of all these problems, back-transformations certainly have a heuristic value. The splitting of complex structures into simpler ones is a widespread method when the SL text is syntactically so complex that it hinders the translator from interpreting its meaning (cf. Wilss 1977: 165).

B. External Criticism

i. Nida's concept of translation as a three-level activity of analysis, transfer, and synthesis cannot capture the translation process adequately and must be regarded as an oversimplification[17]. Especially the discreteness of the three phases and their strict temporal succession seem not to be found in reality. Among others, Hönig (1976), and Hönig/Kußmaul (1982: 25ff.) have shown that translators do not first receive and analyze an SL text and then transfer it into the TL, but that the processes of reception and analysis operate according to the purpose of the translation. Thus, the translator does not receive and analyze the SL text in a neutral way, but with a view to translating it for a certain purpose. Hönig and Kußmaul (1982: 27) point out that while receiving an SL text

> *drängen sich gerade dem erfahrenen Übersetzer 'automatisch', also ohne bewußte Anstrengung, ... zielsprachliche ... Ausdrücke und Formulierungen für Teile und Bruchstücke des AS-Textes auf. Diese automatischen Assoziationen stellen sich ein, ob wir wollen oder nicht.*

The observations made by Hönig and Kußmaul have two consequences for Nida'a model of the translation process:

First, transfer does not represent a discrete phase in the translation process but overlaps with the phases of analysis and synthesis. **Second**, the translator's going back to elementary structures (kernels or near-kernels), as described by Nida, is probably not practiced generally, for economical reasons. Only when the translator does not automatically associate a TL text segment with a respective SL one, and when the syntactic complexity of the SL text segment hinders the translator from understanding its sense, does s/he split the complex SL text

---

16 The kernel-concept in transformational generative grammar has been made obsolete by the hypothetical assumption of a deep structure.

17 Nonetheless, the concept of translation as a three-level activity is rather widespread in translation theory (cf. Koller 1981: 263f.; Kade 1968b: 7; Wilss 1977: 95).

segment into more elementary structures. For practical translating this means that back-transformations can be regarded as problem-solving strategies (cf. section 4.5). To this extent they represent *one* member of a group of strategies for interpreting the meaning of an SL text segment.

ii. Like Diller and Kornelius, Nida does not say anything in his model about what kind of *mental* processes occur in the translator's head when s/he translates. Thus, the model is not a psycholinguistic one in the sense postulated in section 1.2. It only represents schematically the interplay of components which can, but need not, play a part in the translation process. *How* the translator analyzes the SL text, *how* s/he splits it up into elementary structures, and *how* s/he transfers them into the TL thus producing the TL text, all these mental operations of the translator are not captured by Nida's model. The author is well aware of this fact. He sees the problems of his own model in the framework of the general problems of scientific models. These have a metaphorical and heuristic character, or, as Nida (1969: 488) puts it:

> *They are essential aids to comprehension, but they must not be permitted to dictate the nature of what they are supposed to explicate. It is particularly dangerous to employ mechanical models as ways of describing the nature of language and the presumed manner in which the human brain functions in encoding or decoding messages. Elaborate networks with and-or nodes are fascinating devices for suggesting certain logical relationships, but they should certainly not be regarded as having any direct bearing on the way in which the brain actually functions in encoding or decoding.*

3.1.3 Kade

Kade's 1968 model situates translation within a framework of communication theory. According to the author, a communication-theoretical approach to translation has certain advantages because it can isolate the various factors involved in translation and can stimulate their further investigation in related disciplines, such as micro- or macro-linguistics, psychology, neurophysiology, epistemology or aesthetics. Kade points out that a communication-theoretical approach to translation represents an urgent desideratum because to him it is evident that the neglect of the specifics of the various components of translation is one of the greatest disadvantages of earlier investigations (cf. Kade 1968b: 3f.).

Kade distinguishes between a narrow, micro-linguistic concept of translation, which restricts itself to the change of code from SL to TL, and a wider, communication-theoretical concept of translation which the author describes as

> *jenen in einem zweisprachigen Kommunikationsakt eingebetteten Prozeß, der mit der Aufnahme eines AS-Textes* (= Original; Text einer gegebenen Sprache L_1) *beginnt und mit der Realisierung eines ZS-Textes* (= Translat; Text einer gegebenen Sprache L_2) *endet. Die wichtigste Phase dieses Prozesses ist der Kodierungswechsel AS → ZS, der aufgrund seiner Funktion im Kommunikations-*

akt bestimmten Bedingungen unterliegt und den wir als Translation im engeren Sinne auffassen können. (Kade 1968b: 3)

The wider concept of translation in the sense of a communication process in which two languages are involved can be schematically represented as follows (Kade 1968b: 7):

Diagram 3: Kade's Model

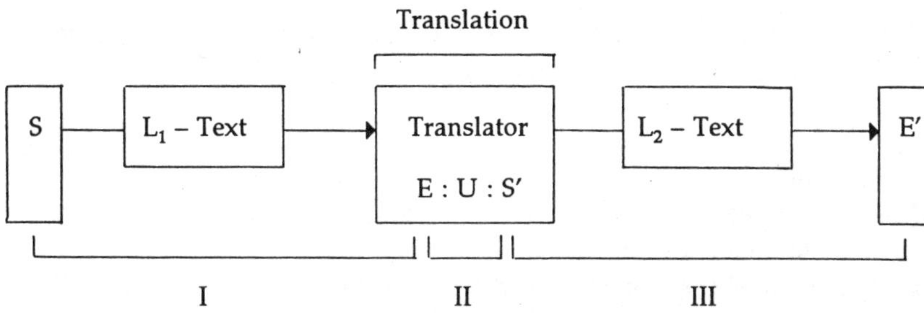

According to the model, communication consists of three phases of which the former has to be successfully completed for the latter to occur. In phase I communication between a sender (S) and the translator in his/her function as receiver (E) takes place. This communication is established via a text in the source-language (L_1). Phase II is characterized by a change of code from SL to TL and is realized by the translator (U). The third phase (III) thematizes the communication between the translator in his/her function as target-language sender (S') and the target-language receiver (E') by means of a target-language (L_2) text.

Thus, translation comprises part of phase I, i.e. the decoding of the SL text by the translator as receiver, the whole of phase II, i.e. the change of code of the SL (L_1) text by the translator (U), and part of phase III, i.e. the translator's realization of the SL text's message in the TL text for the TL receiver (cf. Kade 1968b: 7).

Within the communication-theoretical framework the fundamental problem of translation is how to preserve in the TL text the communicative effect which the SL text produces on the translator and which s/he has to produce on the TL text receiver. This is the precondition for the congruence of the informational content and the communicative value of the SL and TL text.

The communicative value of a text is, however, extremely difficult to determine because intentions exist only in the minds of individuals. What can be determined linguistically, i.e. without recourse to the text producer's intention, is the informational value of a text. It is the *linguistic* realization of the text producer's intention corresponding to the communicative value of the text (cf. Kade 1968b: 9f.).

Thus, according to Kade, from a communication-theoretical point of view it is sufficient to keep the denotation of a text invariant. This invariance is obligatory in translation whereas the significative meaning of a text, its pragmatic value, and its formal level (*Ausdrucksebene*) cannot always be kept invariant in translation (cf. Kade 1968b: 11).

A. *Internal Criticism*

i. From a linguistic point of view, Kade's model, like all communication-theoretical models, reveals a high degree of generality. This is not surprising since communication-theoretical models must be able to capture not only linguistic but *all* types of communication. As a consequence, the specifics of a certain type of communication – for instance the linguistic – cannot be captured adequately.

The consequences for Kade's model of translation which result from the arguments outlined above are twofold:

First, the model can neither capture nor reveal the specifics of *translational* communication adequately. Even though the change of code (U) functions as a component in the model, nothing is said about how it is brought about by the translator. **Second**, the specifics of translation amount to more than communication only. Especially translation strategies, which operate within the translation process, and which are of special interest here, are not represented in the model.

ii. According to Kade, translation is an interdisciplinary phenomenon which can only be investigated in its entirety by a cooperation of various disciplines, such as linguistics, psychology and neurophysiology (cf. Kade 1968b: 36). In other words, the complex whole of translation should be reduced to its factors, which in turn should be investigated by their relevant discipline(s).

On the one hand, it is certainly true that such a complex phenomenon as translation cannot be investigated adequately by means of one discipline alone.

On the other hand, the investigation of another, similarly complex area, i.e. foreign language classroom discourse, has shown that a mere addition of approaches relating to the various relevant disciplines (additive interdisciplinarity) can only reveal certain aspects of the object under investigation. And as the different approaches were mainly carried out in isolation from one another without asking how the results which the research yielded could be related to each other, the investigation of the phenomenon *as a whole* was hindered rather than helped (cf. Bausch/Raabe 1978: 65).

Therefore, an integrative interdisciplinarity must be postulated. The various autonomous, self-sufficient disciplines must be integrated into a unified approach. But whether and how this can be put into practice is hardly more than an open question for the time being. However necessary an integrative interdisciplinarity is, the problems of integrating different disciplines into a unified approach are enormous because – as Hüllen (1976: 21) points out –

> *... die einzelnen Teildisziplinen ... selbst modelltheoretisch organisierte, analytisch arbeitende Wissenschaften* [sind], *die Befunde aus der Wirklichkeit abzubilden versuchen. Sie wählen die Datenkorpora der Erfahrung gemäß ihren eigenen Erkenntnisinteressen aus, sie verengen dabei die Wirklichkeit und schaffen sich ihren Untersuchungsmethoden entgegenkommende Laborsituationen. Sie verändern und kontrollieren jeweils verschiedene Variablen. Was auf diese Weise von den* [Wissenschaften] *... an Erkenntnissen konstruiert wird, sind Abstraktionen über höchst unterschiedlichen Bereichen der Wirklichkeit ...*

B. External Criticism

i. Although, according to Kade, the change of code from SL to TL is the most important phase of the translation process, the author gives no information whatsoever about *how* the translator brings about this change of code. Nothing is said about the mental operations of text processing taking place in the mind of the translator when s/he receives the SL text, organizes it into units of translation, transfers them into the target-language, and thus produces the TL text. So, from a translation-procedural point of view, the most interesting activity of the translator is reduced to a merely static component in the model. Its dynamic character is not considered at all.

ii. Similar to Nida, Kade considers the translation process to be a succession of three partial processes: the decoding of the message of a source-language text, the change of code, and the encoding of the message in a target-language text.

As has already been pointed out under i. in the external criticism of Nida's model, the concept of translation as a process comprising three discrete phases which occur in strict temporal succession has no psychological reality and thus cannot capture the mental translation process adequately. Kade's model is therefore not a process model of translation in the sense postulated in section 1.2. It only represents schematically some of the components involved in the translation process without even thematizing their dynamic interplay.

3.1.4 Stein and Hönig/Kußmaul

Stein was led to develop his model of translation by the deficits of translation theory and its inoperativity, which he had described in detail in 1980. Stein's model is based on the theory of text which was inaugurated by S.J. Schmidt in 1973.

According to Schmidt (1973: 73), text can be defined as an ordered set of instructions to a communication partner. It is only in communication that interlocutors realize the instructions of a text, i.e. its meaning. Thus an isolated text does not *have* any meaning, it only *receives* meaning in communication.

In Stein's view, the concept of text as an ordered set of instructions to an interlocutor in a communication is a fruitful one for both translation theory and translation teaching methodology, for three reasons:

First, Schmidt's instructional-linguistic theory of text deals with what is considered to be the ultimate material for translation, i.e. text. It investigates the transphrastic relations which play an important part in all translating, and which could not be captured adequately before, when linguistics restricted itself to the level of the sentence or even of the word (Stein 1980: 50). **Second**, it could be expected that an instructional-linguistic theory of text would address the problems of text types, which are of crucial importance for the choice of the method of translating (cf. Reiß 1971; 1976; Reiß/Vermeer 1984). And **third**, Schmidt's instructional-linguistic theory of text made the communicative character of text its object of investigation, an object which had hardly been paid any attention in both translation theory and linguistics. It could therefore be expected that the theory of text would open up new perspectives for translation theory in the investigation of its object, and would help to solve problems which could not have been solved by earlier, non-communication-oriented linguistics.

In sum, Stein considers the advantage of the instructional-linguguistic theory of text to be its ability to function as a theoretical framework for translation theory and that it

> [erklärt] *den Bereich sprachlicher Kommunikation in Texten in einer wesentlich umfassenderen Weise zu ihrem Objektbereich ..., insbesondere die Dynamik des Sprachgebrauchs sowie die pragmatische Einbettung von sprachlichen Texten.*

The model developed by Stein attempts to represent the translation process by means of instructional-linguistic categories and to visualize the ideal course of communication between the source-language text producer, the source-language text receiver, the target-language text producer, and the target-language text receiver (cf. Stein 1980: 62).

The model can be schematically represented as follows:

Diagram 4: Hönig and Kußmaul's Model

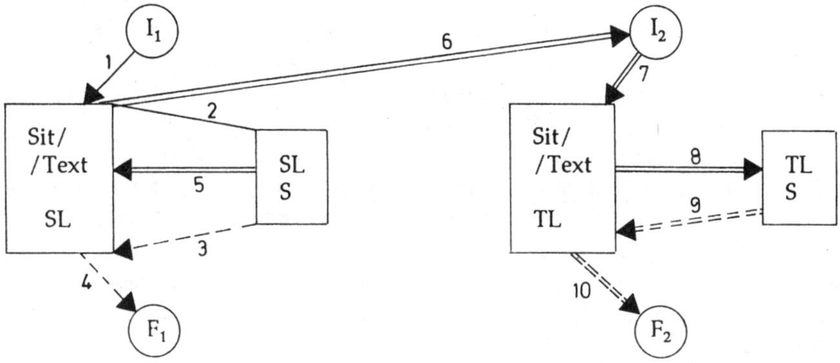

—— steps 1 and 2 made by the SL text producer
-------- steps 3 and 4 made by the SL text receiver
═══ steps 5, 6, 7, and 8 made by the translator
===== steps 9 and 10 made by the TL text receiver
(cf. Stein 1980: 62)

Explanations

A source-language text producer has a certain communicative intention (I_1) and wants to evoke a certain communicative function (F_1) (i.e. action, attitude, etc.) in the source-language text receiver. To make sure that the desired communicative effect is produced on the receiver, the text producer takes into account the situation (Sit) of the addressee. In addition, s/he informs him- or herself about the textual knowledge (Text) which has been built up by the preceding communication. With a view to his/her knowledge about the addressee's situation and textual knowledge, the text producer selects those source-language signs (SL S) from his/her repertoire which most probably make the receiver act according to the text producer's intention. Whilst the text producer must thus calculate prospectively, i.e. how to use language signs in order to optimally realize his/her intention, the translator plays an entirely different part in the translational communication process. His/her first task is to deduce the source-language text producer's communicative intention (I_1). S/he does this by applying a retrospective calculation. Taking into account the SL addressee's situation and textual knowledge, the translator views the SL signs which the text sender has selected and used to produce the SL text. Additionally, the translator focusses on the specific way the language signs are used in the text and thus concludes what intention the source-language text producer probably pursued. According to Stein, the first task of the translator is optimally accomplished when I_2 is identical to I_1, i.e. when the translator wants to evoke in the TL text receiver a communicative function which is maximally similar to that evoked by the initial communicative intention I1 (Stein 1980: 67).

After having deduced the intention of the SL sender (i.e. I_1), the translator acts as text producer in the target-language. Taking into account the TL addressee's situation and textual knowledge, the translator selects those target-language signs which probably produce a communicative effect (F_2) on the TL addressee that is largely similar to the function evoked by the SL text (i.e. F_1).

Thus, the processes of target-language and of source-language text production are analogous, but the communicative intention of the translator is a mediated one. The process of translation can therefore be considered a process of selection and optimization (cf. Levý 1967) with fixed components ($I_1 = I_2$; Sit; Text) and a given repertoire of signs (TL S). The signs are selected with recourse to the fixed components and with a view to optimally achieving the aim (i.e. F_2).

Stein's model of translation represents the starting-point for the strategy of translation developed by Hönig and Kußmaul in 1982. The authors consider the process of translation a process of decision-making and problem-solving. The decisions to be made on the different levels of language (text, sentence, word) are determined by the purpose of the communication, which, according to Hönig and Kußmaul, is the "Archimedean Point" in translation. It makes a description of the process of translation possible and is of considerable help for the translator. Hönig and Kußmaul (1982: 13) point out that neither the information to be conveyed by the translation nor the function of the text result from the individual communicative intention of the translator as sender and text producer. Therefore, all communicative functions – from the function of the text to the function of the single word – become variables which have to be determined according to the specific purpose and aim of the translational communication.

Whilst Stein's model represents the theoretical framework, Hönig and Kußmaul's strategy of translation can be considered the practical application of Stein's model with one important modification. It concerns the status of the communicative intention I_1/I_2. Whereas Stein stipulates the maximal similarity between I_1 and I_2, Hönig and Kußmaul consider this to be *one* type of translation only. Another basic type[18], which is by no means a special case, are translations in which the communicative function differs from that of the original SL text. Those translations are equally important and no less legitimate and justified than translations for which $I_1 = I_2$ holds (Hönig/Kußmaul 1982: 40).

18 Examples of this type are, for instance, translations of Swift's *Gulliver's Travels* or Cervantes' *Don Quixote* as books for children or young people. Furthermore, the translations of novels as scripts, or the translations of advertisements for the information of a target-language readership about advertisements in the source-language culture. (Cf. Diller and Kornelius' (1978: 3ff.) concept of *primäre* and *sekundäre Übersetzung* and House's (^{2}1981: 188ff.) distinction between *overt* and *covert* translation.

A. *Internal Criticism*

The model outlined above belongs to the group of functional models of translation. They are characterized by the dominance of the translation *purpose.* It controls the selection of the language signs on the different levels of translation, from the hierarchically highest level, the text, to the hierarchically lowest level, the word. The language signs thus become variables which have to be determined according to the specific purpose and aim of the communication. This determining becomes problematic, however, when two or more signs can have the same or a similar communicative function. Those functional equivalents which the practical translator often encounters cannot be captured adequately by a functional model of translation. Verbal communication – and translation as a special case of it – always has both a functional and a partially independent formal dimension[19]. Therefore, an entire subordination of the language signs to the communicative purpose, and thus implicitly a lower status of the formal dimension of signs, is neither appropriate for communication nor for translation.

In this context, Reiß (1984) and Reiß/Vermeer (1984: 90) have pointed out that translation *hic* et *nunc* should keep functionally and formally on all levels as close to the source-language text as the translation purpose allows. In other words, the postulate of imitation, of the greatest possible similarity between the signs of the SL and the TL text, is hierarchically directly subordinate to the primacy of the translation purpose[20]. Thus, when functional equivalents occur, the one having the greater formal similarity with the corresponding SL sign would be given preference.

B. *External Criticism*

i. An essential weakness of Hönig and Kußmaul's model concerns its idealized and prescriptive character. The model shows how an *ideal* translator *should* proceed under *ideal* circumstances. But as an ideal translator does not exist, and as every translator has to work under non-ideal circumstances of performance (i.e. a limited memory capacity, an incomplete Sit and/or Text-knowledge, a limited availability of SL- and/or TL signs, deficient mental mechanisms, translational experience, etc. (cf. Königs 1979: 9)), the model cannot adequately capture the real, unvarnished translation performance.

ii. Stein's concept of translation as a process consisting of discrete subprocesses which occur in strict temporal succession must be regarded as an over-simplification. The model assumes an interpretation phase (5, 6) followed

---

19 The importance and (partial) independence of the formal dimension of (verbal) communication is dealt with in e.g. Crystal and Davy's (1969) stylistics and in Hymes' (1972) and Gumperz/Hymes' (1972) ethnography of communication. Cf. also Dirven 1981.

20 For a completely different view, cf. Toury 1982: 35ff. and: 45.

by a production phase (7, 8). Simultaneity of the two phases is not regarded but should be taken into consideration (cf. point I. of the external criticism of Nida's model, and additionally Hönig 1976 and Hönig/Kußmaul 1982: 25ff.)

iii. Compared with the concepts discussed before, the models of Stein and Hönig/Kußmaul are much closer to translation performance. Translation is modelled as SL text reception and TL text production. These processes are represented by their components and their *idealized* interplay is described as the task of the translator. Thus, the two models can be regarded as being *idealized*, even though deficient, performance models, and are therefore much more relevant to the epistemological interest of this study than the concepts outlined before.

iv. In the two models nothing is said about *how* the translator relates the different components to each other when s/he receives the SL text and produces the TL text. This deficit results from the fact that they do not approach their object of investigation in an empirical but rather in a theoretical-speculative way. Translation as a mental process which can be described and investigated psycholinguistically is therefore beyond the reach of these two models as well.

3.2 Critical Remarks on the Process Models

In the preceding section, five models were discussed which claim to capture the translation process. That this claim obviously does *not* coincide with reality was pointed out in the critical remarks on the various models.

In the following section, four critical arguments will be presented in summary. They refer to all the process models outlined above, and, because they are of a fundamental nature, make a performance-analytical approach to the translation process an urgent desideratum.

i. The models discussed approach the translation process either in a prescriptive or in a statically descriptive way (cf. Königs 1987). In the first case, instructions are given which, when followed by an *ideal* translator, would result in what is assumed to be an optimal translation. In the second case, components of the translation process are described and their interplay, as it can theoretically be postulated, is depicted schematically, and thus in a simplified and idealized way, too. Therefore, the dynamics of the translation process as a largely mental activity of an individual can neither be elucidated nor described or explained by the five models.

ii. As a consequence, none of the models of the translation process can account for the psychological reality of translating. No conclusions can be drawn from the models as to *what* goes on in the head of a translator when s/he renders a source-language text into the target-language. Neither is the problem addressed as to *whether* the complex translation process consists of mental subprocesses, *what* their possible nature is, and *how* the translator integrates them during the process of translating.

iii. All the models of the translation process approach their object of investigation in a theoretical-speculative, not in an empirical way. The components of the translation process and their assumed interplay, as outlined in the models, have been construed rationalistically by logical deduction not by empirical induction. Thus, the translation process appears to be completely rational, which, however, it is only in ideality, but not in reality.

iv. The information on the translation process which the models contain refers to the competent, professional translator and his/her fully developed translational competence. The object of this investigation, however, is the non-professional, partly competent translator's rudimentary ability to mediate and its realization in the translation process (cf. section 4.3 of this volume). The latter will be described and analyzed by means of translation performance, as will be discussed in detail in the following chapters. As a consequence of the differences between the models and this study as regards goals, objects, methods, and approaches, hardly any information contained in or gathered by the models can be used in this investigation.

4 The Performance-Analytical Investigation of the Translation Process

In section 1.2, it was pointed out that the goal of this study is to investigate aspects[1] of the mental – and thus not directly observable – translation process. As is customary in psycholinguistics, since it is a mentalist discipline, this investigation is carried out by means of an analysis of translation performance[2], which, to a large extent[3], can be considered the externalization of the translation process. Translation performance in this study comprises both translation as text production and the thinking-aloud data which the test subjects externalize while translating. In the following section (4.1), two preliminary assumptions are made concerning that investigation of language performance which aims at reconstructing aspects of the underlying mental processes. These assumptions are followed by considerations on the empirical investigation of translation performance (4.2). The process of the empirical accumulation of knowledge is described (4.2.1) and the research design is outlined (4.2.2). In section 4.3, the hypothetical construct of a rudimentary ability to mediate, as the basis of all translating, is described and critically evaluated. The methodology of performance-analytical research in general and, with respect to this study, in particular, is dealt with in section 4.4. In its first part (4.4.1), thinking-aloud as a method to gain insights into mental processes is presented and its conditions, possibilities, and limitations are shown. The

---

1 The aspects (i.e. parts) of the translation process which are the object of this investigation are precisely determined and defined as translation ***strategies*** in section 4.5.3.

2 The view is taken here that although translation performance can largely be considered the verbal (and non-verbal, e.g. kinesic, proxemic) manifestation of the translation process, other factors (e.g. context, situation, mental and physical state of translator) may also be responsible for its concrete expression (cf. section 4.4.1). To consider performance the mere externalization of process – perhaps even in analogy to stimulus and response – would be a gross simplification of the very complex relations between mental processes and performance.

3 The notion of performance which is used in this study differs from Chomsky's in one essential aspect. Chomsky (cf. 1965: 3f.) considers performance to be the actual use of language affected by memory limitations, distractions, shifts of attention and interest, and errors. Thus, he emphasizes its unsystematic nature and its variability. He also points out that "investigation of performance will proceed only so far as the understanding of underlying competence permits" (Chomsky 1965: 10). A performance analysis which aims at gaining insights into performance itself, is – according to Chomsky – not the province of linguistics but of psychology.
In contrast to Chomsky's view, it will be argued in the following section (4.1) that besides its variability and its unsystematizable part, performance contains many regularities. They can be described and explained by an investigation of performance. Furthermore, the aspect of performance ***production*** by the language user will be investigated here.

second part of section 4.4 deals with both the interpretive reconstruction of sense, which is a central task of any performance analysis, and with the specific reconstruction of aspects of the translation process, which is the central theme of this investigation. In the last section (4.5) of this chapter, the object of this study is delimited to translation *strategies*. General considerations on the notion (4.5.1) and on different concepts of strategy (4.5.2) are made, which result in the author's definition of translation strategy (4.5.3).

4.1 Introductory Remarks

An investigation of translation *performance* aiming at the reconstruction of aspects of the translation *process* implies at least two general assumptions:

i. An analysis of language performance – and thus also of translation performance[4] – can only be sensible and useful if it yields generalizable results (cf. Dittmann 1979b: 8f.). Therefore, it must be assumed that besides the manifold variables which are effective in performance (e.g. idiosyncrasies, different degrees of competence in the languages involved, psychophysical state of the language user, situational and contextual factors, etc.), regularities in performance exist. To discover them would lead to a considerable accumulation of knowledge. The variables should certainly not be underestimated in their importance, especially because they are probably one cause of the wide differences among the translations and the protocols of thinking-aloud. Nonetheless, the existence of performance regularities and the possibility of systematizing performance at least partially are indispensable prerequisites for any performance analysis.

After the identification, the description, and the analysis of performance regularities, the manifold variables, which are largely uninvestigated themselves and in their interplay, and not all of which are known yet, can be isolated and analyzed in a more systematic, economical, and better way (cf. Lörscher 1983: 188).

ii. In order to gain insights into the mental translation *process* by an investigation of translation *performance*, a relation – even though of an indirect kind

4 When the terms '*language* performance' and '*translation* performance' are used in this study, it is always understood that performance is constituted not only by language alone but also by its concomitant paralinguistic (cf. Crystal 1974; Stammerjohann 1975) and nonverbal (cf. Scherer 1973; Leathers 1976; Siegman/Feldstein 1978) phenomena. It is assumed, however, that in general, language is the *main* component of *language* performance even though paralinguistic and nonverbal components of performance can be of eminent importance in the sense-constitution and in the reconstruction of process aspects both of which can only be achieved by an analysis of performance. The term '*translation* performance' is to denote that the crucial component of this performance is language in a specific interlingual use.

– between these two phenomena must be hypothesized. But as not all performance data allow conclusions on the underlying processes, and as not all these conclusions are obvious, i.e. can be drawn by mere recognition, an interpretive approach to the data is necessary. Such a procedure, which became programmatic in mentalist psychology, is also widely used in the empirically and experimentally oriented branch of psycholinguistics. It has, however, rarely been thematized and even more rarely been critically evaluated (cf. Dascal 1983: 91ff.). With regard to the investigation of the processes of speech planning, Möhle and Raupach describe those difficulties which any process-analytical research is confronted with. They point out (1983: 29):

> *Die Schwierigkeit [...] liegt darin, daß Planung nicht von außen beobachtbar ist. Da sich erhebliche Teile der Planungsaktivitäten nicht einmal im Bewußtsein des Sprechers spiegeln, können auch Sprecheraussagen nur in begrenztem Umfang hilfreich sein. Die Erforschung von Plangsvorgängen kann daher nur indirekt erfolgen durch Rückschlüsse aus der Untersuchung beobachtbarer Merkmale des Sprechprozesses – bzw. einer beliebig reproduzierbaren Aufzeichnung dieses Prozesses – und aus der Untersuchung beobachtbarer Merkmale des produzierten Textes.*

The essence of the quotation above also applies to this study. But as will be outlined in section 4.5, certain supporting measures will be taken so that the conclusions can be made on a potentially most fruitful data basis provided by the speech process, the thinking-aloud procedure, and the produced text.

In his criticism of the behaviourist concept, which rejects all conclusions about mental processes drawn from performance data, Steinberg advocates a mentalist approach which, besides input and output, takes into consideration information that the language users themselves can give about the production of their language output:

> *Just because phenomenal experiences cannot be directly observed, it does not follow that such experiences cannot be incorporated into scientific theory. Phenomenal experiences may be inferred or corroborated by personal reports of the experiencer. Thus, one may infer that someone is experiencing pain based on reliable objective observations concerning the stimuli impinging on him or her and based on the person's behavioral responses to those stimuli.* (Steinberg 1982: 93)

Steinberg, in a hypothetical rather than in an explanatory way, characterizes the interpretive reconstruction which the analyst has to achieve as follows:

> *The making of inferences regarding unobservables should not frighten Behaviorist psychologists. After all, this is done in Physics all the time. Consider the phenomenon of gravity, for example. This theoretical entity is similar in some important respects to mentalistic entities: gravity is inherently unobservable; only its effects can be observed; it controls the behavior of objects which* **can** *be observed. Mental phenomena, however, have an important advantage over physical theoretical entities such as gravity. For, while no one can directly*

> *experience gravity (only its postulated effects), one can directly experience certain mental events such as feelings and images.* (Steinberg 1982: 94)

In the framework of this study, too, it must be postulated that in principle it is possible to reconstruct process aspects from performance data. Although this postulate can hardly be proved in a positivist way at the present time[5], it seems plausible to make such an assumption for the following reason: It is a matter of fact that (language) performance mainly results from a mental process. To a large extent, it is produced intentionally, rationally and with regard to the given aim, and is thus not the product of mere chance. Therefore, the assumption seems justified that (language) performance, like all products, has certain features which it obtained during the process of its production, and which can be systematized. These features should allow insights into the production process and represent the basis for the interpretive reconstruction carried out by the analyst.

4.2 The Empirical Investigation of the Translation Process

4.2.1 On the Process of the Empirical Accumulation of Knowledge

In the empirical disciplines, the process of accumulating knowledge consists of three phases: the observation, the description, and the explanation of phenomena. The accumulation of knowledge in the empirically oriented branch of linguistics[6] proceeds in the same way. But the three-phase-process, which is well-established in the sciences, implies problems which the empirically oriented branch of linguistics is also confronted with:

i. The process of knowledge accumulation is controlled by the investigator's epistemological interest (cf. Habermas 1969), his/her hypothetical assumptions, and anticipated patterns of explanation. These three factors influence observation, description, and explanation.

At the beginning of the first phase, i.e. observation, the object of epistemological interest is determined. The relevant phenomena of a particular segment

---

5 One important reason for this is the lack of relevant neurolinguistic findings (Dechert: personal communication).

6 Wunderlich (1974: 80) and others consider linguistics to be an empirical discipline (cf. Ballmer 1976). Although this is certainly true with regard to more recent trends in linguistics, such as discourse analysis or certain parts of psycho- and sociolinguistics, other well-established domains of linguistics, e.g. the theory of language, mathematical or philosophical linguistics are not empirical subdisciplines.

of reality are selected and their essential features are picked out. The observation is strictly tied to the relevant data. The selection of the phenomena observed and their relevant features is controlled by the epistemological interest, the hypothetical assumptions, and the anticipated patterns of explanation of the analyst[7]. Thus, observation always implies elements of selection and of reduction of complexity. They are necessary for and characteristic of any empirical research.

In order to make the observed phenomena accessible to further investigation, they have to be transcribed. In this way, a second selection takes place. The phenomena are classified, i.e. ordered according to certain dominant features, related to each other, and thus reconstructed in a generalized way and tied to the language of description (i.e. metalanguage). The selection and classification of the data is again dependent on the analyst's epistemological interest, his/her hypothetical assumptions, and his/her anticipated interpretation.

The explanation of the selected and classified data is the third step in the process of knowledge accumulation. In most cases the investigator is not only interested in what kind the selected phenomena are, but also in why they are or have become the way they are.

In order to solve the latter problem, the investigator forms hypotheses, i.e. s/he develops patterns of explanation and interpretation which go beyond the data observed. The hypotheses are formed as a result of the findings which the observation and the description of the phenomena yield, and with regard to the analyst's hypothetical assumptions and knowledge about (similar) phenomena.

The formation of hypotheses is followed by their testing. This requires a further process of observation and description which results in the corroboration, the modification, or the rejection of hypotheses. Especially in the two latter cases, further processes of knowledge accumulation take place. Hypotheses always thus have a preliminary nature.

ii. In point i., the process of the accumulation of empirical knowledge was described as consisting of three phases. However, this implies neither that observation, description, and explanation occur in a strict temporal succession, nor that the three phases are discrete, i.e. have clear-cut borderlines. As has been pointed out above, observation and description can be influenced by the investigator's anticipated, hypothetical patterns of explanation. They can control *what* is being observed and described, and *how* this is done. In addition, the phase of observation is also influenced by the investigator being aware of the fact that s/he has to describe the observed phenomena and their interrelations. In other words, during the process of observation considerations are generally made about how the phenomena observed can be described in the most simple, and/or exact, and/or economical, and/or elegant way, with the epistemological interest in mind.

---

7 Cf. Imhasly et al. 1982: 21f. and section 4.2.2 below.

From the reflections made above it becomes evident that the three phases influence each other, thus having a dialectical relationship, and occur synchronously. Nonetheless, it is sensible to separate the three phases of the process of knowledge accumulation for heuristic reasons. The distinction between any single phase allows the various activities of the investigator to be discerned and described more clearly. But the analyst must also be aware of the danger of manipulating his/her object of investigation by this artificial separation. On the one hand, it allows insights into the process of empirical research, but on the other hand, it can obscure the investigator's awareness of the systematic interplay of his/her activities.

4.2.2 Research Design

From the considerations made above it has become evident that the investigator's epistemological interest, his/her hypothetical assumptions, and certain anticipated, hypothetical patterns of explanation (can) influence the process of knowledge accumulation (decisively).

The *epistemological interest* of this study has already been outlined in section 1.2, and need not be described here again.

The *anticipated patterns of explanation* can probably only be shown for any single case. Here, a case will be presented in which anticipated results of an analysis influence the description of data. In section 5.3, this case will be described in more detail. After the first translations had been performed, (preliminary) categories of a model of analysis were developed. The transcription of further translations was carried out in such a way that utterances corresponding to certain categories of analysis, which had been previously developed and internalized by the analyst, made up one line or one paragraph in the transcript. Thus, in the analysis to come, the corresponding category can be noted beside the transcript. In other words, the ordering and classifying principle for the description was essentially determined by an anticipated interpretation of the data. If those patterns of interpretation formalized to make categories of analysis turn out to be viable, the description of the data largely controlled by them reveals a high degree of economy.

The *hypothetical assumptions* made in this study control the research design in a characteristic way. They will be discussed in the following section.

4.2.2.1 Hypothetical Assumptions

The investigation of translation performance aiming at the reconstruction of aspects of the translation process rests on three basic hypothetical assumptions.

a. It was assumed that every individual who has two or more languages at his/her disposal also possesses a rudimentary ability to mediate between these languages (cf. section 4.3). To furnish proof of this basic hypothetically assumed mediating competence represents an essential part of the epistemological interest of this study. For the research design, this hypothesis has an important consequence. The translations constituting the data corpus were exclusively performed by non-professional translators. Performance analyses of professional translators were not carried out, for two reasons:

First, my epistemological interest was not directed towards trained, developed translation competence, but towards the universal rudimentary ability to mediate which all bilinguals and multilinguals have, and which in turn is the first and foremost precondition for professional translation competence. Second, I was told by both practising translators and teachers engaged in the training of translators that professional translators are especially used to externalizing the finished end products of the translation process in written or spoken form. For this reason, only very few data in their utterances could be expected which would allow conclusions about the translation process. This is easily understandable because professional translators, in comparison with non-professional ones, have reached a much higher degree of automatization in translation (cf. Krings 1986a: 52; Wilss 1977a: 201). As will be shown in section 4.4.1, hardly any thinking-aloud is to be found in phases of automatic language processing. Thus, even if professional translators could be made to think aloud during their translations, hardly any data from which aspects of the translation process could be interpreted would be externalized.

The test subjects, mostly first- or second-year students of English, had little experience of and hardly any training in translating. Besides their mother tongue, German, they had partial competence in a foreign language, English, which has the status of an interlanguage[8] for them. It results from seven or nine years of learning English at school and from one or two years at university.

b. It was assumed that oral text production would yield more data allowing conclusions about the underlying production process than would written text production[9]. In the latter type of language use, there is probably a stronger tendency to record the *result* of the production process, whereas generally the intermediate *phases* are represented only mentally[10]. Oral text production can largely be considered a process of problem solving and optimization. Its intermediate stages are generally verbalized (cf. Antos 1982) and yield valuable data which, together with those of the thinking-aloud and of the produced text

8 Cf. Selinker 1972; Davies et al. 1984. According to the interlanguage-hypothesis, individuals who learn a foreign language at school, i.e. under highly controlled conditions of acquisition, do not normally acquire full competence of the target-language but only an approximation situated between the mother tongue and the foreign language. The systematicity of interlanguages can be seen in fossilizations, i.e. mostly irreversible stand-stills in the development of skills.

9 Cf. Goldman-Eisler 1980; For a different view cf. Krings 1986a: 78.

10 Cf. Black 1982; Gregg/Steinberg 1980; Hayes/Flower 1980; Bereiter 1980: 74f.; Börner 1987.

itself, allow hypothetical conclusions about aspects of the mental process of text production.

The assumption outlined above also applies to *translation* processes, because they are also a type of text production. For the research design this had the consequence that the test subjects were asked to translate *written* texts *orally* into the target-language. This type of translation probably represents a special case in translation practice[11] and the characteristics of *oral* text production may well influence it and be detectable in it. But the same applies to written translations. They are shaped by the characteristics of *written* text production. As translation is a language-bound operation, and as language always occurs in either the oral or the written medium, it can be expected that the respective medium influences translation at least as a *product*. Whether it also influences the mental translation *process* cannot be decided here. However, it does not seem to be very likely that the linguistic medium of the texts to be translated has any decisive influence on those aspects of the translation process which are the object of this investigation, i.e. on translation strategies as procedures for solving translation problems (cf. section 4.5.3). Processes of problem solving are cognitive processes which often employ 'inner speech' (cf. Leontev 1971; 1975; Vygotski 1962; Benediktov 1974; Lewandowski 1976; Wahmhoff 1980; Rühl 1983). When received, oral or written speech is transformed into 'inner speech' (*interiorisation*)[12] to make it accessible for mental (problem solving) processing. Solutions to problems are externalized in oral or written form by means of 'inner speech', too (*exteriorisation*). It can therefore be assumed that the kind of mental representation of 'inner speech' also exerts a considerable influence on speech processing, and thus on the process of problem solving. Relevant investigations into this subject are an urgent desideratum (cf. Průcha 1974: 85).

c. It was assumed that thinking-aloud would yield data which allowed (additional) conclusions about process aspects. As will be shown in section 4.4.1, thinking-aloud is widely considered to be an adequate procedure for collecting data on the basis of which hypotheses on the processing of information can be made. It is generally agreed, though, that thinking-aloud does not provide

---

11 In translation practice, a written source-language text is normally rendered into a written target-language text (cf. Kade 1973; Meyer 1974). Hönig (personal communication) and Snell/Crampton (1983: 118) made the point that professional translators often translate written texts orally on tape in order to have them written down later. This is done for economical reasons, because professional translators often have to work under enormous pressure.

12 This is also maintained by the analysis-by-synthesis models of speech reception (cf. Halle/Stevens 1964; Clark/Clark 1977: 205–207; Hüllen/Jung 1979: 87f.) the strongest version of which is the motor theory of speech reception by Liberman et al. (1963; 1967). Cf. also Hörmann ^{2}1977: 46–48; Clark/Clark 1977: 207–210; Hüllen/Jung 1979: 88f.

information about the mental processes themselves[13]. Procedural knowledge evades its verbalization because it is not within the individual's focus of attention (cf. Dechert 1987; Hölscher/Möhle 1987; Færch/Kasper 1987). What can be verbalized is information which has the form of declarative knowledge. It is within the individual's focus of attention, refers to the intermediate steps of the information processing, and is probably more closely connected with the mental processing of information than any other information which can be elicited (cf. section 4.4.1).

For the research design this consideration has the consequence that the test subjects were asked to think aloud during their translations, i.e. to verbalize whatever came into their minds during the translation of a text from one language into another. Retrospective data stemming from subjects' *ex-post* elicited reports or from *ex-post* thinking-aloud protocols (cf. Wagner et al. 1977) were not collected, mainly because retrospective procedures are generally considered to be less reliable than introspective ones (cf. section 4.4.1).

As the transcription, and thus also the interpretation, of the translations was not carried out immediately after data collection but with a time lag of a few days, it could not be expected that the test subjects would have been able to give reliable information about aspects of their mental translation processes. It could rather be expected that, in order to help the test leader, the subjects would have possibly rationalized their modes of behaviour. They might have interpreted them in a way which complies well with the research project, although at the time of the experiment subjects might have interpreted them in quite a different way. In order to exclude such glossed over data, I decided at the beginning of data collection not to elicit information retrospectively.

During the interpretive reconstruction of the translations, however, cases emerged where it could be expected that *ex-post* elicited reports would have provided information that could have been of help for interpretation. When an item is within the focus of attention of a subject for a long time, it can be assumed that the subject still remembers aspects of its mental processing after a few days, or that s/he can at least partly activate his/her remembrance. This activation can be supported by presenting the respective item to the subject both acoustically on tape and visually in the transcript.

However, it was often not possible to elicit information from the subjects several days after the experiments because many subjects were no longer available. So, to secure comparability of the data, I decided not to elicit any

---

13 White (1980: 105f.), however, points out that no satisfactory definitions of product and process, as mental phenomena, exist: "There are no criteria by which a mental event could be located under one heading and discriminated from the other" (105f.). Thus, the distinction between *process* and *product*, as mental phenomena, is untenable.

ex-post reports at all. The data corpus ascertained in this way consists of three interdependent types of data[14]:

1. The translations, i.e. the respective target-language texts which the subjects externalize as the end products of their process of text production;

2. The thought-aloud utterances in which intermediate stages as preliminary results of text production manifest themselves verbally[15], and in which meta-utterances such as comments on certain passages, realized problems, problem-solving and text processing strategies can be found;

3. The paralinguistic phenomena (e.g. speed, rhythm, key, voice quality, etc.) which accompany the utterances mentioned in 1. and 2. above, and the temporal variables (e.g. rate of articulation, pauses, repetitions, self-corrections, lapses, etc.), which partly overlap with the former.

Two things need to be taken into consideration here:
First, in their entirety, the three types of data constitute the performance which is the object of this investigation. They are interconnected with each other, and often it cannot be decided definitely to which of the three types of data a performance phenomenon is to be assigned. The distinction between the three groups was made here solely for heuristic reasons. It must not obscure our awareness of the concomitance of the phenomena. **Second**, it must be taken into account that in practice, the most frequently occurring kind of translation, i.e. written translation, either contains only the end products of text production or the end products plus certain intermediate steps, i.e. preliminary versions. Meta-utterances as well as data belonging to type 3. are obviously not to be found in written translations.

In addition to the end products of text production, their accompanying paralinguistic phenomena and temporal variables (data of type 3.), orally performed translations probably also contain preliminary translation versions. Meta-utterances, however, are most likely to occur as exceptions only. They result from an individual's personal disposition to verbalize his/her thoughts and to account for his/her behaviour.

The instruction to the test subjects to think aloud and thus to potentially produce meta-utterances, too, is bound to generate a performance which differs from 'normal' performance. But this manipulation of the object results from

14 A possible fourth type of data, i.e. visual information, could not be used because the equipment for making video recordings of the subjects performing the translations was not available. In retrospect, however, it can be doubted whether such video recordings would have been necessary, had they been made. During the performance of the translations, the test leader could detect hardly any visual information which, in addition to the types of data outlined in 1. to 3. above, would have allowed further conclusions to be drawn about aspects of underlying mental processes.

15 The problem of the degree of correspondence between what is thought 'silently' and what is thought 'aloud' will be addressed in detail in section 4.4.1.

and can be justified by the purpose and aim of this study, i.e. the hypothetical reconstruction of aspects of the mental translation process. It is also suggested by the assumption that thinking-aloud yields data that can be interpreted as process indicators (cf. section 4.4.2).

4.2.2.2 Data Collection

The data corpus which was compiled for my research project comprises 52 translations. They were performed by 48 subjects most of whom were first or second year students whom I knew from my seminars and lectures (cf. section 5.1.1). The search for subjects who were willing to produce a translation in an experimental situation was rather difficult. Many of those I asked refused although I assured them that their translations would be dealt with confidentially and anonymously, that they would only be used for research purposes, and that they would not be evaluated according to their quality. Nonetheless, many of the students asked were not prepared to speak into the microphone, perhaps because they feared that, if they did not do well in the task, the teacher would have a bad opinion of them, which in turn could have consequences for his marking their papers in the future[16]. This pattern of thinking and behaving, which is quite common in schools and universities, turned out to be a considerable hindrance.

Those who agreed to act as test subjects produced the translations on their own, either in the presence of the test leader or alone, whichever they preferred[17]. Before the subjects started with their translations, the task which they were to perform was explained in detail. The test leader pointed out that a written text was to be translated orally on tape and that the subjects should verbalize everything that came into their minds while performing the task. The subjects were told that the aim of the investigation was to find out aspects of the mental translation process and that the intermediate steps of the translation would thus yield more important insights into the translation process than the end product, i.e. the final version of the translation.

Therefore, a 'good' final version without further verbalization of what goes on in the subject's mind would be of much less use to the investigation than a 'bad' translation which contained much additional information on the underlying mental processes.

Sometimes the question was asked whether the text should be read first, or whether the translation should be started right away. The answer to this question given by the test leader was that the subject should proceed in the way s/he normally did. It was also pointed out that subjects had as much time for

16 This was pointed out by one of the students, referring to other students who had told him that this was the reason for their refusing to take part in the experiment.

17 Seven of the 48 subjects wanted to perform their translations without the test leader being present. This wish was met in all cases.

their translations as they needed and that even when they had to pause for a long time, the running of the tape should not make them work under pressure.

After these instructions, the subjects were given the written texts. The cassette recorder was switched on and was not switched off until the subjects had declared their translations finished.

The use of aids of any kind, especially of monolingual and bilingual dictionaries, was not allowed. This was to prevent problem-solving processes from being blocked or broken off too early by simply adopting ready-made solutions. As will be shown in section 4.4.1, it is primarily in problem-solving processes that data externalized by thinking-aloud which allow hypothetical conclusions to be drawn about aspects of mental processes can be expected. This is especially valid for problem-solving *strategies*, which go into operation when problems occur, and which are central to the epistemological interest of this study.

After having finished their translations, some of the subjects were additionally asked to read the source-language text again and, when they had finished reading it, to retell it in the target-language as complete in its contents as possible. The aim of this experiment was to get hints to what extent the subjects had interpreted the meaning of the SL text for their translation and had stored it in memory. This was also intended to yield insights on whether the subjects had performed the translations as mediations of sense rather than as interlingual exchanges of signs, or vice versa, and whether the subjects had the meaning of the text mentally available, thus meeting a basic requirement for performing mediations of sense[18].

The retelling of the text in the target-language was to prevent the test leader from receiving the impression that an interpretation of meaning, and thus genuine text processing, had taken place, even though the subjects might have only remembered the wording of the source-language text after having read it and thus produced a verbatim recall (cf. Wolff 1985: 164).

The data elicited by this experiment must certainly be evaluated critically and used in a cautious way. When the task of the experiment is to retell the content of a text in a foreign language, problems of text production may have the consequence that, although the subjects can interpret the meaning of the source-language, i.e. mother tongue, text, they only succeed partially or deficiently in reproducing it in the target-language, i.e. foreign language, text. In the case of the opposite direction of translation, i.e. foreign language into mother tongue, the problem may be less serious. It can be expected that after having interpreted the meaning of a foreign language text, the subjects are in principle able to reproduce it in their mother tongue, even though – as in the former case, too – performance factors such as limited memory, distraction, or momentary mental confusion may well exert a perturbing influence.

18 Cf. section 7.3.

But with all due care in dealing with the data thus elicited, it is likely that they give hints as to whether the source-language text was mentally processed to a greater or lesser extent; whether the meaning of the source-language text is mainly represented conceptually in the subjects or not; and whether the subjects could have performed their translations mainly as mediations of sense or not.

After the translations and reproductions had been recorded on cassette, they were transcribed in order to make them accessible for the subsequent analysis (cf. sections 4.4.2, 5.1.2, and 5.3.1).

4.3 On the Construct of a Rudimentary Ability to Mediate

It is an obvious fact that translation competence, as possessed by professional translators, is the result of a developmental process that is never final. The process is based on a predisposition to translate which every individual is endowed with. This innate predisposition is not controversial in translation theory. What is most controversial, however, is the way translation competence develops from an individual's innate predisposition. At the moment two highly controversial developmental models exist: Harris 1977, Harris/Sherwood 1978, and Toury 1984, 1986a; b.

Harris and Sherwood investigated "natural translation", i.e. ".. *the translation done by bilinguals in everyday circumstances and without special training for it*" (Harris 1977: 99) The authors came to the conclusion that the bilinguals' translation competence develops to the same degree as and parallel to their competence in the two languages involved. According to Harris (1977: 99)

> *... all translators have to be bilingual and ...* ***all bilinguals can translate.*** *In addition to some competence in two languages Li and Lj, they all possess a third competence, that of translating from Li to Lj, and vice versa. Bilingualism is therefore a triple, not a double, competence: and the third competence is bi-directional.*

When they acquire bilingualism children go through four stages in the development of translation competence:

Stage 1 is called **pre-translation**. During this most elementary stage a child names objects in two languages, e.g. French *oeil* and English *eye*. According to Harris and Sherwood (1978: 167), the main function of pre-translations for a child is to build up and practice a co-ordinated bilingual lexicon instead of two autonomous monolingual ones. Stage 2, **intrapersonal autotranslation** is characterized by the child translating utterances which s/he has produced in one language into the other. So the addressee of an intrapersonal autotranslation is the translator him- or herself, not a communication partner. As to the reason or reasons why intrapersonal autotranslations are produced, Harris and Sherwood point out that their subjects found it amusing and enjoyed playing with two languages. Stage 3 is called **interpersonal autotranslation.** Children translate utterances which they have produced themselves from one language into another. In contrast to intrapersonal autotranslations, interpersonal ones are produced and directed towards a communication partner.

According to Harris and Sherwood stages 1 to 3 have to be gone through in order to reach stage 4. This is called **transduction**, i.e. translation in the narrow sense. It is defined by Harris and Sherwood as "*communication in which the translator acts as an intermediary between two people*" (1978: 165).

It should be emphasized again that Harris and Sherwood consider the development of translation competence as running parallel to the development of bilingualism, and that the degree of translation competence increases automatically to the extent to which the child's ability to use the two languages involved develops.

The second developmental model of translation competence was proposed by Toury (1984, 1986a,b). Toury agrees with Harris and Sherwood about an innate human predisposition to translate. He considers it to be "*co-extensive with bilingualism*" (Toury 1986a: 85). The differences between the two concepts become evident when Toury characterizes the innate predisposition as follows (1986a: 85):

> *(a) the **realization** of this potential, which coincides with the onset of a translating career, should be taken as **coextensive with "interlingualism"** (which is the ability to establish similarities and differences, at more than a single level, between items, structures and rules pertinent to those languages that a bilingual speaker has at his disposal) and with the presence of some mental mechanism which enables him to **activate** his ability to establish interlingual relationships, and*
> *(b) the **development** of translating as a skill is not reducible to a mere unfolding of the innate predisposition, but should be regarded as a function of the bilingual speaker's practice in actual translating, at least from the point where his translational behaviour can be characterized as communicative, that is, socially motivated and socially functional.*

According to Toury, translation competence does not develop quasi-automatically and parallel to the development of a child's bilingualism. Bilingualism is considered to be a *necessary*, but not a *sufficient* pre-condition for the development of translation competence. In addition to an individual's bilingual or quasi-bilingual competence a transfer competence must be built up (Toury 1984: 189). Apart from other possible but hitherto unknown factors, it comprises the individual's ability to transfer texts equivalently on various levels according to a given purpose/aim and with regard to sense, communicative function(s), style, text type, and/or other factors; or to deliberately violate postulates of equivalence for a certain purpose (cf. Hönig/Kußmaul 1982; Reiß/Vermeer 1984; Krings 1987).

My research into translation processes is founded on the hypothesis that every individual who has a command of two or more languages (even with various degrees of proficiency) also possesses a rudimentary ability to mediate between these languages. On the one hand, this hypothetical construct takes a medial position between Harris/Sherwood and Toury, on the other hand, it goes beyond Harris/Sherwood and Toury in three important aspects:

1. The question as to whether translation competence is a *natural* phenomenon which comes into being and develops automatically and parallel to an individual's bilingualism can only be answered in terms of the notion of translation which one adopts. In translation theory, it is customary to define translation as a text-based activity which, with respect to the purpose of the translation and its addressees, aims at rendering a source-language text into a target-language text so that equivalence of sense and/or function and/or style and/or text type, etc. will be realized in an optimal way for the various levels of the text (cf. Reiß/Vermeer 1984; Hönig/Kußmaul 1982; Catford 1965). If one adopts such a concept of translation, Harris and Sherwood's hypothesis must obviously be questioned. The data which the authors discuss suggest that their subjects produced approximate mediations of sense rather than translations which correspond to the definitional criteria mentioned above.

In his developmental model, Toury distinguishes between *bilingual* and *interlingual* competence, considering the former a necessary precondition for the latter (i.e. translation competence). Thus Toury also implicitly uses a notion of translation which goes beyond an approximative mediation of sense. In his 1984 paper, however, he points out (p.190):

> *Since the ability to translate presupposes the ability to acquire bilingualism ..., a speaker may be said to be able to make this crucial transition as soon as his bilingualism commences. Admittedly, at the beginning, translating, if indeed performed, is restricted in nature. But "restricted translating" is a form of "translating".*

Those elementary froms of mediation of sense which can be observed in bilingual children at a very early age are neither considered to be translations by translation theory nor are they given any attention by translation theorists. One reason for this may be that translation theory focusses on professional translators and their highly developed translation competence[19]. Another reason may be that professional translators do not wish to see their complex work, for which an extensive training was necessary, placed on the same level and subsumed under the same heading as the very elementary mediations of bilingual children.

With the aim of my research in mind, i.e. a psycholinguistic analysis of the translation process, I think it *is* sensible to subsume bilingual children's media-

19 Cf. Toury 1979, 1980a, 1981, 1984, 1986a,b; cf. also Chapter 3 of this volume.

tions under the heading of translation. It is only after a comparison of the products *and* the mental processes as they are to be found in or can be reconstructed from bilingual children's and professional translators' performance that it would be possible for a model of translation competence with either a wide or a narrow notion of translation to *rationally* be construed.

2. In both Toury's and Harris and Sherwood's developmental model, bilingualism is considered to be a crucial precondition for translating or is taken to comprise the ability to translate (i.e. in *natural translation*). Real bilingualism, i.e. an absolutely equal degree of availability of two languages in any situation and for any information to be communicated, probably only exists in approximations (cf. Crystal 1976; Hüllen 1980b; Secord/Backman 1974).

This is equally true for professional translators. As a rule, their competence in one language is higher than in the other. Furthermore, there seem to be considerable differences among professional translators with respect to their competence in the languages involved.

Since bilingualism and bilingual competence can only be achieved approximately, the logical consequence is to hypothesize as well a rudimentary ability to mediate information between languages for people who are in possession of a mother tongue and an *interlanguage*, and to consider their mediations as translations in a broad sense. This seems to be justified because the transition from an interlanguage to a fully developed second language – as far as this can be achieved by learners – is a continuum rather than a fixed boundary.

3. The elementary forms of mediation which have been outlined occur in *real* mediating situations, in which communication between a source-language text sender and a target-language text receiver is established via a mediator. The data for my research were not collected in *real* mediating situations. First, there was no explicit addressee for whom the translations had been performed, although in the minds of the test subjects the test leader might have played this role. Second, both the subjects and the implicit addressee of the translation (the test leader) share the same languages involved in the translations. There was no language barrier which would have made translations necessary to establish communication. The purpose of the translations for the subjects was rather to externalize data on the translation process, and for the test leader to collect these data[20]. Thus communication in the translations of my corpus resembles didactic communication in the foreign language classroom which I have analyzed elsewhere (Lörscher 1983: 38ff.). In spite of the artificial element inherent in the translational communications and the situations in which they

---

20 This artificial mediating situation was chosen because my epistemological interest focusses on the hypothetical reconstruction of translation strategies (cf. sections 1.2, 4.1, 4.2.2, and 4.5). The methods employed, especially that of thinking-aloud, could either not have been applied in *real* mediating situations or would have caused an even higher degree of artificiality.

were produced, the modes of realization of the subjects' evident rudimentary ability to mediate will be categorized as translations. Since the aim of my research was to analyze translation *processes*, this seems to be sensible because it is still unknown whether translation *processes* in real mediating situations are different – in detail or in principle – from translation *processes* in artificial mediating situations. A distinction between these phenomena would only be justified if a comparison of the data collected in these two kinds of mediating situations revealed significant differences.

As a result of the three arguments outlined above, it can be pointed out that an individual's elementary ability to mediate leads to performance products which are to be classified as translations. As soon as an individual has an even partial command of two or more languages, elementary mediations between them become possible. The rudimentary ability to mediate and its modes of realization function irrespective of the genuine nature of the mediating situation and irrespective of the naturalness of its communication.

The existence of an innate rudimentary ability to mediate and of its realization in elementary translations cannot be proved in the strict positivist sense. But it seems highly plausible in the light of the following two considerations:

i. The rudimentary ability to mediate as realized in elementary translations can be considered a special case of at least two universal innate abilities of the human intellect: that of *categorizing* and and that of *comparing*, of differentiating similarities and dissimilarities. Both these abilities, which also underlie any natural linguistic competence, make it possible for the individual to express sense and/or connections of signs in different ways. The mediations of sense and/or signs can occur within the verbal sphere (V → V), between the verbal and the nonverbal spheres (V ↔ NV) and between different nonverbal spheres (NV → NV). Diagram 5 is a first, preliminary, and certainly incomplete, attempt to systematize the manifold relations which exist between the various factors potentially involved in mediations (cf. also Toury 1986c: 1111ff. especially 1114).

Diagram 5: Factors and Relations Potentially Involved in Mediations

MEDIATION

(primarily sense- or primarily form-oriented)

NV	→	V	V	→	NV	V → V	NV	→	NV
Thoughts	→	Language	Language	→	Thoughts	(see below)	Emotions	→	Music
Mimicry	→	Language	Language	→	Mimicry		Emotions	→	Art
Gestures	→	Language	Language	→	Gestures		Emotions	→	tactile, kinesic, proxemic, behaviour
Body Movements	→	Language	Language	→	Body Movements				
Music	→	Language	Language	→	? Music ?				
Art	→	Language	Language	→	? Art ?		.		.
Photography	→	Language	Language	→	? Photography ?		.		.
.					.		.		.
.					.		.		.
.					.		.		.

V → V

intralingual (*no code change involved*)			
Paraphrase	Change of Style	Change of Register	Others

interlingual (*code change involved*)	
Code Switching (*primarily form-oriented*)	Translation (*primarily sense-oriented*)

As soon as an individual has at least partially acquired the modes of verbal and/or nonverbal behaviour listed in the diagram, rudimentary mediations between them are possible. As a matter of fact it can be observed that a child who has partially acquired his or her mother tongue as well as the meaning and use of gestures, facial expressions, etc. is able to express information available in a verbal code by means of gestures or facial expressions, and vice versa. Admittedly, these mediations differ considerably from those made by experts (e.g. professional mimes) as regards range, quality, and possibly other criteria, but nonetheless they are considered to be mediations even though they are imperfect ones. Something similar is true when emotional complexes are transformed into tactile, kinesic, or proxemic modes of behaviour, and vice versa.

Mediations between language and art or music are probably on a very elementary level. It seems that in these mediations differences between experts and non-experts are especially striking.

ii. The training of students for translation and interpretation never starts from scratch but builds on the skills which the students already possess. These may have been acquired in the foreign language classroom, but they in turn build on even more basic mediating skills. The starting-point of an individual's rudimentary ability to mediate between two or more languages and its realization in elementary translations is probably marked by the beginning of the acquisition process of a second language. During this process – especially when it takes place in the classroom – a widespread phenomenon can be observed: learners often systematically relapse into their mother tongue. It functions like a filter through which the foreign language is received and produced. According to Ringbom (1985b: 9; n.d.[1985]: 4) it is a generally accepted principle that L2-learners constantly seek to facilitate their difficult task by making use of all those parts of their previous knowledge which they consider (potentially) relevant. Their previous linguistic knowledge consists of both what they already know about the target-language and of their knowledge of their L1 and possible other languages. – The learners' recourse to their L1 knowledge and the learners' relating it to their relevant L2 knowledge in order to augment and develop the latter represents a case of a uni-directional mediation of information.

There is, furthermore, a phenomenon of importance which occurs primarily during the initial phase of foreign language learning at school and which resembles Harris and Sherwood's *intrapersonal autotranslation*: it is the learners' translation of target-language material which they have received, in order to be able to (better) decode it; or, in foreign language text production, it is the learners' production of an interim source-language text which they will then translate into the target-language[21]. The latter is often done because directly producing a foreign language text is often considered more difficult than producing it via a translation.

It is no wonder that the two kinds of mediation of information just mentioned and the products which they yield are *not* considered translations in translation theory. They are phenomena which do not occur in professional translating and therefore the models of translation theory either cannot cope with them at all or cannot cope with them satisfactorily. For the reasons mentioned, however, I think it *is* sensible to investigate them when one aims at analyzing translation processes or when one aims at finding out how translation competence develops.

4.4 Methodological Remarks

The methods employed in researching the object of investigation, which was outlined in section 4.2.2, will be dealt with in the following sections. A distinction will be made between methods and procedures for the *elicitation* of data and those for the *analysis and evaluation* of data.

Among the methods for the elicitation of data, thinking-aloud as a procedure for collecting data which yield insights into mental processes is of decisive importance. It will be dealt with in section 4.4.1.

---

21 Cf. Chlenov 1948: 787f.; Wald 1961: 166f.

The analysis and evaluation of data is carried out by means of an interpretive approach, as this is customary in performance analysis (cf. section 4.4.2). The primary aim of this approach is the hypothetical reconstruction of sense relations (cf. subsection 4.4.2.1). It is determined by the epistemological interest of this investigation. In the process of interpretive reconstruction, certain data are interpreted as (observable) indicators of (unobservable, mental) translation strategies (cf. subsection 4.4.2.2). These indicators represent the basis for the formation of hypotheses. The procedures employed in this process will be dealt with in subsection 4.4.2.3.

4.4.1 Thinking-Aloud as a Method for Collecting Data on Translation Processes

During the era of behaviourism, language behaviour was almost exclusively studied in terms of *input* (i.e. stimuli) and *output* (i.e. response, the actual behaviour). The processes of speech reception and speech production taking place inside the human brain, (the *black box*, as the bahaviourists called it), were beyond the reach of the behaviourists' stimulus-response model. They were considered to be beyond any scientific investigation because they are not open to observation and thus cannot be investigated by means of those methods which the behaviourists proclaimed to be the only scientific ones[22]. With the advent of mentalism, however, they developed into a new focus of interest and a considerable part of research in psychology and linguistics was devoted to them (cf. Bense 1973; Chomsky 1959, 1965; Dascal 1983; Katz 1964). According to mentalist psychology, hypotheses on the processes of speech reception and speech production can be formed by taking into account the input and the output together with information on the situation, as well as general knowledge of the nature of mental processes. The problems connected with this approach are well-known and numerous. Here I only want to mention that it is often impossible to determine input precisely in terms of a set of information, and make use of it in a 'workable' way. The same applies to output. Furthermore, different inputs can lead to the same output, and vice versa, which makes reasoning about mental processes problematic, to say the least.

Therefore, the assumption seems justified that the quality of the hypotheses on the processing of information in the brain can be improved by taking into account data from the production process which the language user has been asked to externalize while producing the language output. Such introspective data are more closely linked to the production process than any other data which investigators can currently elicit (cf. Weidle/Wagner 1982: 83).

---

22 Nonetheless, a close, rule-governed connection between stimulus and response was hypothesized. Thus, the behaviourists presupposed a strong hypothesis for which they had hardly any empirical evidence.

The method of introspection as a research tool was developed and introduced into psychology by the Würzburg school in the first decade of this century. (Here I will only mention the names Külpe and Bühler who are probably the most famous representatives of this school.) Starting from a criticism of the then predominant associationist view of thinking, the Würzburg school founded the experimental psychology of thought (*Denkpsychologie*). The main method used to collect data was introspection.

Thinking-aloud as a special case of introspecting, goes back to Karl Bühler and Edouard Claparède (1933; 1934) who developed this method of data collection.

Bühler's aim was to find out what an individual experiences while thinking. He assumed that many processes of thinking are highly automatized and thus not conscious. In order to make an individual think consciously, the most natural way is to ask him/her a question which can be answered with 'yes' or 'no' (cf. Bühler 1907/1971: 64). The data which Bühler elicited in this way can be characterized as follows: First, they are verbalizations in connection with tasks for the solutions of which the subjects had to give reasons and/or explanations; second, they are *ex-post*-verbalizations and thus strictly speaking not thinking-aloud data; and third, they are elicited by the instruction to the subjects to report as precisely as possible what had gone through their minds during the experiment.

Claparède (1932, 1933, 1934) used the method of thinking-aloud in order to find out how hypotheses are formed during the process of problem solving. He gave his subjects the instruction to perform a verbal or pictorial task involving the solution of certain problems, and to verbalize everything which came into their minds during the task performance. As a result of his investigations Claparède found three basic kinds of hypothesis formation (Claparède 1932): First, by carefully looking at a phenomenon, i.e. by an habitual, automatic process. The hypothesis leaps to the eye, so to speak; second, by interpreting, by drawing logical conclusions from the observations made; and third, by simply trying out on the off-chance, without any concept.

When behaviourism became the predominating paradigm in psychology, the method of thinking-aloud was violently criticised (cf. Watson 1913). The behaviourists rejected any kind of introspection as being speculative because the interpretation of the data yielded by introspective methods was not considered to be objective. Only since the beginning of the 1970s has there been a revival and nowadays introspection is widely appreciated as a useful tool for the investigation of mental processes (cf. Cohen 1984; Deffner 1984; Ericsson/Simon 1980, 1984; Færch/Kasper 1987).

In connection with second-language learning, Cohen (1984) distinguishes between three basic categories of learner report data based on introspection:

1. *self-reports*: they are learners' descriptions of what they do, characterized by generalized statements about learning behaviour or labels they apply to themselves. Such statements are usually based on beliefs or concepts that

the learners have about the way in which they learn languages. The reports are often *not* derived from the observation of any specific event.

Examples (from my data): "I always read the text first before I start translating it." "First I always try if I can translate a sentence word-for-word."

2. *self-observation*: this is an inspection of specific language behaviour by the learner. The inspection occurs either *introspectively* (i.e. while the information is still in the short-term memory) or *retrospectively* (i.e. usually after about twenty seconds).

   Examples: "I took the word 'outline' because I think that it means a *short* description of the characteristics." "I use *extent* here, although I am not quite sure whether this is right."

3. *self-revelation*: if a learner's report is neither a description of general behaviours, nor based on inspection of specific ones, but consists of thinking-aloud data, i.e. verbalizations of whatever comes into the informant's mind while carrying out a task, this is referred to as selfrevelation. So the data of thinking-aloud protocols are basically unedited and unanalyzed by the subjects.

   Examples: "'Spite' means 'böser Wille' or 'Böswilligkeit', yes, I think I take that, 'Böswilligkeit'." "Where is the verb here in this sentence?"

These three different types of data externalization usually occur in combination; that is, a given report may contain data of all the three types. Thus it can be difficult to establish whether subjects are thinking aloud, without analysis, or whether they are observing their behaviour introspectively or retrospectively.

In my investigations of the translation process I asked the subjects to think aloud only, to externalize verbally whatever came into their minds during the translation of a text from one language into another. Most of the data I was able to collect by this method fall into the category of 'self-revelation', but a considerable portion (about 10%) can be classified as 'self-observation'. This is not astonishing because the two categories have no clear-cut borderline but overlap to a certain extent. Furthermore, subjects sometimes seem to feel a need to interpret their own behaviour although they were not asked to do so. Data which could be categorized as 'self-reports' are extremely rare in my corpus and can be neglected here.

According to Cohen (1984) six major factors characterize the data from the three categories of verbal reporting:

i. **number of participants**: how many investigators and informants take part in the process of gathering the data? The standard situation is probably that with one investigator and one or more informants. But the informants may also collect data by themselves as is the case in diary studies, for instance.

ii. **research context:** refers to the 'when', 'where', and, to some extent to the 'how' of data collection. The most general distinction to be made here is that between formal and informal settings.

iii. **recency of the event:** whilst thinking-aloud data are obtained at the time of the learning event, self-observational and self-report data can vary with respect to how soon after the learning event they are elicited.

iv. **mode of elicitation and response:** verbal report data can be elicited orally or by means of written instructions. The informants can respond verbally or in writing.

v. **formality of elicitation:** this can vary considerably. The degree of formal structure imposed on the elicitation can be very high, as for example in certain questionnaires, or very low, as for example in interviews which are carried out in a similar way to everyday conversations.

vi. **degree of external intervention:** the extent to which the respondent's reporting process is shaped by the investigator's instructions can vary a lot. On the one hand, informants could be asked to report everything which comes into their minds, on the other hand, the instructor could ask them to report specific information only.

The thinking-aloud data which I have gathered can be characterized as follows: They were collected orally (iv.), from an individual by an investigator (i.), at the moment the thoughts were taking place (iii.), with a low degree of formality of elicitation (ii. v.), and with no external intervention by the investigator (vi.).

Although nowadays introspective methods, and especially that of thinking-aloud, are widely used in psychology and linguistics, two decisive questions have not yet been answered in a fully satisfactory way:

(1.) How close is the correspondence between what is reported verbally by thinking-aloud and the internal processes of thinking?
(2.) How great an influence does thinking-aloud exert on the internal processes of thinking during the performance of a task?

To give at least preliminary answers to these two questions, Ericsson and Simon (1980, 1984) developed a model of how subjects, in response to an instruction to think aloud, verbalize information. The model is based on the assumption that human cognition is information-processing. A cognitive process can be seen as a sequence of internal states successively transformed by a series of information-processing steps.

According to Ericsson and Simon, it is the information about the input and the output of the processing system, not the processes themselves, which are in the subjects' focus of attention. Nonetheless, an individual can monitor these mental processes and can at least partially influence them after an evaluation of the (interim) results which they yield. As a consequence, the data externalized by thinking-aloud refer to the steps of information processing, not to the processing itself[23].

Information can be stored in several memories (cf. Ericsson/Simon 1980, 1984; Craik/Lockhart 1972)[24]. They differ with regard to their capacities, their processing characteristics, the representational characteristics of the information stored, and the speed with which information is taken in and fixed. There are:

a. several **sensory stores** of very short duration, but with large capacity. The sensory stores do not keep information for more than about two seconds and are often referred to as the ultra-short-term memory.

b. a **short-term memory** with limited capacity (about seven unconected items), intermediate duration, and acoustic or visual format of representation.

c. a **long-term memory** with large capacity and relatively permanent storage, but with slow fixation and long accesss times compared with the other memories. The nature of the representation is semantic or propositional.

Information from the long-term memory must first be retrieved, i.e. transferred to the short-term memory, before it can be reported. This is done via an association process. Information from the sensory stores can be brought into the short-term memory by a recognition process. Association processes operate on a step-by-step basis and are much slower than recognition processes. So, for instance, in recalling a name that is not immediately accessible, a person may use a sequence of cues to find an associative path, step-by-step to the desired name.

According to the findings of Artificial Intelligence and modern psycholinguistics, pieces of information are *not* stored independently of each other in the long-term memory, but in clusters, or rather in hierarchically structured networks (cf. Collins/Loftus 1975), which make up an organic whole. Thus, a person can recall a name by searching through his or her long-term memory for pieces of information which were stored in connection with the respective name, e.g. characteristics of a person's outer appearance, of the situation in which one saw, heard or met him or her, and so forth. Such information can activate the semantic network, i.e. the respective script, frame, schema in which the desired name is stored, and can result in recalling the name from the long-term memory.

---

23 Cf. Dechert 1987; Dechert/Sandrock 1986; Cohen/Hosenfeld 1981; for a contrary view cf. White 1980.

24 Although Ericsson and Simon use the conventional multi-store model, they emphasize that their processing assumptions about thinking-aloud are well compatible with other memory models, such as the levels-of-processing approach (cf. Craik/Lockhart 1972; Shiffrin/Schneider 1977) according to which there is only one homogeneous store with different levels of processing.

According to Ericsson and Simon's model, aural information, i.e. strings of phonemes, which is encoded in the short-term memory can be vocalized by automatic verbal translation. Information which is encoded visually can only be reported verbally if it is transformed into the verbal code. As the verbal-encoding processes involved in thinking-aloud evoke a verbal reference to the heeded structure in the short-term memory, thinking-aloud will not change the structure and the course of the task process, although it may slightly slow down the speed of task performance. So, according to Ericsson and Simon, the question as to whether thinking-aloud influences the internal processes of thinking during the performance of a translation as a verbal task can be answered negatively.

Summing up, one can say that concurrent verbalizations, i.e. verbalizations during task performance, fall into three categories:

i. When subjects articulate information directly that is already available to them, thinking-aloud neither changes the course and structure of the cognitive processes, nor does verbalization slow down these processes;

ii. When the information being processed to perform the main task is not verbal or propositional (e.g. visually encoded information), the performance may be slowed down or the verbalizations may be incomplete, but the course and structure of the task performance process remains largely unchanged;

iii. When subjects are not merely asked to think aloud, but are asked for specific kinds of information, their efforts to obey these instructions have more substantial effects on task performance.

As to the question of how close the correspondence is between thinking-aloud and internal thinking, Ericsson and Simon distinguish between three cases:

i. If the task is of a verbal kind and can be performed in a series of steps towards the final goal, the model predicts a close correspondence between the internal processes of thinking and what is externalized by thinking-aloud;

ii. If the task is performed as a highly automatic, overlearned process, such as, for instance, perceptual-encoding and motor processes, the intermediate stages of such processes are not stored in the short-term memory, but only their final product. As a consequence, automatic mental processes are less reportable, and thinking-aloud does not yield useful information about intermediate stages of these processes;

iii. If the task is performed by mental processes which are *not* automatized and which operate on information that is *not* verbally, but visually encoded, it is assumed that verbal reports are incomplete, which means that thinking-aloud and the internal processes of thinking only correspond partially.

The assumptions made by Ericsson and Simon were largely confirmed by an empirical investigation reported on in Deffner (1984). He compared the task performance of a group of subjects who were thinking aloud while performing a task with a group of subjects who were thinking silently. The task was the same in the two groups. Among other things, the comparison yielded two interesting results:

1. Subjects who were thinking aloud during the task performance were the more systematic problem-solvers;

2. Subjects who were thinking aloud during the task performance were the more successful problem-solvers.

So it seems that thinking-aloud does not hinder but rather favours problem-solving. However, more research is needed to find out whether these results can be generalized and/or under what circumstances.

Finally, I would like to sum up what to me seem to be the main points concerning introspective methods in general, and thinking-aloud in particular, as a means for eliciting information about translation processes in my investigation:

I. Subjects can only report what is in their focus of attention (cf. Ericsson/ Simon 1984; Weidle/Wagner 1982; Dechert/Sandrock 1986). It is only information stored in the short-term memory which can be externalized, and which, by definition, is in the individual's focus of attention. There is no way of obtaining information about mental processes which are not given cognitive attention by means of any of the three introspective methods described above.

II. To obtain mainly unedited and unanalyzed data, I asked my subjects to think aloud only. In this way, I wanted to make sure that the method of data collecting exerts the least influence possible on the mental processes of task performance.

III. Thinking-aloud was also requested because it is a type of concurrent verbalization. In contrast to retrospective reports, subjects are not exposed to a memory load, which means that the information they externalize is potentially more complete.

IV. Translation processes mainly operate on verbally encoded data. According to Ericsson and Simon, this is another favourable precondition for thinking-aloud to yield the largest possible amount of information on on-going mental processes.

V. In my analysis of translation processes I concentrated on translators' problems and on what they thought aloud when they found themselves confronted with such problems. There was hardly any thinking-aloud during subjects' automatic, i.e. largely unconscious, substitution of source-language text segments by target-language text segments (cf. Krings 1986a).

VI. Solving translation problems is often carried out as a series of steps. Generally, subjects do not immediately reach solutions which they consider to be optimal. They rather have to work out optimal solutions. In searching through their memories they activate informational networks (scripts, frames, schemata), thus producing interim solutions, and try to optimize these with regard to their expectation structures (cf. Chapter 7).

The step-by-step nature of translational problem-solving is a further favourable precondition for thinking-aloud to yield much reliable data on the ongoing mental processes.

From all these considerations, it becomes clear that verbal report data are useful for making hypotheses[25] about mental processes if we take into account the conditions under which the data are externalized, and their inherent limitations. Or, as Ericsson and Simon (1980: 247) put it:

> *... verbal reports, elicited with care and interpreted with full understanding of the circumstances under which they are obtained, are a valuable and thoroughly reliable source of information about cognitive processes. ... They describe human behavior that is as readily interpreted as any other human behavior. ... To omit them ... is only to mark as terra incognita large areas on the map of human cognition that we know perfectly well how to survey.*

4.4.2 Performance Analysis as an Interpretive Approach

As was pointed out in subsection 4.2.2.3, the translations which constitute the data corpus were produced orally and recorded on cassette in order to make them accessible for subsequent analysis. In performance analysis, this permanent record of utterances is considered to be a necessary precondition for any kind of interpretation of the data. The analysis is carried out on the basis of the transcripts *and* the recordings. It aims at the hypothetical reconstruction of aspects of the translation *process* by interpreting the recorded and transcribed translation *performance* (cf. section 1.2).

Two aspects of the reconstructive analysis will be presented in the following subsections:

i. the aspect of *interpretation as sense constitution*; the analyst interprets the collected data with regard to his/her hypothetical assumptions, his/her anticipated patterns of explanation, and his/her epistemological interest. The process of interpretation will be dealt with in subsection 4.4.2.1.

ii. the aspect of *sense constitution by means of strategy indicators*; data which the analyst considers to be indicators of underlying mental strategies

---

25 Both Ericsson and Simon (1980: 216, 1984: 3) and Dörner (1976: 8) point out that thinking-aloud and other introspective methods can only be used for making hypotheses about mental processes, not for testing them.

allow sense to be ascribed to the phenomena under investigation. The concept of strategy indicators will be discussed in subsection 4.4.2.2.

It must be emphasized here that these two aspects of the reconstructive analysis always occur together in the concrete process of interpretation. They have only been separated for heuristic reasons (cf. section 4.2.1 ii.).

The sociology of knowledge (cf. Schütz 1932; Berger/Luckmann 1966) and ethnomethodology (cf. Cicourel 1964; 1973a; 1973b; Garfinkel 1967; 1973; Mehan/Wood 1975) have convincingly shown that sense is not inherent to the phenomena of the world but that it is ascribed to them by the analyst on the basis of his/her epistemological interest. The sense constitution is thus carried out for a certain purpose and with a certain aim. As a consequence sense is not an objectively given entity[26], but is always predicated sense (cf. Schütz 1932; Holly/Kühn/Püschel 1984).

4.4.2.1 Interpretive Reconstruction

The method of interpretive reconstruction of sense relations is the traditional domain of hermeneutics (cf. Gadamer 1965; 1974; Hartfiel 1972: 263). In the recent past it was developed further by a discipline which is called discourse or conversational analysis (cf. Lörscher 1983: 64ff.). Since about the mid-sixties, developments in both linguistics and sociology have occurred which have been mutually supportive.

Whereas previously, linguistics had concentrated on the systematicity of *langue*, it now (re-)discovered the social nature of language, and the use of language in communicative situations became a focus of interest.

The (re-)discovery by sociologists of the function of language as a means of social interaction, complementing the work of linguists, was characterized by the important part ethnomethodology played (cf. Kallmeyer/Schütze 1976; Giglioli 1973b; Lörscher 1983).

The term *ethnomethodology* was coined by Garfinkel (1967) and denotes the investigation of practical everyday thinking as a constitutive part of any human activity. According to Garfinkel (1972), ethnomethodology is concerned with two things: with the everyday activities which socialized individuals make explicable by using their everyday knowledge in an unreflected but nonetheless methodical way; and with the methods which individuals employ in their everyday life to construct social reality (cf. Psathas 1972: 291f.; Lörscher 1983: 67). Thus, social reality is no longer considered to be a static product or *fait* as in the tradition of Durkheim (1938/1895), but rather to be a dynamic

26 This is also pointed out by Gadamer (1965; 1974). According to him, understanding is more than a mere re-production of a former production. In philosophical hermeneutics, the view is taken that understanding is only possible when the 'understander' brings his/her knowledge into play. This productive contribution of the interpreter is necessary for any interpretation to make sense (cf. Gadamer 1974: 1069).

process of internalization, objectivation, and externalization (cf. Berger/ Luckmann 1966).

Ethnomethodology aims at discovering the structure of the social reality thus construed and at elucidating the process of reality construction. It seeks to understand the world in the same way in which the individual interprets it in his/her everyday life (cf. Psathas 1972: 291f.).

The interpretation and reconstruction of everyday knowledge in the way in which the members of society methodically use it is mainly carried out by an analysis of conversations because social reality is built up by means of communicative processes which, to a large extent, are linguistic processes, too. And since linguistic processes are embedded in interactive processes, the former can only be understood in connection with the latter. Social meaning thus always has a reflexive and indexical nature (cf. Cicourel 1973a; Bar-Hillel 1954), and is characterized by an "essential vagueness". This becomes evident mainly by the fact that utterances in natural conversations almost always have an incomplete and ambiguous meaning (cf. Giglioli 1973b: 13).

Whereas those engaged in conversation *negotiate* reality and *construct* sense(relations), it is the task of the analyst to *interpret* conversation, i.e. to *re-construct* sense(relations). Whilst in conversational and discourse analysis conversations with at least two participants[27] are mainly investigated, the linguistic phenomena to be analyzed here are texts with an *explicitly* mono-logical character. The subjects produced their translations in situations in which generally they had neither any linguistic nor any non-linguistic contact with the only possible communication partner, the test leader. Nevertheless, it can be assumed that *implicitly*, in the minds of the subjects, the test leader was the addressee of the utterances produced (cf. section 4.3 and Chapter 3.). To this extent, the texts have an *implicitly* dialogical character. They are addressed to another person and thus represent a type of social activity in the sense of Weber (1966: 5).

The analyst of the explicitly monological texts to be investigated here is possibly in a less favourable position than somebody who has to interpret (dia-logical) conversations. In conversations, the communication partners negotiate reality and jointly constitute sense. This often manifests itself in the text produced and thus becomes accessible to analysis. In (explicitly) monological texts, however, the text producer implies his/her model of reality and does not usually make it explicit. The same probably applies to sense constitution. It is likely to be verbalized to a lesser degree in monologues than in conversations. In order to compensate for these deficiencies, at least partially, the method of thinking-aloud suggests itself. By means of this procedure it should be possible to obtain information which is generally made explicit in (dialogical) conversa-tions but which is implicit in (monological) texts.

27 Cf. Lörscher 1983: 64–66 where the different notions are discussed and definitional approaches are reported on.

Reconstructive analysis, irrespective of its application to monologues or dialogues, is described by Switalla (1977: 175) as follows:

> *Eine sprachliche Äußerung zu verstehen, ist ... ein komplexer Prozeß der (in Alltagssituationen in der Regel stillschweigend vollzogenen) Deutung von ... sprachlichen Äußerungen als Ausdrücken für bestimmte Mitteilungen, mit denen bestimmte Handlungen in bestimmten Situationen (und zu bestimmten Zwecken) getan werden. Die Basis dieser Deutungsleistungen, die das Verstehen von Äußerungen ausmacht, ist jenes soziale Wissen davon, was denn einer 'üblicherweise' sagen will, wenn er die und die Äußerung tut, welche kommunikative Intention einer 'üblicherweise' hat, wenn er das und das sagt, welche Gründe einer 'üblicherweise' hat, wenn er die und die Handlungs-Intention verfolgt usw. das wir in für uns mit der jeweils gegebenen Situation ähnlichen Situationen erworben haben. – Eine sprachlich-kommunikative Äußerung im konkreten Fall **explizit** zu deuten, kann demnach nur heißen, das eigene sprachlich-kommunikative Erfahrungswissen schrittweise und soweit wie notwendig und sinnvoll darzulegen.*

The interpretive reconstruction as outlined by Switalla will also be used in this investigation. Here, too, (series) of verbal utterances as well as their cooccurring non-verbal and paralinguistic ones will be interpreted on the basis of the analyst's linguistic and communicative experience. It comprises segments of three fields of knowledge:

I. everyday knowledge[28], which is acquired in the process of socialisation. It is possessed by all socialised individuals and represents the basis of any interaction and interpretation.

II. specific knowledge, which the analyst has acquired by observing his/her and other people's production of translations. It is used for the interpretation of those performance phenomena which are similar to the ones in his/her experience.

III. scientific knowledge, which the analyst has acquired during his/her scientific training and as a result of his/her experience in analyzing data. It mainly comprises methodological and research-practical knowledge.

By deliberately and systematically appealing to his/her everyday knowledge, which s/he has basically in common with the investigated subjects, the analyst can interpret their linguistic performance in a way not constantly affected by subjective distortions. This is even more valid because the analyst with his/her scientific and specific knowledge thus participates in two more fields of knowledge which s/he partially shares with other analysts.

---

28 According to Günther/Habel/Rollinger (1983) everyday knowledge can be divided into three subtypes:
i. factual knowledge, i.e. knowledge of events and facts in the real world,
ii. rule-based knowledge, i.e. knowledge of relations between objects in the real world,
iii. object-based knowledge, i.e. knowledge of objects and human beings in the world.

In the interpretive reconstruction of sense(relations), observable verbal and non-verbal actions are explained teleologically, i.e. with regard to their aims and purposes. In the domain of conversational analysis, Dittmann (1979b: 23ff.) deals with the problems connected with teleological hypotheses under formal and research-practical points of view. As the interpretive reconstruction of an action is carried out by means of an implicit, circular logical conclusion, the validation of the results which the analysis yields represents a considerable problem (cf. Brunner 1982). It cannot be solved logically. Only a consideration of plausibility seems possible, a consideration based on the analyst's everyday knowledge, which s/he has largely in common with the investigated subjects, as well as on his/her specific and scientific knowledge, which s/he has at least partly in common with other analysts. For these reasons, conversational analysis, according to Ramge (1977: 120), can never be *objective*. It can only be *methodologically controlled* when suitable measures are taken to ensure a high degree of intersubjective validity. The same also applies to performance analysis.

In order to gain hints on how great differences in interpretation might be among different analysts, I asked seven students of mine[29] to analyze a sample of translations with me but independent of one another. The students were to listen to the recorded translations several times and then to analyze them by means of the categories of analysis which I had developed (cf. sections 5.2.2 and 5.2.3). As a result of the experiment, a high degree of agreement in interpretation became evident. This is also corroborated by observations made by Ramge (1977: 122, 127).

4.4.2.2 Strategy Indicators

In the interpretation of the available data corpus, the analyst has recourse to those observable data which s/he considers signs or indicators of not directly observable, mental translation strategies. In anticipation of the definition of strategy suggested in section 4.5.3, and of the translation strategies and their elements discussed in section 5.2.3, it must be kept in mind that translation strategies range from a subject's realization of a translational problem to its solution or to the subject's realization of its insolubility for him or her.

The concept of indicator as it will be used in this investigation is based on Sager (1981). According to him, an indicator is an observable or measurable object or event which reveals something, or refers to something. It is, at least at the time of the investigation, not observable or accessible, but exists or can exist independent of the indicator.

According to this definition, indicators represent a subgroup of signs. With the latter they share their function of representation (*aliquid stat pro aliquo*).

---

29 As these students had taken part in a seminar on analyzing translation processes, which I had taught, they had acquired knowledge which was partly in common with my own.

Specific for indicators is the fact that they refer to non-observable phenomena and that specific relations exist between them and the entities they indicate. Sager (1981: 351) distinguishes between four possible types of indicator-entity-relations:

1. An indicator results from a causal connection in inanimate nature. Thus, lightning is an indicator of thunder, smoke indicates fire, rain a low-pressure area, etc.

2. An indicator results from a biological process within organisms. Thus, a sore throat, fever, and other symptoms indicate a cold, trembling hands refer to nervousness or excitement, certain sounds of animals are signs of aggression, hunger, etc.

3. An indicator results from a change of a relation in nature which was brought about by an organism. Thus, skid-marks on a road refer to abrupt breaking of a vehicle, footprints and remains of bones indicate the existence of animate beings, trees with gnawed off bark are signs of the occurrence of rodents, etc.

4. An indicator results from an intentional use of signs by individuals. Thus, a specifically wrong answer to a question indicates a (semantic or acoustic) misunderstanding, the use of certain expressions refer to the speaker belonging to a certain regional or social group, a specific use of signs indicates the intention of the sign user[30], etc.

From the types of possible indicator-entity-relations outlined above, three facts become evident:
First, different indicators have different degrees of vagueness (cf. Sager 1981: 353). Smoke can indicate fire as well as certain chemical reactions, a sore throat and fever can be signs of a cold but also of diphtheria, a specifically wrong answer to a question can indicate misunderstanding but also an intentional misleading. All these cases show that the indicators of types 4. and 5. have inherently an especially high degree of vagueness compared with the ones of types 1. and 2. One reason for this may be the fact that social reality is controlled by rules and norms, whereas nature is governed by natural laws and, as far as animate nature is concerned, by biological laws. Social rules and norms allow functionally equivalent behaviour and are characterized by a certain degree of flexibility and by the existence of options. Natural and biological laws, however, are largely determined in the sense of causal chains and are either valid without exceptions (natural laws) or with only very few exceptions (biological laws) and allow hardly any options for the individual. ***Second***, indicators generally have a higher degree of reliability when they are made up

30 Cf. Hönig and Kußmaul's retrospective calculation being the translator's interpretive achievement.

of several pieces of information or even when they constitute whole sets of symptoms of something. Thus, a sore throat and fever can indicate a cold or diphtheria. But when further pieces of information are given, such as headache, sweet-smelling breath, inflammation of the palatine tonsils, tumefaction of the mandible lymph glands, trouble in the abdomen, in breathing and speaking, and albumin in the urine, a set of symptoms is constituted which typically indicates diphtheria. ***Third***, indicators are always bound to an interpreter. S/he must be able to interpret certain signs and complexes of signs as indicators of certain entities. This presupposes the interpreter's knowledge of the relationship between an underlying segment of reality and the sign(s) to be interpreted as indicator(s) of this segment of reality. In this connection Sager (1981: 352) points out:

> *Indikator zu sein, ist daher nicht eine Eigenschaft von Objekten an sich, sondern eine "funktionale Eigenschaft" ..., die Entitäten nur von bestimmten Interpreten zugeschrieben werden kann, und zwar im Rahmen eines diesem Interpreten bekannten Konzepts von Wirkungszusammenhängen.*

With regard to the specifics of the knowledge involved in interpretation, two extreme cases can be distinguished:
In the first case, everyday knowledge as well as specific and scientific knowledge are required for the interpretation. This is true for the symptoms indicating diphtheria, for certain performance phenomena which function as an indicator of a person belonging to a certain regional and social group, etc. In the second case, the interpreter only has recourse to his/her everyday knowledge and possibly to some rather unspecific knowledge acquired by experience. This is true for the interpretation of smoke indicating fire or lightning indicating thunder, etc.

The arguments put forward above are valid for indicators in general. They have important consequences for the interpretation of verbal and non-verbal signs as indicators of mental translation strategies.

As regards the *vagueness* of strategy indicators, they are likely to belong to type 4. (intentional use of signs), in general, and are accordingly vague. Nonetheless, a distinction must be made between *explicit* and *implicit* indicators (cf. Krings 1986a, b; Færch 1984). With respect to the localisation of the first step of a strategy, the realization of a translational problem (cf. sections 5.2.2 and 5.2.3), a pause in the production of the target-language text can be interpreted as being an implicit indicator, whereas the verbalization of a translational problem by the subject is to be interpreted as an explicit indicator. Thus, implicit indicators are obviously more vague than explicit ones. As regards the degree of *reliability* of implicit indicators, it must be assumed that it is higher when several pieces of information which the analyst considers relevant constitute the indicator. A pause in target-language text production may indicate a translational problem, but also a momentary distraction, lack of concentration, etc. If, however, the pause occurs at a point in the text which the analyst interprets to be difficult to translate, and if further signs such as *handicap-*

signals – e.g. "I don't know." (cf. Færch 1984: 60) – phatic utterances such as "hm" or "oh" with a fall-rise intonation contour, drawls, repetitions, and/or self-corrections can be found in the environment of that point, all the signals in their entirety are most likely to indicate a translational problem of a subject. But it is at the analyst's discretion to interpret the signals as an indicator or not. The basis of this interpretive achievement is, as pointed out by Sager (1981: 352), the analyst's knowledge of the relationship between the sign(s) s/he interprets to be an indicator and the underlying segment of reality. The interpreter's knowledge comprises relevant parts of the three types of knowledge described in the preceding section, i.e. everyday knowledge, specific knowledge, and scientific knowledge. The specific knowledge of the interpreter is of special importance in this respect. By the systematic and purposeful observation and analysis of translations which s/he and others have produced, the interpreter has acquired knowledge of what signs generally or often indicate or are likely to indicate translation strategies or their elements[31]. But this knowledge of the analyst is not entirely comprehensive. Signs which are not represented in the analyst's experience and which are not in analogy to represented signs are likely to be interpreted as indicators, or not, in a largely speculative way on the basis of considerations of probability. As a consequence, these considerations of probability must be made explicit step by step and to a degree which is necessary and sensible (cf. Switalla 1977: 175).

An essential differentiation of the concept of indicator was proposed by Sager (1981: 353ff.). He distinguishes between object and concept indicators. The former indicate concrete segments of reality (objects) which exist independently of the indicators. Thus, a footprint refers to an animate being which exists independently of the footprint. The same applies to smoke and fire. The latter (concept indicators) function as observable manifestations or components of an abstract, not directly observable, concept (system). It does not exist independently of its indicators but is constituted by them. Thus, for example, the speed with which problems can be solved can indicate the abstract concept of intelligence; the knowledge of those facts and of their relations to each other which are considered relevant by society, having good manners, etc., indicate the abstract concept of good education and upbringing.

With regard to the differentiation of object and concept indicators, Sager (1981: 254) points out that there is no clear-cut borderline but rather an area of overlap between the two kinds of indicators. The more differentiated a concept (i.e. model) of a segment of reality becomes, the more object indicators become concept indicators.

Translation strategies, as they will be defined in section 4.5.3 and documented in section 5.2, represent entities which are indicated by concept indicators. They are abstract in nature, not accessible to direct observation, and, for

31 Cf. subsection 4.4.2.1, as well as Switalla 1977: 175 and Schulze 1986.

the analyst, they do not exist independently of their indicators but rather they are constituted by those signs which are interpreted to be their indicators.

This means that the process of knowledge accumulation with respect to translation strategies has a dialectical nature. On the one hand, the analyst must have some knowledge of the concept of translation strategy in order to be able to ascribe the status of strategy indicators to certain signs. On the other hand, it is only by their indicators that translation strategies are constituted, so that knowledge of them can, to a very large extent, only be gained by means of strategy indicators. Therefore, the analyst must often proceed in a speculative and hypothetical way. S/he often does not interpret certain signs to be indicators as a result of his/her knowledge of the respective entity or of the relationship between an indicator and a segment of reality, but rather on the basis of considerations of probability. They can be corroborated or turn out to be false in the course of accumulating further knowledge of the phenomena and of gathering more experience in intepretation.

Therefore, the following list of signs which can function as strategy indicators is of a preliminary kind. It remains for further empirical investigations to possibly modify or complete the list of possible indicators. In the relevant literature, the following potential strategy indicators are given (Færch 1984: 60f.):

Diagram 6: Færch's Potential Strategy Indicators

– temporal variables
  – rate of articulation
  – pauses
  – drawls
  – repetitions
  – self-repairs
  – slips
	implicit strategy markers

– handicap signals (e.g. "I don't know" as an aside)	explicit strategy markers

The signs listed above can indicate strategies that operate in oral text production in general. They mainly refer to the realization of problems and thus to the very first step of strategies. They are, however, not specific to the translation process. But as this investigation focusses on translations produced orally, and as translation strategies, like any other text production strategies, have their starting-point in the identification of a problem (cf. section 4.5), the potential strategy indicators compiled by Færch can also be made usable for the analysis of my data corpus. Specific problem indicators which can be localized in the translation process were compiled by Krings (1986b: 267). He lists the following eleven indicators:

Diagram 7: Krings' Specific Problem Indicators

- The subjects' explicit statement of problems (1)
- The use of reference books (2)
- The underlining of source-language text passages (3)
- The semantic analysis of source-language text items (4)
- Hesitation phenomena in the search for potential equivalents (5)
- Competing potential equivalents (6)
- The monitoring of potential equivalents (7)
- Specific translation principles (8)
- The modification of written target-language texts (9)
- The assessment of the quality of the chosen translation (10)
- Paralinguistic or non-linguistic features (e.g. groaning or sighing) (11)

In his monograph on the investigation of the translation process (1986a: 121ff.), Krings distinguishes between primary (*primäre*) and secondary (*sekundäre*) problem indicators and thus comes close to the distinction between explicit and implicit strategy markers made by Færch. With regard to the differentiation between primary and secondary indicators Krings (1986a: 121) points out:

> *Primäre sind 'starke' Indikatoren, d.h. solche, die in so hohem Maße Problemevidenz schaffen, daß bei der Analyse der Daten bei Vorliegen von nur einem dieser Indikatoren das fragliche item als Problem klassifiziert worden ist. Sekundäre sind 'schwache' Indikatoren, d.h. solche, die zwar auf Probleme hinweisen können, aber einzeln nicht als ausreichend betrachtet werden, um das fragliche item als Problem zu klassifizieren.*

The following primary and secondary problem indicators are mentioned by Krings (1986a: 121):

Diagram 8: Krings' Primary and Secondary Problem Indicators

A. *primäre*
  1. *explizite oder implizite Problemidentifikation durch den Übersetzer*
  2. *Hilfsmittelbenutzung*
  3. *Lücken im zielsprachlichen Text*

B. *sekundäre*
  1. *konkurrierende tentative Übersetzungsäquivalente*
  2. *Änderungen im zielsprachlichen Textmanuskript (ZTM)*
  3. *Unterstreichungen im ausgangssprachlichen Text*
  4. *Unzufriedenheit des Übersetzers mit dem Übersetzungsprodukt (negative Übersetzungsproduktbewertung)*
  5. *Metaproblematisierung [Problematisierung des Zusammenhanges zwischen der Funktion des Ausgangstextes, der Funktion des Zieltextes und den sich daraus ergebenden unterschiedlichen Äquivalenz- und Adäquatheitsparametern (Krings 1986a: 136)]*
  6. *ungefüllte Pausen*
  7. *paralinguale Indikatoren*
  8. *Fehlen einer primären Äquivalentassoziation ...*

According to Krings' research design, the indicators listed above occur in the oral translation process (1, 2, 4–8, 10, 11, A1–A3, B1, B4–B8) or in the subsequent writing down of the translation (3, 9, A3, B2, B3). They refer both to subjects' realization of problems (1, (3), 11, A1, B3, B5–B8) and to steps of problem solving (2, 4–10, A2, (A3), B1, B2, B4, (B5)).

Although the signals listed under 3, 9, A3, B2, and B3 refer to written text production, they can be assumed to have counterparts in oral text production, too. Thus, 3/B3 may correspond to 'emphasizing source-language text segments, for example by one or more of the markers mentioned by Færch'; 9/B3 may correspond to 'modification of a target-language text segment by paraphrasing it or by altering it syntactically or semantically'; and A3 may correspond to 'gaps in the orally produced target-language text'. Therefore, the problem indicators compiled by Krings can also be useful for the analysis of my data which will be carried out in Chapter 5.

As was pointed out above, indicators are only constituted by the analyst's interpretive approach to the data. As a consequence, the signs in the lists quoted above are not strategy or problem indicators *by themselves* but *potential* indicators. In the process of interpretive reconstruction they can be interpreted as being strategy or problem indicators by the analyst. Therefore, Krings' view that the problem indicators can be *read* from the thinking-aloud protocols and hence allow a consistent and widely intersubjective identification of translation problems (1986a: 120) must be contradicted. Krings' instruction to the analyst of data from the translation process according to which an item is generally to be classified as a translation problem when at least one primary or two secondary problem indicators can be detected must also be considered critically. It implies that translation problems can automatically be read from the data by a mere numeric distribution of certain signs without recourse to the analyst's interpretive reconstruction.

Nonetheless, the potential problem or strategy indicators compiled by Krings are relevant for the analysis to follow because they can sensitize the interpreter for potential problems in subjects' translation process.

4.4.2.3 Hypothesis Formation

For the domain of conversational analysis, Dittmann (1979b: 32) distinguishes between two kinds of hypothesis formation: one is *inductive*, the other is *deductive*. These two kinds are not mutually exclusive but rather complementary in nature. When proceeding inductively, the analyst starts from the transcript of the conversation. S/he makes generalizations about single phenomena in the transcript which have the status of hypotheses. Such generalizations can be of a qualitative and/or of a quantitative kind. In the first case, the description of the transcript has a heuristic function; in the second case, it is a precondition for a subsequent analysis of the phenomena described. As any inductive procedure contains certain assumptions made by the analyst (cf. (sub)sections 4.2.1, 4.2.2, and 4.2.2.1), it always inherently has a deductive element, too (cf. Dittmann 1979b: 32; Lörscher 1983: 193).

When proceeding deductively, the analyst forms hypotheses by having recourse to relevant parts of his/her everyday knowledge and of his/her scientific and specific knowledge of the phenomenon to be analyzed. The hypotheses made in this way are then tested in the data corpus.

The two kinds of hypothesis formation described by Dittmann are also valid for the analysis of translation performance as carried out in this study. Here, as well as in conversational analysis, the approach to the data is of an empirical kind. The translation strategies and their elements, which will be discussed in the following sections and which will be formalized to make categories of analysis, were found by a combined inductive and deductive procedure of a qualitatively hypothetical kind. Starting from the empirical data elicited (inductive aspect), and using as a basis the analyst's assumptions about the translation process which s/he had developed as a result of his/her observing his/her own and other people's production of translations (deductive aspect), hypotheses about translation strategies and their elements will be proposed. When formalized, they make up a system of categories for analysis (cf. section 5.2.2, 5.2.3, and 5.2.5).

My approach to the data can be characterized as qualitatively insofar as the system of categories for analysis is heuristic in nature. Its application to transcribed translations allows a qualitative analysis of the data, which logically precedes any quantitative analysis. The latter, which will be carried out in Chapter 6, is essential for a comprehensive analysis of the translation process (cf. Lörscher 1983: 193; 283ff.; Arbeitsgruppe Fremdsprachenerwerb Bielefeld 1987).

4.5 Translation Strategies as the Object of Investigation

As was outlined in section 1.2, the aim of this study is to document and describe aspects of the translation process which can be reconstructed interpretively from the empirical data available. In the following sections, the object of this investigation will be determined more precisely.

Section 4.4.1 has yielded two essential results: First, it became evident that the quality of the hypotheses about mental processes can be improved when introspective data, especially those externalized by language users' thinking-aloud during their production of texts, are taken into account. Second, it became clear that thinking-aloud can yield much reliable data about procedures of problem-solving. Therefore, it seems sensible to limit the empirical investigation of the translation process to those aspects which are connected with the solution of translational problems and which can be documented in and interpreted from the data. Such a limitation accords with both the nature of the data (translations as text production *and* protocols of thinking-aloud) and the methodology employed (interpretive reconstruction).

The problems and procedures of problem-solving represent the object of a certain concept of strategy relevant in psycholinguistics. With one essential modification, this concept of strategy can be made use of in this investigation. Its object can thus be limited to those aspects of the translation process which can be interpreted as translation strategies, according to a definition which will be elaborated in section 4.5.3.

In the domain of performance analysis, within which this study is to be situated, the ontological status of strategy has not yet been definitely clarified (cf. Selinker 1972; Tarone et al. 1976; Bialystok 1984; Færch 1984), and highly differing notions of strategy are used. Therefore, it is necessary to develop a notion of strategy which can be applied to both the translations under investigation and other forms of oral text production. The notion must allow the phenomenon denoted by it (strategy) so much variability with regard to its internal structure that the specifics of strategies in one domain, and thus also of translation strategies, become recognizable and can be compared with strategies in another domain.

In the following section (4.5.1), the problems of the identification of strategies will be dealt with. Section 4.5.2 presents different concepts of strategy from translation theory and second language acquisition research, and thus of areas of investigation which are closely related to the object of this study. In the concluding part of this section (4.5.3), a concept of strategy will be developed which is in accordance with both the aim and the epistemological interest of this investigation, and which comes close to the psycholinguistic concept of strategy from second language acquisition research.

4.5.1 On the Notion of 'Strategy'

The notion of 'strategy' originated in military science and denotes the comprehensive preparatory planning of a war including all essential military as well as non-military factors. In a metaphorical sense, the notion of strategy is used in various disciplines, such as economics, psychology, and political science; it is also used in non-technical, colloquial language.

The notion, however, denotes highly different phenomena, and very rarely is it defined precisely (cf. Lee 1977: 41). In the following sections, the notion of strategy will be delimited from other related notions with which the term 'strategy' is often confused or equated in an unreflected way. These notions are: method, plan, rule, and tactics.

The meaning of the term 'strategy' as it occurs in non-technical contexts reveals how unspecific the notion is used and how wide its spectrum of usage is. According to *Duden* (vol. 6, p.2517), 'strategy' denotes an exact plan of one's actions which aims at achieving a certain military, political, psychological, or similar, goal, and which takes into account those factors that might influence one's actions.

A further constitutive element of 'strategy' is mentioned in *Brockhaus* (1984, vol. 6, p.96), according to which the planning is done *on a large scale, in order to reach superordinate, fundamental goals.*

Thus, the following four structural elements are constitutive of the non-technical use of 'strategy':

1. Strategies are procedures carried out by an individual (cf. distinction i.: *strategy* and *method*);
2. Strategies contain an element of planning (cf. distinction ii.: *strategy* and *plan*);
3. Strategies aim at reaching certain goals (cf. distinction iii.: *strategy* and *rule*);
4. Strategies refer to a sequence of actions during the process of goal realization (cf. distinction iv: *strategy* and *tactics*).

i. *Strategy and Method*

Both strategies and methods are procedures for reaching goals. Methods, like algorithms, are supraindividual, tried and tested procedures with which goals can be achieved with a high degree of probability. Strategies, however, are more individual by their very nature and select from the resources available to an individual those means which are considered to be the most suitable and/or effective for achieving the given aim. Thus, any strategy has an element of optimization (cf. Königs 1987; van Dijk/Kintsch 1983: 67).

ii. *Strategy and Plan*

According to Miller/Galanter/Pribram (1960: 16), a plan controls a prescribed series of actions so that they occur in the right order. It is thus a global mental representation of sequences of actions (cf. van Dijk/Kintsch 1983: 65; Rehbein

1977: 146ff.). In contrast to a plan, a strategy, according to van Dijk and Kintsch (1983: 65), is

> *a global mental representation of a style, that is,* ***a way of doing this global action in the most effective way****. ... A strategy is merely a global instruction of each necessary choice to be made along the path of the course of action* ... (my emphases)

Whereas plans represent actions mentally, strategies contain procedural knowledge (cf. Ryle 1946; 1949; Kurcz 1984: 135) about the realization of plans in sequences of actions.

A distinction between plan and strategy which differs considerably from that of van Dijk and Kintsch is made by Færch and Kasper (1980; 183c; 1984a). Following Klaus and Buhr (1976) and Sharwood-Smith (1979), strategies are considered to be a subcategory of plans:

> *a strategy is a potentially conscious plan for solving what to the individual presents itself as a problem in reaching a particular goal.* (Færch/Kasper 1980: 60)

According to this definition, problem-orientedness and potential consciousness are the definitional criteria of strategies[32].

iii. *Strategy and Rule*

Rules are generally defined as norms of society or of a group of society which aim at controling human behaviour in such a way that it will be accepted socially, or considered to be correct and/or adequate (cf. van Dijk/Kintsch 1983: 67; Lörscher/Schulze 1988). Violations of rules mostly result in sanctions.

Strategies also control human behaviour, but they have no socially prescriptive element. They represent mostly individual, procedural knowledge about how human behaviour, in accordance with social rules, should be organized in the most effective way to reach (a) certain aim(s). Strategies thus differ from rules by their goal- and efficiency-oriented, their procedural, and their mostly individual nature.

iv. *Strategy and Tactics*

As outlined above, strategies operate on a large scale in order to achieve superordinate, fundamental goals. Being molar entities (cf. Miller/Galanter/Pribram 1960) strategies refer to sequences of actions. Tactics, however, are molecular entities and control a concrete action or part of it within the entire process. Like strategies, they are oriented towards achieving a certain aim, and the criterion for their evaluation is their efficiency/expediency.

---

32 More detailed information about this concept of strategy will be given further down in this section as well as in section 4.5.3.

The following example may elucidate the relationship between plan, strategy, and tactics: In certain situations, the plan for a football match may be both to win and to win without conceding a goal. A possible strategy, i.e. procedure for the realization of this plan, could be to attack the opposing team out of a massed defence. This strategy may apply to the whole match or to large parts of it. Within the strategy chosen, possible tactics can be to draw the wingers back into the penalty area to support the defenders when the opposing team predominates, or, when the predominance decreases, to order the defenders into the midfield in support of the forwards.

A concept of tactics which is completely different from the one outlined above is maintained by van Dijk and Kintsch. They argue that tactics refer "to relatively large segments or periods of our lives and actions". Thus, the term denotes "an organized set, a system, of strategies" (van Dijk/Kintsch 1983: 66). Such a concept of tactics as a molar, and of strategy as a molecular entity is, however, neither customary in non-technical language nor is it used in academic disciplines such as psychology, economics, political science, or linguistics.

4.5.2 Concepts of Strategy

After the delimitation of the notion of strategy from other related notions in the preceding section, concepts of strategy from the domains of translation theory (Hönig/Kußmaul) and psycholinguistically oriented second language acquisition research (Færch/Kasper 1980; 1983a;c; 1984a; Tarone 1981; 1983) will now be presented and critically commented upon.

Translation strategies are of potential interest because this study aims to investigate the translation process with regard to the strategies which operate within it.

Communication strategies, as described in psycholinguistically oriented second language acquisition research, are also of potential interest, because the subjects of this investigation are second (or rather foreign) language learners whose translation processes will be analyzed psycholinguistically.

a. **Translation Strategy**

In translation theory, the notion of translation strategy plays only a minor role. When it is used at all, it is neither defined precisely nor is it delimited from other related notions, such as translation method or translation rule. Only Königs (1987) and Wilss (1983) distinguish between translation strategies and translation methods. The former denote procedures, often of a highly individual kind, which are applied when a source-language text is transferred into the target-language. These procedures can, but need not, result in an optimal translation. The latter (translation methods) are supraindividual, tried and tested procedures which, when applied systematically by the translator, guarantee a high degree of success (cf. Königs 1987).

Even though this distinction is theoretically reasonable, it must be acknowledged that translation strategies have hardly been investigated in translation theory and that practicable translation methods are not much more than a desideratum at the moment.

A concept of strategy which differs considerably from the one outlined above is maintained by Hönig and Kußmaul. In their 1982 publication, the authors develop a strategy of translation which, when acquired by an individual, enables him/her "Texte problembewußt auf verschiedenen sprachlichen Ebenen zu analysieren und zielgerichtet zu übertragen" (Hönig/Kußmaul 1982: back cover). Although the authors do not explicitly define their concept of translation strategy, they give many hints on their use of the term.

On the one hand, a translation strategy is considered to be a procedure "die uns den jeweils optimalen Weg zur Lösung der übersetzerischen Probleme zeigt" (Hönig/Kußmaul 1982: 13). According to this quotation, a translation strategy appears to be a problem-solving device which can be applied when a translator is faced with a translation problem. The application of the strategy then results in an optimal solution to the problem. On the other hand, the authors consider it to be strategic when a translator carries out a certain sequence of steps in translation:

> *Er nimmt den AS-Text zur Kenntnis und bezieht ihn auf seine Situation als Übersetzer. Er präzisiert den Übersetzungsauftrag und legt die kommunikative Funktion des ZS-Textes fest, wobei er sich an den pragmatischen Erwartungen seiner Adressaten orientiert. Aus dieser kommunikativen Funktion leitet er den notwendigen Grad der Differenzierung ab, indem er die relevante Grenze zwischen Verbalisierung und soziokulturellem Situationshintergrund im AS-Text bestimmt, und dann als Sender des ZS-Textes auf dem Hintergrund der soziokulturellen Situation seiner Adressaten den notwendigen Grad der Differenzierung seiner Verbalisierung festlegt.* (Hönig/Kußmaul 1982: 58)

Translation strategy in this sense denotes a global procedure which a translator uses in making the considerations quoted above, which influence the selection of verbal (and non-verbal) means for the production of the target-language text. As a consequence, a translation strategy logically (but not necessarily temporally) precedes the process of transfer and of target-language text production.

From a decision-theoretical perspective, the strategic considerations thus concern the hierarchically highest decisions to be made by the translator (i.e. the communicative function of the TL text, its orientation towards the addressees of the translation, and the determining of the necessary and sufficient degree of differentiation of the translation). They partly determine and partly delimit the decisions which are to be made on the hierarchically lower levels, such as syntax and lexis[33].

---

33 The concept of translation as a hierarchical process of decision-making is also dealt with in Levý 1967.

Translation strategies in the sense described above are prescriptive in nature. They reflect Hönig and Kußmaul's concept of translation and are meant to give the professional translator instructions about how to proceed in order to produce a translation which the authors consider to be optimal.

In contrast to Hönig and Kußmaul's view, a descriptive concept of strategy will be developed in this study. It should be able to capture the concrete ways in which non-professional translators mentally proceed when they translate a text from one language into another. In other words, it is *not* of interest here what considerations an individual *should* make in order to translate optimally, but rather what considerations s/he does in fact make while translating a text from one language into another.

b. Communication Strategy

In second language acquisition research, the notion of communication strategy plays an important role (cf. Færch/Kasper 1983a; Færch 1984). Like the term strategy, the notion of communication strategy is not unanimously defined either. In the following parts of this section, two relevant definitions of communication strategies will be presented and critically commented on with regard to their usability for this investigation. The first definition, as found in the works of Tarone (1980; 1981; 1983; 1984), situates communication strategies in an interactional framework, whereas the second definition, as suggested by Færch and Kasper (1980; 1983c; 1984), deals with communication strategies as psycholinguistic phenomena.

i. Interactional Definition

According to Tarone (1983: 63), communication strategies comprise the foreign language learner's knowledge of how s/he can use his/her linguistic knowledge when communicating with a native speaker. As they represent knowledge of the use of knowledge, communication strategies are procedural by their very nature (cf. Ryle 1946; 1949; Kurcz 1884). They must comply with the following requirements (Tarone 1983: 65):

1. *a speaker desires to communicate a meaning X to a listener;*
2. *the speaker believes the linguistic or sociolinguistic structure desired to communicate meaning X is unavailable, or is not shared with the listener;*
3. *the speaker chooses to:*
   (a) avoid – not attempt to communicate meaning X; or
   (b) attempt alternate means to communicate meaning X.
   The speaker stops trying alternatives when it seems clear to the speaker that there is shared meaning.

Communication strategies, in the sense of Tarone, have an interactional function because they refer to the negotiation of meaning[34] as a joint activity of the communication partners: "the term relates to a mutual attempt of two interlocutors to agree on a meaning in situations where requisite meaning structures do not seem to be shared." (Tarone 1983: 65)

Production strategies, in contrast to communication strategies, lack the interactional element of meaning negotiation. They focus on the efficiency and economy of language use. According to Tarone (1983: 66), "[a] production strategy [is] an attempt to use one's linguistic system efficiently and clearly, with a minimum of effort."

The definition of communication strategy outlined above can hardly be used for this investigation in view of its specific aim. In my research design, the translations which constitute the data corpus were produced as monologues. There was no interlocutor with whom the subjects could have negotiated meaning[35]. Thus, an essential requirement for the existence of communication strategies is not complied with. Nonetheless, some of the criteria which characterize communication strategies can be documented in my data corpus. The types of behaviour listed under point 3. of the above quotation by Tarone can often be observed. In section 5.3, it will be shown that, for example, subjects often give up their attempts to express a certain meaning in the target-language after several unsuccessful trials, or that they search for alternative ways of expressing a certain meaning in the target-language, for example by paraphrase or by approximation. These cases are to be considered elements of translation strategies, according to a concept of strategy which will be developed in the following section.

The notion of production strategy is also of very little use for the psycholinguistic investigation of the translation process, mainly because production strategies denote rather unspecific phenomena. Economy, efficiency, and clarity of language use are such general and all-encompassing aims of the text producer that their investigation can hardly elucidate the specifics of text production in general, and of translational text production in particular.

---

34 The concept of the social construction of reality and of the negotiation of meaning is also current in ethnomethodology (cf. Garfinkel 1967; Cicourel 1973a; Mehan/Wood 1975; section 4.4.2).

35 A phenomenon similar to the negotiation of meaning in communication is that of optimization in processes of monological text production. As will be described in section 7.2, the text producer generally tries to optimally express meanings in a target-language text. If s/he does not succeed in doing so straight away, a process is started in which specific means of expression are searched for, tested with respect to the text producer's expectation structure, and in which the target-language text is thus successively optimized in the view of the text producer.

ii. Psycholinguistic Definition

The concept of communication strategy which is probably most widespread in second language acquisition research is the one expounded by Færch and Kasper (1980; 1983c; 1984a). According to the authors, communication strategies are mental structures within second language learners' processes of language use. Following Klaus and Buhr (1976) and Sharwood-Smith (1979), strategies are considered to be a subgroup of plans which must fulfil certain conditions: "... a strategy is a potentially conscious plan for solving what to the individual presents itself as a problem in reaching a particular goal." (Færch/ Kasper 1980: 60) Problem-orientedness and potential consciousness are thus the definitional criteria of strategies.

Problem-Orientedness

Of the multitude of plans, only those are considered strategies which a second language learner uses for solving a communication problem. A problem occurs when an individual realizes that his/her knowledge and skills are not sufficient for reaching a certain goal but that this requires an extension of knowledge and an elaboration of skills (cf. Klaus/Buhr 1976: 974; Færch/Kasper 1983c: 32).

After the realization of a problem, a learner can make use of different strategies for its solution. Færch and Kasper mention two main types: *achievement strategies* and *reduction strategies*[36] (cf. also Knapp-Potthoff/Knapp 1982: 135–149). The former are used when the communicative goal is retained and an alternative plan for reaching it is developed. Learners thus creatively expand the linguistic resources available to them. The latter (reduction strategies) are used when a problem is evaded by altering (parts of) the goal and by setting a (partially) new goal which, the learner assumes, can be reached by means of the linguistic resources available to him or her.

Potential Consciousness

Færch and Kasper consider the criterion of potential consciousness to be a secondary one, subordinate to that of problem-orientedness. It does not necessarily apply to the strategies themselves but rather to the situation in which strategies are used, i.e. to the realization of problems.

According to the authors, there are two reasons for not considering consciousness to be a definitional criterion of strategies: First, consciousness, in most cases, is not a matter of 'either or', but of 'more or less'. Mental plans seem to potentially contain conscious, as well as less conscious and unconscious, elements. Lexical, syntactic, semantic, and pragmatic elements in co-occurrence with patterns of articulation in opposition to them are examples of

---

36 These two main types of problem-solving strategies can also be documented for the translation process. Cf. sections 5.2 and 5.3.

conscious, less conscious, and unconscious elements of planning given by Færch and Kasper (1980: 60; 1983c: 35). Second, there seem to be considerable individual differences as regards the consciousness of using mental plans. Færch and Kasper (1980: 60; 1983c: 35) distinguish between three categories:

1. plans which are always used consciously,
2. plans which are never used consciously,
3. plans which, depending on the situation and on the individual circumstances of the learner, are either used consciously or unconsciously.

The plans of categories 1. (consciously used ones) and 3. (potentially consciously used ones) can represent strategies, when the criterion of problem-orientedness applies. According to Færch and Kasper, it is only these two types of plans which can be investigated by means of introspective methods[37]. In order to cover categories 1. and 3., it thus seems necessary to consider *potential* consciousness a definitional criterion of strategies.

The plans of category 2., however, cannot function as strategies. They are not open to empirical investigation. Their existence and characteristics can at best be speculated about on the basis of general behavioural data and of results yielded by neuro-psychological investigations (cf. Færch/Kasper 1980: 60; 1983c: 36).

Among the strategy concepts discussed above, the one developed by Færch and Kasper is certainly the most fruitful for this investigation in view of its particular goal and purpose, for at least four reasons:

1. The concept is psycholinguistic in nature. Only those behavioural plans which operate within the mental processes underlying language use and which fulfil certain requirements (problem-orientedness, potential consciousness) are considered strategies. Thus it becomes possible to analyze essential aspects of mental processes by isolating and describing the strategies which operate within them. This is largely similar to the aim of this investigation.

2. The concept is descriptive in nature. Certain phenomena within mental processes which fulfil the definitional criteria are considered to be strategies, and are described with regard to their types of realization. Unlike Hönig and Kußmaul's translation strategy, the concept of Færch and Kasper does not contain any prescriptive element. The strategy user is given no instructions as to how strategies should be employed correctly and efficiently. Instead, it describes how and what strategies s/he uses. Since the aim of this study is to investigate psycholinguistically those aspects of the translation process, which can be documented empirically, a specific strategy concept is called for. It must enable us to investigate what strategies are in fact used by the subjects, and in what way, not how they ought to have used strategies. Færch and Kasper's strategy concept fulfils this requirement.

---

37 Cf. also section 4.4.1 above.

3. The concept can be documented empirically. In concrete performance, verbal and non-verbal phenomena are recognizable which can be interpreted as being manifestations of mental strategies. The limitation of the concept of strategy to procedures for problem-solving has a definite advantage as regards the documentability of strategies. Subjects can gain information about their mental plans for solving problems by introspection and can verbalize it. In contrast to automatized, and thus nonstrategic, speech production, problems are within the subjects' focus of attention, and thus reportable. In addition to explicit and implicit (potential) strategy indicators (cf. subsection 4.4.2.2), protocols of thinking-aloud can be used to obtain reliable information about subjects' problems and the strategies they employ to solve them.

4. The concept is of a comprehensive, all-embracing kind but, nonetheless, can capture the specifics of strategies from different domains. Although it was developed in connection with second-language acquisition research, the strategy concept is so general that it can be applied to all domains in which an individual is faced with problems for the solutions of which s/he develops behavioural plans. But in spite of this high degree of generality, Færch and Kasper's concept can grasp the specific ways in which strategies can be built up. The variability of the internal structure of strategies can be determined by such factors as the domain to which they are applied (e.g. translation, second-language acquisition, the building of a house, the preparation of a meal), the individual mental and physical dispositions of different strategy users, the nature of the problems, or the different contexts of situation which strategy users are exposed to. Whether specific translation strategies exist, and if so, what their specifics are, can be investigated by comparing their internal structures with those from different domains[38].

4.5.3 Translation Strategy: A Definition

As was pointed out in the preceding section, Færch and Kasper's psycholinguistically motivated concept of strategy contains many features which are relevant to the aim and epistemological interest of this study. The concept will therefore be used here, but with two essential modifications. Accordingly,

> *a translation strategy is a potentially conscious procedure for the solution of a problem which an individual is faced with when translating a text segment from one language into another.*

---

38 Strategies (in the sense of the psycholinguistic definition or comparable to it) have been documented for language use within *interlanguage*. Strategies of text production have been investigated by Færch and Kasper (1980; 1983c), Corder (1983), Tarone (1983), Færch (1984), and others; strategies of text reception have (rarely) been investigated by Kasper (1984) as well as by Færch and Kasper (1986a).

According to this definition, problem-orientedness, potential consciousness, and goal-orientedness are criteria of translation strategies as well as of interlanguage communication strategies.

Problem-orientedness is to be seen in connection with the empirical documentability of strategies.

Potential-consciousness results from an axiom according to which only those phenomena are interpreted to be problems which the subjects consider to be problems (cf. sections 5.2 and 5.3). In other words, strategies are defined from the perspective of the language user, the subject, not from the perspective of the analyst. In this investigation, and in contrast to Færch and Kasper, potential consciousness applies to the problem *and* the procedure employed for its solution. Both are in the subject's focus of attention.

Goal-orientedness is a criterion of a general kind and applies not only to processes of language use but to human behaviour in general[39].

The most important difference between my definition of strategy and the psycholinguistic one concerns the ontological status of strategy. Whereas Færch and Kasper consider strategies a subgroup of plans, I subsume them under the more neutral category 'procedure'. Færch and Kasper distinguish between goal, planning phase, plan, and execution (of plan), and point out: "The aim of the planning phase is to develop a plan, the execution of which will result in an action which will lead to the actional goal."[40] Plan and action as well as planning process and execution process are thus strictly separated from each other. Even though the authors assume feedback to take place between the planning and the execution process in their general model of speech production in a second language, this feedback can only result in the *ad hoc*-correction of errors in planning or execution. The possibility of other, further-reaching modifications of a plan by systematically taking into consideration interim results of the execution[41] is not provided for; the distinctness of a planning and an execution phase is, in principle, retained in the model.

A concept which is different from Færch and Kasper's is proposed by Rehbein (1976a; 1977). He also distinguishes between a planning phase and a plan execution phase. The former consists of three subphases:

i. the developing of the actional focus; the actor concentrates his/her cognitive attention on a specific sector of reality and specifies his/her actional goal (cf. Rehbein 1976a: 14).

---

39 Cf. Færch 1984: 51; As regards goal-orientedness of language use in translation, cf. Holz-Mänttäri 1984 and Reiß/Vermeer 1984.

40 Færch/Kasper 1980: 55; Cf. also Clark/Clark 1977: 223ff. and Rehbein 1977: 41ff. and 146ff.

41 Cf. Miller/Galanter/Pribram 1960 and Rehbein (1977: 188) who assumes a "wechselseitige Determinierung zwischen *Planbildung und Ausführung* .." According to him, a plan can be refined, corrected, or revised during the execution phase (1977: 217).

ii. the developing of an actional schema; the actor construes a rough plan, an outline of the whole course of the action (cf. Rehbein 1976a: 17).

iii. the generating of the complete actional plan; the actor develops a pre-organization of the future action, s/he construes the (expected) course of the action (cf. Rehbein 1976a: 31ff.).

In contrast to Færch and Kasper, Rehbein points out that the distinction between planning and plan execution is of an analytic, heuristic kind and that in reality, it only occurs in certain types of planning. In communicative situations, however, plans are often developed during the execution phase (Rehbein 1977: 147f.). When a speaker starts with an utterance, s/he often searches for the complete plan or has only a vague conception of it[42].

A further-reaching, essential criticism of the conception, according to which speech performance can be modelled as a process consisting of a planning phase and a plan execution phase, is put forward by Antos (1982). He investigated the process of formulating, i.e. a type of (oral or written) text production, and points out (1982: 92):

> *Bei sprachlichen Prozessen ist im Gegensatz zu anderen komplexen Handlungen die Unterscheidung von 'Planen' und 'Ausführen' unter semiotischem Aspekt unscharf!*

For complex non-verbal actions, such as the building of a house or the cooking of a meal, plans can be represented semiotically (as drawings or recipes) and are clearly distinct from the finished house or the cooked meal. This distinction, however, cannot be made for the planning and the realization of a text with regard to their semiotic representation (cf. Antos 1982: 92; Hölscher/Möhle 1987). Every text produced can be the basis for (a) revised version(s) of it, or it can function as a final version of a process of text production which, in principle, is never complete.

When, however, the distinction between plan and execution of plan does not indicate any semiotic and communicative difference, such a distinction is not sensible. What is sensible, is to distinguish between different degrees and states of formulating.

The criticism put forward by Antos is reasonable. Accepting it means giving text production the status of a domain of investigation in its own right, which cannot be described in the same way as the building of a house or the cooking of a meal. Therefore, a more complex approach is needed; an approach which regards text production as an integrative process of planning and plan execu-

---

42 Cf. Möhle/Raupach 1983: 21ff.; Fromkin 1971; Clark/Clark 1977: 292.

tion[43] and which takes into account the dialectical relationship of the components in developing and modifying each other. As a model-theoretical framework for such an approach, problem-solving concepts (cf. Kummer 1972; 1975) and especially the concept of dialectical problem-solving, as analyzed by Dörner (1975; 1976), could be used (cf. Antos 1982: 133ff.)[44].

The inadequacy of those text production models which separate a planning phase from an execution phase has important consequences for the description of translation strategies. As a certain type of text production is obviously also involved in translation, the distinction between plan and execution causes problems here, too. For this reason, it is hardly sensible to define translation strategies as a type of plan. Rather, the more neutral term 'procedure' is used. Procedures in this sense are systems with feedback in which mental (i.e. planning) aspects and verbal (i.e. execution) aspects operate integratively.

A further deficit of most strategy concepts concerns the vagueness of the notion of problem which underlies them. What the authors consider to be a problem is often not made explicit. Nonetheless, an implicit use of the term 'problem' in a colloquial sense can be detected. The term denotes a difficulty or a difficult task to perform.

In the following section, translation strategies – and translation problems which initiate these strategies – will be documented empirically and investigated psycholinguistically. Therefore, an exact definition of 'problem' is essential and allows the interpretation of the collected data with regard to the translation strategies used by the subjects.

A definition of 'problem' which can be operationalized for this investigation is offered by Dörner (1976: 10). According to it, an individual is faced with a problem

> *wenn es sich in einem inneren und äußeren Zustand befindet, den es aus irgendwelchen Gründen nicht für wünschenswert hält, aber im Moment nicht über die Mittel verfügt, um den unerwünschten Zustand in den wünschenswerten Zielzustand zu überführen.*

According to this definition, a problem consists of three components:

1. an undesirable initial state;
2. a desirable goal state;

43 This also becomes evident in the psycholinguistic investigations by Kempen (1977) and Danks (1977). Kempen (1977: 262ff.) has shown that the production of cognitive concepts (conceptualization) does not need to precede in time the production of syntactic forms (formulation). Rather, conceptualization and formulation make up a feedback system in which the interactions of the components can be modelled by means of search-and-formulate programs. According to Danks (1977: 229ff.), the generation of thoughts and the production of sentences represents the same functional process. The processes of thinking which occur during the production of speech and the processes of syntactic sentence production are fully integrated: "Our ideas come into being as we select the words and construct the sentences we utter" (Danks 1977: 255; cf. also Antos 1982: 94f.).

44 Cf. section 7.2.

3. a barrier which prevents the transformation of the initial state into the goal state.

A *problem* thus defined must be distinguished from a *task*. Dörner considers tasks to be "geistige Anforderungen, für deren Bewältigung Methoden bekannt sind." In contrast to problems, which require innovative thinking for their solution, the managing of tasks only requires reproductive thinking.

The barriers between an initial state and a goal state which constitute a problem can be of very different kinds. Nonetheless, three main types can be distinguished and correspond to three types of problems (cf. Dörner 1976: 11ff.):

i. The means for the transformation is/are unknown. This type of barrier is implied in problems such as the one which the alchemists had been preoccupied with for centuries, i.e. how to make gold. Problems of this kind are called *synthesis problems*.

ii. An abundance of means and combinations of them for the transformation are known. The possibilities are so large in number that they cannot systematically be tried one after the other. This type of barrier is implied in problems such as the one every chess player is confronted with, i.e. how to checkmate one's opponent. Problems of this kind are called *interpolation problems*.

iii. The goal state is only vaguely known or unknown. An initial state is considered to be undesirable but one neither knows how a desirable goal state should be nor does one know how it could be realized. This type of barrier is implied in problems such as the ones which occur in the production of a lyrical work. But it is also to be found in many problems in everyday life, for example in the writing of a letter. Problems of this kind are called *dialectical problems*.

The general remarks on the problems made above must now be made specific with regard to translation problems. For the investigation of the available data corpus, a translation problem is considered to occur when a subject realizes that, at a given point in time, s/he is unable to transfer or to transfer adequately a source-language text segment into the target-language[45].

It should be emphasized here that, according to the psycholinguistic orientation of this investigation, translation problems are defined from the perspective of the subjects, not of the analyst. In other words, only those text segments which *the subjects* cannot translate or which *the subjects* have tried to translate but whose results they then consider to be inadequate, represent translation problems.

The three components which, according to Dörner, constitute problems in general can also be detected in translation problems where they have a specific

---

45 Cf. section 5.2.1 for a more detailed discussion of the concept of 'translation problem'.

nature. On the one hand, the undesired initial state corresponds to the whole of the source-language text which has to be translated; on the other hand, it corresponds to a specific unit of translation which a subject has separated from the SL text at a given time in order to translate it into the target-language[46]. In analogy to this, the desired goal state is represented by the whole of the translation (i.e. TL text) on the one hand, and by a unit of translation rendered into TL on the other.

It must be taken into account, here, that the attributes 'desirable' and 'undesirable' hardly reflect the subjects' individual intentions and needs. Rather, they are to be seen in connection with the task of the experiment in which the subjects participated. There was neither a 'genuine' mediating situation in which communication between an SL text sender and a TL text receiver would have to be established by a mediator[47], nor are the translations likely to be manifestations of the subjects' communicative desire.

As concerns the types of barriers which hinder or prevent the transformation of the initial state into the goal state, translation problems mainly contain dialectical barriers for the subjects. As pointed out by Antos (1982: 138ff.), the crucial point about creative text production is the fact that the criteria by which it can be judged whether a goal has been achieved or not are themselves 'created' in the process of text production, and are not given in a quantified way in advance. This also applies to translation. As will be discussed in more detail, translation can largely be modelled as a process of text production. The definition of 'translation problem' developed above takes this fact into account. Furthermore, a distinction between a target-text and the verbal means for its realization is probably largely untenable for text production because the verbal means chosen are themselves elements of the target-text. The translator's processes of searching and selecting are directed towards target-language text segments and thus concern the degrees and states of the formulation of the TL text which can, in principle, reach a preliminary, but not a definite completion (cf. Antos 1982: 93).

As will be shown in section 7.2, translators as text producers build up within themselves an expectation structure with regard to the target-language text during the process of source-language text reception and target-language text production. It represents an essential control mechanism during the search for and the selection of target-language text segments and thus allows dialectical barriers in the production of translations to be surmounted.

46 Following Krings (1986a: 178ff.), a distinction can be made between a macro- and a micro-level of translation. Aspects concerning the whole of the SL or TL text of a translation represent the macro-level. Aspects concerning segments of the SL or TL text represent the micro-level of translation.

47 Cf. also section 4.3 point 3).

5 An Empirical Investigation Into the Translation Process

As was pointed out in section 1.1 and in Chapter 3, the psycholinguistic, empirical investigation of the translation process is hardly more than a desideratum at the moment. From the first pilot studies[1] it already emerges that this area of investigation will develop into an important object of research in the future because of its complex nature and the relevance of the results which its investigation has yielded so far. These results have important implications for translation theory, translation teaching methodology (cf. Krings 1986a: 500ff.), as well as for research into text reception and text production.

In this section, an investigation will be presented whose aim is to analyze translation *performance*, as represented empirically in a corpus of data, in order to reconstruct hypothetically strategies operating within the translation *process* (cf. section 1.2 and Chapter 4).

In the following subsection, two preliminary remarks are made. The first (5.1.1) is about the data corpus and the second (5.1.2) is about the characteristics, problems, possibilities, and limitations of corpus analysis. In section 5.2, after several remarks on the concept of 'translation problem' (5.2.1), a model for the strategic analysis[2] of the translation process will be construed on the basis of empirically documented translations. It captures the elements of translation strategies (5.2.2), i.e. steps which can be distinguished within problem-solving processes, and the translation strategies themselves (5.2.3). Translation versions, which can comprise strategic and non-strategic phases[3] of the translation process, will be dealt with in section 5.2.4.

An outline of the model of analysis in which both the elements of translation strategies and the translation strategies themselves are formalized to yield categories of analysis will be presented in section 5.2.5. The model will be applied to recorded translations in section 5.3. These translations did *not* serve as the empirical basis on which the model was construed. Thus, it is possible to test whether the model can analyze translations which are different from but analogous to those by means of which it was developed. After several introductory remarks on the transcription used (5.3.1), four exemplary analyses of

---

1 Cf. Dechert/Sandrock 1986; Feldmann/Stemmer 1987; Gerloff 1986; 1987; Hölscher/Möhle 1987; Krings 1986a; b; Lörscher 1986; 1987; n.d. [1987]; Sandrock 1982.

2 'Strategic analysis' means the analysis of (language) performance which aims at hypothetically reconstructing mental strategies (cf. subsection 4.4.2.1).

3 Within 'strategic phases' of the translation process, subjects are faced with translation problems for the solution of which they employ strategies. Within 'non-strategic' phases, subjects do not realize translation problems and thus do not use strategies.

translations will be made and commented on. In two of the translations (5.3.2; 5.3.3), subjects orally transfer a written text from their mother tongue (German) into English, which they possess as an *interlanguage* (IL). In the other two translations (5.3.4; 5.3.5), two written texts from the subjects' *interlanguage* (English) are rendered orally into the subjects' mother tongue (German).

5.1 Introductory Remarks

5.1.1 The Data Corpus

As mentioned in 4.4.2.2, the data corpus collected comprises fifty-two translations which were produced orally and recorded on cassette. Half of them are translations into English: Twenty-four subjects whose mother tongue is German translated three German texts into their *interlanguage* (IL); and half of them are translations into German: Twenty-four subjects translated six texts from English into their mother tongue. The fifty-two translations were produced by forty-eight subjects. Forty-two of them are first or second year's students of English whom I personally know from the lectures and seminars I taught. Six of the subjects (S47–S52) are pupils from the 11th or 12th form of a German *Gymnasium*.

All the subjects have German as their mother tongue and have a medial to high command of English as an *interlanguage*. It results from seven to nine years learning English as a foreign language at school and, as far as the students are concerned, from learning English at the university[4]. The subjects (S) and texts (T) are distributed over the translations as follows:

4 Cf. (sub)sections 4.2.2.1 a., 4.2.2.2, and 4.3.

Diagram 9: Distribution of Subjects and Texts over the Translations

I. Translations *from* the mother tongue (German – English)

S 1	–	S 16	:	T1 (Kurzgeschichte)
S 17	–	S 22	:	T2 (Tagebuch)
S 23	–	S 26	:	T3 (Österreich)

II. Translations *into* the mother tongue (English – German)

S 27	–	S 32	:	T4 (Sale of Honours)
S 33	–	S 38	:	T5 (History of the English Language)
S 39	–	S 42	:	T6 (Tourism)[5]
S 43	–	S 46	:	T7 (Berlin)[5]
S 47	–	S 49	:	T8 (Shakespeare)[6]
S 50	–	S 52	:	T9 ('Correct English')[6]

After the translations had been performed, several subjects were additionally asked to retell the contents of the source-language text as completely as possible in the target-language[7]. The subjects who performed this task were S24–S27 and S29–S38.

The following written texts had to be translated orally into the target-language:

Text 1

In jüngerer Zeit sind mehrfach Versuche unternommen worden, Eigenschaften und Merkmale der *short story* zu beschreiben, die sich aus ihrer Kürze ergeben, die andererseits aber auch eine bestimmte Geisteshaltung (attitude) spiegeln und so auch auf unsere Zeit verweisen. Dabei scheint Übereinstimmung darüber zu herrschen, daß kurzes Erzählen dem Autor besondere Fähigkeiten abverlangt und die *short story* eine der einfachsten, aber auch gleichzeitig schwierigsten Formen der Erzählliteratur darstellt, wenn sie versucht, mit einem Minimum an Erzählung ein Maximum literarischer Wirkung zu erreichen. Die Frage, 'Was macht eine *short story* kurz?', ist dabei verhältnismäßig leicht zu beantworten. Die Kurzgeschichte ist einmal das Ergebnis verschiedener Reduktionen auf dem Gebiet der Handlung, der Charakterdarstellung und -entwicklung sowie der Zeit und des Raumes.
(......)
(Source unknown; from a collection of texts for translation)

5 These translations were elicited by Ms Andrea Reichart.

6 These translations were elicited by Mr Peter Szczotok.

7 Cf. subsection 4.2.2.2 for a more detailed description of this experiment.

Text 2

Sagt man, es sei nicht der erste Besuch in den Vereinigen Staaten, so kommt fast immer die Frage: Finden Sie's verändert? Dabei erwarten sie alles andere als die Antwort, es habe sich zum Guten verändert. Das finde ich aber. ... Ein Antikommunismus ohne Kenntnis, was Kommunismus ist, in Verbindung mit einem repressiven Patriotismus (nicht viel anders als bei uns), ist nicht geschwunden; im Schwinden ist trotzdem die Arroganz der Macht, auch wenn sie sagen: Wir sind das reichste Land der Welt. Das stimmt ja. Sie sind erschreckt. Luftverschmutzung ist ja nur eine Metapher für alle anderen Realitäten, die sie erschrecken. Zumindest ist man nicht mehr sicher, daß alles, was größer und größer wird, auch erfreulich sein.

(......)

(Max Frisch: *Tagebuch 1966–1971.*)

Text 3

Obwohl wir Ansätze heranziehen, die in Frankreich, in der BRD und in Skandinavien entwickelt worden sind, müssen wir von der spezifischen sprachlichen Situation ind Österreich beziehungsweise in Wien ausgehen, die sich zum Teil durch die Anwesenheit des Dialekts von manchen der oben genannten Länder unterscheidet: Danach sind die jugoslawischen beziehungsweise türkischen Kinder nicht mit einer Fremdsprache konfrontiert, sondern eigentlich mit drei Sprachen, von denen zwei für eine adäquate kommunikative Verständigung wesentlich sind: die deutsche Norm (Hochsprache), wie sie in der Schule unterrichtet wird, die österreichische Norm oder Umgangssprache, wie sie in systematischer Variation auftritt, und schließlich der Dialekt.

Die Kinder müssen also mit einer mehrfachen Sprachbarriere zurechtkommen lernen; wissen, wann welches Deutsch mit wem gesprochen wird. Dies setzt einen Unterricht voraus, der sich explizit mit diesem Problem beschäftigt; einen kommunikationsorientierten Unterricht, der vor allem die Verständigung in wesentlichen Sprechsituationen im adäquaten Sprechstil fördern würde.

(......)

(R. Wodak: "'Gastarbeiterdeutsch': Probleme des Zweitsprachenerwerbs für Gastarbeiterkinder." *Die Sprache* 27,2 (1981), 129–140; here: 135f. with minor alterations)

Text 4

Sale of Honours

There is no possible argument on which the decision by the congregation of Oxford University to refuse Mrs Thatcher the proposed honorary degree ist worthy of respect. It is the culmination of a nasty campaign which has oscillated between political spite and logic-chopping. Every Oxford graduate, of whatever party, who has previously attained the high office of Prime Minister since the war has been awarded an honorary doctorate. Mrs Thatcher alone has been refused because the dons campaigning against her resent her government's policies and particularly those which affect education. By doing so, Oxford has

made it clear that an honorary doctorate for everyone in public life who is concerned with politics is now no more than a political award.
(......)
The Times 30.1.1985, p.13

Text 5

The History of the English Language a Cultural Subject

It was observed by that remarkable twelfth-century chronicler, Henry of Huntington, that an interest in his past was one of the distinguishing characteristics of man as compared with the other animals. And in these days when the cultivated man or woman is conscious of deficiencies in his education without some knowledge of economics, medieval history, recent advances in the basic natural sciences, so also he may discover a desire to know something of the nature and development of his mother tongue. The medium by which he communicates his thought and feelings to his fellow men, the tool with which he conducts his business or the government of millions of people, the vehicle by which have been transmitted to him the science, the philosophy, the poetry of the race is surely worthy of study.
(......)
(A.C. Baugh/T. Cable: *A History of the English Language.* London 1981, p.1)

Text 6

A drive to encourage more tourists to visit the regions of Britain rather than spending all their holiday in London is planned by the Government. Areas of high unemployment with tourist potential could be the first to benefit from the initiative, MPs were told yesterday. This year, out of the estimated 15 million overseas visitors to Britain, most of whom are tourists, 44 per cent will not leave London. Lord Young of Graffham, Secretary of State for Employment, told the Commons trade and industry select committee that a new British Travel Centre opening in London next April would have a "key role" in encouraging a greater dispersal of visitors to destinations outside London. Lord Young, who believes tourism has an important role to play in creating more jobs, is also setting up regional enterprise units within his department to boost tourism.
(......)
The Times 20.4.1985, p.5)

Text 7

Berlin is an island economy. Geographically isolated from the rest of West Germany, it has special needs. It has also developed a unique economic structure characterized and determined by its large number of small and medium size companies. Of the 2,300 companies based and registered in Berlin, more than 90 per cent employ fewer than 200 people. In short, it is just the sort of regional small company-based economy that can most benefit from closer co-operation between universities and industry. The Technical University of Berlin has established a Technology Transfer Office to meet this aim. It was founded in 1980 and has since identified six essential transfer sections: information transfer,

technology transfer, personnel transfer, support and establishment of new technology oriented enterprises, further education, evaluation and research.
(......)
(*The Times* 30.10.1985, p.21)

Text 8

Say it with Shakespeare

The plays of Shakespeare have been read and seen by so many millions since the time they were written that countless phrases from them have become part of the English language. People often quote them, but half the time they do so quite unconsciously. "Much ado about nothing", says the ten-year-old boy angrily when he sees his mother paying too much attention to his new-born baby brother, though he does not know that this is the title of one of Shakespeare's comedies. "The rest is silence", quotes the teacher when the schoolboy stops in his translation because he has not learnt his lesson. The pupil after school will refer to his teacher's explanations and say "It was Greek to me", though he may not have read 'Julius Caesar'.
Thus the great poet has come into our daily life, where he will stay for ever.
(......)
(K. Eckermann/W. Piert: *Einführung in die englische Sprache.* Stuttgart 1966, p.68; with minor alterations and slightly abridged)

Text 9

How to speak 'Correct English'

Well, the first thing I must tell you is that there is no such thing as ideally 'correct English'. In Great Britain you would not find any two persons who speak exactly alike. I am a member of a committee established by the BBC (radio and TV), and we are to find out how the speakers of the BBC should pronounce what they say in order that they should be a model of correct English speech for the British Islands. Now, the interesting fact is that the members of our committee do not even agree as to the pronunciation of some of the simplest words in the English language: 'yes' and 'no'. That means, they all speak differently, and it is nonsense to say that they all speak correctly. But, certainly, they all speak 'good English', and if you speak as they do you will be understood and accepted in any English-speaking country.
(......)
(G.B. Shaw: "Spoken English and Broken English." from: *Learning English A3.* Stuttgart [3]1973, p.128; with minor alterations and slightly abridged)

The essential criterion for the selection of the texts derives from the epistemological interest of this investigation. As pointed out in section 1.2, the strategies operating within the translation process will be reconstructed hypothetically. In section 4.5.3, translation strategies were defined as potentially conscious procedures which the subjects employ when faced with translation problems. Thus, *strategic translating* is translating in which problem-solving is involved, whereas *non-strategic translating* is characterized by a problem-free, automatic replacement of source-language text segments by target-language text segments[8]. In order to be able to document translation strategies in the sense defined above, it is necessary to use source-language texts containing translation problems for the solutions of which the subjects must employ strategies. This causes certain difficulties for the selection of texts for translation:

1. On the one hand, the texts must contain a sufficient number of translation problems to make sure that a sufficient number of (potentially different) problem-solving strategies will be used. On the other hand, the texts must not contain too many translation problems. Otherwise the subjects would lose their motivation to make an effort to solve them.

2. The nature of the translation problems must be such that the subjects with their specific source- and target-language competence must be able to solve them, in principle. Furthermore, the subjects must consider the problems solvable to ensure that they will make an effort to solve them.

3. Although the subjects had participated in English-as-a-foreign language lessons for seven or nine years, their competence in English, which is the foreign language involved in the translations, is by no means homogeneous. The recognizable differences are not only between the groups of subjects with seven and nine years training but also within these two groups. Nevertheless, a measurement of the subjects' foreign language competence, however desirable it would have been, was out of the question because it would have introduced a strongly evaluative element into the investigation. As a consequence, the subjects, when thinking aloud, would probably have externalized only those data of whose linguistic correctness they were strongly convinced (cf. Krings 1986a: 105). The selection of information that accompanies this consequence would not have been desirable and would also have had a substantial influence on the translations (cf. Ericsson/Simon 1980: 226f. and section 4.4.1 above).

Therefore, I decided to choose as subjects students whom I knew personally and whose competence in English I knew about, at least approximately. Nonetheless, many, partly considerable, differences in the subjects' level of competence in the foreign language, i.e. English, can be detected and become evident in the translations (cf. section 6.3.6).

4. In view of the subjects' heterogeneous competence in the foreign language, it was difficult to find adequate texts for translation. They should be of non-professional registers, stylistically unmarked, and their length should not exceed about 15 typewritten lines to make sure that they were not beyond the subjects' powers of concentration. Furthermore, they should contain an adequate number of translation problems with an adequate degree of difficulty. When searching for such texts, my knowledge of the subjects' foreign language

8 Cf. section 7.3 for more details.

competence was very helpful. After I had selected texts which I considered potentially adequate I translated the texts myself and paid attention to possible problems for the subjects, especially those concerning lexis and syntax. These two problem areas were given special attention because in a pilot-experiment it had become evident that the lexical and syntactic problems played the most important part for the subjects, whereas problems of stylistic and text-type adequacy were hardly given any attention. This may be explained by the fact that the subjects had only produced translations for purposes of language practice and language testing in foreign language lessons at school and at university. There, the main emphasis was laid on lexical and syntactic correctness, and questions of stylistic and text-type adequacy, if at all dealt with, played quite a minor role.

If I considered a text difficult for the subjects after I had tested it on myself, there was the choice of two possibilities:

a. When the text could *not* be transformed to an adequate level of difficulty by a few minor alterations, i.e. lexical and/or syntactic simplifications, the text was excluded from the corpus of potential source-language texts.

b. When the text could be transformed to an adequate level of difficulty by a few minor alterations, i.e. lexical and/or syntactic simplifications, it was altered accordingly. Although such a procedure is widely criticised (cf. Krings 1986a: 52), I do consider it justified. The argument that translating, in the sense of translation theory, can only be practised when using unabridged, authentic texts, may apply to professional translators. They may act according to the postulate that *texts* are the object of translation and that translating has to be text-oriented (cf. Diller/Kornelius 1978: 1f.). In this study, however, the performance of non-professional translators will be investigated. In contrast to professional translators, they generally do not make a text-oriented but a sentence-oriented approach to translation (cf. Krings 1986a: 198 as well as section 5.3 and subsection 6.3.5.2 below).

Furthermore, the mental translation *strategies* employed by the subjects represent the epistemological interest of this study. It seems to be very unlikely that they are dependent on the authenticity[9] of the source-language text. Rather, they seem to depend on the kind of problems, their number and degree of difficulty, as seen by the subjects.

---

9 A further theoretical argument against the postulate of authenticity comes from research into text production. Antos (1982: 92), for example, has shown that the formulation process must be considered a process which has no termination, in principle. Different versions of a text can function as planning bases for and, at the same time, as final versions of the formulation process at a given time (cf. section 4.5.3 above). Thus, authenticity is to be considered a quality which characterizes the relation between a text and its producer/author. It is not an intratextual feature which characterizes the content or form of a text.

After the selection of the texts, the translations were performed. It was my intention, to no longer use a text in the experiment if it turned out to be either too difficult or too easy for three or more subjects. In both these cases, a considerable deficit of translation strategies would have been detectable in the data. But none of these cases occurred and the selected texts could all be used in the experiment.

The source-language texts which had to be translated can be characterized as follows: Text 1 is abridged, but quasi authentic. Only one possibility for the translation of the lexeme "Geisteshaltung", i.e. "attitude" was given as a help. Text 3 is also abridged and quasi authentic. Instead of the abbreviations "bzw." (lines 3 and 5), "z.T." (line 3), and "v.a." (line 14), the complete lexemes were used. "Danach" (line 5) is used instead of "demnach" and "fördern" (line 15) instead of "forcieren". Texts 2, 4, 5, 6, and 7 are authentic but abridged, whereas texts 8 and 9 are not authentic and abridged.

The following diagram represents the distribution of texts and subjects over the translations and characterizes these by means of the criteria pointed out above.

Diagram 10: Characteristics of the Translations

	T1	T2	T3	T4	T5	T6	T7	T8	T9
Direction of Translation	G→E	G→E	G→E	E→G	E→G	E→G	E→G	E→G	E→G
Subjects No.	1–16	17–22	23–26	27–32	33–38	39–42	43–46	47–49	50–52
Student/ Pupil	St	St	St	St	St	St	St	Pu	Pu
Content of text	Kurzgesch.	Tagebuch	Österreich	Sale of Hon.	Engl. Lang.	Tourism	Berlin	Shakespeare	Correct Engl.
authentic	(+)	+	(+)	+	+	+	+	–	–
abridged	+	+	+	+	+	+	+	+	+

Abbreviations used: T = Text; G = German; E = English;

5.1.2 Corpus Analysis

In the following section, a model for the strategic analysis of the translation process will be presented which was developed on the basis of fourteen translations. Nine of them (S 1–5; 8; 17; 18; 26) are translations into the foreign language, five of them (S 29–32; 37) are translations into the mother tongue.

As a first test of the model's validity and in order to obtain hints as to whether it can be applied to translations other than those for which it was developed, analyses of all the translations of the corpus were made. Two of the translations into the foreign language (S 15; 24) and two of the translations into the mother tongue (S 28; 34) plus their analyses, made using the model are to be found in sections 5.3.2 to 5.3.5. As the model was developed on an empirical basis, it is necessarily to a certain extent corpus-bound. In the complex, empirical domain of translation with its manifold forms which depend on individual, situational and other factors, there will certainly be elements, structures and processes which are not represented in the corpus of my model and which therefore cannot be (adequately) captured by it. This, however, applies to any model construed for a domain of empirical reality.

Furthermore, the model was developed on the basis of a relatively small corpus (fourteen translations). When applied to further translations, the model may be modified and/or supplemented and, as a result, applied to a larger segment of the domain of translation. To this extent, the process of model construction has probably only come to a preliminary end (cf. Lörscher 1983: 239f.).

5.2 Conception of a Model for the Strategic Analysis of the Translation Process

5.2.1 On the Concept of 'Translation Problem'

In section 4.5, strategies were defined as procedures used to solve strategy users' problems. Thus, translation strategies are procedures which the subjects employ in order to solve the translation problems they realize. As the concept of 'translation problem' will play a crucial role in the following sections, considerations will first be made which critically discuss this concept and which operationalize it for the analysis to be carried out in section 5.3.

The concept of 'translation problem' which manifests itself empirically has hardly been paid any attention by translation theory. The reason for this may be the fact that translation theory has had a strong theoretical, speculative, and thus non-empirical orientation (cf. section 1.1 and Chapter 3. above). Although taxonomies or typologies of translation difficulties are sometimes given in the relevant literature (cf. e.g. Wilss 1977a: 192ff.), they are theoretical constructs which are based on single, individual, and largely unsystematic observations or, what is more likely, are hypothetically derived from a comparison of source- and target-language phenomena in a contrastive-linguistic way. Only very recently, with the development of a new empirical and process-oriented paradigm within translation studies[10], has the concept of 'translation problem' – and with it, that of 'translation strategy' – gained crucial importance.

The most comprehensive discussion of these concepts is probably to be found in Krings 1986a. In his empirical study on the analysis of the translation

10 Cf. e.g. the studies by Dechert and Sandrock (1986), Feldmann and Stemmer (1987), Hölscher and Möhle (1987), Gerloff (1986, 1987), Krings (1986a, b), Sandrock (1982), and Lörscher (1986, 1987, n.d. [1987], 1989).

process, Krings distinguishes between three types of problems occurring within translations (1986a: 112–171):

1. *translation problems*
2. *L2-competence problems*
3. *translation-competence problems*

According to this distinction, translation problems represent the most general category. It comprises all linguistic problems which occur within translations. Translation problems are subdivided into L2-competence problems and translation-competence problems. The former occur when "eindeutig ein *intra*linguales Wissens- oder Beurteilungsdefizit ... vorliegt" (Krings 1986a: 163). As examples of L2-competence problems, Krings discusses cases in which subjects search for translation equivalents in bilingual dictionaries and, after having looked up the mother tongue lexemes and read the lexical entries, verbalize the fact that the given foreign language lexeme or lexemes is or are unknown to them, independent of the translation task.

Problems "(mit einer) *inter*lingualen äquivalenzbezogenen Fragestellung" (Krings 1986a: 163) are considered to be translation-competence problems. According to the author, it is the task of the analyst to classify actually occurring problems as L2- or translation-competence problems. This requires a process of interpretation in which the analyst acts according to the maxim that a problem must be considered a translation-competence problem as long as no clear evidence can be produced of it being an L2-competence problem. As a result of this maxim, only 6.5% of the problems in the four translations into the foreign language elicited by Krings can definitely be classified as mere L2-competence problems (Krings 1986a: 165).

The distinction between the three kinds of problems outlined above will not be made use of in this investigation, for essentially two reasons:

i. The distinction is characterized by a low degree of practicability and operationality on the one hand, and by a high degree of speculation on the other hand. As Krings himself points out several times (e.g. 1986a: 163ff.), a clear, unambiguous, and intersubjectively valid categorization of problems as L2- or translation-competence problems is often impossible, because neither from the translations themselves nor from the protocols of thinking-aloud which are interwoven with them can the necessary information be interpreted. Therefore Krings categorizes translation problems as translation-competence problems in all doubtful cases. These are very large in number compared with the relatively few clear and unambiguous cases of L2-competence problems. As a consequence, the distinction loses much of its meaningfulness. One possibility of increasing its practicability and intersubjective validity could be to elicit specific information from the subjects by means of special techniques of elicitation and/or retrospection on the basis of which differentiations of problems could be made *in a well-founded way*. However, the disadvantages of such far-reaching procedures have already been pointed out in (sub)sections 4.2.2.1 and 4.4.1.

In view of the manifold practical difficulties of differentiation which the analyst is faced with and because of the low degree of meaningfulness which accompanies these problems, it does not seem to be sensible to further subcategorize translation problems at present.

ii. In addition to these practical considerations, I cannot see any theoretical necessity for a differentiation of translation problems as proposed by Krings. His main reason for such a differentiation is closely connected with his epistemological interest. It is directed towards translation teaching and research into foreign language teaching and learning. The differentiation of translation problems is considered to be of direct relevance for a more precise determination of the essence of translation competence. As a consequence, the role of translation in foreign language teaching and of foreign and native language instruction in translation teaching can also be determined more precisely (Krings 1986a: 153). Krings' argumentation is plausible but of hardly any relevance for this study since its epistemological interest and its theoretical assumptions are psycholinguistically motivated. Accordingly, the investigation of the data and the definition of the notions and concepts used are carried out from the perspective of the *subjects* and the analyst tries to reconstruct them from the data. But neither in the subjects' translations nor in their thinking-aloud, could hints be detected that L2-competence problems and translation-competence problems were given a different status and/or were treated in a different way. As a consequence, I assume that – until contrary evidence should arise – the differentiation of problems discussed above does not play any role *for the subjects*. Rather, I assume that the subjects, after having realized a translation problem – in the sense of Krings' definition – employ problem-solving strategies which are independent of the analytical artefacts of L2-competence problems and translation-competence problems[11].

As a result of the arguments put forward in i. and ii., I shall only refer to 'translation problems' in the following sections. The term denotes all those (linguistic) problems which a subject is faced with when performing a translation.

A further differentiation of problems suggested by Krings (1986a: 144–152) could, however, be important within the framework of this investigation. It is the distinction between *reception problems*, *production problems* and combined *reception-production problems*.

---

11 In Chapters 6. and 7., the question of what factors the structure and quality of the translational problem-solving strategies are dependent on will be discussed.

Reception problems occur when a subject has difficulties in receiving a source-language text segment, i.e. in the intake of information from an SL lexeme or combination of lexemes, and in the subsequent sense constitution[12].

Production problems occur when a subject has difficulties in finding a target-language text segment which s/he considers equivalent to the corresponding source-language text segment. As will be shown in section 7.3, equivalent target-language text segments can be found by two basically different procedures: First, by separating the sense from the forms of source-language text segments. The sense constituted in this way thus becomes the basis on which target-language equivalents can be searched for. Second, by searching for equivalent target-language text segments primarily on the basis of the forms of source-language text segments. This often occurs in the form of an interlingual equation of lexemes, as learned in vocabulary lessons at school. Mixtures of these two procedures are also frequently to be found in the data.

From the considerations above it becomes apparent that the subjects often do not comply with the postulate maintained by translation theory according to which any translation must be preceded by an understanding of the sense of the SL text[13]. Rather, translations are often performed in a primarily form-oriented way, which, as a consequence, does not require an understanding of the SL text. Thus, problems in the reception of the source-language text need not necessarily cause problems in the production of the target-language text. Furthermore, subjects could have latent problems in SL text reception which would become manifest if the task was to understand the SL text, but which remain latent in translation and do not cause problems in TL text production either.

Combined *reception-production problems* occur when a subject has difficulties in both the reception of an SL text segment and in the production of an equivalent TL text segment. In view of the considerations made above, such combined reception-production problems can be expected to occur when a subject performs a translation in a primarily sense-oriented way, either because form-oriented procedures have turned out to be unsuccessful or impossible, or because s/he usually translates in a sense-oriented way.

As a first inspection of the data collected has revealed, a clear, intersubjectively valid distinction between *reception problems*, *production problems*, and

12 In most recent theories and models of speech reception, it is emphasized that receiving speech in the sense of understanding it is not a mere *intake* of information but rather a goal-oriented *processing* of information, which implies a constitution of sense. Cf. e.g. Clark/Clark 1977: 210ff.; Hüllen/ Jung 1979: 81ff.; McDonough 1981: 45ff., as well as those studies which, in connection with *cognitive science*, model the understanding of text as a goal-oriented combination of *top-down* and *bottom-up processing*. Cf. Ballstaedt et al. 1981; de Beaugrande 1980a; Collins et al. 1975; van Dijk/Kintsch 1983; Müller 1984; Neubert 1983; Norman/Rumelhart 1975; Palmer 1975; Rihs-Middel 1982; Rumelhart 1975; 1980; den Uyl/van Oostendorp 1980; Schank 1978; Wolff 1985; n.d.; 1987. Cf. also section 7.2.

13 Cf. Wilss 1977a: 72; 1981d: 460; Koller 1983: 52; Stolze 1982: 157–160.

especially combined *reception-production* problems can often neither be made from the translations nor from the protocols of thinking-aloud. In these cases, translation problems will not be further subcategorized. In the great majority of the cases, however, it will be possible to assign translation problems to either *reception-* or *production problems*.

As concerns the practical use of this distinction of problems in the analyses of translation processes carried out in section 5.3, the following assumption is made: Subjects are primarily faced with *production problems* when translating *into the foreign language*, and with *reception problems* when translating *from the foreign language* (cf. Krings 1986a: 147ff.). Accordingly, a differentiation of problems will only be made explicit in the categories of analysis developed below in those cases which do *not* correspond with the assumption made[14].

However, the question of whether the distinction between the three kinds of problems described above is in fact of importance for the *psycholinguistic* analysis of the translation *process* can only be answered after the data have been analyzed qualitatively and quantitatively. Only when it becomes apparent that, in order to solve the different kinds of problems, the subjects employ strategies which differ from one another with respect to their quality, their quantity, and their distribution, will a distinction between reception-, production-, and combined reception-production problems be justified.

5.2.2 Elements of Translation Strategies

In section 4.5.3, translation strategies were defined as procedures which the subjects employ in order to solve translation problems. Accordingly, translation strategies have their starting-point in the realization of a problem by a subject, and their termination in a (possibly preliminary) solution to the problem or in the subject's realization of the insolubility of the problem at the given point in time.

Between the realization of a translation problem and the realization of its solution or insolubility, further verbal and/or mental activities can occur which can be interpreted as being strategy steps or elements of translation strategies. Their verbal and nonverbal manifestations, in so far as they can be interpreted from the fourteen translations constituting the data basis for the analysis, will be presented below. They can be formalized to yield categories of a model for the strategic analysis of the translation process. Such a model contains the following twenty-two categories:

---

14 E.g. when a *reception problem* occurs in a translation *into the foreign language*, or when a *production problem* occurs in a translation *into the mother tongue*. Cf. also section 5.2.2.

RP : Realizing a Translation Problem

A subject recognizes a problem connected with the transfer of an SL text segment into TL. After realizing a problem, the subject's search for a solution (→SP) usually begins. To the analyst this is often interpretable by a pause and/or hesitation during the production of the TL text.

Example /S1/ *Text*	Category of *Analysis*
`(...) there seems to be, ehm`	
`(2s)`	RP
`agreement about the fact that short`	
`(2s)`	RP
`narrating (...)`	

(2s) = pause of two seconds; /S1/ = subject one;

Of course, not every pause or hesitation necessarily indicates a translational problem. The mental organization of SL and TL text segments as well as problems in SL text reception (definitions below!) can also lead to pauses or hesitation. It is, therefore, the task of the analyst to interpret pauses and hesitations as indications of either translational or other problems.

VP : Verbalizing a Translational Problem

A subject verbalizes a problem connected with the transfer of an SL text segment into TL. Translational problems are verbalized either before or during the search for their solution. When a subject additionally verbalizes part of the context in which the problematic SL text segment is embedded VP + CT is noted.

Example /S1/ *Text*	Category of *Analysis*
`in recent times (1s)`	
`ja, jetzt 'mehrfach unternommen worden'`	VP

→SP : Search for a (possibly preliminary) Solution to a Translation Problem

The search for a (possibly preliminary) solution to a translational problem normally begins after realizing the problem (RP). When a translational problem is verbalized (VP), the search for a solution can already start before the verbalizing, i.e. after realizing the problem.

After verbalizing a problem, subjects normally start or continue searching for a solution. Therefore, →SP is only noted in those cases in which the process of searching lasts for a longer time (at least four seconds).

Example /S8/ *Text*	Category of *Analysis*
(...) which	
(2s)	RP
'ergeben'	VP
(9s)	→ SP

SP : Solution to a Translational Problem

A subject considers a text segment realized in TL to be an optimal solution to a translational problem *under the given circumstances.* When a subject considers a TL text segment to be an approximation to a solution and perhaps substitutes it by a more adequate TL text segment in the course of the translation, the approximation is noted as PSP (definition below!).

Example /S1/ *Text*	Category of *Analysis*
(...) the short story is the result of different, ehm, reductions (...) in action	
(4s)	RP / → SP
'Charakterdarstellung und -entwicklung'	VP
presentation and development of characters	SP
as well as (...)	

PSP : Preliminary Solution to a Translational Problem

A subject considers a text segment realized in TL to be a preliminary or approximate solution to a translational problem, a solution which is to be improved on, if possible. The adequacy of preliminary solutions is often checked in the course of the translation. The result of this checking is either a corroboration of the preliminary solution (PSP+), which thus acquires the status of a solution (SP) for the subject, or its rejection (PSP–) and (the search for) a new (preliminary) solution (PSP2/SP).

Example /S8/ *Text*	Category of *Analysis*
(...) and therefore	
hint at	PSP1
show at	PSP2
(5s)	
hint at	PSP1+ / SP
our time.	

SPa,b,c.. : Parts of a Solution to a Translational Problem

When a complex translational problem is solved successively, the different parts of the solution are noted as SPa, SPb, SPc, etc.

Example /S1/ *Text*	Category of *Analysis*
(...) 'mit einem Minimum an Erzählung ein Maximum literarischer Wirkung zu erreichen'	VP
(...)	
to gain	SPa
(...)	
a maximum of literary	SPb
(...)	
impression	SPc
(...)	
by a minimum of	SPd
(...)	
narrating.	SPe

SP∅ : A Solution to a Translational Problem is still so be found (∅)

A subject considers a translational problem to be insoluble at a given point in time. Its insolubility is either realized immediately or is the result of a process in which preliminary solutions to a problem (PSP) have been worked out, tested and rejected.

SP∅ is also used when a subject (consciously) leaves a problem aside in order to try to solve it in a second version of the translation.

Example /S15/ *Text*	Category of *Analysis*
(...) to (1s) describe	
(20s)	RP / → SP
Tja, 'Eigenschaften und Merkmale' Hm [↑↓]	VP
(15s)	→ SP
Ja, das würd ich jetzt erst mal weglassen.	SP∅

[↑↓] = rise-fall intonation

SP = ∅ : Negative (∅) Solution to a Translational Problem

A subject verbalizes a TL text segment which s/he does *not* consider to be the or a possible solution to a translational problem. Negative solutions occur when a certain inadequate TL text segment suggests itself as a solution to a problem, e.g. because it is a literal translation of an SL text segment, and when the subject realizes its inadequacy. Negative solutions often represent the basis on which the search for a solution continues *ex negativo*.
Parts of a negative solution are noted as SPa,b.. = ∅.

Example /S1/ *Text*	Category of *Analysis*
(3s)	RP / → SP
'kultivierter Mensch' kann man nicht sagen	SP = Ø
'cultivated man or woman'	VP
(3s)	→ SP

PSL : Problem in the Reception of the SL text

The problem which the subject is faced with is not a transfer problem but a problem in the comprehension/interpretation of an SL text segment. These problems mostly occur in translation *from* the foreign language. According to the definitions above, RPSL, VPSL, SPSL, etc. may be noted if applicable.

Example /S1/ *Text*	Category of *Analysis*
(SL text segment: (...) müssen wir von der spezifischen sprachlichen Situation in Österreich beziehungsweise in Wien ausgehen, die sich zum einen durch die Anwesenheit des Dialekts von manchen der oben genannten Länder unterscheidet.) (...) from	
'manchen' (2s) worauf bezieht sich jetzt 'manchen'?	VPSL

The categories listed above refer to entities which exclusively occur within strategic phases of the translation process. They are original elements of translation strategies. The categories listed below refer to entities which frequently, but not exclusively, occur within strategic phases of the translation process (i.e. MSL, MTL, REPHR.SL, REPHR.TL, CHECK, $[TS]_{com}$, TRANS or to entities which can, but generally do not, occur within strategic phases of the translation process (i.e. OSL, OTL, REC, T, ORG). They are potential elements of translation strategies.

MSL / MTL : Monitoring of SL- or TL Text Segments

A subject repeats exactly verbatim SL or TL text segments which s/he has already received in SL or verbalized in TL. In contrast to Rehbein (1977: 216ff.), the function of monitoring is to relate a partial, verbalized sequence to the appropriate part of its mental plan. This is done in order to recognize the remaining part of the plan and to further its realization in TL, or in order to find an appropriate continuation to the partial sequence which had already been verbalized. In contrast to verbalizing translational problems (VP), monitoring of SL text segments always occurs in *retrospective* phases of the translation process (cf. section 7.1)

a. when a subject repeats an SL text segment which s/he had already received (= *antecedent* text segment) in order to obtain (possible) hints for the continuation of the sentence structure of the TL text (= translation);

b. when a subject repeats an *antecedent* SL text segment in order to obtain (possible) hints for the solution to a (mostly lexical) problem or for an optimization or repair of a preliminary solution to a translational problem which the subject had found before.

VP is noted when a subject verbalizes a problem in a *prospective* phase of the translation process (cf. section 7.1). After VP, a process of searching for a solution to the problem normally starts. When a problem is verbalized a second, third, etc. time during this process of searching, and before the translation goes on, the categories VP1, VP2, etc. are used.

Example (MSL) /S24/ *Text*	Category of *Analysis*
Obwohl wir Ansätze heranziehen (2s) Ehm, although (1s) we	
(2s) ehm (3s)	RP / → SP
take into account	SP
(1s) oder 'heranziehen' (7s) ehm (3s)	RP / → SP
'Ansätze'	VP
(11s)	→ SP
'Obwohl wir Ansätze heranziehen'	MSL<VP2>

< > The element in the pointed brackets is embedded in the preceding element. Here, MSL contains a second verbalization of the problem 'Ansätze'.

Example (MTL) /S8/ *Text*	Category of *Analysis*
(...) which (2s)	
'ergeben'	VP
(9s)	→ SP
which, which	MTL
comes out of	SP

REPHR.SL : Rephrasing of SL Text Segments

A subject takes up SL text segments and verbalizes them, not verbatim but in a form different from that of the original. The function of SL rephrasings is to try to find an adequate translation for a problematic SL text segment. This is attempted by changing the form (= surface structure) of the text segment but keeping its meaning invariant to the greatest possible extent. In primarily form-oriented translations, the changed surface form can lead to a recall of an interlingual equation of lexemes which the subject had learned. In primarily sense-oriented translations, the separation of form and meaning, which is necessary for any rephrasing, enables the subject to search for TL equivalents on the basis of the sense thus constituted[15]. Rephrasings of SL text segments are used in order to find a solution to a translational problem, to check a (possibly preliminary) solution to a translational problem, or to optimize approximations to solutions.

Example /S8/ *Text*	Category of *Analysis*
In jüngerer Zeit' (1s)	
müßt ich passen;	SPØ
würd ich sagen 'heutzutage'	REPHR.SL

REPHR.TL : Rephrasing of TL Text Segments

A subject takes up TL text segments and verbalizes them in a form different from that of the original. The functions of TL rephrasings are to *correct* or *optimize* a previous (preliminary) solution, or to *add an alternative solution* to a previous (preliminary) one.

Example /S1/ ***Text***	Category of ***Analysis***
(...) 'verweisen'	VP
point out	PSP
ehm, and thus	MTL
ja, something like 'reveal certain characteristics'	REPHR.TL

15 Cf. section 7.3 for more detailed information on *form-* and *sense-oriented* translation.

CHECK : Discernible Testing (= Checking) of a (preliminary) Solution to a Translational Problem

After a (preliminary) solution has been found, a subject tries to corroborate it or, if certain findings contradict it, rejects it and tries to bring about a new (preliminary) solution. CHECKS can be subclassified according to their structure. This leads to the following types of CHECK:

CHECK SL/TL[16] : testing by comparing an SL text segment with the corresponding (preliminary) solution verbalized in TL;

Example /S8/ *Text*	Category of *Analysis*
(...) 'Maximum'	VP
'greatest extent'	PSP
(1s)	CHECK SL/TL
gibt es bestimmt nicht.	PSP-

CHECK TL/TL : testing by comparing two (preliminary) solutions verbalized in TL with each other;

Example /S8/ *Text*	Category of *Analysis*
(...) and therefore	MTL
hint at	PSP1
show at	PSP2
(5s)	CHECK TL/TL
hint at	PSP1+ / SP

CHECK BSL/SL : testing by comparing a (preliminary) solution translated back into SL with the corresponding SL text segment;

Example /S8/ *Text*	Category of *Analysis*
(...) 'abverlangen'	VP
Hm [↑↓] (9s)	→ SP
expects	PSP
'erwarten', 'abverlangen' (1s)	CHECK BSL/SL
ja, okay.	PSP+ / SP

16 As this is by far the most frequently occuring type of CHECK, it will generally be noted as *CHECK* only.

CHECK CT : **testing by finding out whether a (preliminary) solution fits into its context;**

Example /S34/ *Text*	Category of *Analysis*
'tool', ist das nicht so ne Art (2s)	VP
Spule oder was?	PSP
(3s) Wie paßt das jetzt hierein?	CHECK CT

CHECK ANALOG : **testing by analogy and by drawing a conclusion of probability;**

Example /S8/ *Text*	Category of *Analysis*
'Reduktionen'	VP
(...)	
reductions	PSP
(...)	
'to reduce', 'reduzieren' (1s) 'Reduktion'	CHECK ANALOG

STRUCTURE:

Since	verb X SL	=	verb Y TL	*known to the translator*
	reduzieren	=	reduce	
it is highly probable that	noun Y SL	=	noun Y TL	*PSP*
	Reduktion	=	reduction	

OSL : Mental Organization of SL Text Segments

A subject mentally organizes SL text segments for translation into TL. Three cases can be distinguished:

i. The subject extracts a unit of translation, i.e. an SL text segment which, at a given point in time, s/he puts into his/her focus of attention in order to render it into the TL *as a whole*.

ii. The subject sorts out the parts of an SL text segment that cannot be translated word-for-word into the TL.

iii. The subject sifts an SL text segment in order to find out the point from which to proceed with the translation. This sifting mostly occurs in complex SL text segments which the subject splits up into several units of translation, or after a complex solution of a translation problem has been brought about.

Example /S1/ *Text*	Category of *Analysis*
(SL text segment: "In jüngerer Zeit sind mehrfach Versuche unternommen worden, Eigenschaften und Merkmale der *short story* zu beschreiben ...) In recent times, ehm (2s) many attempts have been made	
(2s) ehm, jetzt gehts weiter mit hier 'zu beschreiben' (...)	OSL

OTL : Mental Organization of TL text segments

A subject mentally organizes text segments which s/he has already translated into TL but which have to be combined in a certain way to make an adequate stretch of TL discourse.

Example /S28/ *Text*	Category of *Analysis*
(SL text segment: "There is no possible argument on which the decision by the congregation of Oxford University to refuse Mrs Thatcher the proposed honorary degree is worthy of respect.") Translation: "Es gibt kein wie auch immer geartetes Argument (...)"	
Vielleicht fang ich nochmal ganz anders an (1s) ehm (4s) vielleicht fangen wir mal so an mit dem 'on which the decision'.	OTL

REC : Reception of SL Text Segments

A subject receives SL text segments by reading them either silently or aloud. It is only the *first* reading of the whole text, of a paragraph, or of a sentence, clause or phrase which is categorized as REC. Further readings either fall under MSL or, if they aim at mentally organizing SL text segments for translation, under OSL.

Example /S28/ *Text*	Category of *Analysis*
Okay, ich les mir den Text erst mal durch.	
Reading aloud: "There is no possible argument (...)"	REC

$[TS]_{com}$: Comment on a Text Segment

A text segment is commented on by making a metastatement about it. In the case of an SL text segment, the comment mostly refers to its translation into TL. TL text segments are mostly commented on as regards their adequacy. According to the definitions given above, $[P]_{com}$, $[SP]_{com}$, $[\rightarrow SP]_{com}$, etc. are noted, if applicable.

Example /S15/ *Text*	Category of *Analysis*
`Das Schwierige an dem Satz ist also, daß ich, daß der verschiedene Teile enthält.`	$[TS(SL)]_{com}$

TRANS : Transposition

A subject reorders lexemes or combinations of lexemes within a (complex) TL unit (i.e. text, paragraph, sentence, clause, or phrase). Transpositions are made in order to correct or optimize TL text segments.

Example /S1/ *Text*	Category of *Analysis*
`(TL text segment: "(...) die sich bewegt hat (...) zwischen (...) politischem (...) Trotz (...) und Haarspalterei (...)"`	
`die sich zwischen (5a) politischem Trotz und Haarspalterei bewegt hat.`	TRANS<OZS>

T : Translation

Non-strategic rendering of SL text segments into TL. Immediately after the reception of an SL text segment, it is translated into TL without any problem-solving involved.

Example /S28/ *Text*	Category of *Analysis*
`"(...) is worthy of respect"`	REC
`was respektwürdig ist`	T

→T2,3,..n : Conceiving a second, third, etc. Translation version

A subject endeavours to conceive a new translation version for an SL text, paragraph, sentence, clause, or phrase. The new translation version is either explicitly announced, or performed only. Its end is noted as T2,3,..n#. Whereas rephrasings (REPHR.TL) always refer to *one* text segment only, which is captured by *one* category of analysis and thus represents *one* recognizable step within the translation process, a new translation version always contains several TL text segments. They either occur as verbatim repetitions (MTL), or in a form different from the original. In the latter case, the new translation version contains one or more rephrasings (REPHR.TL).

Example /S1/ *Text*	Category of *Analysis*
(First translation version: "Jeder Absolvent der Universität Oxford, welcher Partei er auch immer angehörte") (...)	
(1s) also jeder (5s) Absolvent der Universität Oxford, (4s)	MTL → T2
	<OTL>
von welcher Partei auch immer	REPHR.TL T2#

ORG : Organization of Translational Discourse

Subjects sometimes break the (monological) discourse by which the translations are produced into parts, for example after a unit of translation has been rendered into TL, or before the reception of an SL text segment. This structuring of the translational discourse is indicated by certain organizing utterances.

Example /S1/ *Text*	Category of *Analysis*
Okay, ich les mir den Text erst mal durch.	ORG
(Reads text aloud)	REC
(2s) Okay.	ORG

5.2.3 Translation Strategies

As pointed out in section 1.2, the epistemological interest of this investigation is directed towards the subjects' use of translation strategies. They will be described and analyzed in this section.

Translation strategies are constituted by those minimal problem-solving steps which were described in the previous section. As the data shows, the elements of translation strategies combine in specific ways only to build up structures. Accordingly, translation strategies contain one or more of these structures.

Following a model for the analysis of discourse, which I developed in a different context (Lörscher 1983: 223), a distinction will be made between *basic structures*, *expanded structures*, and *complex structures* of translation strategies. This is based on the fact that although translation strategies can be highly complex and thus difficult to document and describe in their manifold forms, they can be reduced to a fairly small number of simpler structures. The application of a generative principle allows the transformation of *basic structures* into *expanded-* and *complex structures.*

As regards their description, basic structures are the simplest structural types. This, however, does not necessarily imply that *in the course of the translation* the subjects consider those *problems* which they tackle with strategies consisting of one basic structure only to be especially easy to solve. As a consequence, the *linguistic* complexity of the analytical constructs need by no means be identical with the *psychological* complexity of the problems, as assessed by the subjects (cf. Lörscher 1983: 283). It can be assumed, however, that, *in retrospect*, the subjects consider those problems to be especially complex, and thus difficult to solve, which they have tackled with linguistically complex strategies requiring a great amount of time and mental effort. Retrospective reports[17] could possibly supply further information.

Whether the subjects can already assess or estimate the complexity and difficulty of translational problems immediately after they have realized them, and whether they accordingly employ more or less complex strategies for solving them, has not been investigated yet. It will be dealt with in Chapter 7.

In my data corpus, a tendency seems to be recognizable according to which the subjects generally use (linguistically) simple strategies first, and only when they turn out to be unsuccessful do the subjects employ more complex strategies. This procedure of the subjects complies with the generative principle whereby complex translation strategies are constituted by and can be derived from simpler structures.

Basic Structures

In the data basis of the corpus, five types of basic structures are to be found. According to the generative principle, types II to IV can be derived from type I.

---

17 In subsection 4.2.2.1 it was pointed out that retrospective data stemming from subjects' ex-post elicited reports or from ex-post thinking-aloud protocols were not collected, mainly because retrospective procedures are generally considered to be less reliable than introspective ones.

Type I : RP – (P)SP# / SP∅[18]

Immediately after the realization of a translational problem, a subject finds a (preliminary) solution to the problem or realizes its insolubility at that particular time.

As concerns the descriptive complexity, type I is the simplest of the five types. When (P)SP is reached, the boundary is fluid between this type of strategic translation and non-strategic translation, in which a subject quasi-automatically finds a corresponding TL text segment for an SL one. For the analyst, a short pause of not more than two seconds[19] and/or a filler such as 'Hm' with a rise-fall intonation contour [↑↓] are possible indicators of a subject's realization of a problem. A TL text segment immediately following these indicators can be interpreted as being a solution to the problem previously realized. If a subject cannot find a solution to a problem, s/he must verbalize this. Otherwise, there is no indicator of the occurrence of a strategy for the analyst.

Example /S28/ *Text*	CoA/Type of *Structure*[20]	
Ehm, jeder	T	
(2s)	RP	I
Absolvent	SP	SP
(8s)		
(...)		

Type II : RP – →SP (P)SP# / SP∅

After the realization of a translational problem, a subject searches for a solution, finds and verbalizes it, or realizes that s/he cannot solve the problem at that particular time. Pauses lasting for three or more seconds which go beyond the mere realization of a problem are interpreted as being a search for a solution and are categorized accordingly.

Type II differs from type I only in that the former additionally contains a phase of searching for a solution to a problem.

18 Elements in round brackets are optional; thus, (P)SP means SP *or* PSP. The termination symbol # indicates the end of a structure.

19 Pauses of more than two seconds are interpreted as being elements of strategies, such as the mental organization of SL or TL text segments (OSL/OTL), or the search for a solution to a problem (→SP).

20 Square double brackets in the transcript indicate strategies. The outcome of the strategy (PSP, SP, or SP∅) is noted after or beneath the number of the type of structure (I, II, III, IV, V). CoA stands for Category of Analysis.

Example /S28/ *Text*	CoA/Type of *Structure*	
(...) der bisher das hohe Amt des Premier-ministers		
(5s)	RP/→ SP	II
inne hatte (1s)	SP	SP
(...)		

Type III : (RP) – VP – (P)SP# / SP∅

A subject realizes a translational problem and verbalizes it. Immediately afterwards, s/he finds a (preliminary) solution to the problem or realizes that s/he cannot solve the problem at that particular time. As any verbalization of a problem must logically be preceded by a realization of it, RP is only noted when there is a pause of one or two seconds between the realization and the verbalization of a problem. In this case, RP and VP can be identified as two elements of the strategy.

Type III differs from type I only in that the former additionally contains a verbalization of a problem.

Example /S6/ *Text*	CoA/Type of *Structure*	
(...) of different reductions	T	
(2s)	RP	III
'auf dem Gebiet' (2s)	VP	
concerning	SP	SP
(...)		

Type IV : (RP – (→SP)) – VP – (→SP) – (P)SP# / SP∅

A subject realizes a translational problem, possibly starts searching for a solution, and verbalizes it. After the verbalization, the subject may find a (preliminary) solution either immediately or after a (further) phase of searching, or the subject may realize that s/he cannot solve the problem at that particular time.

Type IV differs from type I only in that the former additionally contains a verbalization of the problem and two potential phases of searching for a solution, one of which must occur so that the structure can be distinguished from type III.

Example /S24/ *Text*	CoA/Type of *Structure*	
Ehm, the German norm	T	
(3s) ehm (2s)	RP/→ SP	IV
'Hochsprache'	VP	
'standard German' irgendwie	PSP	PSP

Type V : **(...) (P)SPa / SPa∅ (...) (P)SPb / SPb∅ (...) (P)SPc / SPc∅ (...)**

A subject solves a translational problem by successively solving the parts which constitute it ((P)SPa, (P)SPb, (P)SPc, etc.), or s/he realizes the insolubility of parts of the problem at that particular time. Three subtypes can be distinguished:

Type Va : **RP – (→SP) – (P)SPa / SPa∅ – (→SP) – (P)SPb / SPb∅ – (→SP) – (P)SPc / SPc∅ (...)**

The subject realizes a translational problem and solves it by working out solutions for the parts which constitute it ((P)SPa, (P)SPb, (P)SPc, etc.). There can either be short pauses (up to two seconds) or separate phases of searching (→SP) between the parts of the solution.

If the subject does not succeed in solving certain parts of the problem, SPa∅, SPb∅, SPc∅, etc. is noted.

Example /S24/ *Text*	CoA/Type of *Structure*	
'wie sie in systematischer Variation auftritt'	OSL	
(2s) ehm (2s)	RP/→ SP	
as it appears	SPa	Va
(5s) ehm (1s)	→ SP	SP
in systematical variation	SPb	
(...)		

Type Vb : **RP – (→SP) – VPa – (→SP) – (P)SPa / SPa∅ – (→SP) – VPb – (→SP) – (P)SPb / SPb∅ (...)**

The subject realizes a translational problem and solves it by alternately verbalizing the parts which constitute the problem (VPa, VPb, etc.) and successively working out solutions for them (SPa, SPb, etc.). There can be phases of searching (→SP) between the various elements of the structure. If the subject does not succeed in solving certain parts of the problem, SPa∅, SPb∅, SPc∅, etc. is noted.

The decisive difference between Va and Vb is that the various parts of the problem are verbalized in the latter type of structure.

Example /S25/ *Text*	CoA/Type of *Structure*	
'mit einer mehrfachen Sprachbarriere'	VP	
nehm ich erst das Hauptwort (1s)	→ SPa	
	<OSL>	
'Sprachbarriere'	VPa	Vb
'language barrier'	SPa	PSP
und dann guck ich mir eventuell noch an, ob en Adjektiv davor steht, also	OSL	
hier 'einer mehrfachen'	<VPb>	
wie wäre es mit 'double'	PSPb	

Type Vc : RP – (→SP) – (VPa) – (→SP) – (P)SPa / SPa∅ – (→SP) – (VPb) – (→SP) – (P)SPb / SPb∅ (...)

Type Vc represents a mixture of Va and Vb. The subject realizes a translational problem and solves it by partially verbalizing and working out solutions for parts of the problem, and by partially working out solutions for parts of the problem without prior verbalizations.

Example /S1/ *Text*	CoA/Type of *Structure*	
'mit einem Minimum an Erzählung ein Maximum literarischer Wirkung zu erreichen'	VP	
(2s) ehm (4s)	→ SP	
to gain	SPa	
(...)		Vc
(3s)	→ SP	SPa,
a maximum of literary	SPb	b,d,
(2s)	→ SP	SPc∅
'Wirkung'	VPc	
(4s)	→ SP/ SPc∅	
with a minimum of (1s) narrating	SPd	

The basic structures described and listed above are translation strategies in their simplest, pure and unadulterated forms. Besides these structures, others can be found in my data corpus which differ from the former in two respects: First, certain elements can be embedded in the structures; second, certain elements can be bound to them.

Embedded elements occur within a translation strategy, i.e. between two steps in the problem-solving process. Embedded elements are not original parts of a strategy. They are indicated by pointed brackets < > in the transcript.

Example /S3/ *Text*	CoA/Type of *Structure*	
(...) people have tried (1s) to describe	T	
(6s)	RP/→ SP	II
to describe	MTL	<MTL>
aspects and features of the short story	SP	SP
(...)		

The transcribed part of a translation contains a type II structure (RP – →SP – (P)SP) with an exactly verbatim repetition of a previously produced TL text segment (MTL) embedded in it, i.e. between the search for a solution and the solution brought about. Elements which often function as embeddings are monitoring, rephrasing, and mentally organizing SL and TL text segments (MSL, MTL, REPHR.SL, REPHR.TL, OSL, and OTL), as well as non-strategic elements of translation (T), transpositions (TRANS), and comments ($[TS]_{com}$).

Whereas embeddings occur between steps of a strategy, *bound elements* are appended to one of the five basic structures described above. When, for example, a subject checks a solution to a problem, this checking is considered to be a bound element, and noted by square double brackets in broken form. This is to indicate the double nature of these elements. On the one hand, they are not original parts of strategies in the sense of the five basic structures. Strategies terminate when a solution to a problem has been found, or when the insolubility of a problem has been realized. On the other hand, bound elements are closely connected with their preceding strategies. When a subject checks a solution to a problem, for example, s/he gives to understand that although the element to be checked is considered to be a solution to a problem at that time, it has to be corroborated in order to be relevant in the continuation of the translation. It is only after its corroboration that the subject considers the problem solved and directs his/her cognitive attention to the continuation of the translation.

Example /S8/ *Text*	CoA/Type of *Structure*	
(2s)	RP	
narrative literature	SP	I +
(1s) 'Erzählliteratur' (2s)	CHECK	CHECK
narrative literature	SP+	SP
(2s)	RP	
'darstellen'	VP	

The transcribed part of a translation contains a type I structure (RP – (P)SP), with two elements appended to it: a checking of the solution (CHECK) and its corroboration (SP+) being a precondition for the continuation of the translation.

Besides CHECKS and corroborations (SP+), rephrasing and monitoring of TL text segments (REPHR.TL, MTL), comments on ($[(P)SP]_{com}$) and repetitions of (preliminary) solutions to a problem ((P)SP1,2,..) can function as bound elements. Each of these types can occur in four structural forms: i. as a pure and unadulterated basic structure, ii. as a basic structure with (an) embedded element(s), iii. as a basic structure with (a) bound element(s), or iv. as a basic structure with (an) embedded element(s) and (a) bound element(s).

Expanded Structures

Besides the basic structures described above, there are expanded structures of translation strategies. They consist of a basic structure which contains one or more expansions. In contrast to embeddings, which are intrastructural elements and not components of the strategy itself, expansions are defined as additional elements of a strategy itself. They are indicated by the symbol *EX* in the transcript.

Example /S2/

Text	CoA/Type of *Structure*	
(2s)	RP	
'auf dem Gebiet der Handlung'	VP	
(24s)	→ SP	IV +
'auf dem Gebiet der Handlung'	VP2	2EX
(8s)	→ SP	PSP
wörtlich: 'on the area of action'	PSP	

The example above contains a type IV structure (RP – (→SP) – VP – (→SP) – (P)SP) with two additional elements of the structure itself (→SP, VP2), i.e. with two expansions.

As the five basic structures listed above consist of at most RP, VP, →SP, and (P)SP, only VP and →SP can function as expansions. The realization of a translational problem can in principle only occur once within a strategy and can thus not function as an expansion. Nor can a repetition of a (preliminary) solution to a problem. It does not occur within a strategy, but at its end, and is thus a bound element, by definition.

Accordingly, type I cannot have any expansions. Types II and III can only occur as expanded structures if they additionally have at least one embedded element after which →SP and/or VP can occur again.

Expanded structures, like basic structures, can thus have embedded and/or bound elements.

Complex Structures

Complex structures of translation strategies are built up of at least two basic and/or expanded structures and/or translation versions (cf. section 5.2.4).

Example /S25/

Text	CoA/Type of *Structure*	
In recent times	T	
(11s) ja, jetzt 'mehrfach unternommen worden'	OSL	
'mehrfach'	VP	III SPØ
attempts have been made	T/SPØ	
(2s)	→ SP	II + 1EX
in recent times	MTL	<MTL> SP
(3s)	→ SP	
many	SP	
(...)		

The example above contains a type III and a type II structure. The former is terminated with the subject leaving the problem aside in order to try to solve it later. The second part of this complex translation strategy is a type II structure. It reveals a characteristic trait of complex structures in general. As can be seen in the example, type II starts with a search for a solution to the problem. The first step of the strategy, the realization of the problem, does not occur. It is implicit in VP in the preceding type II structure, since any verbalization of a problem logically implies that the problem has already been realized.

This fact can be generalized as follows: When a translation strategy consists of two or more structural types, the *last* element of the first part of the structure ((P)SP, SP_x, SPØ), and the *first obligatory* element of the second part and of all further parts of the structure can be missing. If RP is the first element, it must be missing, as a rule. A further example may illustrate this:

Example /S24/

Text	CoA/Type of *Structure*	
(2s) ehm (3s)	RP/→ SP	VA +
'einen kommunikationsorientierten Unterricht'	VP	1 EX
(13s)	→ SP	<VP>
ja, entweder 'a communi.., communicative'	PSPa1.	PSPa
(4s)	CHECK	CHECK
or 'communication oriented'	PSPa2./	
	REPHR.TL	REPHR
(5s) ehm (2s)	→ SPb	Va
lesson	SPb	
oder (2s)	→ SP2	
'kommunikationsorientierter'	VPa	IV SP
(8s)	→ SP	
ja, 'lesson oriented (2s) on communication	SP2	

The transcribed part of a translation contains two structures of the type Va, and one type IV structure. The first (Va with VP embedded and expanded by →SP) starts with the realization of a translational problem and ends with the first preliminary solution to the first part of the problem (PSPa1.). A solution to the second part of the problem is still to be found. Va has two bound elements, CHECK and REPHR.TL, appended to it. The second structural type is also Va. It contains a phase of searching for a solution to the second part of the problem (→SPb), and the solution itself (SPb). RP is missing because it occurred at the very beginning of the strategy. This also applies to the third structural type (IV). It starts with a search for a further solution to a problem (→SP2), and ends when the solution has been found and verbalized (SP2).

A phenomenon which can often be observed in complex translation strategies is the occurrence of *free elements*. Whereas embeddings occur intrastructurally, i.e. within structural types, free elements are to be found interstructurally, i.e. between two structural types of a complex structure. The following example may elucidate this:

Example /S1/ *Text*	CoA/Type of *Structure*
(4s)	RP/→ SP
'auf unsere Zeit verweisen'	VP
(2s) ja (1s)	→ SP
'verweisen'	VPa
'point to'	SPa
ehm, and thus	MTL
(3s) ja, something like	→ SP
reveal certain characteristics	SP
of our time.	<REPHR.TL(SPa)>

In the example transcribed above, the free element occurs between the type Vb and the type II structure. It is a verbatim repetition of a previously produced TL text segment (MTL). Besides MTL, OSL, OTL, REPHR.SL, and $[(S)P]_{com}$ occur as free elements in my data.

The translation strategies discussed so far are by their very nature *continuous*. The translation problems to be solved are always tackled *in one go*. This means that the subjects reach a (preliminary) solution, or a further (more adequate) solution to a problem, or realize the insolubility of a problem without having shifted their *global* focus of attention from the problem under consideration to another strategic or non-strategic phase of the translation. There can, however, be *local* shifts of attention within continuous strategies, as is the case when embeddings or free elements are to be found. Such shifts, which mostly last for a short time only, occur between two strategy steps. They are brought about with the aim of solving the problem under consideration and thus of producing an adequate TL text.

Global shifts of attention occur between the parts of *discontinuous* strategies. After the strategy has come to a preliminary end (SPØ, PSP), the subject does not direct any further attention towards the problem's solution or towards an optimization of the preliminary solution. Rather, s/he directs his/her cognitive attention towards another strategic or non-strategic phase of the translation. It is not before its termination that the initial problem or the optimization of its preliminary solution again becomes the subject's focus of attention. The example below may illustrate this:

Example /S13/

Text	*CoA/*	Type of *Structure*	*Part*
when it tries	T		
(6s) ehm (2s)	RP/→ SP		
'erreichen'	VP	IV SPØ	Sa
(8s)	→ SP/SPØ	>>>.........	
with a minimum	T		
(2s) of nar (..)	RP'		
(6s)	→ SP'		
'Erzählung' mit	VP'	IV' PSP'	
(12s)	→ SP'		
ja, eventuell 'written words'	PSP'		
'geschriebenen	CHECK	+ CHECK	
Worten' (4s)	TL/BSL		
ich weiß nicht, das ist ja k (..)			
(1s) im Grunde keine Erzählung,	[P']com	+ [P']com.	
wie eben eine Erzählung oder die			
Erzählung als en literarischer			
Stil oder irgendwas			
(7s) ehm (2s)	OSL/OTL	OSL/OTL	
when she tries	MTL	MTL	
(4s)	→ SP	IV SP<<<...	
'erreichen', 'to reach'	VP2/SP		Sb
(4s)	CHECK	+ CHECK	
to reach	SP+	+ SP+	
(...)			

The above example contains a discontinuous strategy consisting of two parts, i.e. Sa and Sb. The continuation symbol >>> / <<< indicates that Sa will be continued and that Sb is the continuation of Sa. The first part of this discontinuous strategy consists of a type IV structure with SPØ at its end. The subject cannot find a TL equivalent for the SL lexeme 'entsprechen'.

In the part of the translation between Sa and Sb, the subject shifts his focus of attention to another translation problem (P'). In order to solve P', a strategy consisting of the structural type IV is used and results in a preliminary solution to the problem. The strategy has two bound elements: a checking of the preliminary solution (CHECK) and a comment on the problem $[P']_{com}$. They are followed by two free elements: OSL/OTL and MTL. After monitoring, the subject shifts his focus of attention back to the initial problem and realizes the second part of the discontinuous strategy, i.e. Sb. It consists of a type IV structure with CHECK and SP+ following as bound elements.

In the concluding part of this section, the translation strategies described above will be represented in a flow chart. Thus, the interplay of the strategies' components as well as the decision paths available to the subjects when they are engaged in solving translational problems can be visualized.

It goes without saying that the diagram cannot (adequately) capture all the possible forms of realization of translation strategies. However, it claims to represent the essential *types* of strategy in an adequate way.

Diagram 11: Flow Chart of Strategic Translating

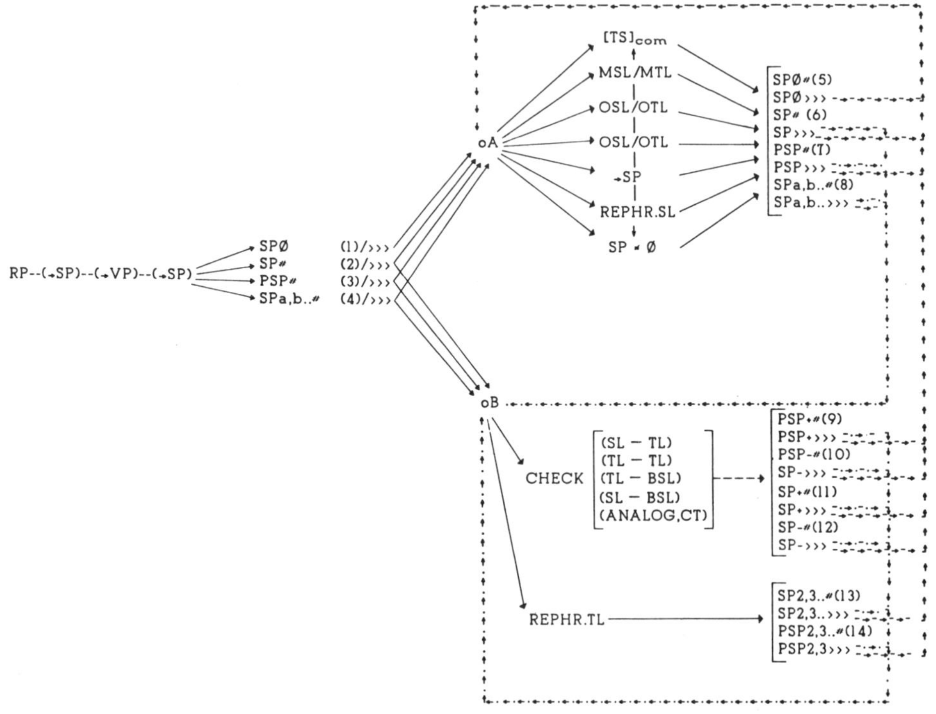

Explanatory Remarks to Diagram 11

After realizing (RP) and possibly verbalizing (VP) a translational problem, and after a potential search for a solution (→SP), a subject may achieve a solution (SP, SPa,b..) or a preliminary solution (PSP) immediately (2), (3), (4), in which cases the problem-solving process may come to an end (#). This may also be the case when the subject considers a problem insoluble (1).

Having found a (preliminary) solution (2), (3), (4), the subject may go on dealing with the problem (>>>) and proceed to either decision node A or B (oA, oB). When the subject cannot find a solution (SPØ), s/he can only proceed to decision node A. Having reached decision node A, the subject may try to bring about a solution by monitoring SL or TL text segments (MSL, MTL), and/or by rephrasing SL text segments (REPHR.SL), and/or by (further) searching for a solution (→SP), and/or by mentally organizing SL or TL text segments (OSL, OTL), and/or by commenting on text segments ($[TS]_{com}$), and/or by conceiving a negative solution (SP=Ø).

As a result of these problem-solving activities, the subject may either find a (preliminary) solution to the problem (PSP, SP, SPa,b..) or not (SPØ). Here again, the problem-solving process may come to a successful (6), (7), (8) or to an unsuccessful (5) end.

When the subject decides to continue, s/he may either go back to decision node A, which is possible after SPØ, PSP, SP, and SPa,b..; or s/he may proceed to decision node B, which, however, is not possible after SPØ.

Having reached decision node B, the subject continues by rephrasing (REPHR.TL) the respective TL text segment (SP, PSP, SPa,b..) or by testing it (CHECK).

The result of the rephrasing is a new (preliminary) solution ((P)SP2,3.., SPa2,3.., SPb2,3.. ..). Here again, the problem-solving process may come to an end, as in (13) and (14), or the subject may proceed to one of the decision nodes again.

After the testing of a TL text segment, the (preliminary) solution may either be corroborated ((P)SP+) or rejected ((P)SP–). In both these cases, the subject may terminate the problem-solving process (9), (10), (11), (12) or proceed to either decision node A or B.

5.2.4 Translation Versions

As shown in the previous sections, the translation process contains both strategic phases, which are directed towards solving translational problems, and non-strategic phases, which aim at accomplishing tasks[21]. The former range from the realization of a translational problem to its solution or to the realization of its insolubility at a given point in time. The latter start with the extraction of a unit of translation and terminate when it has been (preliminarily) rendered into TL or when a translational problem arises. Whereas translation strategies can, by definition, only occur within strategic phases of the translation process, translation versions can be located within strategic or non-strategic phases, or can extend from strategic into non-strategic phases or *vice versa*.

As my data reveal, the subjects often produce several translation versions. They can comprise the entire text or only parts of it (e.g. paragraphs, sentences, clauses, or phrases). The production of several translation versions can have various reasons, of which at least four can be interpreted from the data:

21 Cf. Dörner 1976: 10, and section 4.5.3 above.

i. If a subject does not succeed in solving a translational problem at the first attempt, s/he may try to solve the problem ***in its further context.*** This may require a second, third, etc. translation version which potentially also contains nonstrategic parts of the translation.

ii. If, at the first attempt, a subject does not succeed in rendering a strategic or non-strategic part of an SL text into TL in a way which is considered adequate, the subject may try to optimize the TL text production by conceiving a more adequate second, third, etc. translation version.

iii. If a subject, while checking a complex TL text segment, finds an alternative for it, s/he may conceive a further translation version which contains the alternative TL text segment plus part of its context.

iv. If a subject translates a complex SL text segment consisting of several strategic and/or non-strategic parts by successively rendering its components into TL, the subject may produce a further version of the TL text segment. Thus, s/he may become aware of the complex interrelationships between the components of the TL text segment. S/he may realize that the components, in order to make an adequate stretch of TL discourse, cannot be put together in the same way as they were successively translated from the SL.

As far as the investigation of translation strategies is concerned, the potential conception of several translation versions by a subject plays an important part because translation strategies and translation versions are interconnected in various ways. Two cases are of special interest here: In the ***first case***, a further translation version contains one or more translation strategies. They are called *intraversional strategies* and are indicated by a marker (') after the symbol of their structural type(s). In the ***second case***, a translation strategy contains one or more translation versions. They are called *intrastrategic versions* and are indicated in the same way as intraversional strategies.

I. Example of an *intraversional translation strategy* /S28/

Text	Category of *Analysis*	Type of *Structure*
vielleicht fang ich nochmal *ganz*	→ TRANS	
anders an	→ T4	
(1s) ehm (4s)		
vielleicht fangen wir man so an	OTL	
mit dem 'on which the decision'	<MSL	
(1s) ehm (2s)	RP/→ SP	II'
Für die Entscheidung	SP	SP
(9s)	OSL/OTL	
der Versammlung	MTL	
(3s)	OSL	
der Universität Oxford	T	
(3s)	OSL	
Mrs Thatcher (1s)	Ti.	
das vorgeschlagene	Tii.	
(5s)	CHECK	
Nee	Tii.-	
den vorgeschlagenen (1s)	REPHR.TL(Tii.)	
Ehrengrad zu verweigern	T	
gibt es kein wie auch immer		
geartetes mögliches Argument.	MTL T4#	

The example above contains the fourth translation version of a complex text segment which consists of several clauses and phrases and which can only be rendered into TL by a transposition of its parts. Within the fourth translation version, a strategy is to be found. The subject realizes a translational problem, i.e. the transfer of the SL text segment 'on which the decision' into TL. After a phase of searching, the subject finds a solution and verbalizes it. The translation strategy thus consists of a type II structure, which, because of its intraversional occurrence, is noted as II'.

II. Example of an intrastrategic translation version /S24/

Text	Category of *Analysis*	Type of *Structure*
ach, 'mit wem' hab ich doch vergessen (4s)	→ T3	
they have to know (1s)	MTL	
when	MTL	
(7s)	RP/→ SP	
to use (2s)	SPa=MTL	Va +
to whom, no, ah	SPb=∅ T3#	<SPb=∅,
(3s)	→ SP	
'wann welches Deutsch mit wem gesprochen wird'	VP	VP> -
(2s)	OTL → T4	T4' [OTL,
they have to know	MTL	
(1s) when	MTL	3MTL]-
(2s) they have (1s) to use	MTL T4#	
(10s)	→ SP	+ 1EX-
oder (1s)	→ T5	T5'
when	MTL	[MTL,
(2s) ehm (4s)	→ SP	
to	SPai2	Va']
when to talk	REPHR.TL = SPa2	
(1s) with whom (1s) in which (1s) kind of German.	T5# SPb	SP

The segment of translation transcribed above contains a strategy which ranges from the realization of a translational problem to the solution of its last part (SPb). The strategy is complex in nature. It contains a type Va basic structure expanded by a phase of searching (→SP), two embedded elements (SPb=∅, VP), as well as a fourth and fifth (intrastrategic) translation version of a previously verbalized problematic SL text segment (VP). Version 4 contains a phase of mental organization of TL text segments (OTL) and verbatim repetitions of three TL text segments (MTL). Version 5 comprises a phase of monitoring of a TL text segment (MTL) and a type Va basic structure strategy which is thus an intraversional translation strategy (Va').

The discussion of the two examples of intraversional strategies and intrastrategic versions has revealed an aspect of the translation process which is probably of eminent importance for a comprehensive investigation comprising the strategic *and* non-strategic dimension of the translation process: the hierarchical organization of the translation process which manifests itself above all in the fact that certain elements and structures bear a relationship of super- and subordination.

As this investigation is concerned with the *strategic analysis* of the translation process, its hierarchical nature will only be dealt with briefly.

In example I., the subject's endeavour to conceive a new translation version (→T4) is superordinate to the entire part of discourse which follows[22]. All utterances between →T4 and T4# are produced under the subject's superordinate aim. This also applies to the intraversional strategy (II' SP). The subject's endeavour to conceive a further translation version can be considered to be a realization of his/her global aim which is superordinate to the entire translation[23], i.e. to produce a TL text which is as adequate as possible and which not only conveys the sense of the SL text, but which also corresponds to the TL norms of language use and its conventions of text production. This aim, which has the character of a maxim (cf. Krings 1986a: 429–434), is, however, not pursued by all the subjects. Lack of knowledge and/or inability may be the reason(s) for this[24].

Example II. reveals an even more complex structure of relations of super- and subordination. The transcribed segment of a translation starts with a subject conceiving a third translation version for an SL text segment. Within this version, a translation strategy is initiated by a problem which the subject is faced with when conceiving the version. The strategy continues after the version has been completed. It thus has a partly intraversional character and is dominated by the superordinate aim of the version (→T3). The translation strategy itself is superordinate to the versions 4 and 5. They are dominated by the subject's aim of solving the translation problem which s/he has realized and verbalized.

5.2.5 A Formalized Model for the Strategic Analysis of the Translation Process

In this section, the results of the sections 5.2.2, 5.2.3, and 5.2.4, to the extent that they can be formalized to yield categories of analysis, will be presented in the form of a synopsis. In their totality, they make up a model for the strategic analysis of the translation process. It consists of three hierarchical levels. The first contains the *elements of the translation strategies*, i.e. the smallest detectable problem-solving steps. These were discussed in detail in section 5.2.2. The second level comprises the *translation strategies* presented in section 5.2.3. The third level of the model contains the *translation versions*, which can either be located within strategies or can extend from one strategy into another strat-

22 In the transcript, elements which are superordinate to a part of a translation are marked with a frame ( ).

23 Cf. also my remarks on the hierarchy of illocutions in foreign language classroom discourse which is rather similar to superordinate aims and dominating elements within the translation process (Lörscher 1983: 115–128, 228–232 and 280–283; Hüllen/Lörscher 1987; Hüllen/-Lörscher 1989).

24 Cf. also Chapter 7.

egy, or from a strategic phase into a non-strategic phase of the translation process, or *vice versa*. Translation versions were discussed in section 5.2.4.

I. Elements of Translation Strategies

Ia. Original Elements of Translation Strategies

RP	:	Realizing a Translational Problem
VP	:	Verbalizing a Translational Problem
→SP	:	Search for a (possibly preliminary) Solution to a Translational Problem
SP	:	Solution to a Translational Problem
PSP	:	Preliminary Solution to a Translational Problem
SPa,b,c..	:	Parts of a Solution to a Translational Problem
SP∅	:	A Solution to a Translational Problem is still to be found (∅)
SP = ∅	:	Negative (∅) Solution to a Translational Problem
PSL	:	Problem in the Reception of the SL Text

Ib. Potential Elements of Translation Strategies

MSL	:	Monitoring of SL Text Segments
MTL	:	Monitoring of TL Text Segments
REPHR.SL	:	Rephrasing of SL Text Segments
REPHR.TL	:	Rephrasing of TL Text Segments
CHECK	:	Discernible Testing (= Checking) of a (preliminary) Solution to a Translational Problem
OSL	:	Mental Organization of SL Text Segments
OTL	:	Mental Organization of TL Text Segments
REC	:	Reception of SL Text Segments
[TS]com	:	Comment on a Text Segment
TRANS	:	Transposition of lexemes or combinations of lexemes
T	:	Translation of Text Segments
→T2,3,..n	:	Conceiving a Second, Third, etc. Translation Version
ORG	:	Organization of Translational Discourse

II. Translation Strategies

IIa. Basic Structures

i. Pure Forms

Type I	:	RP – (P)SP#/SP∅
Type II	:	RP – →SP – (P)SP#/SP∅
Type III	:	(RP) – VP – (P)SP#(SP∅
Type IV	:	(RP) – (→SP) – VP – (→SP) – (P)SP#/SP∅; at least one →SP must be realized.

Type V : (...) (P)SPa/SPa∅ (...) (P)SPb/SPb∅ (...) (P)SPc/SPc∅ – (...)
Type Va : RP – (→SP) – (P)SPa/SPa∅ – (→SP) – (P)SPb/SPb∅ – (→SP) – (P)SPc/SPc∅ – (...)
Type Vb : RP – (→SP) – VPa – (→SP) – (P)SPa/SPa∅ – (→SP) – VPb – (→SP) – (P)SPb/SPb∅ – (→SP) – (...)
Type Vc : RP – (→SP) – (VPa) – (→SP) – (P)SPa/SP∅ – (→SP) – (VPb) – (P)SPb/SPb∅ – (→SP) – (...)

ii. Pure Forms with Embeddings

Type I + <MSL/ MTL/ REPHR.SL/ REPHR.TL/ ...>
Type II + <MSL/ MTL/ REPHR.SL/ REPHR.TL/ ...>
Type III + <MSL/ MTL/ REPHR.SL/ REPHR.TL/ ...>
Type IV + <MSL/ MTL/ REPHR.SL/ REPHR.TL/ ...>
Type V + <MSL/ MTL/ REPHR.SL/ REPHR.TL/ ...>

iii. Pure Forms with Bound Elements

Type I + CHECK/ (P)SP+/ MTL/ REPHR.TL/ ...
Type II + CHECK/ (P)SP+/ MTL/ REPHR.TL/ ...
Type III + CHECK/ (P)SP+/ MTL/ REPHR.TL/ ...
Type IV + CHECK/ (P)SP+/ MTL/ REPHR.TL/ ...
Type V + CHECK/ (P)SP+/ MTL/ REPHR.TL/ ...

iv. Pure Forms with Embeddings and Bound Elements

Type I + <MSL/ MTL/ REPHR.SL/ REPHR.TL/ ...> + CHECK/ (P)SP+/ MTL/ REPHR.TL/ ...
Type II + <MSL/ MTL/ REPHR.SL/ REPHR.TL/ ...> + CHECK/ (P)SP+/ MTL/ REPHR.TL/ ...
Type III + <MSL/ MTL/ REPHR.SL/ REPHR.TL/ ...> + CHECK/ (P)SP+/ MTL/ REPHR.TL/ ...
Type IV + <MSL/ MTL/ REPHR.SL/ REPHR.TL/ ...> + CHECK/ (P)SP+/ MTL/ REPHR.TL/ ...
Type V + <MSL/ MTL/ REPHR.SL/ REPHR.TL/ ...> + CHECK/ (P)SP+/ MTL/ REPHR.TL/ ...

IIb. Expanded Structures

i. Pure Forms

Type IV + 1,2,3,...EX (VP, →SP)
Types Vb,c + 1,2,3,...EX (VPa,b,c..., →SP)

ii. Pure Forms with Embeddings

Type II + <MSL/ MTL/ REPHR.SL/ REPHR.TL/ ... > + 1,2,3,...EX
Type III + <MSL/ MTL/ REPHR.SL/ REPHR.TL/ ... > + 1,2,3,...EX
Type IV + <MSL/ MTL/ REPHR.SL/ REPHR.TL/ ... > + 1,2,3,...EX
Type V + <MSL/ MTL/ REPHR.SL/ REPHR.TL/ ... > + 1,2,3,...EX

iii. Pure Forms with Bound Elements

Type IV + 1,2,3,...EX + CHECK/ (P)SP+/ MTL/REPHR.TL/ ...
Types V + 1,2,3,...EX + CHECK/ (P)SP+/ MTL/REPHR.TL/ ...

iv. Pure Forms with Embeddings and Bound Elements

Type II + 1,2,3,..EX + <MSL/ MTL/ REPHR.SL/ REPHR.Tl./ ...> + CHECK/ (P)SP+/ MTL/ REPHR.TL/ ...
Type III + 1,2,3,..EX + <MSL/ MTL/ REPHR.SL/ REPHR.Tl./ ...> + CHECK/ (P)SP+/ MTL/ REPHR.TL/ ...
Type IV + 1,2,3,..EX + <MSL/ MTL/ REPHR.SL/ REPHR.Tl./ ...> + CHECK/ (P)SP+/ MTL/ REPHR.TL/ ...
Type V + 1,2,3,..EX + <MSL/ MTL/ REPHR.SL/ REPHR.Tl./ ...> + CHECK/ (P)SP+/ MTL/ REPHR.TL/ ...

IIc. Complex Structures

Complex structures are built up of several basic and/or expanded structures.

IIa.i. IIa.ii. IIa.iii. IIa.iv. IIb.i. IIb.ii. IIb.iii. IIb.iv.	(+ free + elements)	IIa.i. IIa.ii. IIa.iii. IIa.iv. IIb.i. IIb.ii. IIb.iii. IIb.iv.	(+ free + elements)	IIa.i. IIa.ii. IIa.iii. IIa.iv. IIb.i. IIb.ii. IIb.iii. IIb.iv.	+...

Discontinuous Strategies:

Strategic or non-strategic parts of a translation occur between two or more parts of a strategy (Sa, Sb, ...):

Sa	Basic Structure i. - iv. Expanded Structure i. - iv. Complex Structure	SPØ / (P)SP -

further strategic or non-strategic part of translation	- Sb	Basic Structure i. - iv. Expanded Structure i. - iv. Complex Structure	...

III. Translation Versions

Translation versions are derived from a maxim which dominates an entire translation and according to which a translation should not merely convey the sense of the SL text into TL, but should be an adequate piece of discourse produced according to the TL norms of language use. Translation versions can consist of strategic and/or non-strategic components. They can be located within strategies (i.e. intrastrategic versions), between strategies, and can range from one into another strategy. The latter case is called intraversional strategy.

5.3 Application of the Model of Analysis

In the preceding sections, a model for the strategic analysis of the translation process was developed on the basis of a corpus of fourteen orally produced translations. In the following section, the model will be exemplified by applying it to four translations. Two of them (S15, S24) are *translations into the foreign language* (= English), and the other two (S28, S34) are *translations into the mother tongue*. The analyses will be reproduced in detail and commented on in the sections 5.3.2 to 5.3.5.

As was pointed out by Switalla (1977: 175) in connection with interpretive reconstruction (cf. subsection 4.4.2.1), carrying out a sense-constituting analysis of language performance can only mean for the analyst to make explicit step by step and as much as is necessary his/her linguistic-communicative knowledge which is the basis of interpretation. The analyses to be presented in the following sections will also be carried out according to this maxim.

5.3.1 Preliminary Remarks on the Transcription

In the domain of performance analysis, it is generally agreed that orally produced utterances must first be transcribed and that the transcript is the basis of any interpretive approach to the data (cf. Bergmann 1981; Dittmann 1979b: 14f.; Ehlich 1980b: 23; Ehlich/ Switalla 1976; Lörscher 1983: 240–243; Ramge 1977: 120ff.; 1978). Bergmann (1981: 19) states two essential reasons for producing transcripts:

> *Erstens ist die Arbeit am Material darauf angewiesen, daß das Material selbst in einer problemlos verfügbaren, bearbeitbaren, zergliederbaren, memorierbaren (?) und rasch rezipierbaren Form präsent ist, und diese Bedingungen werden am ehesten dadurch erreicht, daß aus dem Nacheinander des Interaktionsablaufs das Nebeneinander eines fixierten Beschreibungstextes wird, daß also, mit anderen Worten, der transitorische Charakter eines Gesprächsgeschehens in der 'eingefrorenen' Dauerhaftigkeit eines Notats aufgehoben wird. Zweitens werden Transkripte deshalb benötigt, weil ethnomethodologische und konversationsanalytische Arbeiten der Verpflichtung unterworfen sind, dem Leser einen Nachvollzug der Analyse anhand des dem Autor selbst zur Verfügung stehenden Datenmaterials zu ermöglichen.*

Any transcription thus necessarily implies a twofold reduction of the object of investigation:

1. In order to produce a transcript, it is generally necessary to make a recording of the utterances under investigation[25]. This recording, be it on audio- or on video-tape, inevitably implies a loss of information because only part of the entire reality of the produced utterances can be recorded visually and/or acoustically. All other data are inevitably lost (cf. Söffner 1982).

With regard to my data corpus, this loss of information especially concerns visual data. Since the translations were recorded on audio-tape, no information on gestures, mimicry, body movements, or proxemic behaviour of the subjects is available. In retrospect, however, it can be doubted whether video recordings would have been necessary, had they been made. During the performance of the translations, the test leader could detect hardly any visual information which, in addition to the acoustic data available, would have allowed further conclusions to be drawn about aspects of underlying mental processes.

2. The recorded utterances, which are thus reduced in their complexity but still provide manifold verbal and nonverbal information, must then be transformed into written language. Even the most subtle transcription, whose degree of readability and operationality is, however, very low (cf. Pittenger et al. 1960; McQuown 1971), can only capture fragments of the profusion of perceivable information and can only reproduce it indirectly by means of written language, possibly supplemented by additional signs.

From these theoretical and practical considerations, it follows that the task of transcription cannot be to reproduce performance in as much of its entirety as possible. Rather, the necessary degree of exactness and comprehensiveness of the transcription depends on the use of the transcript, i.e. on the aim of the analysis to follow. To this extent, the transcription is already fully integrated into the interpretive process (cf. Ehlich/Switalla 1976; Ehlich 1980b: 23).

As a consequence, it is not the utterances themselves[26] but rather a simplified model[27] of them, partly pre-interpreted by the notational conventions, which represents the *starting-point* and *basis* for the analysis. By means of certain supporting measures, such as the exact and explicit transcribing by several transcribers working independently, the similarity between the transcript and the original utterances can be increased; but its natural limit is reached when the simplicity and operationality of the model are affected. For this (and other)

---

25 This, however, does not apply to interaction analysis (cf. Flanders 1970; Lörscher 1983: 147-154), in which conversations were analyzed at the time of their production.

26 Cf. Söffner (1982: 11) who points out: "Aufgezeichnete Texte ... sind zu verstehen ... als Protokolle von Handlungen, die unwiderruflich vorbei sind, die sich aus der verschrifteten Textform als Real- oder Ursprungshandlungen nie wieder hervorzaubern lassen, sondern nur noch als Protokolle repräsentiert sind. Dieser Protokolltext stellt eine feststehende, unumkehrbare Sequenz von Aktion und Reaktion dar."

27 The term 'model' is used here in the sense of Stachowiak (1965, 1973) and denotes an analogous representation of structures of a segment of reality.

reason(s), the analysis must not be carried out on the basis of the transcript alone.

Rather, the transcript *and* the recording should be used together in the analysis of performance data (cf. Lörscher 1983: 241).

For reasons of standardization of the transcription the following notational conventions will be used in this study:

1. Utterances in the mother tongue (= German) will be transcribed literally according to the acoustic impression they produce on the transcriber.
2. Utterances in the foreign language (= English) will be transcribed in standard orthography. Deviations from standard pronunciation will be noted in phonemic transcription.
3. Utterances which relate to one category of analysis will be noted continuously, comprising one or several lines in the transcript.
4. Utterances shorter than a line in the transcript which relate to one category of analysis occupy the particular line alone.
5. The lines will be numbered consecutively so that a transcribed utterance or part of it can be found without difficulty.
6. Broken off or continuing utterances will be indicated by (...).
7. Incomprehensible utterances or parts of utterances will be indicated by (...?...).
8. Additional information like 'quickly', 'aloud', etc. is noted in round brackets together with the respective utterance; e.g. (quietly: 'Obwohl wir Ansätze heranziehen (...)').
9. Metalanguage is indicated by single quotation marks ('..').
10. Emphatic or wrong stress is indicated by an accent on the respective vowel, e.g. (sécure).
11. Pauses are noted by the number of seconds and the small letter 's' both in round brackets, e.g. (4s).
12. Intonation contours, when they are relevant for the analysis, will be noted as follows: [↓] = falling; [↑] = rising; [↓↑] = falling-rising; [↑↓] = rising-falling.

In the *analyses* of the translations, the following notational conventions will be used in addition to those mentioned in sections 5.2.2 to 5.2.4:

1. When an utterance corresponds to more than one category of analysis, the two or more categories are noted with an oblique line (/) between them, e.g. RP/→SP.
2. When an utterance can be related to two different categories of analysis from two different aspects of analysis, the symbols of the two categories are connected by the equals sign (=), e.g. REPHR.TL = SP2.
3. Elements embedded in other elements are indicated by pointed brackets (<>), e.g. SP<ORG>.

4. When utterances relate to other utterances, as is the case with comments, monitorings, rephrasings, and others, the related utterance is indicated after the category of the relating utterance. Thus, the categories $[(TS)]_{com}$, MTL, REPHR.TL, etc. either have the categorial symbol or the line number of the utterances they relate to appended to them in round brackets, e.g. MTL(SP2); REPHR.TL(38). When the related utterance immediately precedes the relating utterance, the former is *not* noted specifically.

5.3.2 Translation L1 → IL (T1, S15)

In the following subsection (5.3.2.1), the translation produced by subject 15 will be reproduced in transcript and analyzed with regard to its strategies and their elements. The analyst's linguistic-communicative knowledge which is the basis of his interpretation will be made explicit as much as is necessary and sensible by means of the comments.

A detailed description of the translation *strategies* employed by the subject will be given in subsection 5.3.2.2.

5.3.2.1 Qualitative Analysis

No.	T1 S15 Text	Category of Analysis	Comments
	(Reads text aloud) (152s)	REC	The subject receives the text by reading it.
1 2 3	Also (2s) um anzufangen jetzt hier würd ich den ersten Teil- satz übersetzen mit (1s)	OSL	The subject extracts the first unit of translation from the text, which falls under the category OSL.
4 5	Recently there have been (1s) some trials	T	The first unit of translation is transferred to TL.
6	(3s)	OSL	The German text segment 'Eigenschaften und Merkmale der *short story* zu beschreiben' cannot be translated word-for-word into English because of the different syntaxes of the two languages. The object-predicate construction in German has to be transformed into a predicate-object construction in English. The subject mentally organizes the SL text segment for translation in such a way that he starts with the predicate. It is translated in No. 7.

No.	T1 S15 Text	Category of Analysis		Comments
7	to (1s) describe	T		Translation of the predicate as the first part of the text segment which the subject considers as a unit of translation.
8	(20s)	RP/→SP	S	The subject realizes a problem and starts searching for a solution. This interpretation is suggested by the verbalization of the problem in No. 9.
9	Tja, 'Eigenschaften und Merkmale'	VP	1	The translation problem is verbalized.
10	Hm [↑↓] (15s)	→SP		The subject searches for a solution to the problem.
11 12	Ja, das würd ich jetzt erst mal weglassen.	SPØ		The subject cannot find a solution to the problem. He leaves the problem aside to try to solve it in a second version of the translation.
13	(2s)	OSL		After having focussed on the previous problem, the subject looks through the SL text segment to find the point from which the translation must proceed.
14	of the short story.	T		The subject proceeds with the translation.
15	(1s) ehm (7s)	RP/→SP		This filled pause of eight seconds is to be interpreted as the realization of a problem, followed by a search for a solution. This interpretation is suggested by the verbalization of the problem in Nos. 17/18.
16	ehm which (1s)	SPa	S 2	The first part of the problem realized in No. 15 and verbalized in Nos. 17/18 is solved here.
17 18	'die sich aus ihrer Kürze ergeben'	VP		The whole of the problem is verbalized here.
19	(2s) Hm (36s)	→SPb		The pause is to be interpreted as a search for a solution to the remaining part(s) of the problem.

No.	T1 S15 Text	Category of Analysis		Comments
20 21 22	Das Schwierige an dem Satz ist also, daß ich, daß der ver- schiedene Teile enthält	$[TS(SL)]_{com}$		SL text segments are commented on with a view to translating them into TL.
23 24 25	man muß da also (2s) erst mal das sortieren, was man zuerst übersetzt. (68s)	OSL/→SPb		The subject mentally organizes the SL text segment for translation, extracts the unit of translation and goes on searching for a solution to the problem verbalized in Nos. 7/8.
26 27 28 29	Ich wüßt im Moment nicht, wie man 'aus, die sich aus ihrer Kürze ergeben' übersetzen sollte. (2s)	SPbØ	S	The subject considers the translation problem insoluble.
30 31 32 33	Das is natürlich en Problem, weil der darauf folgende Satz sich darauf bezieht (1s) das is	$[SPbØ]_{com}$	2	The insolubility of the translation problem verbalized in Nos. 7/8 is commented on here.
34	(29s)	→SPb		In Nos. 30–32, the subject realized that a solution to the problem (Nos. 17/18) had to be found in order to proceed with the translation. Although the insolubility of the problem had already been stated (Nos. 26–29), the utterances 30–32 strongly suggest a continuation of the search for a solution.
35 36	Am besten mach ich einfach mal weiter.	SPbØ2		As the preceding search for a solution was unsuccessful, the subject states again the insolubility of the problem.
37	(6s)	OSL		Here, the subject informs himself in the SL text as to where to proceed with the translation.
38 39 40	but on the other side (1s) they show (1s) a certain attitude	T		The subject proceeds with the translation.
41	(2s)	RP		This pause is interpreted as being the realization of a problem ('verweisen').
42	and point (...) and (2s)	PSP	S 3	A preliminary solution to the problem realized in 41 is ver balized.

No.	T1 S15 Text	Category of Analysis		Comments
43	and point to	REPHR.TL = SP	S 3	The preliminary solution is rephrased. Apparently, the subject has realized the inadequacy of PSP and corrected it.
44	(4s)	RP/→SP		Here, the subject realizes a further translation problem and starts searching for a solution.
45	our	SPa		The first part of the problem is solved.
46	(3s)	→SPb		During this pause, the subject searches for the second part of the solution.
47 48	'our time' wär da nicht richtig	SPb = ∅	S 4	The subject verbalizes a TL text segment which he considers to be a 'negative solution'. The subject is aware of the inadequacy of the literal translation (*unserer Zeit – our time*) and rejects it as a solution.
49	(21s)	→SPb		An adequate solution to the second part of the problem is searched for.
50 51	'period' würd ich dann viel- leicht sagen	PSPb		A suggestion for a solution is made.
52	(24s)	REC/OSL		This pause is interpreted as being a reception of an SL sentence. But as the mere reading hardly takes 24 seconds, the subject probably also organizes the sentence mentally for the translation.
53	It seems to be clear	T		The subject starts translating the complex sentence.
54	(reads text silently)	REC		The *first* reception of an SL text segment is categorized as REC.
55	(23s)	OSL		After its reception, the SL text segment is mentally organized for its translation into TL.

No.	T1 S15 Text	Category of Analysis		Comments
56 57	Ehm, das ist schon wieder so en Wumrsatz	$[TS(SL)]_{com}$		The subject comments on the complex sentence received in No. 54.
58 59 60 61	(2s) (reads silently: 'daß kurzes Erzählen dem Autor (...) Formen der Erzähllite- ratur darstellt.') (46s)	OSL		The mental organization of the SL text segment is continued here. The two rather long phases of organization (Nos. 55 and 58–61) can be explained by the complex nature of the SL sentence.
62	It seems to be clear that	MTL(53)		The subject repeats a TL text segment which he originally uttered in No. 53.
63 64	the autor ehm (1s) has to (1s) have (1s) certain	Ta		The first part of the complex SL text segment is translated.
65	(3s) Tja (2s)	RP/→SP	S	This filled pause is interpreted as being the realization of a problem. The length of the pause (5s) suggests that the subject also starts searching for a solution.
66	certain	MTL(64)	5	Verbatim repetitions of TL text segments are categorized as MTL.
67	(9s)	→SP		Here, the subject searches for a solution to the problem realized in No. 65.
68	'Fähigkeiten'	VP		The problem realized in 65 is verbalized here.
69	(5s)	→SP/SP∅		This pause is interpreted as being a search for a solution to the problem. As the translation proceeds in No. 70 without a solution, the subject probably also realizes here that he cannot solve the problem at the moment.
70	to narrate in a short way	Tb		The translation continues.

No.	T1 S15 Text	Category of Analysis	Comments
71	(3s)	OSL	During this pause, the subject looks through the SL text to find the point from which to proceed with the translation. The SL clause "und die *short story* eine der einfachsten aber auch gleichzeitig schwierigsten Formen der Erzählliteratur darstellt" cannot be translated into English word by word. The subject mentally organizes the clause for translation and realizes that the predicate at the end of the SL clause must immediately follow the subject in English.
72	and the short story is	Tc	The translation goes on.
73	the pro (...) easiest	Td	The translation goes on.
74	(3s)	OSL	Here again, the subject probably orients himself in the SL text where to continue, in order to extract the next unit of translation.
75	but at the same time (1s)	Te	Continuation of translation.
76	also the (1s)	Tf	Continuation of translation.
77	difficul (...)	Tg	Continuation of translation.
78	most difficult	REPHR.TL→ T2	The TL text segment in 77 is considered inadequate and is corrected.
79	(11s)	CHECK(73–78)	During this pause, the subject probably tests the TL text segments 73–78. This interpretation is suggested by the utterances 80–83. Td, Te, and Tf are rejected and replaced by rephrasings: 80 replaces 73, 81 replaces 75, and 82 replaces 76. Only 78 is corroborated: TS(TL) (78)+.
80	one of the easiest	REPHR.TL(73)	
81	and at the same time (2s)	REPHR.TL(75)	
82	one of the (1s)	REPHR.TL(76)	
83	most difficult	TS(TL) (78)+ T2#	
84	(3s)	RP S6	The pause of 3 seconds indicates the realization of a translational problem.

No.	T1 S15 Text	Category of Analysis		Comments
85	Ehm, 'Form'	VP	S 6	The problem realized in 84 is verbalized.
86	(8s)	→SP/SP∅		This pause is interpreted as a search for a solution to the problem. As the translation continues without a solution, No. 86 must also be considered a realization of the problem's insolubility.
87 88	of (2s) narrating (1s) narrative (2s) literature	Th		The last part of the complex SL text segment received in 54 is translated.
89	(10s)	OSL		Here, the subject mentally organizes the remaining part of the sentence received in 52 for translation. He probably extracts the first unit of trans lation.
90	if it tries	T		The first unit of translation is transferred to TL.
91	(6s)	RP/→SP		This pause can be interpreted as being the realization of a translational problem, followed by a search for its solution. The fact that the German Clause "mit einem Minimum an Erzählung ein Maximum an literarischer Wirkung zu erreichen" cannot be translated literally into English probably represents the problem. This is interpreted from the following utterances.
92	with a	SPa	S 7	When uttered, this text segment is considered the first part of a solution to the problem realized in 91.

No.	T1 S15 Text	Category of Analysis		Comments
93	(3s)	→ TRANS(SPa)		The subject recognizes that a literal translation of the TL text segment is not possible. A transposition must be made according to which the utterance 92 (SPa) must *follow* an utterance which is still to be found (SPb).
94 95	to, to (1s) maintain with a	SPb TRANS SPa		The transposition is realized by the change in sucession of the two text segments.
96	(3s)	OSL		During this pause, the mental organization of an SL text segment takes place. The subject informs himself in the SL text as to where to proceed from, and extracts the next unit of translation.
97 98	minimum (1s) of narrative (2s) a (1s) maximum (1s) of	SPc		The third part of a solution to the complex problem realized in 91 is verbalized.
99	(5s)	RPd/→SPd	S 7	Within the complex translation problem, the subject realizes a further problem. The realization is followed by a search for a solution.
100	ehm literary (1s) effect.	SPd		A solution to the problem realized in 99 is found and verbalized.
101	(9s)	REC		The subject reads the sentence which is to be translated next
102 103 104	The question what is it (1s) that makes (1s) the short story short (1s) is	T		and starts with the translation.
105	(4s)	RP/→SP		During the translation, the subject realizes a problem and starts searching for a solution.
106	quite easy (1s) to	SPa		The problem's first part is solved.
107	(5s)	→SPb	S 8	A solution to the problem's second part is searched for.

No.	T1 S15 Text	Category of Analysis		Comments
108	answer [↑]	PSPb		A preliminary solution to the second part of the problem is verbalized. The preliminary nature of the solution is interpreted from the rising intonation contour [↑].
109	(2s)	CHECK/PSPb+ = SPb		The subject checks on the adequacy of the preliminary solution PSPb. As the translation proceeds in 110, it is to be assumed that the result of the checking is a corroboration of PSPb, which thus becomes SPb.
110 111	(reads quietly: Die Kurzgeschichte (...))	REC		Receiving (part of) the text by quietly reading it is categorized as REC.
112	(4s)	OSL		The subject mentally organizes the last sentence of the SL text for translation.
113	The short story is	T		The first part of the sentence is translated.
114	(7s)	RP/→SP	**S 9**	A translation problem is realized and a solution is searched for. It is probably the lexeme 'einerseits' which represents the problem.
115	first of all	SP		The subject verbalizes a solution to the problem.
116	(4s)	RP/→SP		A further problem is realized and a solution is searched for.
117 118	(quietly: 'Das Ergebnis verschiedener (...))	VP		The translation problem is verbalized.
119	(26s)	→SP		Here, the subject probably goes on searching for a solution to the problem.
120 121 122 123 124 125	Hm, ich wüßt jetzt auch nicht, wie man 'das Ergebnis verschiedener Reduktionen (3s) auf dem Gebiet der Handlung' übersetzen sollte.	VP2/SPØ	**S 10**	The problem is verbalized a second time, and its insolubility is stated.

No.	T1 S15 Text	Category of Analysis		Comments
126	(2s) Hm [↑↓] (48s)	→SP		Again, the subject searches for a solution to the problem realized in No. 116 and verbalized in Nos. 117/118.
127 128 129 130 131	Nein, diesen se (...) letz- ten Satz würd ich also ganz weglassen (2s) weil der (3s) ich schon einige Teile davon nicht übersetzen kann.	[TS(SL)Ø]$_{com}$	**S** **10**	Here, the subject explains why he gives up translating the last sentence. He comments on the untranslatability of the SL text segment for him.
132	(4s)	→SP		Nonetheless, the subject tries to find a solution to the problem by searching for it.
133 134 135	Wüßt ich im Moment nicht, wie ich den (2s) überset- zen sollte.	SPØ		The subject states a second time that he cannot translate the problematic SL text segment into TL.

5.3.2.2 Comment

The translation contains ten strategies:

S1 : Nos. 8–12
This is a realization of a type IV basic structure. The strategy terminates without the subject having found a solution to the translational problem.
Type: IV SPØ#

S2 : Nos. 15–36
Strategy 2 realizes a complex structure. Its first part, an expanded type Va structure (1 x →SP) with three embedded elements <VP, [TS(SL)]$_{com}$, OSL>, terminates without a solution to part b of the problem. The second part of the complex strategy is a basic structure of the type II which contains <[SPbØ]$_{com}$> as an embedded element. At its end, the subject realizes for the second time that he cannot solve part b of the translational problem (SPbØ2).
Type: Va + 1EX + <VP, [TS(SL)]$_{com}$, OSL> SPbØ – II + <[SPbØ]$_{com}$> SPbØ#

S3 : Nos. 41–43
This strategy is based on a type I structure. It terminates with a solution to the problem which is, at the same time, a rephrasing of a previously verbalized preliminary solution (PSP).
Type: I SP#

S4 : Nos. 44–51

Strategy 4 realizes an expanded structure (1 x →SPb) of the type Va, with one element embedded in it <SPb = Ø>. As the result of the strategy, PSPb, and thus an entire solution to the problem, is found.

Type: Va + 1EX + <SPb = Ø> SP#

S5 : Nos. 65–69

This is a type IV expanded structure (1 x →SP) which contains MTL as an embedded element. The strategy does not provide a solution to the translational problem.

Type: IV + 1EX + <MTL> SPØ#

S6 : Nos. 84–86

Strategy 5 is a realization of a type IV simple structure. It terminates without a solution.

Type: IV SPØ#

S7 : Nos. 91–100

This strategy is based on a structure of the type Va, with three elements embedded in it <→ TRANS, TRANS, OSL>. At the end of the strategy, part d, and thus the entire translational problem, is solved.

Type: Va + <→ TRANS, TRANS, OSL> SP#

S8 : Nos. 105–109

Strategy 8 realizes a type Va basic structure. It has a bound element (CHECK+) and provides a solution to the problem.

Type: Va + CHECK+ SP#

S9 : Nos. 114–115

This strategy belongs to the basic structures, type II. A solution to the translational problem is found.

Type: II SP#

S10 : Nos. 116–135

S10 is a complex structure. Its first part, an expanded structure (1 x VP) of the type IV terminates without a solution. Its second part is also an expanded structure (1 x →SP), but of the type II. It contains an embedded element <[TS(SL)Ø]$_{com}$> and ends with the subject's realization of the problem's insolubility.

Type: IV + 1EX SPØ – II + 1EX + <[TS(SL)Ø]$_{com}$> SPØ#

5.3.3 Translation L1 → IL (T3, S24)

5.3.3.1 Qualitative Analysis

No.	T3 S24 Text	Categories of Analysis		Comments
	(Reads text silently)	REC		Reading (part of) a text for the first time is categorized as REC.
1 2	Obwohl wir Ansätze heran- ziehen (2s)	OSL		The subject extracts the first unit of translation.
3	Ehm, although (1s) we	Ta		The first part of the unit of translation is transferred into TL.
4	(2s) ehm (3s)	RP/→SP		The filled pause is interpreted as the realization of a translational problem followed by a search for its solution. This is suggested by the progression of the translation, especially by the CHECK in No. 6.
5	take into account	SPa		The first part of the problem is solved.
6	(1s) oder 'heranziehen'	CHECK/SPa+	S 1a	SPa is tested by a comparison with the respective SL text segment. As the translation proceeds without the subject verbalizing another solution, the result of the checking is interpreted as being a corroboration of SPa.
7	(7s) ehm (3s)	→SPb		The subject searches for the remaining part of the solution to the problem.
8	'Ansätze'	VPb		The remaining part of the problem is verbalized.
9	(11s)	→SPb		The search for an adequate solution continues.

No.	T3 S24 Text	Categories of Analysis		Comments
10 11	(Quietly: obwohl wir Ansätze heranziehen)	MSL (1)/ <VP>	S 1a	During the search for a solution, the subject goes back in the SL text and repeats verbatim the SL text segment in which the problem is embedded.
12	(14s)	→SPb		During this pause, the subject searches for a solution to the problem.
13 14	Naja, also 'Ansätze' weiß ich nicht.	SPbØ		At the moment of this utterance, the subject considers the problem insoluble.
15	Although we take into account	MTL(3,5)		In order to proceed with the translation, the preceding TL text segment is repeated verbatim.
16	(4s)	CHECK		Here, the subject probably checks on the adequacy of the preceding TL text segment. As a result of the checking, the TL text segment is rephrased.
17	or 'for'	REPHR.TLa		This is the first part of the rephrasing.
18	(5s)	→ REPHR.TLb		The subject searches for the second part of the rephrasing.
19	Although we	MTL (15) → T2		An antecedent TL text segment is repeated verbatim. A second translation version commences.
20	(2s) draw for our	REPHR.TLa+b/ SPa2 T2#		The entire rephrasing is verbalized. The second translation version ends.
21	(11s)	→SPb	S 1b	Here, the subject probably goes on searching for a solution to the problem verbalized in No. 8.
22	also 'Ansätze'	SPbØ2		For the second time, it becomes apparent that the subject cannot solve the problem. She takes the SL word instead of the TL word.
23	which in	T		The translation proceeds.

No.	T3 S24 Text	Categories of Analysis	Comments
24	(3s)	OSL	The subject informs herself in the text, as to where the translation must be continued from.
25	in France, in the German (1s)	T	The translation proceeds.
26	the federal German Republic	REPHR.TL	The preceding TL text segment is rephrased and thus corrected.
27	(6s)	CHECK(23–26)	The TL text segment 23–26 are tested. This is suggested by the fact that they will be transposed in Nos. 29–32.
28	Nee	TS(TL)(23–26)–	As a result of the checking, the succession of the TL text segments 23–26 is negatively evaluated.
29 30 31 32	which are developed (1s) in the (1s) in France, in the Federal German Republic	Ta(23) TRANS Tb Tc(25,26)	The subject performs a transposition of the utterances 23, 25, and 26.
33	(2s) and in Scandinavia	T	The translation goes on.
34 35 36	(2s) ehm 'müssen wir von der spezifischen (...) (3s) ausgehen'	OSL	The subject informs herself in the SL text as to where to proceed from, and extracts the next unit of translation.
37 38 39 40	(2s) ehm, we have to start (2s) from (1s) the specific (3s) ehm, linguistic situation in Austria	Ta	The subject translates the first part of the extracted unit of translation.
41	(3s)	RP/→SP	A problem is realized and the search for a solution commences.
42	'beziehungsweise' (3s)	VP/→SP	The problem is verbalized and the search for its solution continues.
43 44	'such relation' (2s) 'beziehungsweise'	PSP/VP2	S 2 — A first preliminary solution is found and compared with the problematic SL text segment for the purpose of testing the former.

No.	T3 S24 Text	Categories of Analysis		Comments
45	(8s)	CHECK-====	S 2	The result of the checking is a negative evaluation of the preliminary solution. This becomes apparent from the fact that the subject continues tackling the problem.
46	'beziehungsweise'	VP3		The translation problem is verbalized for the third time.
47	or better (1s)	REPHR.TL(43)/ SP ====		This is the correction of the rephrasing in No. 43, and thus a solution to the problem.
48	in Vienna	T		The translation proceeds.
49 50	(2s) ehm, 'die sich zum Teil (...)' (7s)	OSL		The subject mentally organizes the next SL text segment and extracts the next unit of translation.
51 52	which, eh, differs (2s) partly	T		The translation continues.
53	which partly differs	REPHR.TL		The preceding TL text segment is rephrased.
54 55	(3s) ehm, 'durch die Anwe- senheit'	OSL		The next unit of translation is determined.
56	(2s) through the presence	T		The translation proceeds.
57	(4s)	OSL		The subject mentally organizes the SL text and extracts the next unit of translation.
58	of a dialect	T		The translation continues.
59	(5s)	OSL		The next unit of translation is determined.
60 61	of some (1s) of the (1s) countries named above	T		The translation goes on.
62	(7s)	CHECK+		Here, the subject probably tests the adequacy of the text segments she has translated into TL. As the translation proceeds, it is assumed that the result of the checking is a positive evaluation of the TL text segments.

No.	T3 S24 Text	Categories of Analysis		Comments
63 64	(Quietly: 'Danach sind (...) (5s)	REC		The subject reads the next sentence to be translated.
65	'Danach'	VP		A translation problem is verbalized.
66	(5s)	→SP		The subject searches for a solution.
67	'following from that' sogar	PSP	S 3	A preliminary solution is verbalized.
68	(1s) 'danach' (9s)	CHECK-==		The preliminary solution is tested by comparing it with the respective SL text segment. As a result of the checking, PSP is rejected
69	Though	SP		and an adequate solution to the problem is found.
70	(1s) ehm (4s)	OSL		The subject mentally organizes the sentence received in 63 for translation.
71	the Yugoslavian	T		The translation continues.
72	(3s)	RP/→SP		This pause is interpreted as being the realization of a problem followed by a search for its solution.
73	or better	SP		A solution to the problem is found.
74	(2s)	CHECK-==		The solution is tested and rejected.
75	or	MTL(73)	S 4	An antecedent TL text segment is repeated verbatim.
76	(1s) ach 'beziehungsweise'	VP		The problem realized in 72 is verbalized.
77	(3s)	→SP		A solution is searched for.
78 79	'beziehungsweise türkische Kinder'	VP + CT		The translation problem and part of its context is verbalized (again).
80	(3s)	→SP		The search for a solution is continued.
81	or even	SP		For the subject, the problem is solved.

No.	T3 S24 Text	Categories of Analysis		Comments
82	(2s) ehm Turkish children	T		The translation goes on.
83	(2s) ehm (5s)	RP/→SP	S	During this filled pause, the subject realizes a further problem and searches for a solution.
84 85	'sind nicht mit einer Fremdsprache konfrontiert'	VP	5	The subject verbalizes the problem realized in 83.
86	(8s)	→SP		She searches for a solution.
87 88	are not confronted (1s) with one foreign language	SP		The problem is solved.
89	(3s) ehm	OSL		The subject informs herself as to where to proceed from and determines the next unit of translation.
90	but	Ta		The first part of the unit of translation is transferred into TL.
91	(3s) ehm (1s)	RP/→SP		A translation problem is realized and a solution is searched for.
92	indeed	SP	S 6	This is considered to be the solution to the problem.
93	(1s) 'eigentlich' (4s)	CHECK		The solution is tested by comparing it with the respective SL text segment.
94	indeed	SP+		The solution is corroborated.
95	with three languages	Tb		The second part of the unit of translation determined in No. 89 is transferred to TL.
96	(2s) 'von denen zwei (...)'	OSL		Extraction of the next unit of translation.
97	(6s) ehm (2s)	RP/→SP	S	The subject realizes a translational problem and starts searching for a solution.
98	of (5s)	SPa/→SPb	7	The first part of the problem is solved, and the second part is searched for.
99	of which (2s)	SP		The entire problem is solved.

No.	T3 S24 Text	Categories of Analysis		Comments
100 101	ehm two (3s) are essen- tial for a adequate	T		The translation of the text segment extracted in 96 continues.
102	(3s) ehm (1s)	RP/→SP		A problem is realized and a solution is searched for.
103	communicative	PSPa		This is considered to be a part of a solution.
104	(3s)	→SP	S 8	The search for an entire solution continues.
105	oder vielleicht			(see No. 107)
106	for a adequate (1s)	MTL(101)		An antecedent TL text segment is repeated verbatim.
107	communication	PSP		The subject considers this text segment a possible solution. Utterance 105 suggests that the subject considers it a *preliminary* solution.
108 109	(2s) ehm 'Verständigung' (1s) sag is 'communication'	CHECK+		The preceding text segment is tested. The continuation of the translation suggests that the text segment is corroborated.
110	(4s)	OSL		The next unit of translation is determined.
111	Ehm, the German norm	T		The translation starts.
112	(3s) ehm (2s)	RP/→SP	S 9	The subject realizes a translation problem and searches for a solution.
113	'Hochsprache' (2s)	VP		The problem is verbalized.
114	'standard German' irgendwie	PSP		The subject verbalizes a possible solution.
115	(3s) ehm (2s)	OSL		The next unit of translation is determined.
116 117	as it is (1s) ehm, taught (1s) in (1s) schools	T		The unit of translation is transferred to TL.
118 119	(2s) ehm (1s) 'die österrei- chische Norm' (1s)	OSL		The subject extracts the next unit of translation.
120	the Austrian norm (1s)	T		The unit of translation is transferred to TL.
121	or the	T		The translation goes on.

No.	T3 S24 Text	Categories of Analysis		Comments
122	(2s) ehm (1s)	RP/→SP		A translation problem is realized and a solution is searched for.
123	colloquial	SPa		The first part of the problem is solved.
124	(4s)	→SP	S	The search for a solution is continued.
125	li (...) ehm language	SPb	10	The second part of the problem is solved.
126	Umgangssprache	VP		The translation problem is verbalized.
127	(3s) ehm (5s)	CHECK		The text segment 123 and 125 are checked on.
128 129	ja, col (...) ja, colloquial language	SPa+ SPb+		The two parts of the solution are corroborated.
130 131	'wie sie in systematischer Variation auftritt'	OSL		The subject determines the next unit of translation.
132	(2s) ehm (2s)	RP/→SP		The subject realizes a translational problem and searches for a solution.
133	as it appears	SPa	S	The first part of the problem is solved.
134	(5s) ehm (1s)	→SPb	11	The subject searches for a solution to the second part of the problem.
135	in systematical variation	SPb		The second part of the problem is solved.
136	(3s)	OSL		The last unit of translation of the sentence received in No. 63 is determined.
137	and at least the dialect.	T		The unit of translation is transferred to TL.
138 139 140	(5s) 'Die Kinder müssen also mit einer mehrfachen Sprach- barriere zurechtkommen'	OSL		The next unit of translation is extracted from the SL text.
141	(82s) Ehm, the children	Ta		The first part of the unit of translation is transferred to TL.
142	(1s) ehm (3s)	CHECK		The adequacy of the preceding utterance is checked.

No.	T3 S24 Text	Categories of Analysis		Comments
143	oder: Thus the children	REPHR.TL(141)		As a result of the checking, utterance 141 is rephrased.
144	have to cope	Tb		The second part of the unit of translation is transferred to TL.
145	(2s) ehm (2s)	CHECK		The adequacy of the preceding utterance is checked.
146	have to learn to cope	REPHR.TL(144)		As a result of the checking, utterance 144 is rephrased.
147	(1s) ehm (2s)	RP/→SP		The subject realizes a translational problem and starts searching for a solution.
148	with (1s) a multiple	SPa		The problem's first part is solved.
149	(3s)	→SP		The subject searches for the remaining part of the solution.
150	language barrier (1s)	SPb	S 12	The second part of the solution is verbalized.
151	or 'barrier'	REPHR.TL= = SPb2		The preceding utterance is rephrased. Thus, an alternative solution to the second part of the problem is given.
152 153	or 'linguistic barrier' ist besser	REPHR.TL = SPb3		The rephrasing is rephrased again and represents an optimization of utterance 151.
154	(2s) 'Sprachbarriere' (1s)	CHECK =		The adequacy of utterance 152 is checked by comparing it with the respective SL text segment.
155	ja, 'linguistic barrier'	SPb3+		The checked utterance is corroborated.
156 157 158	(3s) 'wissen, (1s) wann welches Deutsch mit wem gesprochen wird'	OSL		The next unit of translation is determined.
159 160	(2s) Ehm, they have to know (1s)	Ta		The first part of the unit of translation is transferred to TL.
161	oder einfach 'to know'	REPHR.TL		The preceding TL text segment is rephrased.
162	(2s)	RP	S 13	This pause is interpreted as being the realization of a problem.

No.	T3 S24 Text	Categories of Analysis		Comments
163	when	SPa		The first part of a solution is verbalized.
164	(5s)	→SP		Search for the remaining part of the solution.
165	ehm, what	SPb		The second part of a solution is verbalized.
166	(4s)	CHECK		The subject checks the two parts of the solution.
167	when they have to	SPa2 <MTL(163)>		Utterance 163 is repeated verbatim and a new first part of a solution is verbalized.
168	(3s) ehm (2s)	→SP		The search for an entire solution is continued.
169	use (2s) what (1s)	SPb2 <MTL(165)>	S	A new second part of a solution is verbalized. It contains utterance 165.
170	type	SPc	13	The third part of a solution is given.
171	oder 'kind'	REPHR.TL = SPc2		The preceding TL text segment is rephrased.
172	of language (1s)	SPd		The fourth part of a solution is verbalized.
173	kind of German (2s)	REPHR.TL = SPd2 <MTL(171)>		The subject rephrases the preceding utterance. Additionally, she repeats utterance 171 verbatim, which is part of its context.
174	Nochmal	→ T2		The subject announces the production of a second translation version. The utterances 175–170 represent the second, incomplete, version. The text segments of the first version, which are combined in a different way to make up the second version, are noted in brackets after MTL.
175	Ehm, they have to know	MTL(159)		
176	(2s) when	MTL(163)		
177 178	(2s) ehm to use (2s) what (1s) kind of German	MTL(169–173) T2#		
179	(2s) ach 'with'			
180 181	(1s) ach 'mit wem' hab ich doch vergessen (4s)	→ T3		The subject realizes the necessity of producing a third translation version.

No.	T3 S24 Text	Categories of Analysis		Comments
182	They have to know	MTL(175)		The third translation version consists of utterances 182–187.
183	(1s) when	MTL(176)		
184	(7s)	RP/→SP		The subject realizes a translation problem and starts searching for a solution.
185	to use (2s)	SPa = MTL(177)		The first part of the problem is solved. The solution is a verbatim repetition of utterance 177.
186	to whom,	SPb		A second part of a solution is verbalized but immediately rejected.
187	no, ah	SPbØ — T3#		
188	(3s)	→SP		The subject goes on searching for an entire solution.
189 190	'wann welches Deutsch mit wem gesprochen wird'	VP		The problem realized in No. 184 is verbalized here.
191	(2s)	OTL — → T4	S 14	The subject realizes the necessity of a fourth translation version. She mentally organizes the TL text segments, i.e. puts them in a correct order.
192	they have to know	MTL(182)		This fourth translation version comprises utterances 192–194. They are verbatim repetitions of antecedent utterances. The translation problem remains unsolved.
193	(1s) when	MTL(183)		
194	(2s) they have (1s) to use	MTL(167,185) —T4#		
195	(10s)	→SP		The search for a solution continues.
196	oder (1s)	— → T5		The necessity for a fifth translation version to solve the problem is realized.
197	when	MTL(193)		The fifth translation version consists of the utterances 197-202 and brings about a solution to the translational problem (utterances 200-202).
198	(2s) ehm (4s)	→SP		
199	to	SPai2		
200	when to talk	SPa2 = REPHR.TL (193–194)		

No.	T3 S24 Text	Categories of Analysis		Comments
201 202	(1s) with whom (1s) in which (1s) kind of German	SPb T5#		
203 204	(3s) 'Dies setzt einen Un- terricht voraus'	OSL		The subject determines the next unit of translation.
205	(4s)	RP/→SP		During this pause, the subject realizes a problem and starts searching for a solution.
206	'voraussetzen'	VP		The problem is verbalized.
207	(2s) ehm (5s)	→SP		The search for a solution goes on.
208 209	(Quietly: 'Dies setzt einen Unterricht voraus')	VP2 + CT		The translation problem is verbalized again, this time embedded in part of its context.
210	(2s)	→SP		The search for a solution continues.
211	'voraussetzen'	VP3		The problem is verbalized for the third time.
212	(3s)	→SP	S 15	The subject goes on searching for a solution.
213	Ehm, this (1s) takes	SPa		The subject verbalizes the first part of a solution.
214	(2s)	CHECK		During this pause, the subject probably tests the preceding TL text segment.
215	Nee	SPa–		As a result of the checking, the utterance is rejected.
216	(4s)	→SP		Continuation of the search for a solution.
217	(Quietly: 'Dies setzt einen Unterricht voraus')	VP3 + CT		For the third time, the problem and part of its context are verbalized.
218	(11s)	→SP		Continuation of the search for a solution.
219	'voraussetzen'	VP4		The translation problem is verbalized for the fourth time.

No.	T3 S24 Text	Categories of Analysis		Comments
220	(8s) ehm (5s)	→SP/SPØ		This pause is interpreted as being another phase of searching for a solution. The proceeding of the translation suggests that the subject realizes the insolubility of the problem here.
221	ich müßt das umändern	→ T2		The subject realizes the necessity of a second version for the translation of the text segment verbalized in Nos. 208-209.
222 223	(1s) 'Voraussetzung' fällt mir nicht ein	$[SPØ]_{com}$		The subject states that she cannot solve the translation problem, thus giving the reason why she produces a second translation version.
224	(2s) ehm (6s)	OTL	S 15	The subject mentally organizes the first TL text segments for the second translation version.
225	For that problem	SPa2		The first part of a solution is uttered.
226	(3s) ehm (6s)	→SPb		The search for the remaining part of the solution continues.
227	a kind of lesson is needed	SPb T2#		The remaining part of the solution is found and verbalized. The second, successful translation version terminates here.
228	(1s) ehm (1s)	OSL		Here, the subject extracts the next unit of translation.
229	that's (1s)	Ta		The first part of the unit of translation is transferred to TL.
230	that	REPHR.TL		The preceding utterance is rephrased.
231	(3s) ehm	RP/→SP	S	The subject realizes a problem and searches for a solution.
232	deals	SP	16	A solution to the problem is found and verbalized.

No.	T3 S24 Text	Categories of Analysis		Comments
233 234	(1s) explicitly (1s) with this problem	Tb		The second part of the unit of translation is transferred to TL.
235	(2s) ehm (3s)	RP/→SP		A further translation problem is realized and a solution is searched for.
236 237	'einen kommunikationsori- entierten Unterricht'	VP		The problem realized in 235 is verbalized.
238	(13s)	→SP		This pause is interpreted as being a phase of searching for a solution.
239 240	ja, entweder 'a communi (...) communicative'	PSPai		A possible first part of a solution is verbalized.
241	(4s)	CHECK		The preceding text segment is tested during this pause.
242	or 'communication oriented'	PSPaii/ REPHR.TL(240)	S	As a result of the testing, the text segment is rejected, and a new first part of a solution is verbalized.
243	(5s) ehm (2s)	→SPb	17	The subject searches for a second part of a solution.
244	lesson	SPb		The solution is found.
245	oder (2s)	→SP2		The subject announces a further possibility of solving the problem.
246	'kommunikationsorientierter'	VPa		She verbalizes the first part of the problematic SL text segment.
247	(8s)	→SP		A (second) solution is searched for.
248 249	Ja, 'lessons oriented (2s) on (1s) communication'	SP2		The subject verbalizes a second possibility of solving the problem.
250 251	(2s) 'der vor allem die Ver- ständigung (1s) fördern würde'	OSL		The next unit of translation is determined.
252	(2s) ehm (5s)	RP/→SP		A translation problem is realized and a solution is searched for.
253	'fördern'	VPa		A part of the problem is verbalized.

No.	T3 S24 Text	Categories of Analysis		Comments
254	(10s)	→SP		The subject searches for a solution.
255 256	'die Verständigung fördern würde'	VP		The entire translation problem is verbalized.
257	(1s) ehm (2s)	→SP		A solution is searched for.
258	that would (2s)	SPa	S 18	The first part of a solution is found.
259	that would above all	SPa2/T		The subject repeats the preceding text segment and proceeds with the translation.
260	(2s) ehm (4s)	→SP		The search for the remaining part of the solution continues.
261	help (1s) with the problem	SPb		The second part of the solution is verbalized.
262	(1s) of (1s) communication	SPc		The third part of the solution is verbalized.
263	'Verständigung' (2s)	CHECK		The preceding TL text segment is checked.
264 265	or (1s) 'intelligibility' vielleicht	REPHR.TL(262) = SPd2		As a result of the checking, a further possibility of solving the problem is found and verbalized.
266	(2s) ehm (2s)	→T2		As the following utterances constitute a second translation version, the subject probably realizes here that the various parts have to be combined in a specific way to form an adequate solution to the problem.
267	that would (1s) above all	MTL(259)		The second translation version consists of the utterances 267–269.
268	(2s) help with the problem	MTL(261)		
269	of (1s) intelligibility	MTL(264) —T2#		
270	(2s)	RP		The subject realizes a problem during this pause.
271 272	'in wesentlichen Sprech- situationen'	VP	S	The problem is verbalized.
273	(3s)	→SP	19	The subject searches for a solution to the problem.

No.	T3 S24 Text	Categories of Analysis		Comments
274	in	SPa		The first part of a solution is uttered.
275	(3s)	→SPb		The subject searches for a second part of a solution.
276	'wesentlich' (1s)	VPb		The second part of the problem is verbalized.
277	essential	SPb		The second part of the problem is solved.
278	(2s) oder 'wesentlichen' (2s)	CHECK		The adequacy of the preceding text segment is checked.
279	ja, vielleicht 'important'	REPHR.TL = SPb2	S 19	As a result of the checking, a second possibility of solving the problem is found.
280	(3s) essential	CHECK TL/TL		The second possibility is tested by comparing it with the first possibility.
281	important	SPb2+		The checking corroborates the second possibility.
282 283	(1s) speech (1s) situations (2s) in an (1s) adequate	T		The translation proceeds.
284	(2s) ehm (1s)	RP/→SP		The subject realizes a problem and searches for a solution.
285	style	PSP		A preliminary solution is found.
286	(2s) speech style, nee	REPHR.TL/ SP = Ø		A further solution is uttered and immediately rejected.
287	(2s)	→SP	S 20	The search for a solution continues.
288	style of speech	SP2		A second possibility of solving the problem is found.
289	(2s) 'Sprechstil' (3s)	CHECK		The two possibilities are tested by comparing them with the SL text segment.
290	just 'style'	PSP+ = SP		The preliminary solution is corroborated and thus becomes SP.
291	in an adequate style.	SP + CT		The solution is uttered within its context.

5.3.3.2 Comment

The translation contains twenty strategies:

S1 : Nos. 4–14; 21–22

This discontinuous strategy consists of two parts, 1a and 1b. Between them a non-strategic phase is located. Part 1a realizes a type Vc basic structure with two expansions (→SPb, VP) and two embeddings <CHECK, MSL>, and terminates without a solution to the second part of the problem.

Part 2 of the discontinuous strategy belongs to the structural type II. It also terminates without a solution to the second part of the problem.

Type: 1a.: Vc + 2EX + <MSL, CHECK> SPb∅ –
1b.: II SPb∅#

S2 : Nos. 41–47

Strategy 2 is the realization of a complex structure. Its first part belongs to the type IV expanded structures (1 x VP2). It is followed by a free element (CHECK–). Part 2 of the strategy, a type III basic structure, terminates with a solution to the problem.

Type: IV + 1EX + CHECK– – III SP#

S3 : Nos. 65–69

This strategy is based on a complex structure. It consists of two basic structures and a bound element (CHECK). The first basic structure belongs to type IV and terminates with a preliminary solution to the problem. The second basic structure belongs to type I and ends with a definite solution.

Type: IV PSP + CHECK + I SP#

S4 : Nos. 72–81

Strategy 4 realizes a complex structure. Its first part is a type II basic structure followed by two free elements (CHECK–, MTL). The strategy's second part belongs to the expanded structures (1 x VP, 1 x →SP) of the type IV and terminates with a solution to the translational problem.

Type: II + CHECK– + MTL – IV + 2EX SP#

S5 : Nos. 83–88

This is a type IV basic structure strategy which terminates with a solution to the problem.

Type: IV SP#

S6 : Nos. 91–92/94

This strategy is the realization of a type II basic structure with two free elements (CHECK, SP+) appended to it.

Type: II + CHECK + SP+#

S7 : Nos. 97–99
Strategy 7 realizes a basic structure of the type Va and ends with an entire solution to the translational problem.
Type: Va SP#

S8 : Nos. 102–107/109
This is a type Va basic structure strategy. It contains MTL as an embedded element and is followed by CHECK+ as a bound element.
Type: Va + <MTL> + CHECK+ SP#

S9 : Nos. 112–114
This strategy realizes a basic structure of the type IV. As the result of the strategy, a preliminary solution is found.
Type: IV PSP#

S10 : Nos. 122–125/129
Strategy 10 belongs to the type Va basic structures and contains VP as an embedded element. Two free elements, CHECK and SPa,b+ are appended to the strategy.
Type: Va + <VP> + CHECK + SPa,b+ SP#

S11 : Nos. 132–135
Here again, a type Va basic structure is realized. The strategy ends with a solution to the translational problem.
Type: Va SP#

S12 : Nos. 147–150/155
This strategy is also a realization of a type Va basic structure with four bound elements appended to it; two rephrasings of SPb, CHECK , and SPb3+.
Type: Va + 2 REPHR.TL + CHECK + SPb3+ SP#

S13 : Nos. 162–172/173
Strategy 13 is based on a complex structure. Its first part, a type Va basic structure, is followed by a bound element, CHECK–. The strategy's second part is also a basic structure of the type Va. It contains three embeddings, <2 x MTL, REPHR.TL>, and is followed by a bound element (REPHR.TL) with another <MTL> embedded in it. The strategy terminates with a solution to the problem.
Type: Va + CHECK– – Va + <2MTL, REPHR.TL> + REPHR.TL<MTL> SP#

S14 : Nos. 184–201
This strategy is commented on in section 5.2.4: II. Example of an *intrastrategic translation version.*
Type: Va + 1EX + <SPb=∅, VP> – T4' [OTL, 3MTL] – T5' [MTL, Va'] SP#

S15 : Nos. 205–227
Strategy 15 is based on a complex structure which consists of two expanded structures and a further translation version. The first expanded structure belongs to type IV and contains four expansions (2 x →SP, VP2+CT, VP3). CHECK and SPa– follow as bound elements. The second expanded structure (VP, →SP) also belongs to type IV. As a result of the strategy's second part, the subject realizes that the problem is insoluble for her, and produces a second translation version. Besides $[SP\emptyset]_{com}$ and OTL, it contains an intraversional strategy of the type Va'. The strategy terminates with an entire solution to the translational problem.
Type: IV + 4EX + CHECK + SPa– – IV + 2EX SP∅ – T2' [$[SP\emptyset]_{com}$, OTL, Va'] SP#

S16 : Nos. 231–232
Here, a type II basic structure is realized. A solution to the problem is found.
Type: II SP∅#

S17 : Nos. 235–249
Strategy 17 is the realization of a complex structure consisting of three parts. Part 1 belongs to the type IV basic structures. It is followed by a bound element, CHECK. Part 2 of the strategy belongs to the basic structures of the typeVa and ends with SPb. The strategy's last part is a type IV basic structure. As the result of the strategy, the entire translational problem is solved.
Type: IV + CHECK – Va – IV SP#

S18 : Nos. 252–262/265
This strategy is based on a type Vc structure and contains one expansion (→SP) and two embedded elements <VP, T>. CHECK and REPHR.TL follow as bound elements. The strategy ends with a solution to the problem.
Type: Vc + 1EX + <VP, T> + CHECK + REPHR.TL SP#

S19 : Nos. 270–277/281
This is the realization of a type Vc basic structure. It contains <VP> as an embedded element, and is followed by four bound

elements: 2 x CHECK, REPHR.TL, and SPb2+. At the end of the strategy, the problem is solved.

Type: Vc + <VP> + CHECK + REPHR.TL + CHECK + SPb2+ SP#

S20 : Nos. 284–288/291
Strategy 20 realizes a complex structure. Its first part, a type II basic structure, is followed by a bound element, i.e. REPHR.TL/SP=∅. The strategy's second part is also a basic structure of the type II. Three bound elements are appended to it: CHECK, PSP+, and SP+CT.

Type: II + REPHR.TL/SP=∅ – II + CHECK + PSP+ + SP+CT SP#

5.3.4 Translation IL → L1 (T4, S28)

5.3.4.1 Qualitative Analysis

No.	T4 S28 Text	Categories of Analysis		Comments
1 2	Okay, ich les mir den Text erst mal durch	ORG		The subject organizes (initiates) the discourse.
3	(Reads text aloud)	REC		The first reading of the text is categorized as REC.
4	(2s) Okay.	ORG		This organizing utterance marks the beginning of the translation.
5	Sale of Honours	OSL		The first unit of translation is determined.
6	(2s)	RP		The subject realizes a translational problem.
7	vielleicht 'Ausverkauf von	PSPa	S	The subject verbalizes the first part of a possible solution.
8	(2s)	→SP	1	The remaining part of the solution is searched for.
9	ehm Ehrentiteln'	PSPb		The remaining part of the solution is verbalized.
10	(3s)	CHECK(7,9)+		During this pause, the subject probably checks the two parts of the solution. As the translation proceeds, the result of the checking is probably a corroboration of the utterances 7 and 9.

No.	T4 S28 Text	Categories of Analysis		Comments
11 12 13 14 15 16	'There is no possible argument (2s) on which the decision by the congregation of Oxford University to refuse Mrs Thatcher the proposed honorary degree is worthy of respect.'	REC		Reading is categorized as REC.
17	(4s) ehm (3s)	RP/→SP		The subject realizes a problem and starts searching for a solution.
18	Es gibt keinen (1s) Grund	SP	S 2	A solution to the translation problem is found.
19	(7s)	CHECK		Here, the subject probably tests the preceding TL text segment.
20 21	ja, oder 'es gibt kein Argument'	REPHR.TL(18)/ SP2		As a result of the checking, the subject finds another solution to the problem. It is a rephrasing of utterance 18.
22	(8s)	OSL		The next unit of translation is determined.
23	für die Entscheidung [↑]	T		The translation continues.
24	(7s)	RP/→SP		The subject realizes a problem and searches for a solution.
25	der	SPa		This is interpreted to be the first part of a solution.
26	(2s)	→SP		The search for the remaining part of the solution goes on.
27 28	congregation of Oxford University	VPb+CT	S 3	The remaining part of the translational problem and part of its context are verbalized.
29	congregation	VPb2		The problem is verbalized a second time.
30	(4s)	→SPb		The subject searches for a solution.
31	nicht 'Zusammenschluß'	SP = ∅		A negative solution is uttered.
32	congregation	VPb3		The problem is verbalized a third time,
33	(4s)	→SPb		and the search for a solution is continued.

No.	T4 S28 Text	Categories of Analysis		Comments
34	'Versammlung' vielleicht	PSPb		The subject utters a possible solution.
35	(9s)	→SPb	S 3	Nonetheless, the search for a definite solution is continued.
36	oder 'Beschlußorgan' (1s)	SPb		This text segment is interpreted as being the solution to the problem. The translation proceeds without the subject's further searching for a solution.
37	Also nochmal	→ T2		A second translation version is announced.
38	Es gibt kein	MTL(20)		Part of the text segment No. 20 is repeated verbatim.
39	(4s)	RP/→SP		The subject realizes a problem and searches for a solution.
40	mögliches (1s)	SP	S 4	The problem is solved by producing a TL text segment which was not contained in the first version.
41 42	there is no possible argument	VP + CT		The problem and part of its context are verbalized.
43	(11s)	CHECK(40)		The solution uttered in No. 40 is tested.
44 45	irgendwas mit 'wie auch immer'	REPHR.TL(40)/ SP2 —T2#		As a result of the checking, the subject finds another solution to the problem. It is a rephrasing of No. 40.
46	Es gibt kein	→T3 MTL(38)		The subject starts producing a third translation version. Here, utterance 38 is repeated verbatim.
47	wie auch immer	MTL(45)		Verbatim repetition of utterance No. 45.
48	geartetes	T		The translation is continued.
49	Argument	MTL(21)		Verbatim repetition of utterance No. 21.
50	(22s)	CHECK(46–49)		The adequacy of the TL text segments 46–49 is tested.

No.	T4 S28 Text	Categories of Analysis		Comments
51	Nee,	TS(TL)(46–49)– --- T3#		As a result of the checking, the subject realizes that the TL text segments 46–49 do not represent an adequate stretch of TL discourse but that they have to be combined in a different way.
52 53	Vielleicht fang ich nochmal *ganz* anders an	→ TRANS →T4		Therefore, the subject announces a transposition by producing a further translation version.
54 55 56	(1s) ehm (4s) Vielleicht fangen wir mal so an mit dem 'on which the decision'	OTL <MSL>		The subject mentally organizes the succession of the TL text segments in order to produce an adequate translation.
57	(1s) ehm (2s)	RP/→SP	S5	Here, the subject realizes a translational problem and starts searching for a solution. The problem concerns the SL text segment 'on which the decision', which cannot be translated word for word into the TL.
58	Für die Entscheidung	SP		A solution to the problem is found and verbalized.
59	(9s)	OSL/OTL		During this pause, the subject probably organizes the various parts of the sentence received in 11–16 and those parts of the sentence he has already translated. He searches for an adequate combination of the TL text segments.
60	der Versammlung (1s)	MTL(34)		Verbatim repetition of the text segment No. 34.
61	der Universität Oxford	T		This is the first translation of the respective SL text segment.
62	(3s)	OSL		Here, the subject probably informs himself in the SL text about the remaining part of the sentence received in 11–16.
63	Mrs Thatcher (1s)	T		The translation proceeds.
64	das vorgeschlagene	T		The translation proceeds.

No.	T4 S28 Text	Categories of Analysis		Comments
65	(5s)	CHECK		The subject tests the adequacy of the preceding TL text segment and rejects it.
66	Nee,	Ts(TL)(64)-		
67	den vorgeschlagenen (1s)	REPHR.TL(64)		Utterance 64 is rephrased. This is necessary because the gender of the noun which will be translated in No. 68, and which is already mentally available to the subject, is masculine, and the adjective has to have masculine gender accordingly.
68	Ehrengrad	T		The translation goes on.
69	zu verweigern	T		The translation goes on.
70	gibt es kein	MTL(46)		This is a case of monitoring because the two utterances 46 and 70 only differ in their word order. This is caused by a grammatical rule in German according to which there has to be a predicate-subject word order in surordinate clauses.
71	wie auch immer geartetes	MTL(47,48)		Verbatim repetition of 47 and 48.
72	mögliches	MTL(40)		Verbatim repetition of 40.
73	Argument	MTL(49) – – –T4#		Verbatim repetition of 49.
74 75	(3s) und jetzt (3s) 'is worthy of respect'	 OSL/OTL		Here, the subject looks through the SL sentence received in 11–16 as well as through the text segments of the third translation version. He realizes that only the SL text segment vebralized in 75 has still to be translated.
76	was respektwürdig ist	T		Translation of the preceding utterance.
77	oder 'was Respekt	REPHR.TLa		Part of the preceding utterance is rephrased.
78	(2s)	RP/→SP	S 6	A problem is realized and a solution is searched for.

No.	T4 S28 Text	Categories of Analysis		Comments
79	abverlangen würde'	SP/ REPHR.TL(76)b	S 6	The solution verbalized here is also the second part of a rephrasing of utterance 76.
80	(3s)	OSL		The subject informs himself in the SL text as to where to proceed from with the translation.
81 82 83 84	'It is the culmination of a nasty campaign which has os- cillated between political spite and logic-chopping.'	REC		Reading is categorized as REC.
85	(1s) Ehm (3s)	OSL		The subject determines the first unit of translation.
86 87	Es ist der Höhepunkt einer häßlichen Kampagne	T		The unit of translation is transferred to TL.
88 89 90	(2s) which has oscillated between political spite and logic-chopping (2s)	OSL		The second unit of translation is extracted from the SL sentence.
91	die sich bewegt hat	Ta		The first part of the unit of translation is transferred to TL.
92	(2s)	OSL		The subject informs himself as to where to proceed from with the translation.
93	zwischen	Tb		The second part of the unit of translation is transferred to TL.
94	(2s)	OSL		Again, the subject informs himself as to where to proceed from with the translation.
95	politischem	Tc		The third part of the unit of translation is transferred to TL.
96	(3s)	RP/→SP	S 7	The subject realizes a problem and searches for a solution. This is interpreted from the fact that the adequacy of the solution to this problem which the subject finds in 97 is checked in No. 99.
97	Trotz	SP = Td		The subject finds a solution to the problem.
98	(1s) und Haarspalterei	Te		The last part of the unit of translation is transferred to TL.

No.	T4 S28 Text	Categories of Analysis		Comments
99	(3s) 'politischem Trotz'	CHECK(97)	S	The adequacy of the text segment 97 is tested,
100	ja	TS(TL)97+	7	the solution is corroborated
101	(3s)	OTL —→ T2		The subject mentally organizes the various translated parts of the unit of translation determined in 88–90. By the following utterances, the subject tries to combine the various translated parts in a coherent, second translation version.
102	die sich bewegt hat	MTL(91)		Verbatim repetition of 91.
103	die sich zwischen	MTL(91,93)		The utterances 103, 105 and 106 are a transposition of the text segments 91, 93, 98, and 99 of the first version.
104	(5s)	OSL/OTL		
105	politischem Trotz und	MTL(99)		
106	Haarspalterei bewegt hat.	MTL(98,91) —T2#		
107	Okay. (2s)	ORG		This organizing utterance marks the end of the second translation version.
108 109 110 111 112 113	'Every Oxford graduate, of whatever party, who has pre- viously attained the high of- fice of Prime Minister since the war has been awarded an honorary doctorate.'	REC		Reading is categorized as REC.
114	(1s) Ehm, jeder	T		The translation continues.
115	(2s)	RP	S	The subject realizes a problem here.
116	Absolvent	SP	8	A solution is uttered.
117	(8s)	RP	S 9	Here again, the subject realizes a problem, i.e. the translation of 'Oxford' into German, and searches for a solution.
118	der Universität Oxford	SP		The subject verbalizes a solution to the problem.
119	(3s)	OSL		The subject mentally organizes the SL text and determines the next unit of translation.

No.	T4 S28 Text	Categories of Analysis		Comments
120 121	welcher Partei (1s) er auch immer angehörte,	T		The translation proceeds.
122	(12s)	CHECK		Here, the adequacy of the preceding text segment is tested.
123 124	ja, ist ne etwas seltsame Konstruktion jetzt	TS(TL)(120, 121)		The following utterances suggest that the TL text segment is rejected.
125	(1s) also jeder	→ T2 MTL(114)		The subject starts producing a second translation version by a verbatim repetition of utterance 114.
126	(5s)	RP/→SP	S 10	A translation problem is realized and a solution is searched for.
127 128	Absolvent der Universität Oxford	SP = MTL(116,228)		The solution verbalized is a verbatim repetition of utterances 116 and 118.
129	(4s)	RP/→SP	S 11	The subject realizes a problem and searches for its solution. This is suggested by the fact that the SL text segment 'of whatever party' which represents the problem here, has been inadequately translated into TL, previously (Nos. 120/121).
130 131	von welcher Partei auch immer	SP = REPHR.TL(120, 121) T2#		A solution to the problem is found. The second translation version ends here.
132	(2s)	OSL		The subject informs himself in the SL text as to where to proceed from with the translation.
133	der	T		The translation goes on.
134	(4s)	RP/→SP	S	During this pause, the subject realizes a translation problem and searches for a solution.
135 136	jetzt sag ich trotzdem hier 'bisher'	SP + $[SP]_{com}$	12	The subject verbalizes the solution to the problem and comments on it.

No.	T4 S28 Text	Categories of Analysis		Comments
137 138	(3s) 'previously', ja.	CHECK+		The solution is tested and corroborated.
139	der bisher (1s)	MTL(133,136)		Verbatim repetition of utterances 133 and 136.
140 141	das hohe Amt des Premier- ministers	T		The translation continues.
142	(5s)	RP/→SP	S 13	The subject realizes a problem and starts searching for a solution.
143	inne hatte (1s)	SP		A solution is found.
144	ehm, der früher	REPHR.TL(139) → T2.2		The subject considers the text segment 139–143 to be inadequate or not optimal and produces a second translation version for the relative clause. It starts with a rephrasing of No. 139.
145	der bisher	REPHR.TL = MTL(139)		Nonetheless, the subject repeats utterance 139, probably because it is taken to be more adequate than the preceding utterance.
146 147	das hohe Amt des Premier- ministers	MTL(140,141)		Verbatim repetition of utterances 140 and 141.
148	(1s) seit (2s) dem Krieg	T		This is the first translation of the respective SL text segment.
149	nee (1s)	TS(TL)(145–148)– —T2.2#		The subject considers the succession of the TL text segments 145–148 to be inadequate or not optimal. He starts producing a further translation version.
150	der	MTL(145) → T2.3		Its first utterance is a verbatim repetition of a part of utterance 145.
151	(2s)	OSL/OTL		Looking at the SL utterance the subject mentally organizes the succession of the TL text segments within this translation version.

No.	T4 S28 Text	Categories of Analysis	Comments
152	der seit dem Krieg	MTL(150,148) —T2.3#	The two TL text segments 150 and 148 are repeated verbatim.
153 154	dann lassen wir, dann machen wirs ganz anders	TS(TL)(152, 145)–	The subject realizes the inadequacy of the preceding text segment and thus of the succession of utterances 150 and 148.
155 156	dann lassen wir das 'previously' so weg	TS(TL)(145) = Ø	The subject realizes that because of the text segment 152, utterance 145 is superfluous.
157	Also nochmal.	→ T3	The subject announces a third translation version of the whole sentence.
158 159	Jeder ehm(1s) Absolvent der Universität Oxford (1s)	MTL(125, 127,128)	Verbatim repetition of utterances 125, 127, and 128 of the second version.
160	welcher Par (...)	REPHR.TL(130)	The subject rephrases utterance 130 but rejects the rephrasing immediately. This interpretation is suggested by the breaking off of this utterance and by the following utterance.
161 162	von welcher Partei auch immer (1s)	MTL(130)	The utterance 130 is repeated verbatim.
163 164	der (1s) das (1s) hohe Amt des Premierministers	MTL(150, 146,147)	Verbatim repetition of the TL text segments 150, 146, and 147.
165	(7s)	OSL/OTL	Here, the subject probably informs himself in the SL text and in the TL text as to where to proceed from with the translation.
166	seit dem Krieg	MTL(150)	Part of 150 is repeated.
167	inne gehabt hat	REPHR.TL(143)	Utterance 143 is rephrased.
168	(4s)	CHECK CT (158–167)/ TS(TL)(158)– T3#	The subject tests the text segments 158–167 with respect to the part of the context that follows them. He realizes that utterance 158 must be altered with regard to its grammatical case.

No.	T4 S28 Text	Categories of Analysis		Comments
169 170	Jetzt müssen wir wiederum an, neu anfangen (1s)	——→ T4		A fourth translation version of the whole sentence is announced.
171	Jedem	REPHR.TL(158)		Utterance 158 is rephrased so that it syntactically fits into its context.
172	(2s)	CHECK CT		The preceding text segment is tested with regard to whether it fits into its context.
173	Jedem	TS(TL)(171)+		The utterance is corroborated.
174	(2s) ehm (3s)	RP/→SP	S 14	The subject realizes a problem and searches for a solution. The translation of 'graduate' is interpreted as being the problem. Although the subject has already translated this lexeme three times (116, 127, 158) it is probably not mentally available to him (cf. 176/177).
175	Graduierten	PSP		A preliminary solution is found.
176 177	oder was hatten wir eben gesagt?	→SP		The subject searches for the solution which has already been verbalized several times.
178	Jedem	MTL(173)		Verbatim repetition of 173.
179	(2s) ehm (2s)	→SP		The search for the solution is continued.
180	Absolvent	SP = MTL(158)		The subject finds the solution.
181	der Universität Oxford	MTL(158/159)		Verbatim repetition of utterance 158/159.
182 183 184	der seit dem Krieg das (1s) hohe Amt des (1s) Premierministers inne gehabt hat	TRANS: MTL(163,166, 163,164,167)		The TL text segments 163, 164, 166, and 167 are repeated verbatim but in a different succession.
185	(4s)	OSL/OTL —T4#		The subject mentally organizes the respective SL text segment and focusses on the point in the TL text from where to proceed.
186	ist	T		The translation goes on.

No.	T4 S28 Text	Categories of Analysis		Comments
187 188	(2s) jetzt ergänz ich hier 'bisher'	OTL/T		The subject focusses on the respective TL text segment and completes it by a further TL text segment which has no correspondence in the SL text but which is necessary in order to constitute an adequate stretch of TL discourse.
189 190	ein Ehrendoktor verliehen worden.	T		The last part of the complex SL sentence is transferred to TL.
191 192 193 194 195 196	'Mrs Thatcher alone has been refused because the dons cam- paigning against her resent her government's policies and particularly those which af- fect education.'	REC		The SL sentence is read for the first time.
197 198 199 200	(3s) ehm (4s) ja, der Anschluß war (1s) 'ein Ehrendoktor verliehen worden'	OSL/OTL		The subject informs himself in the SL text and in the TL text from where to proceed with the translation.
201	Alleine Mrs Thatcher	T		Continuation of the translation.
202	(5s)	RP/→SP	S 15	The subject realizes a problem and starts searching for a solution.
203	wurde er (1s) verweigert	SP		A solution is verbalized.
204	(4s)	OSL		The next unit of translation is determined.
205	weil die	Ta		The first part of the unit of translation is transferred to TL.
206	(3s)	RP/→SP	S 16	A problem is realized and a solution is searched for.
207	Dozenten	SP		Solution to the problem.
208	(3s)	OSL		The subject informs himself what text segment must be translated next.
209 210	die gegen sie (1s) eine (2s) Kampagne führten	Tb		The second part of the unit of translation is transferred to TL.

No.	T4 S28 Text	Categories of Analysis	Comments
211	(11s)	OSL	The subject mentally organizes the remaining part of the unit of translation for its transfer to TL.
212 213	die (2s) Politik ihrer Regie- rung und besonders	Ta	Part one of the unit of translation determined in 211 is transferred to TL.
214	(5s)	OSL	The remaining part of the unit of translation is mentally organized,
215 216 217	soweit sie (2s) das Ausbil- dungswesen betrifft, ablehnen (1s)	Tb	and transferred to TL.
218 219 220 221 222 223 224 225 226 227 228	Ich übersetz hier 'education' mit 'Ausbildungswesen', weil ich meine, daß (2s) 'Erzie- hung' hier (2s) ja doch wohl nicht nur gemeint ist, sondern (1s) wohl das, was institu- tionalisiert ist, und innerhalb dessen sich (1s) die Erzie- hung, Ausbildung, (1s) Weiterbildung und so weiter, vollzieht. (1s)	$[TS(TL)(215\text{–}216)]_{com}$	The subject comments on the preceding TL text segment and thus explains his translation of 'education'.
229 230 231 232 233 234	'By doing so, Oxford has made it clear that an honorary doctorate for anyone in public life who is concerned with politics is now nor more than a political award.'	REC	Reception of a part of the SL text.
235	(3s)	OSL	The subject mentally organizes part of the SL text and determines the next unit of translation.
236 237 238	Ja, ich glaube, da kann man hier jetzt einfach sagen 'dadurch'	$T + [T]_{com}$	The subject's first unit of translation is transferred to TL and commented on.
239	oder 'damit'	REPHR.TL	The preceding TL text segment is rephrased.
240	(4s)	OSL	The next unit of translation is determined.
241	hat	Ta	The first part of the unit of translation is transferred to TL.

No.	T4 S28 Text	Categories of Analysis		Comments
242 243	jetzt würd ich auch sagen 'Oxford'	Tb + $[Tb]_{com}$		The second part of the unit of translation is transferred to TL and commented on.
244	(10s)	RP/→SP		The subject realizes a problem and searches for a solution.
245	Damit hat Oxford	MTL(239,241, 243)		The TL text segment 239, 241, and 243 are repeated verbatim.
246	(6s)	→SP		The search for a solution is continued.
247	deutlich gemacht	SP	S 17	A solution to the problem is found and verbalized.
248	Damit hat Oxford (1s)	MTL(245)		Verbatim repetition of 245.
249	klar gemacht	REPHR.TL(247) = SP2		This text segment is a rephrasing of utterance 247.
250	(2s)	CHECK TL/TL		During this pause, the subject probably tests the adequacy of the preceding text segment by comparing it with the text segment No. 247.
251	ja	SP2+		As a result of the checking, the text segment No. 249 is corroborated.
252 253	Damit hat Oxford klar gemacht	MTL(248,249)		Verbatim repetition of text segments 248 and 249.
254 255	daß ein Ehren (1s) doktor- titel	T		The translation is continued.
256	(10s)	RP/→SP		The subject realizes a problem and searches for a solution.
257	daß ein Ehrendoktortitel	MTL(254,255)		The text segments 254 and 255 are repeated verbatim.
258	(4s)	→SP	S	The search for a solution is continued.
259	für jedermann	SPa	18	The first part of a solution is verbalized.
260	(7s)	→SP		The remaining part of a solution is searched for.
261	der im öffentlichen Leben	SPb		The second part of a solution is verbalized.

No.	T4 S28 Text	Categories of Analysis		Comments
262	Nee	SPa,b–		The two parts of a solution are considered inadequate and rejected.
263 264	Damit hat Oxford es klar gemacht	REPHR.TL = (252,253) → T2		The subject produces a second translation version in order to solve the problem. The version starts with a rephrasing of the utterance 252 and 253.
265	(3s)	→SP		The subject continues searching for a solution to the problem realized in 256.
266	that an honorary doctorate	MSL		An SL text segment is repeated verbatim.
267	for anyone in public life	VP		The problem realized in 256 is verbalized.
268	(3s)	→SP	S	Continuation of the search for a solution.
269	daß ein Ehrendoktortitel	MTL(257)	18	Verbatim repetition of 257.
270 271	(5s) Wie sagt man da im Deutschen jetzt? (1s)	→SP		The search for a solution goes on.
272	for anyone in public life	VP2		The problem is verbalized a second time.
273	(15s)	→SP		The subject continues searching for a solution.
274 275	da gibt es doch auch noch en feststehenden Begriff	$[SP]_{com}$		The solution to be found is commented on.
276 277 278	(1s) für, also Leute des (1s) ja, für Leute des	SPa2		Another first part of a solution is verbalized.
279 280	oder 'für Personen des öf- fentlichen Lebens'	REPHR.TL = SPa3 /SPb2		The subject rephrases part a2 of a solution and thus verbalizes a further first part of a solution. The utterance also includes a second possibility of the second part of a solution.
281	ja, das ist es, ja	SPa3+/SPb2+ = SP —T2#		The preceding text segment is considered to be a solution and is emphasized.

No.	T4 S28 Text	Categories of Analysis	Comments
282	Also, dadurch hat Oxford es	REPHR.TL(263) → T3	A third translation version is produced. It starts with a rephrasing of No. 263.
283 284	dadurch hat Oxford klar ge- macht	REPHR.TL/ MTL(264)	The preceding TL text segment is rephrased, and No. 264 is repeated verbatim.
285	daß ein Ehrendoktortitel	MTL(269)	Verbatim repetition of 269.
286 287	für Personen des öffent- lichen Lebens (1s)	MTL(278,279)	Verbatim repetition of 278 and 279.
288	die	T	The translation continues.
289	(9s)	OSL	The next unit of translation is determined.
290 291	in der Politik (1s) tätig sind	T	The translation goes on.
292	(5s)	OSL	The next unit of translation is determined.
293	fortan nicht mehr	T	The translation continues.
294	(5s)	OSL	The next unit of translation is extracted.
295 296	als eine politische Aner- kennung ist	T	The translation goes on.
297	(2s)	CHECK(293,295, 299)	The TL text segments 293, 295, and 296 are tested.
298 299 300	oder 'nichts anderes als eine politische Anerken- nung ist'.	REPHR.TL(293, 295,296) T3#	As a result of the checking, the subject verbalizes an alternative for the text segments 293, 295, and 296.
301	Ja, okay.	TS(TL)(298- 300)+	The rephrasing is corroborated.
302	So lassen wirs.	ORG	The translational discourse is terminated.

5.3.4.2 Comment

The translation contains eighteen strategies:

S1 : Nos. 6–9/10
This strategy realizes a type Va basic structure. It is followed by CHECK+ which functions as a bound element. At the end of the strategy, a solution to the translational problem is found.
Type: Va + CHECK+ SP#

S2 : Nos. 17–18/21
Strategy 2 is the realization of a type II basic structure with two bound elements, CHECK and REPHR.TL.
Type: II + CHECK + REPHR.TL SP#

S3 : Nos. 24–36
This strategy is based on a complex structure consisting of an expanded and a basic structure. The expanded structure belongs to type Vc and contains three expansions (2VP, →SP) and one embedded element <SPb = ∅>. As a result of the expanded structure, PSPb is found. The second part of the strategy is a basic structure of the type II. SPb and thus an entire solution to the problem is found.
Type: Vc + 3EX + <SPb=∅> – II SP#

S4 : Nos. 39–40/45
This is an intraversional strategy realizing a type II basic structure. Three bound elements are appended to it: VP+CT, CHECK, and REPHR.TL.
Type: II' + VP+CT + CHECK + REPHR.TL SP#

S5 : Nos. 57–58
S5 is also an intraversional strategy. It belongs to the type II basic structures and terminates with a solution to the translational problem.
Type: II' SP#

S6 : Nos. 78–79
Realization of a type II basic structure.
Type: II SP#

S7 : Nos. 96–97/100
This strategy represents a basic structure (type II) with three bound elements (Te, CHECK, TS(TL)+) appended to it.
Type: II + Te + CHECK + TS(TL)+ SP#

S8 : Nos. 115–116
S8 realizes a type I basic structure.
Type: I SP#

S9 : Nos. 117–118
This is the realization of a basic structure (type II).
Type: II SP#

S10/S11 : Nos. 126–127/129–130
Both these strategies are intraversional and realize basic structures of the type II.
Type: II' SP#

S12 : Nos. 134–138
Strategy 12 belongs to the type II basic structures. It has one embedding <$[SP]_{com}$> and one bound element, CHECK.
Type: II + <$[SP]_{com}$> + CHECK SP#

S13 : Nos. 142–143
Realization of type II.
Type: II SP#

S14 : Nos. 174–180
This intraversional strategy is based on a complex structure. Its first part is a basic structure (type II), its second part an expanded structure (1 x →SP) of the type II. The latter contains an embedded element <MTL>. The strategy terminates with a solution to the translational problem.
Type: II' + II' + 1EX + <MTL> SP#

S15/S16 : Nos. 202–203/206–207
Both these strategies realize type II basic structures.
Type: II SP#

S17 : Nos. 244–247/251
Strategy 17 belongs to the type II structures. It contains one expansion (→SP) and one embedding <MTL>, and has four bound elements appended to it: MTL, REPHR.TL, CHECK, and SP2+.
Type: II + 1EX + <MTL> + MTL + REPHR.TL + CHECK + SP2+ SP#

S18 : Nos. 256–281
This complex translation strategy consists of an expanded structure and a second, intrastrategic, translation version. The expanded structure (1 x →SP) of the type Va contains one embedding <MTL> and two bound elements, SPa,b– and REPHR.TL. It is followed by the second translation version. This comprises an expanded and a basic structure. The former belongs to the type IV structures and contains one expansion (→SP) and two embedded elements <MSL, MTL>. The latter also belongs to the type IV structures and contains one embedding <$[SP]_{com}$>. Two bound elements, REPHR.TL and SPa3+/SPb2+, are appended to the

translation version. The strategy ends with a solution to the problem.

Type: Va + 1EX + <MTL> + SPa,b– + REPHR.TL + T2' [IV + 1EX + <MSL> – IV + <[SP]$_{com}$> + REPHR.TL + SPa3+/SPb2+] SP#

5.3.5 Translation IL → L1 (T5, S34)

5.3.5.1 Qualitative Analysis

No.	T5 S34 Text	Categories of Analysis	Comments
1	(Reads text aloud)	REC	Reading is categorized as REC.
2	(2s) ehm	ORG	The beginning of the translational discourse is marked.
3 4 5	(1s) Also Überschrift 'The history of the English lan- guage as cultural (...)'	OSL	The first unit of translation is determined.
6 7 8	Die Geschichte der engli- schen Sprache (1s) als ein kulturelles Thema.	T	The first unit of translation is transferred to TL.
9	(2s)	CHECK+	The preceding TL text segment is tested. As the translation proceeds, the result of the checking is probably a corroboration.
10 11 12 13 14 15 16 17	'It was observed by that re- markable twelfth century chronicler, Henry of Hunting- don, that an interest in his part (sic!) was one of the distinguishing characteris- tics of man (1s) as compared with the other animals.'	REC	The subject receives the first sentence by reading it.
18 19 20 21 22	(5s) ja, it's (1s) um da eine Chronologie reinzubringen (1s) fangen wir von vorne an (1s).	OSL	The subject mentally organizes the first sentence and determines the first unit of translation.
23	Es würde	T	The first part of the unit of translation is transferred to TL.

No.	T5 S34 Text	Categories of Analysis		Comments
24	(3s)	RP/→SP	S 1	The subject realizes a problem and searches for a solution.
25	beobachtet	SP		A solution is verbalized.
26	bei dem bemerkenswerten	T		The translation continues.
27	(3s)	RP/→SP	S 2	Another problem is realized and a solution is searched for.
28	ja, 'chronicler' (1s)	VP		The problem is verbalized.
29	Geschichtsschreiber	SP		A solution to the problem is found.
30 31	im zwölften Jahrhundert (1s) Henry (1s) von (3s)	T		The translation goes on.
32	von	MTL		Part of the text segment 31 is repeated verbatim.
33	Hungtingdon	T		The translation proceeds.
34	(2s)	OSL		The next unit of translation is determined.
35	daß ein Interesse	T		The first part of the unit of translation is transferred to TL.
36	(2s)	OSL		The subject informs himself in the SL text as to where to proceed from with the translation.
37	an seiner Vergangenheit	T		The translation goes on.
38	(2s)	OSL		Cf. 36
39	war eine	T		Cf. 37
40	(3s)	CHECK		The preceding TL text segment is tested.
41 42	nein, 'war' darf man nicht (...)	TS(TL)(39)–		As the result of the checking, the text segment 39 is considered inadequate and is rejected.
43	daß ein, das Interesse	REPHR.TL(35)		The subject goes back to the TL text segment No. 35 and rephrases it.
44	an seiner Vergangenheit	MTL(37)		Verbatim repetition of utterance 37.

No.	T5 S34 Text	Categories of Analysis	Comments
45	(2s)	OSL	The subject informs himself in the SL text as to where to proceed from with the translation and extracts the next unit of translation.
46	eine der	T	The translation continues.
47	(2s)	RP	During this pause, the subject probably realizes a translational problem.
48 49	'distinguishing' (1s) oh Hilfe	VP + $[P]_{com}$	The problem is verbalized and commented on.
50	(2s)	→SP	A solution is searched for.
51	to distinguish	REPHR.SL(48)	The problematic text segment is rephrased.
52	(4s)	→SP	The search for a solution is continued.
53 54	characteristics of man as compared	MSL(15/16)	Verbatim repetition of an SL text segment received in 15/16.
55	(3s)	→SP	S3 The subject continues the search for a solution.
56 57	unterschiedlichen Ab(...) (1s)	PSP	The subject verbalizes a preliminary solution.
58	distinguish something	REPHR.SL(51)	The problematic SL text segment is rephrased again.
59	(2s)	→SP	The search for a solution goes on.
60	etwas unterscheiden	PSP2 = REPHR.TL(56)	A further preliminary solution is found. It is a rephrasing of No. 56.
61	(5s)	OTL → T2	The subject mentally organizes the TL sentence for a second translation version.
62	daß ein Interesse (1s)	MTL(35)	Verbatim repetition of 35.
63	an seiner Vergangenheit	MTL(44)	Verbatim repetition of 44.
64	(1s) ein (1s)	REPHR.TL(46)	Utterance 46 is rephrased.
65	unterscheidendes (1s)	SP = REPHR.TL(56) T2#	A solution is verbalized. It is a rephrasing of utterance 56. The second translation version terminates here.

No.	T5 S34 Text	Categories of Analysis		Comments
66	Merkmal	T		The translation proceeds.
67	(3s)	OSL		The subject determines the next unit of translation.
68 69 70	war (1s) wenn man Menschen mit anderen Tieren ver- gleicht (1s)	T		The unit of translation determined in 67 is translated into TL.
71 72 73	And in these days when the cultivated man or woman is conscious of (2s)	REC <RP(SL)>		The subject receives an SL text segment. During this reading, he realizes a problem in the SL text.
74 75	das Wort kann ich weder aus- sprechen, noch kenn ich das	$[P(SL)]_{com}$		The SL reception problem is commented on.
76	of [di'fain..] (2s)	VP(SL)	S 4a	The problematic SL text segment is verbalized.
77	(Quietly: [di'faintsiz])	VP(SL)2		The problem is verbalized a second time.
78	[di'faintsiz]	REPHR.SL >>> 102		The problematic SL text segment is rephrased.
79	(2s)	OSL		The subject informs himself in the SL text as to where to continue receiving it.
80 81 82 83 84 85	in his education without some knowledge of economics, medieval history, recent advances in the basic natural sciences, so also he may dis- cover a desire (...)	REC		Reception of the second part of the SL text.
86	Das ist ein langer Satz	$[TS(SL) (80–85)]_{com}$		The received SL text segment is commented on.
87	(3s) And in these days (1s)	OSL		The subject mentally organizes the SL text and determines the next unit of translation.
88	In jenen Tagen (1s)	T		The unit of translation is transferred into TL.
89	oder 'damals' (1s)	REPHR.TL		The preceding TL text segment is rephrased.
90	wenn der	T		Continuation of the translation.
91	(3s)	RP/→SP	S 5	A problem is realized and a solution is searched for.

No.	T5 S34 Text	Categories of Analysis		Comments
92 93	'kultivierte Mensch' kann man nicht sagen	SP = Ø		A text segment is verbalized which is considered to be a zero solution.
94	'cultivated man or woman'	VP	S	Verbalization of the translational problem.
95	(3s)	→SP	5	Search for a solution.
96	wenn der	MTL(90)		Verbatim repetition of 90.
97	(2s)	→SP		Continuation of the search for a solution.
98	cultivate, gebildeter	REPHR.SL (94)/SP		The subject rephrases the problematic SL text segment and verbalizes a solution immediately after the rephrasing.
99	(1s) Mann oder die Frau	T		The translation continues.
100	(2s)	OSL		The subject determines the next unit of translation.
101	sich bewußt ist (1s) über	T		The translation goes on.
102	(2s)	RP	<<< 78	The subject realizes a problem.
103 104	jetzt das Wort, das fehlt mir, Lücke	SPØ	S	The subject points out that he cannot solve the problem.
105	(2s)	OSL/OTL	4b	The subject mentally organizes the next part of the SL text and orients himself about where to proceed with the translation.
106	über	MTL(101)		Verbatim repetition of part of utterance 101.
107 108	vielleicht kriegt mans so raus (1s)	$[\rightarrow SP]_{com}$		The subject comments on his searching for a solution.
109	in seiner Erziehung	T		The translation continues.
110	(2s)	OSL		The subject determines the next unit of translation.
111 112	ohne (1s) das Wissen über Ökonomie (1s) Geschichte	T		The translation goes on.
113	(4s)	RP/→SP	S	A translation problem is realized and a solution is searched for.
114	recent advances	VPa	6	A part of the translation problem is verbalized.

No.	T5 S34 Text	Categories of Analysis		Comments
115	(2s)	→SP		The search for a solution continues.
116	advanced learner's dictionary	REPHR.SL (114) + CT		A part of the SL text segment 114 is rephrased and embedded into a context known to the subject.
117	(2s)	→SP		The search for a solution goes on.
118	recent advances	VPa2		Part of the problem is verbalized a second time.
119 120	in the basic natural sciences	VPb		The second part of the complex translational problem is verbalized.
121	(2s)	→SP		Continuation of the search for a solution.
122	recent	VPai	S	A part of utterance 118 is verbalized (again).
123	über die neuesten	MTL(106)/ SPai	6	A part of the text segment 106 is repeated verbatim, and a solution to the problem verbalized in 122 is found.
124	(5s)	→SP		The search for the remaining parts of a solution continues.
125	advances	VPaii		The second subpart of the problem's first part is verbalized again.
126 127	in the basic natural sciences	VPb2		The second part of the translation problem is verbalized again.
128	(4s)	→SP		The subject searches for a solution to the remaining part of the problem.
129	in den neuesten	REPHR.TL (123) = SPai2		The text segment 123 is rephrased, and thus a second solution to part Pai of the problem is verbalized.
130	Grundlagen (1s)	SPaii		This text segment is considered to be a solution to part Paii of the problem.

No.	T5 S34 Text	Categories of Analysis		Comments
131 132 133 134	der (2s), ja nochmal 'Grundlagen', der grundle- genden Naturwissenschaften geht auch nicht.	SPb = ∅	S 6	A TL text segment that might suggest itself as a solution to the problem's second part is rejected because it is considered inadequate.
135 136	in the basic natural sciences	VPb3		The last part of the problem is verbalized again.
137 138 139 140	(3s) so also he may discover a desire to know something of the nature	<SPb∅> OSL		The subject does not suceed in achieving a solution to the verbalized part of the problem. He continues by determining the next unit of translation.
141	(3s)	OTL		Here, the subject probably informs himself as to where to proceed from with the TL text.
142 143	und so mag er gleichzeitig einen	Ta		The first part of the unit of translation is transferred to TL.
144	(2s)	OSL		The subject orients himself in the SL text as to where to proceed from with the translation.
145	Wunsch entdecken	Tb		The second part of the unit of translation is transferred into TL.
146	(3s)	OSL		The subject informs himself in the SL text as to where to proceed from with the translation.
147 148	etwas zu erfahren über die Natur	Tc		The last part of the unit of translation is transferred to TL.
149 150	und die Entwicklung seiner Muttersprache	T		The translation proceeds.
151 152 153	(3s) and the development of his mother tongue	CHECK+		The preceding TL text segment is tested. As the translation proceeds, the result of the checking is probably a corroboration of the TL text segment.
154	(2s)	OSL		The subject orients himself in the SL text as to where to proceed from.

No.	T5 S34 Text	Categories of Analysis		Comments
155 156 157 158 159 160 161	the medium by which he com- municates his thought and feelings to his fellow men, the tool with which he conducts his business or the govern- ment of millions of people, the vehicle (...)	REC T → 168ff.		The subject receives a part of the SL text by reading it. At first, he leaves it aside but starts translating it in No.168ff.
162 163	Das ganze ist sicherlich wert	T		The translation goes on.
164	(3s)	RP/→SP		The subject realizes a problem and searches for a solution.
165	bearbeitet zu werden	PSP	S 7	A preliminary solution is uttered.
166	worthy of study	VP+CT/ CHECK= =		The translation problem is verbalized and the preliminary solution is tested.
167	erforscht zu werden.	REPHR.TL (165) = SP		As a result of the checking, the text segment 165 is rephrased. The rephrasing is considered to be the solution to the problem.
168	Also, das Medium	T(155)		The translation of the SL text segment which was left aside at first, starts.
169	(3s)	OSL		The subject mentally organizes the SL text segment and determines the next unit of translation.
170 171	mit welchem man (1s) seine Gedanken und Gefühle	T(155– 157		The translation proceeds.
172	(2s)	RP	S	A translation problem is realized,
173	kommuniziert	SP	8	and a solution is found.
174	oder ausdrückt	REPHR.TL= = SP2		The preceding solution is rephrased, and thus a second solution is verbalized.
175	(2s)	OSL		The next unit of translation is extracted.
176	zu seinen	T(157)		A part of the text segment in 157 is translated.
177	(2s)	RP	S 9	Realization of a problem.

No.	T5 S34 Text	Categories of Analysis		Comments
178	to his fellow men	VP + CT		The problem and a part of its context are verbalized.
179	(2s)	→SP	S	The subject searches for a solution.
180	zu seinen	MTL(176)	9	Utterance 176 is repeated verbatim.
181	Gesprächspartnern	SP		A solution to the problem is found.
182	oder Umgangspartnern	REPHR.TL = SP2		The preceding TL text segment is rephrased, and thus a second solution to the problem is found.
183 184 185 186	(2s) the tool with which he conducts his business or the government of mil- lions of people	OSL		The next unit of translation is determined.
187	(7s)	OSL/OTL		Here, the subject probably organizes mentally both the various parts of the received SL sentence and those parts of it which have already been translated. He reflects on how to combine the various TL text segments in an optimal way.
188 189 190 191	Jetzt überleg ich, soll ich doch noch mal anfangen mit dem letzten 'is surely worthy of study' (2s)	$[\text{TRANS}]_{\text{com}}$		Here, the subject considers the transposition of TL text segments.
192 193	Das müßte eigentlich den Satz einleiten also	TRANS → T2		The subject thinks that an adequate translation requires a transposition, which will be realized in a second translation version.
194	(2s)	OSL/OTL		With a view to the respective SL text segments, the subject reflects on how to combine the various TL text segments for the second translation version.
195 196	Es ist sicherlich (1s) wert	REPHR.TL(162/ 163)		Utterance 162/163 is rephrased.
197	(1s) zu erforschen	REPHR.TL(167)		Utterance 167 is rephrased.

No.	T5 S34 Text	Categories of Analysis		Comments
198	(3s)	RP/→SP	S	The subject realizes a problem and searches for a solution.
199	das Medium	SP	10	A solution is verbalized.
200	(1s) the medium	VP/CHECK		The problem is verbalized and its solution is tested.
201	das Medium	SP+		As the result of the checking, the solution is corroborated.
202 203	mit dem man seine Gefühle und Gedanken	REPHR.TL(170/ 171		Utterances 170 and 171 are rephrased.
204	(2s)	OTL		The subject orients himself as to where to proceed from with the translation.
205	kommuniziert	MTL(173)		Verbatim repetition of the TL text segment No. 173.
206	oder austauscht	REPHR.TL		The preceding text segment is rephrased.
207	(1s) mit Gesprächspartnern	REPHR.TL(180/ 181)		The subject goes back to the utterances 180 and 181 and rephrases them.
208 209	oder mit Partnern allgemein	REPHR.TL —T2#		The preceding utterance is rephrased.
210 211	(3s) tool (1s) with which he conducts his business	OSL		The subject determines the next unit of translation.
212	(3s)	RP/→SP		Within the unit of translation, the subject realizes a problem and starts searching for a solution.
213	also 'the tool' (1s)	VP		The subject verbalizes the translational problem.
214 251 216 217 218 219 220 221 222 223 224	ehm 'tool' ist doch (2s) ist das nicht ein Ausdruck (4s) Wo kommt der her? Das hab ich doch schon mal gehört? 'tool' das hat irgendwas (8s) das ist ein technischer Ausdruck 'tool' ist das nicht so ne Art (2s)	→SP VP2 →SP VP3	S 11	The utterances 214–224 are interpreted as representing a phase of searching for a solution. The subject tries to remember in what context he has already met the problem atic word 'tool'.

No.	T5 S34 Text	Categories of Analysis		Comments
225	'Spule' oder was?	PSP		The subject verbalizes a preliminary, hypothetical solution.
226 227	(3s) Wie paßt das jetzt hierein?	CHECK CT=		The preliminary solution is tested by finding out whether it fits into its context.
228 229	Also 'tool with which he conducts his business'	VP4 + CT		The problem is verbalized for the fourth time, this time together with part of its context.
230	(4s)	→SP	S	The search for a solution continues.
231	das Instrument	SP	11	A solution is found and verbalized.
232 233	Ja, 'tool', 'Instrument' kann das sein? (2s)	CHECK = =		The subject checks on the adequacy of the solution.
234	das Instrument	SP+ = =		As the result of the checking, the solution is corroborated.
235 236 237 238	mit dem er (1s) seine Geschäfte führt (1s) oder die Regierung Millionen (1s) von Menschen	T		The translation goes on.
239 240	(2s) the vehicle by which have been transmitted to him	OSL		The next unit of translation is extracted.
241	(2s)	RP		The subject realizes a translational problem,
242	the vehicle	VP		and verbalizes it.
243	(2s)	→SP		He searches for a solution.
244 245	ehm, das könnte man hier (1s) als Metapher verstehen	$[P]_{com}$	S 12 a	The translational problem is commented on.
246	(1s) 'the vehicle' also	VP2		Second verbalization of the problem.
247 248 249	auch wieder 'die Art und Weise' oder 'der Mechanismus'	SP REPHR.TL = SP2 = >>>255		The subject verbalizes two TL text segments (248, 249) which he apparently considers to be two alternative solutions to the problem.

No.	T5 S34 Text	Categories of Analysis	Comments
250	(2s)	OSL	The subject informs himself in the SL text how far the translation has proceeded and determines the next unit of translation.
251	mit welchem (1s) man ihm	T	The translation goes on.
252 253	(2s) 'by which have been transmitted to him'	CHECK	The adequacy of the preceding text segment is tested.
254	mit welchem ihm	REPHR.TL(251)	As the result of the checking, No. 251 is rephrased.
255 256	(5s) Was soll man jetzt sagen?	249<<< →SP ===	Here, the subject continues searching for a solution to the problem originally verbalized in 242.
257	einfach 'Merkmale'	REPHR.TL (249) = SP3	A third alternative solution is verbalized.
258	(2s)	CHECK=== S	The preceding text segment is tested.
259	'Grundlagen'	REPHR.TL== 12 (267) = SP4 b	and another alternative solution is verbalized.
260	(2s)	OSL	The subject determines the next unit of translation.
261	mit welchem ihm	MTL(264)	Verbatim repetition of 254.
262	(3s)	→SP	The subject continues searching for a solution.
263	'the vehicle' (1s)	VP3	For the third time, the problem is verbalized.
264	ach nein!	TS(TL) (257–261)–	The negative evaluation probably refers to utterances 257-261, because in the following second translation version an attempt is made to improve these utterances.
265 266 267	the vehicle by which have been transmitted to him the science	MTL(239/ 240) <VP4> — → T2	Verbatim repetition of the TL text segment 239/240 with a fourth verbalization of the problem embedded in it.
268	(2s)	→SP	The search for a solution continues.

No.	T5 S34 Text	Categories of Analysis		Comments
269 270	also doch 'die Art und Weise'	SP5 = SP1(248)+	S 12	This solution to the problem is also a corroboration of the TL text segment 248.
271	oder 'das Instrument'	REPHR.TL = SP6	b	With the rephrasing of the preceding utterance, a sixth solution is verbalized.
272	mit dem (1s) man ihm	REPHR.TL(251) T2#		Utterance 251 is rephrased. The second translation version terminates here.
273 274	die Naturwissenschaften, die Philosophie	T		The translation proceeds.
275	(2s)	OSL		The next unit of translation is determined.
276	und die	T		The translation continues.
277	(2s)	RP		The subject realizes a translational problem,
278	the poetry of the race	VP		and verbalizes it.
279	Was ist das denn wieder	$[P]_{com}$		The problem is commented on.
280	(3s)	→SP		A solution to the problem is searched for.
281	the race	VPa		A part of the problem is verbalized again.
282	Wie kann man das verstehen?	$[P]_{com}$		The problem is commented on again.
283 284	Das ist ja hier sicherlich hier kein sportliches Rennen	SPa = Ø	S 13 a	The subject verbalizes a TL text segment which can*not* function as a solution.
285	(1s) the poetry of the race	VP2		The entire problem is verbalized again.
286	(3s)	→SP		The search for a solution continues.
287	Ist das überhaupt ein Rennen?	$[SP]_{com}$		The subject implicitly comments on what might be a possible solution.
288	(1s)	→SP		The subject continues searching for a solution.
289	race	VPa2		A part of the problem is ver balized a second time.

No.	T5 S34 Text	Categories of Analysis		Comments
290	Was gibt's noch für 'race'?	→SPa		The search for a solution goes on.
291	Ist das auch 'die Rasse'?	$[SPa]_{com}$		The subject implicitly comments on what might be a possible solution.
292	(2s)	CHECK===		The possible solution is tested,
293	Nee	SPa– ===		and rejected.
294	(4s)	→SPa		The search for a solution continues.
295	Das ist interessant	$[P]_{com}$		The problem is commented on.
296	the poetry of the race	VP3		The subject verbalizes the entire problem for the third time.
297	(4s)	→SP		Continuation of the search for a solution.
298 299	'poetry' als 'die dichtende Kunst'	SPb		A solution to the problem's second part is verbalized.
300	(2s)	→SPa	S 13 a	The subject searches for a solution to the remaining part of the problem.
301	aber 'of the race'	VPa3 + CT		The remaining part of the problem is verbalized a third time, this time embedded in part of its context.
302	(2s)	→SPa		Continuation of the search for a solution.
303 304	da sehe ich ja total keinen Zusammenhang	SPØ		The subject points out that he cannot solve the problem.
305	(2s)	→SPa		Nonetheless, the search is continued.
306 307 308	(Quietly: the poetry of the race is surely worthy of study)	VPa4 + CT		The problem is verbalized for the fourth time, this time embedded in part of its context.
309	(9s)	→SPa		The search for a solution continues.
310 311	Das müßte hier metaphorisch gemeint sein.	$[P]_{com}$		The problem is commented on.

No.	T5 S34 Text	Categories of Analysis		Comments
312 313 314	Ich überleg die ganze Zeit, wo ich das 'race' unterbrin- gen kann (2s)	→SPa <VPa5>		Continuation of the search for a solution with the fifth verbalization of the problem embedded.
315	the poetry of the race	VPa6 + CT		The problem is verbalized for the sixth time, this time embedded in part of its context.
316 317	(5s) welche 'race' um Himmels Willen? (4s)	→SP <VPa7>		The subject continues searching for a solution and verbalizes the problem again.
318	(Quietly: race)	VPa8		The problem is verbalized for the eighth time.
319	(2s)	→SPa		Continuation of the search for a solution.
320 321 322 323	Ich kann mich auch nur immer auf die Bedeutung halt des, des Rennens, des sportlichen Wettbewerbs (4s) beziehen	$[Pa]_{com}$/ SPaØ		The subject comments on the problem and realizes its insolubility.
324 325 326	(Quietly: the poetry of the race is surely worthy of study.)	VPa9 + CT	S	Nonetheless, the problem and part of its context are verbalized for the ninth time.
327	(8s)	→SP	13 a	The search for a solution continues.
328	der Dichtung	REPHR.TL(299) = SPb2		Here, the subject verbalizes an alternative solution to the second part of the problem. The text segment is also a rephrasing of utterance 299.
329	'the poetry', 'die Dichtung'	CHECK+		The solution is tested and corroborated.
330	der	T		The translation goes on.
331 332	(2s) ehm, Pünktchen, Pünktchen	SPaØ >>>379		The subject states again that the problem he has verbalized nine times cannot be solved.
333	is surely worthy of study.	OSL		The next unit of translation is extracted.
334 335	Am besten den ganzen Satz nochmal,	→ T3		A third translation version is announced.

No.	T5 S34 Text	Categories of Analysis		Comments
336	das war alles nichts	TS(TL) (195–330)–		The negative evaluation concerns the text segments 195 to 330, which constitute the problematic sentence.
337	(5s)	OSL/OTL		The subject mentally organizes the SL sentence and those parts of it which he has already translated.
338	Das Medium	MTL(168)		The TL text segment 168 is repeated verbatim.
339 340 341	(1s) eventuell auch vorne anfangen, warum nicht mal anders rum.	TRANS		The subject announces a transposition of text segments with respect to the first translation version.
342	Das Medium	MTL(338)		Verbatim repetition of utterance 338.
343 344 345	mit welchem er (1s) seine Gedanken, Gefühle (1s) kommuniziert	REPHR.TL (170–173)		The TL text segments 170–173 are rephrased.
346	(2s)	OSL		The subject informs himself in the SL text as to where to proceed from with the translation.
347	das Instrument	MTL(271)		Verbatim repetition of 271.
348 349	wenn man hier 'tool' als 'Instrument'	CHECK+		The preceding TL text segment is tested and corroborated.
350 351 352 353 354	mit welchem er seine Ge- schäfte führt (1s) oder mit welchem eine Regie- rung (1s) Millionen von Menschen	REPHR.TL (235–238)		This is a rephrasing of the TL text segments 235–238.
355	(2s)	RP		During this pause, the subject probably realizes a translation problem.
356 357	ja, nicht schon wieder 'führt'	SP = ∅	S 14	The subject verbalizes a TL text segment which might suggest itself but cannot function as a solution.
358	Also (1s) das Instrument	MTL(347)		Verbatim repetition of 347.

No.	TS S34 Text	Categories of Analysis		Comments
359 360 361 362	mit welchem er seine Ge- schäfte (1s) oder eine Re- gierung Millionen von Men- schen führt	SP / REPHR.TL (350–357)		The TL text segments 350–357 are rephrased, and thus the problem realized in 355 is solved.
363	(3s) the vehicle	OSL		The next unit of translation is determined.
364 365	das ist auch wieder das, die Maschinerie,	REPHR.TL(349)		This is a rephrasing of utterance 349.
366	das Instrumentarium	REPHR.TL		The preceding text segment, and thus also No. 349, is rephrased.
367 368 369	mit welchem (1s) ihm die Naturwissenschaften, die Philosophie und die Dichtung	REPHR.TL (272–276, 328)		The subject rephrases the TL text segments 272–276, and 328.
370	übermittelt werden	T		The translation continues.
371	(4s)	OSL		The subject extracts the next unit of translation.
372 373	ist es sicherlich wert, erforscht zu werden.	REPHR.TL(162/ 163,167)		The text segments 162/163, and 167 are rephrased.
374	(3s)	CHECK		The subject checks on the utterances 342–373.
375 376 377	Ja, das ist besser, das könnte man noch hinten dran tun	TS(TL) (342–373)+		As a result of the checking, the sequence of utterances 342-373 is corroborated.
378	(..?..)			Utterance inaudible.
379 380 381 382	Aber dieses verflixte 'the poetry of the race' krieg ich ja mit dem besten Wil- len nicht unter	332<<< SP(278)∅	S	The subject points out that even in the third translation version he cannot find a solution to the problem verbalized in No. 278.
383	(3s)	→SP	13 b	Nevertheless, he continues searching for a solution.
384 385 386	Aber wenn man das alles, 'science', 'Naturwissen- schaften', 'Philosophie'	(SP)CT		The subject verbalizes the context within which a solution must be embedded.

No.	T5 S34 Text	Categories of Analysis		Comments
387	warum nicht nur 'poetry'	REPHR.SL (278) SPa,b = SPb	S 13 b	This is a rephrasing of the problematic SL text segment 278. The subject thinks that because of the context, the entire problem will be solved when a solution to its first part will be found.
388	(2s) (..?..)			Utterance inaudible.
389	of the race	SPa∅		As the problem Pa cannot (and need not) be solved, the problematic SL text segment in taken over into TL.
390 391	ist es sicherlich wert, erforscht zu werden	MTL(372/373) T3#		Verbatim repetition of utterance 372/373.
392	Okay.	ORG		Organizing utterance which terminates the discourse.

5.3.5.2 Comment

The translation contains fourteen strategies.

S1 : Nos. 24–25
This strategy realizes a type II basic structure and terminates with a solution to the problem.
Type: II SP#

S2 : Nos. 27–29
Strategy 2 represents a basic structure of the type IV. At the end of the strategy, the subject finds a solution to the translational problem.
Type: IV SP#

S3 : Nos. 47–65
This strategy is based on a complex structure consisting of an expanded structure, a basic structure, and a second translation version. The expanded structure (2 x →SP), a realization of type IV, contains two embeddings <REPHR.SL, MSL>, and REPHR.SL as a bound element. The type II basic structure which follows terminate with a further, preliminary solution. The last

part of the strategy is a second translation version at the end of which a definite solution to the problem is achieved.

Type: IV + 2EX + <REPHR.SL, MSL> + REPHR.SL – II – T2 [OTL, 2MTL, SP=REPHR.TL] SP#

S4 : a. Nos. 73–78; b. Nos. 102–104/108

Strategy 4 is discontinuous and consists of two parts. Part 4a belongs to the structural types III. It contains an expansion (VP(SL)2), and two embedded elements <[P(SL)]$_{com}$, REPHR.SL>. A solution to the problem is *not* found.

Part 4b realizes a type I basic structure followed by three bound elements: OSL/OTL, MTL, and [→SP]$_{com}$.

At the end of the strategy, the problem is still unsolved.

Type: a. III + 1EX + <[P(SL)]$_{com}$, REPHR.SL> –
b. I SPØ + OSL/OTL + MTL + [→SP]$_{com}$ SPØ#

S5 : Nos. 91–98

This is the realization of a type IV expanded structure (1 x →SP) with three embedded elements: <SP=Ø, MTL, and REPHR.SL>. The strategy terminate with a solution to the problem.

Type: IV + 1EX + <SP=Ø, MTL, REPHR.SL> SP#

S6 : Nos. 113–137

This strategy realizes the structural type Vb. It contains seven expansions: (2 x →SP, VPa2, VPai, VPaii, VPb2, VPb3) and four embedded elements: <REPHR.SL+CT, MTL, REPHR.TL, SPb=Ø>. At the end of the strategy, the second part of the problem remains unsolved.

Type: Vb + 7EX + <REPHR.SL+CT, MTL, REPHR.TL, SPb=Ø> SPbØ#

S7 : Nos. 164–165/167

S7 realizes a type II basic structure. It is followed by two bound elements: VP+CT/CHECK and REPHR.TL. The strategy ends with a solution to the translational problem.

Type: II + VP+CT/CHECK + REPHR.TL SP#

S8 : Nos. 172–173/174

This is the realization of a type I basic structure. It is followed by REPHR.TL as a bound element.

Type: I + REPHR.TL SP#

S9 : Nos. 177–181/182

Strategy 9 is based on a type IV structure. It contains an embedded <MTL> and a bound element (REPHR.TL).

Type: I + <MTL> + REPHR.TL SP#

S10 : Nos. 198–199/201
This intraversional strategy represents the type II basic structures. It is followed by two bound elements: VP/CHECK and SP+
Type: II' + VP/CHECK + SP+ SP#

S11 : Nos. 212–231/234
S11 is based on a complex structure. It comprises an expanded structure (2 x VP, →SP) of the type IV with CHECK as a bound element, and a type IV basic structure which is followed by two bound elements: CHECK and SP+.
Type: IV + 3EX + CHECK – IV + CHECK + SP+ SP#

S12 : a. Nos. 241–248/249; b. Nos. 255–271
This discontinuous strategy belongs to the complex structures and consists of two parts.
Part a. realizes a expanded structure (VP2, →SP) with <$[P]_{com}$> as an embedded and REPHR.TL as a bound element.
Part b. is based on a complex structure and consists of three partial structures: i. a type II basic structure with CHECK, REPHR.TL, OSL, and MTL appended to it; ii. an expanded structure (VP4) of the type IV with <[TS(TL)]– and MTL> as embedded elements; and iii. a second, partially intrastrategic translation version which is built up of a type II basic structure and REPHR.TL as a bound element. The strategy terminates with a solution to the problem.
Type: a. II + 2EX + <$[P]_{com}$> + REPHR.TL –
b. II + CHECK + REPHR.TL + OSL + MTL – IV + 1EX + <[TS(TL)]–, MTL> – T2' [II + REPHR.TL] SP#

S13 : a. Nos. 277–332; b. Nos. 379–389
S13 is a discontinuous strategy and consists of two parts. Part a. is of a very complex kind and realizes five structural types: i. a type IV with an embedded <$[P]_{com}$>; ii. an expanded structure (2 x →SP, VPa) of the type Vb with <$[P]_{com}$, SPa = ∅, VP2, $[SP]_{com}$, and $[PSPa]_{com}$> as embeddings, and CHECK and PSPa– as bound elements; iii. a type Vc expanded structure (2 x →SP) with two embeddings <$[P]_{com}$, VP3> which terminates without a solution to the problem; iv. an expanded structure (3 x →SPa, 2 x VPa) with two embedded elements <$[P]_{com}$, $[P]_{com}$> which again ends without a solution to Pa; v. a type Vb basic structure which contains three bound elements: CHECK, T, and SPa∅.
The intraversional part b. of the strategy comprises a type Va basic structure with two embeddings: <(SP)CT and REPHR.SL>.

The strategy ends without a solution to the first part of the problem: SPa∅.

Type: a. IV + <[P]$_{com}$> –
Vb + 3EX + <[P]$_{com}$, SPa = ∅, VP2, [SP]$_{com}$, [PSPa]$_{com}$> + CHECK + PSPa– –
Vc + 2EX + <[P]$_{com}$, VP3> SP∅ –
Vb + 5EX + <[P]$_{com}$, [Pa]$_{com}$> SPa∅
Vb + CHECK + T + SPa∅
b. Va + <(SP)CT, REPHR.SL> SPa∅#

S14 : Nos. 355–362

This is the realization of a type I structure. It contains two embedded elements: <SP = ∅ and MTL> and terminates with a solution to the translational problem.

Type: I + <SP = ∅, MTL> SP#

6 A Quantitative Analysis of the Data

In the preceding chapter, a model for the strategic analysis of the translation process was developed and applied to four translations from my data corpus. The exemplary analysis carried out in this way is *qualitative* by its very nature. It captures and makes visible the translation strategies, their elements, and the translation versions.

In this chapter, the essential results which the *qualitative* analysis has yielded will be analyzed *quantitatively*. This leads to the following subdivisions of Chapter 6:

After a few introductory remarks on the quantitative analysis of data (6.1), the translation *problems* contained in the corpus will be analyzed quantitatively (6.2). The preliminary remarks (6.2.1) are followed by an investigation of the types of translation problems (6.2.2), and of their frequency, occurrence, and distribution (6.2.3). The section terminates with remarks on individual and supraindividual translation problems (6.2.4).

Section 6.3 contains the quantitative analysis of the translation *strategies* and thus represents the main part of this chapter. After the preliminary remarks (6.3.1), the basic and expanded structures (6.3.2) as well as the complex structures (6.3.3) will be analyzed quantitatively. In the subsequent subsection (6.3.4), the success of the translation strategies employed by the subjects is investigated. The preliminary remarks on the concept of 'success' which is used in this study (6.3.4.1) are followed by an analysis of the translation strategies according to whether (or to what extent) they are successful or not (6.3.4.2).

Subsection 6.3.5 contains a quantitative investigation of selected elements of translation strategies. These are Checks (6.3.5.1), Monitorings (6.3.5.2), Rephrasings (6.3.5.3), and Multiple Verbalizations of Translation Problems (6.3.5.4). The chapter is terminated by an investigation of individually caused differences in strategy use (6.3.6) as well as by a summarizing comparison of strategies for translation *into* and *from* the mother tongue (6.3.7).

6.1 Introductory Remarks

In the preceding chapter, a qualitative analysis of translation strategies, their elements, and of translation versions was made. In this chapter, it will be supplemented by a quantitative analysis of its essential results. As pointed out in subsection 4.4.2.3, any quantitative analysis of data must be preceded, in practice as well as logically, by a qualitative analysis. Both are essential for a comprehensive investigation of the translation process.

The results which the quantitative analysis will yield do not claim to permit statistically valid and far-reaching generalizations. Neither is the data corpus large enough for this, nor were the relevant statistical methods and procedures used. The aim of this study is therefore not to present statistically valid results. Rather, the numerical and percentage results are to show and make plausible the fact that the subjects' use of translation strategies is not the product of mere chance, but is based on and controlled by rules and regularities. These can be revealed by a comprehensive quantitative and qualitative analysis.

The rules and regularities yielded by the analysis are certainly only valid for the translation(s) of the respective subject(s). Nonetheless, I will try to show, with all due care and wherever it seems possible, supraindividual trends and tendencies in strategy use which are valid for all or a large proportion of the subjects or which may even be valid for non-professional translators in general. These trends and tendencies are not the product of a statistical analysis; but they are plausible, nonetheless.

The data corpus compiled for this investigation consists of fifty-two translations. It turned out to be extremely rich[1] with respect to the phenomena which are of interest here. The abundance of data made a selection necessary; a selection with regard to what data should be analyzed quantitatively and with regard to the aspects under which the quantitative analysis should be carried out. The criteria for the selection are derived from the epistemological interest of this study. As it aims at reconstructing the subjects' translation strategies, it is primarily the internal structure, the frequency, the distribution, and the success of the translation strategies which will be analyzed quantitatively[2].

Whilst the entire data corpus available comprises 52 translations, it is 45 translations which constitute the corpus on the basis of which the quantitative, and partly the qualitative, analyses were carried out: 25 translations *into*, and 20 translations *from* the foreign language. The translation produced by subject 9 could not be transcribed because of damage to the tape. The translations by the subjects 47 to 52 are available in transcript but were neither analyzed qualitatively nor quantitatively. These subjects were pupils at a German *gymnasium* whom, in contrast to all the other subjects, I did not know personally. Furthermore, they produced their translations under conditions which were rather different from those of the other subjects[3].

---

1 The amount of data available is so large that it takes approximately ten hours to play all the translations recorded on cassette. In transcript, the translations cover about 150 fully written pages.

2 What other criteria controlled the selection of certain phenomena for the quantitative analysis will be pointed out in sections 6.3.1, 6.3.5, 6.3.6, and 6.3.7.

3 One of the differences was that the pupils were given more detailed information on thinking-aloud and that they had the chance of practising the thinking-aloud technique in a pre-experiment.

6.2 Translation Problems

In this section, the subjects' translation problems will be analyzed with respect to their frequency, their types, and their distribution in the corpus. Additionally, possible supraindividual tendencies as well as consequences which the results of the quantitative analysis suggest will be outlined.

6.2.1 Preliminary Remarks

As regards the epistemological interest of this study, translation problems are of eminent importance because they function as both the starting-point of and the reason for the use of translation strategies. As a consequence, translation strategies only occur when translation problems exist. The reverse conclusion, the fact that translation problems always lead to translation strategies and that thus the former do not exist independent of the latter, is theoretically not necessary, but must be presupposed in practice. It can well be imagined though that a subject realizes a translation problem but neither gives it any cognitive attention nor makes any effort to solve it; for any practical analysis, however, it must be assumed that the subjects in principle endeavour to work out solutions for the translation problems they realize and that they thus behave in a rational way with regard to their task. Only on this assumption can a performance-analytical investigation be carried out in a sensible way. In my data, there is no indication of subjects not fulfilling this requirement. The case that a translation problem is realized but not given any further cognitive attention would have to be categorized as non-strategic behaviour. It would thus be beyond the reach of the model of analysis developed in the preceding chapter and would be outside the epistemological interest of this study. Furthermore, it could hardly be documented empirically because, if at all, there will only be very vague indicators for the mere realization of translation problems without any subsequent strategic behaviour.

Translation problems manifest themselves in source-language text segments which correspond to strategic parts of the translation. It is extremely difficult to determine precisely the percentage of the problems in relation to the entire text. One procedure which will be made use of in this investigation, is to determine the ratio of the problematic text segments to the non-problematic ones on the basis of the number of lexemes. This procedure is adequate where lexical problems are concerned. It is not convincing, however, when the problems are of a purely syntactic or of a mixed lexico-syntactic kind (cf. section 6.2.2). An example may elucidate this. During the translation of text 5, subject 38 considers the SL text segment "by which have been transmitted to him" problematic and verbalizes it. The data externalized during the subsequent problem-solving process suggest that the problem is not the lexemes which constitute the text segment but the syntactic structure of the passive voice construction. This is why the problem cannot be (adequately) determined by focussing on the lexemes of which it is built up.

Nonetheless, the procedure of counting up the lexemes of a problematic text segment and of determining the ratio of the problematic lexemes to the non-problematic ones is used here, mainly for three reasons:

i. According to a close inspection of the syntactic problems represented in the corpus, the respective SL text segments mostly consist of two or three lexemes only. When determining the percentage of the problems on the basis of the lexemes, the biases will thus be on a much smaller scale than with the exemplary text segment consisting of seven lexemes.

ii. As will be discussed in detail in section 6.2.3, the data corpus mainly contains lexical problems. Purely syntactic problems are very rare. If one additionally takes into account what was pointed out in i., it does not seem to be inadequate to use a procedure which adequately captures the great majority of the phenomena and which only causes difficulties with respect to a very small number of cases.

iii. Last but not least, the procedure of counting the lexemes and of determining the ratio of the problematic lexemes to the nonproblematic ones is very easy and controllable and only takes a small amount of time compared with other possible methods. As the aim of the quantitative analysis is only to show supraindividual trends and tendencies (cf. section 6.1), it seems to be justifiable to use the procedure described above for reasons of practicability. With the aim of this chapter in mind, and in view of its shortcomings, the procedure does, nonetheless, provide valuable information about one aspect of the occurrence of translation problems.

6.2.2 Types of Problems

The translational problems to be found in the data corpus can be grouped into three categories[4]:

a. lexical problems
b. syntactic problems
c. lexico-syntactic problems.

Lexical problems refer to single lexemes of the SL text for which the subject has no corresponding TL lexemes available.

---

4 There is only one single problem which does not fall into either of these categories. It occurs in the translation of subject 34. He considered the repetition of a verb in a complex TL sentence which was evoked by the syntactic structure of the respective SL sentence to be stylistically poor. The subject solved this problem by a syntactic rephrasing of the respective TL text segment. In the quantitative analysis of the data, the problem was grouped among the *syntactic problems*.

Example / T1, S15, No. 9 (cf. subsection 5.3.2.1)
Text: Tja, *'Eigenschaften und Merkmale'* Hm [↑↓]

Syntactic problems refer to the syntactic structure of an SL text segment for which the subject has no corresponding TL structure available. It is not the transfer of the lexemes, but their syntactic arrangement to make an adequate TL text segment, which constitutes the problem.

Example / T3, S24, Nos. 189–190 (cf. subsection 5.3.3.1)
Text: *'wann welches Deutsch mit wem gesprochen wird'*

Lexico-syntactic problems occur when both lexical and syntactic phenomena constitute the translational problem for the subject, or when it is not possible to differentiate between either of these phenomena. The latter case frequently occurs with metaphors and idioms which (often) cannot be translated literally into a TL.

Example 1 / T3, S24, Nos. 236–237 (cf. subsection 5.3.3.1)
Text: *'einen kommunikationsorientierten Unterricht'*

*Explanation:*This is an example of a problem which consists of both lexical and syntactic phenomena. As the continuation of the translation shows, the subject is faced with three subproblems: i. the translation of the lexeme 'kommunikationsorientiert'; ii. the rendering of the lexeme 'Unterricht' into English, and iii. the syntactic structure. The third subproblem occurs because a literal translation of the SL text segment into TL is considered to be impossible by the subject. Rather, a syntactic re-arrangement is necessary so that the noun precedes the attribute.

Example 2 / T5, S34, No. 288 (cf. subsection 5.3.5.1)
Text: *'the poetry of the race'*

*Explanation:*This is an example of a translational problem for which a definite differentiation with respect to *lexical* or *syntactic* cannot be made. As the translation shows, the subject has no problem in translating the single lexemes 'poetry' and 'race'. Rather, the problem lies in combining the lexemes translated into TL so that they constitute a sensible text segment.

6.2.3 Frequency, Occurrence, and Distribution of Translation Problems

On examining the data, a phenomenon can be realized which is considered to be an empirical fact. It is the translation process consisting of problematic and non-problematic phases[5]. In the former, the subjects are faced with barriers which prevent or delay, or which only partially or inadequately allow the transformation of SL text segments into TL. Within such phases, a strategic, i.e. problem-solving approach by the subjects is called for.

The latter, non-problematic phases are characterized by the subjects' performing their task in an automatized or partly automatized way without being faced with barriers during the transformation of SL text segments into TL.

Both the problematic and non-problematic phases refer to segments of the underlying SL text. In section 6.2.1, the difficulties of precisely determining the percentage of the problematic text segments with regard to the seven SL texts of the corpus were mentioned. It was also explained why the controversial procedure of counting the lexemes and of determining the ratio of the problematic lexemes to the non-problematic ones is used.

In order to minimize the distortions which occur when the procedure of counting the lexemes is applied to syntactic and lexico-syntactic problems, the following supporting measure was taken: When counting the lexemes, syntactic problems and, if isolatable, the syntactic part(s) of lexico-syntactic problems were counted as one problem unit. A syntactic problem consisting of several lexemes was thus addressed in the same way as a single lexical problem. The counting yielded the following results:

5 Cf. above all Krings 1986a: 113. In connection with second-language reception and production processes, Dechert (1983: 183f.), following Lesser and Erman (1977: 794f.), speaks of "islands of reliability", i.e. "stretches of speech ... which run smoothly and fluently." They correspond to the non-problematic phases of the translation process.

Diagram 12: Frequency, Percentage, and Distribution of Translation Problems.

Text	Number of problematic lexemes	Total number of lexemes	Percentage
1	57	111	51.35%
2	34	117	29.05%
3	45	144	31.25%
4	44	124	35.48%
5	34	143	23.78%
6	28	141	19.86%
7	23	129	17.83%

The percentages of problems in texts 1 and 7 represent extreme values. This is understandable in the case of text 1. It was translated by sixteen subjects whose individual problems naturally add up to much higher numbers than, for example, those of the four subjects who translated texts 3, 6, and 7. The question of whether the other values are more conditioned by the respective texts or by the individual subjects can, however, not be answered from the diagram above.

In order to eliminate those problems which must be interpreted as individual, the following procedure is used: Problems which do not occur with *more* than 25% of the subjects who translated the respective text are considered to be individual problems and are not dealt with any further (cf. section 6.2.4). With respect to text 1, which was translated by fifteen subjects, only those problems were counted as supraindividual which occurred with four or more subjects. As concerns texts 2–7, which were translated by four and six subjects respectively, a problem must occur with two or more subjects in order to be taken into consideration for the analysis.

The following diagram represents those problems which are interpreted as supraindividual, according to the procedure outlined above.

Diagram 13: Frequency, Percentage, and Distribution of Supraindividual Translation Problems.

Text	Number of supraindividual problematic lexemes	Total number of lexemes	Percentage
1	19	111	17.12%
2	22	117	18.80%
3	34	144	16.67%
4	22	124	17.74%
5	15	143	10.49%
6	14	141	9.93%
7	1	129	0.78%

By comparing the respective values of the diagrams 12 and 13, it is possible to calculate the percentage of individually caused problems: ca. 34% for the translations of text 1, ca. 10% for the translations of texts 2 and 6, ca. 14% for the translations of texts 3 and 5, and ca. 18% for the translations of texts 4 and 7.

As is apparent from diagram 13, the percentage of supraindividual problems is almost the same in the texts 1 to 4. It amounts to ca. 17%, which means that about every sixth element of these texts represents a problem for the respective subjects.

In the texts 5 and 6, the rate of problematic elements is approximately 7% lower and amounts to 10%. As the percentage of individually caused problems is rather high in these texts (14% and 10%, respectively), it can be assumed that the texts 5 and 6 were less problematic for the subjects who translated them than the texts 1 to 4 were for the respective subjects.

The translations of text 7 are entirely exceptional because 96% of their problems are individually caused (17.83–0.78 = 17.05; 17.05 ≙ 96% of 17.83). Both these subjects' competence in the foreign language and their experience in translating obviously differ so much that supraindividual problems can hardly be detected in these translations.

In the 45 translations which constitute the corpus of the investigation, 206 different translation problems are contained. As will be shown in section 6.2.4, a considerable amount of these problems are supraindividual in nature, which means that one and the same problem occurs with several subjects. Thus, it is not astonishing that the subjects are faced with the 206 translation problems 394 times. For the quantitative analysis of the data, the number of occurrences of translation problems (394) is of special importance. According to my epistemological interest, which is motivated psycholinguistically, the analysis of the data is carried out from the perspective of the subjects which the analyst tries to reconstruct. Therefore, when one and the same translation problem occurs with several subjects, the various *instances* of the problem are treated as data for the analysis. In the terminology used in this study, a distinction is made between a *problem* and an *instance of a problem.* The distinction corresponds to that between *type* and *token*[6]. The *different problems* of the corpus of investigation represent the *types*, the entire number of *instances of problems* corresponds to the number of *tokens*. The analysis of the data of this investigation focusses on the *instances of problems* and thus is *token-oriented.*

In addition to the number of problems and the number of instances of problems, a third number is of importance for the analysis of the data, i.e. the number that indicates how often the subjects address one and the same problem. In five cases, subjects addressed problems again in a second or third translation version, either because they could not achieve solutions in the first version or because the solutions achieved in the first version turned out to be inadequate or not optimal for the subjects. For the analysis of the translation *problems* carried out in this section, it is of subordinate importance how often one and the same problem is addressed by the subjects. For the analysis of the translation *strategies*, however, the number of times a problem is addressed plays an essential role.

Of the 394 documented instances of problems, 274 are purely lexical, 88 are lexico-syntactic, and 32 are purely syntactic problems. In other words, about 70% of all the instances of problems refer to lexical items for which the subjects have either no or only inadequate TL items available. Approximately 22% of all the instances of problems have both a lexical and a syntactic component, and only 8% are of a purely syntactic kind.

The percentages mentioned above represent mean values with reference to the 45 subjects and the seven texts used. Individually caused differences will mainly be discussed in section 6.2.4. The distribution of the instances of problems over the seven texts is represented in the following diagram:

6 For the *type/token*-concept cf. Herdan 1956; 1960; 1966; Heger 1971; Lyons 1977: 13ff.; Peirce 1933; ^{5}1980: 537.

Diagram 14: Distribution of the Instances of Problems over the Seven Source-Language Texts

TEXT 1	Instances of Problems (15 Subjects)	:	159	=	100.00%
	Instances of Lexical Problems	:	111	=	69.81%
	Instances of Lexico-Syntactic Problems	:	36	=	22.64%
	Instances of Syntactic Problems	:	12	=	7.55%
TEXT 2	Instances of Problems (6 Subjects)	:	34	=	100.00%
	Instances of Lexical Problems	:	17	=	50.00%
	Instances of Lexico-Syntactic Problems	:	11	=	32.35%
	Instances of Syntactic Problems	:	6	=	17.65%
TEXT 3	Instances of Problems (4 Subjects)	:	51	=	100.00%
	Instances of Lexical Problems	:	35	=	68.63%
	Instances of Lexico-Syntactic Problems	:	12	=	23.53%
	Instances of Syntactic Problems	:	4	=	7.84%
TEXT 4	Instances of Problems (6 Subjects)	:	68	=	100.00%
	Instances of Lexical Problems	:	51	=	75.00%
	Instances of Lexico-Syntactic Problems	:	11	=	16.18%
	Instances of Syntactic Problems	:	6	=	8.82%
TEXT 5	Instances of Problems (6 Subjects)	:	38	=	100.00%
	Instances of Lexical Problems	:	26	=	68.42%
	Instances of Lexico-Syntactic Problems	:	10	=	26.32%
	Instances of Syntactic Problems	:	2	=	5.26%
TEXT 6	Instances of Problems (4 Subjects)	:	24	=	100.00%
	Instances of Lexical Problems	:	18	=	75.00%
	Instances of Lexico-Syntactic Problems	:	5	=	20.83%
	Instances of Syntactic Problems	:	1	=	4.17%
TEXT 7	Instances of Problems (4 Subjects)	:	20	=	100.00%
	Instances of Lexical Problems	:	16	=	80.00%
	Instances of Lexico-Syntactic Problems	:	3	=	15.00%
	Instances of Syntactic Problems	:	1	=	5.00%

As the number of subjects varies between 4 and 15 with respect to the texts translated, a determination of the average number of instances of problems per subject per text suggests itself. This is represented in the following diagram:

Diagram 15: Average Number of Instances of Problems per Subject per Text

TEXT 1:	10.60
TEXT 2:	5.67
TEXT 3:	12.75
TEXT 4:	11.33
TEXT 5:	6.33
TEXT 6:	6.00
TEXT 7:	5.00

Diagram 15 above shows that the texts 3, 4, and 1 are the richest and the texts 7, 2, and 6 are the poorest in problems. This statement is valid only for an *idealized* subject who is faced with an *average* number of translation problems. Individually caused deviations from the mean of instances of problems of the respective text are not considered in the diagram.

It should be pointed out again here that the percentages of translation problems, as represented in diagrams 12 and 13, are determined on the basis of the *types* of problems which manifest themselves in the lexemes of a text. The values which diagram 15 shows are determined on the basis of the *instances* of problems (*tokens*) which an idealized subject is faced with, independent of their percentages of the SL texts.

The most obvious deviations from the mean concern the translations of the texts 2 and 7. As is apparent from diagram 15, the translations of text 2 contain 20% fewer instances of lexical problems, but 10% more instances of lexico-syntactic and purely syntactic problems. In other words, half of the instances of problems the subjects are faced with in text 2 are of a lexical kind; about one third have both a lexical and syntactic component; and one sixth are of a syntactic kind.

The translations of text 7 reveal the opposite picture. They contain 10% more instances of lexical problems than the mean, but 7% fewer instances of lexico-syntactic, and 3% fewer instances of purely syntactic problems.

The statements made above are certainly valid only for those translations of the two texts which were produced by the respective, individual subjects. Text 2 was translated by six, text 7 by four subjects. Merely because of these small populations any far-reaching generalizations have to be ruled out. If one additionally takes into account that within the ten sample translations considerable differences occur with respect to the distribution of the instances of problems, any generalization, however cautious it may be, seems to be misplaced. As the translations of the texts 2 and 7 reveal, the differences in the distribution of the instances of problems are mainly, if not exclusively, caused by individual factors.

Thus, the translation produced by subject 19 contains five of the eleven instances of lexico-syntactic problems inherent in text 2, which makes it exceptional. If this extreme value is not considered, the mean for the other subjects amounts to 1 (rounded down). If this mean is used instead of the extreme value for the calculation of the percentage of instances of lexico-syntactic problems, it comes to 22.58%. This value is nearly identical with the mean of instances of lexico-syntactic problems calculated for *all* the subjects of the investigation (ca. 22%).

Analogous considerations apply to subject 20's instances of syntactic problems. They are three in number and thus make 50% of all the instances of syntactic problems in text 2. If this extreme value is not considered, and if the mean of the other subjects (1, rounded up) is used in its place, the percentage amounts to 12.90. This is nearly 5% above the mean of instances of syntactic problems calculated for all the subjects of the corpus (ca. 8%).

The instances of lexical problems are distributed in a smilar way. It is noticeable that subject 22 is not faced with any lexical problem at all. If this extreme value (0) is not considered, the mean for the subjects 17 to 21 amounts to 3. Again, if this mean is used instead of the extreme value, the instances of lexical problems in text 2 add up to 20, i.e. 64.52%. This is nearly 6% below the mean of instances of lexical problems (70%) calculated for *all* the subjects of the investigation.

The three percentages cleared of the extreme values are calculated on the basis of the reference number 31. It results from the sum of all instances of problems in text 2, i.e. 34, minus the four instances of lexico-syntactic problems *above* the mean and the two instances of purely syntactic problems *below* the mean.

As a result of the considerations made above, it must be pointed out that the percentages of the instances of problems in text 2 largely correspond to the mean values calculated if the extreme values are not considered. There is only a deviation of 5% for instances of syntactic and a deviation of 6% for instances of lexical problems. It is only these deviations which can be interpreted as being caused not by individual factors but by the respective text.

Among the translations of text 7, that produced by subject 46 reveals an extreme distribution of instances of problems. Whilst the subjects 43, 44, and 45 are faced with six instances of lexical problems altogether, the translation of subject 46 alone contains ten of these instances of problems. Because of this extreme value, which is most probably caused by individual factors, it is not only the number of instances of lexical but of instances of problems in text 7 altogether which thus increases above the mean. As a consequence, the percentages of the instances of lexico-syntactic and of purely syntactic problems turn out to be accordingly low.

If the extreme value 10 is not considered and if the mean of the other subjects (2) is used in its place, the percentage of instances of lexical problems amounts to 66.67. This value is calculated on the basis of the reference number 12, which results from the sum of all instances of problems in text 7 after being cleared of the extreme value 10. The percentage of instances of lexico-syntactic problems amounts to 25.00, that of instances of syntactic problems to 8.3 when calculated in the way described above. Here again, it can be seen that if the respective extreme values of subjects are replaced by the means calculated for the other subjects, the percentages of the instances of problems in text 7 largely correspond to the mean values calculated for the entire corpus.

The remaining deviations of approximately 3% for the instances of lexical and of lexico-syntactic problems are minimal and probably caused by the respective text.

To conclude this section, the distribution of the instances of problems will now be examined with respect to whether there are differences in the translations *into* and *from* the mother tongue. Texts 1 to 3 represent the basis for the twenty-five translations *from* the mother tongue, texts 4 to 7 underlie the twenty translations *into* the mother tongue. As diagram 14 shows, the percentage of the instances of lexical problems for the translations *into* the mother tongue (texts 4, 6, and 7) is slightly higher than the mean. In addition, the percentage of the instances of lexico-syntactic problems in text 4 is slightly lower than the mean. In the translations of text 5 the percentage of the instances of lexico-syntactic problems is slightly higher and the percentage of the purely syntactic problems is accordingly lower than the mean. As concerns the translations of text 7, the reader is referred to the considerations above.

With respect to the translations of text 6, it is remarkable that subject 39 is faced with eleven instances of lexical problems, whereas all the other subjects who translated text 6 are faced with seven instances of lexical problems altogether. If, however, the extreme value 11 is replaced by the mean, the percentages look entirely different. The instances of lexical problems amount to 62.50%, and thus nearly 8% *below* the total mean, and the instances of lexico-syntactic problems come to 31.25%, i.e. 9% *above* the total mean.

When replacing the extreme values by mean values in the translations of text 5, the distribution of the instances of problems remains about the same as in diagram 14. The percentage of the instances of lexical and of syntactic problems is slightly lower, that of the instances of lexico-syntactic problems is slightly higher than the mean.

Text 4 contains a good 5% more instances of lexical problems for the subjects who translated it. If the procedure of replacing extreme values by mean values is used here again, the percentage of instances of lexical problems even increases to 76.71%, and that of lexico-syntactic problems to 15.07%.

The following diagram represents the deviations from the mean values in the translations *into* and *from* the mother tongue.

Diagram 16: Deviations from the Mean Values in the Translations from and into the Mother Tongue

Translation from the Mother Tongue

TEXT 1	lexical: 0%;	lexico-syntactic: 0%;	syntactic: 0%
TEXT 2	lexical: -6%;	lexico-syntactic: 0%;	syntactic: +5%
TEXT 3	lexical: -1%;	lexico-syntactic: +1%;	syntactic: 0%

Translation into the Mother Tongue

TEXT 4	lexical: +7%;	lexico-syntactic: -7%;	syntactic: 0%
TEXT 5	lexical: -3%;	lexico-syntactic: +4%;	syntactic: -1%
TEXT 6	lexical: -8%;	lexico-syntactic: +9%;	syntactic: -2%
TEXT 7	lexical: -3%;	lexico-syntactic: +3%;	syntactic: 0%

As a result of the considerations above, it can be pointed out that, after being cleared of their extreme values, the translations *into* the mother tongue of texts 5, 6, and 7 reveal a slightly diminished percentage of instances of lexical problems and a slightly increased percentage of instances of lexico-syntactic problems. The deviations from the mean values in the translations of text 4 are considerable and represent exceptions. As far as the translations *from* the mother tongue are concerned, the percentages largely correspond to the mean values calculated. Only the translations of text 2 contain a slightly lower percentage of instances of lexical problems and a slightly higher percentage of instances of lexico-syntactic problems. All this goes to document the fact that there are no supraindividually significant differences between the translations *from* and *into* the mother tongue as regards the distribution of the instances of problems. Again, it must be emphasized here that the aim of this chapter is not to present statistically valid results. The question as to whether what I call 'extreme values' are really extreme values *in the sense of statistics* can hardly be decided here. In order to make statistically valid generalizations, the populations would have to be much larger. In relatively small populations, such as mine, individually caused values naturally produce a much stronger effect than in larger populations. Furthermore, the procedure of replacing extreme values by mean values is not permissible in statistics. Nonetheless, this procedure is employed here in order to 'correct' values which are obviously or strongly supposed to be caused by individual factors. Even though this procedure is statistically problematic, it is both plausible and sensible if one takes into consideration the fact that the results are only valid for the respective sample population.

6.2.4 Individual and Supraindividual Translation Problems

In the preceding section it has already become clear what a crucial role the individual factors play in the quantitative analysis of the data. Neither the problematic elements of an SL text nor the distribution of the translation problems over the underlying texts can be determined without taking the individually caused values into consideration. Especially in relatively small data corpora, individual factors can cause extreme values which can considerably distort the mean values of the sample population. In these cases, it is necessary to clear the data if one wants to obtain supraindividually valid results. As pointed out in section 4.1, the assumption that such results can be produced is an essential precondition for any sensible performance analysis.

The question of how large the percentage of individual and supraindividual translation problems is in the data corpus implies many difficulties. They result from the fact that the criteria for interpreting a translation problem as being individual or supraindividual are not fixed in advance but have to be developed and determined by the analyst. The data necessary for doing this are listed in the following diagram. It contains the number and percentage of shared translation problems for each of the seven texts used, as well as the number of subjects who are faced with the respective problem. Additionally, the entire number of problems and subjects for any text is listed.

Diagram 17: Individual and Supraindividual Translation Problems

	Common Problems: *Number*	Common Problems: *Percentage*	Common Problems: *Number*	Common Problems: *Percentage*	Entire Number of Problems	Entire Number of Subjects
TEXT 1	2	4%	9	60%	51	15
	1	2%	8	53%		
	1	2%	6	40%		
	4	8%	5	33%		
	10	20%	4	27%		
	10	20%	3	20%		
	14	27%	2	13%		
	9	18%	1	7%		
TEXT 2	2	10%	3	50%	21	6
	9	43%	2	33%		
	10	48%	1	17%		

	Common *Number*	Problems: *Percentage*	Common *Number*	Problems: *Percentage*	Entire Number of Problems	Entire Number of Subjects
TEXT 3	3	9%	3	75%	34	4
	11	32%	2	50%		
	20	59%	1	25%		
TEXT 4	1	3%	6	100%	36	6
	1	3%	5	83%		
	1	3%	4	67%		
	7	19%	3	50%		
	6	17%	2	33%		
	20	56%	1	17%		
TEXT 5	1	4%	4	67%	26	6
	3	12%	3	50%		
	3	12%	2	33%		
	19	73%	1	17%		
TEXT 6	5	26%	2	50%	19	4
	14	74%	1	25%		
TEXT 7	1	5%	2	50%	19	4
	18	95%	1	25%		

In the preceding section, translation problems were considered to be supraindividual when their instances occurred with more than 25% of the respective subjects. This limitation is justified insofar as the analysis of the data must be carried out by means of criteria which are the same for the whole of the corpus. With a text translated by four subjects, a limit of 25% or less would have meant that translation problems of which instances occurred with only one subject would have been considered supraindividual. Such a concept is obviously in contradiction to any notion of supraindividuality.

Although the limitation discussed is sensible for the analysis of the data carried out in the last section, one must, in principle, assume a fluid boundary between the concepts of *individuality* and *supraindividuality*. Additionally, it is sensible to consider supraindividuality not to be a discrete concept but to assume different degrees of supraindividuality of data.

In a strict theoretical sense, only those translation problems would be of an individual kind which occur with one subject only. All other problems would thus be supraindividual by their very nature. But such a purely theoretical concept has no recourse to any data corpus and does not take into account the requirements of any practical, empirical work. In the quantitative analysis carried out in this chapter, single data are investigated and interpreted with recourse to the whole of the data corpus of which they are part. Which of the data are interpreted as being caused individually, and thus as having the status of extreme values, and which are of a supraindividual kind is crucially dependent on the purpose of the investigation and on the size and structure of the data corpus. An example may elucidate this. When a corpus of 100 data contains two extreme values, these can be interpreted as being caused individually. They amount to 2% of the data. In a corpus of 20 data, however, two extreme values make 10% of the data. They mark the boundary between individually caused and supraindividual data.

As regards the corpus of investigation *as a whole*, considerations will now be made on the number and percentage of individual and supraindividual translation problems as well as on the degrees of supraindividuality. If, as was done in the preceding section, the boundary between individual and supraindividual problems is fixed at 25%, the corpus contains 134 (= 65%) individual and 72 (= 35%) supraindividual translation problems. This ratio may be surprising, but can be explained by various facts:

1. The calculation made above is *type-* not *token-oriented*, which means that it operates on the basis of the *problems*, not of the *instances of the problems*. Furthermore, it does not take into account *to what degree* problems are individual or supraindividual, i.e. with how many subjects they occurred. If this is taken into consideration, a second calculation yields the following values, which are nearly the reverse of the first:

Instances of Individual Problems: 168 (= 43%)
Instances of Supraindividual Problems: 226 (= 57%)

2. The translations into the mother tongue of texts 5, 6, and 7 are very heterogeneous and contain a large number of individual problems which occur with one subject only:

TEXT 5:	Individual Problems:	19 (= 73%)
	Supraindividual Problems:	7 (= 27%)
TEXT 6:	Individual Problems:	14 (= 74%)
	Supraindividual Problems:	5 (= 26%)
TEXT 7:	Individual Problems:	18 (= 95%)
	Supraindividual Problems:	1 (= 5%)

As the three texts were only translated by four and six subjects respectively, further translations must show whether the interpretation of specific problems as being individual or supraindividual is also valid with respect to a larger data corpus. The values listed above have a considerable effect on the entire corpus of investigation, resulting in a falsely increased percentage of individual problems.

3. The 25% boundary between individual and supraindividual translation problems is sensible with respect to both the corpus of investigation *as a whole* and the translations of the texts 2 to 7. It causes problems, however, with regard to the translations of text 1. As a result of the boundary fixed at 25%, only those problems in text 1 are considered to be supraindividual which occur with four or more subjects. The percentages of the 33 individual and 18 supraindividual problems amount to 65 and 35, respectively.

If the boundary is lowered to 20%, for example, those problems which three subjects are confronted with will also be considered supraindividual. In that case, 28 (= 55%) supraindividual problems and 23 (= 45%) individual problems are contained in text 1. The respective values for the entire corpus change accordingly. Although a lowering of the boundary between individual and supraindividual problems seems sensible with respect to the translations of text 1, again further translations must show whether the interpretation of specific problems as being individual or supraindividual is also valid for a larger data corpus.

As already pointed out at the beginning of this section, the boundary between individual and supraindividual phenomena is fluid and must be determined by the analyst. This implies that individuality and superindividuality are not discrete but continuous concepts and that they always occur with certain degrees. This also applies to the 72 translation problems of the corpus which were interpreted as being supraindividual on the basis of the 25% boundary. In order to find out with what degree these 72 translation problems are supraindividual, three groups were formed:

i. Problems which occurred with at least *one third* of the subjects who translated a given text;

ii. Problems which occurred with at least *half* of the subjects who translated a given text;

iii. Problems which occurred with at least *two thirds* of the subjects who translated a given text.

Group i. contains 62 problems, thus amounting to 86% (with reference to all the 72 supraindividual problems). Group ii. comprises 39 problems and thus a percentage of 54. In other words, more than half of the supraindividual translation problems occur with half or more than half of the subjects of a given text. Group iii. contains 7 problems which make up a percentage of 10.

On balance, the result of this section is the fact that the translation problems which the subjects of this investigation were confronted with are highly individual. This applies especially to the translations *into* the mother tongue of the texts 5, 6, and 7, as pointed out above. Whether the same or similar also applies to the *translation strategies* which are employed in order to solve the *translation problems* will be discussed in section 6.3.6.

6.3 Translation Strategies

Now that the translation *problems* contained in the data corpus have been analyzed in the preceding section, the *strategies* used by the subjects to solve these problems will be considered in this section. The *qualitative* analysis carried out in Chapter 5 has yielded a differentiation of types of strategies with different internal structures. In the following sections, a *quantitative* analysis of the different translation strategies will be made in order to gain insights into the frequency and distribution of the strategies in the corpus, their internal structuring, and into how successfully they are employed by the subjects for solving translation problems.

6.3.1 Preliminary Remarks

As pointed out in section 5.2, translation strategies can occur as basic, expanded, and complex structures. According to a generative principle, complex structures are built up of several basic and/or expanded structures. The quantitative analysis carried out in the following section includes all the basic and expanded structures of the types I. to V. which occur in the corpus. The complex structures, however, cannot be analyzed in such an extensive and detailed way. As pointed out in section 5.2.3, complex structures can be built up in very many different ways. As a result of their diversity, it would hardly be fruitful to divide them into types. Not only would such an endeavour be extremely laborious, since the types derived in this way would be very large in number, but it would also hardly be sensible because it would scarcely yield any generalizable results. For these reasons, the complex structures will not be analyzed quantitatively with respect to their entire internal organization. The analysis carried out in the following sections will restrict itself to the number, the distribution, and the success of the complex structures in the translations as well as to their essential elements[7].

6.3.2 Basic and Expanded Structures I–V

The forty-five translations which constitute the corpus of investigation contain 399 strategies altogether. 248 (= 62%) of them occur in the translations *from* the mother tongue, and 151 (= 38%) occur in the translations *into* the mother tongue. In other words, each of the twenty-five translations *from* the mother tongue contains an average of ten, and each of the translation *into* the mother tongue contains an average of eight translation strategies[8].

The 399 translation strategies are employed by the subjects in order to solve 282 (= 70.68%) lexical, 85 (= 21.30%) lexico-syntactic, and 32 (= 8.02%) syntactic problems. If the translation strategies are differentiated according to the *direction* of the translations in which they occur, the following values are obtained:

Translations *from* the mother tongue: The 248 strategies are used to solve 172 (= 69.35%) lexical, 56 (= 22.58%) lexico-syntactic, and 20 (= 8.06%) syntactic problems.

Translations *into* the mother tongue: The 151 strategies are employed to solve 110 (= 72.85%) lexical, 29 (= 19.21%) lexico-syntactic, and 12 (= 7.95%) syntactic problems.

Of the 399 strategies documented, 286 are basic or expanded structures. This is surprising in so far as the subjects employed *linguistically* simple strategies in about 70% of the cases in order to solve the problems they were faced with during the translations, and only in about 30% of the cases did they use *linguistically* complex strategies. However, what was pointed out in section 5.2.3, must be taken into consideration, i.e. the fact that *linguistically* simple strategies need not necessarily be regarded as simple and *linguistically* complex strategies as complex by the subjects during the translations. The same applies to the translation problems. Those which are addressed by means of simple and complex strategies respectively, need not necessarily be regarded as simple and complex respectively, by the subjects.

The distribution and the percentages of the basic and expanded structures on the one hand, and of the complex structures on the other yield a further important insight into the translation process. As pointed out in section 5.2.3, basic and expanded structures constitute complex structures. Therefore, a basic or expanded structure followed by at least one more basic or expanded structure must be produced so that a complex structure can be constituted. Thus, when

---

7 Cf. section 6.3.5 for more detailed information.

8 Individually caused differences in the use of strategies will be dealt with in section 6.3.7.

a subject achieves a solution to a problem or realizes its insolubility by means of a basic or expanded structure, the translation strategy is terminated. As mentioned above, this applies to ca. 72% of all the translation strategies, and thus also of the instances of translation problems[9].

When a subject cannot bring about a solution to a translation problem by means of a simple or expanded structure but continues his/her problem-solving activities and produces (a) further basic or expanded structure(s), a complex structure is thus constituted. Therefore, the assumption suggests itself that the high percentage of basic and expanded structures in the corpus indicates the fact that the subjects can either solve the great majority of the problems they face or realize their insolubility after having made a comparatively low strategic effort. Only relatively few translation problems require a high strategic effort before they can be solved or their insolubility be realized.

Of the 286 basic and expanded structures of the corpus, 171 occur in the translations *from* the mother tongue and 115 in the translations *into* the mother tongue. In other words, about 69% of all the strategies contained in the translations *from* the mother tongue and about 76 of all the strategies contained in the translations *into* the mother tongue realize basic or expanded structures. For reasons of clarity, the exact numerical values and percentages which are important for the quantitative analysis of the basic and expanded structures are recorded in the following diagram.

Diagram 18: ***Basic and Expanded Structures in the Translations from and into the Mother Tongue***

Strategies in Translations *From* Mother Tongue		Strategies - Total		Strategies in Translations *Into* Mother Tongue
248		399		151
	62.16%		37.84%	
68.95%		71.68%		76.16%
	59.79%		40.21%	
171		286		115
Basic and Expanded Structures in Translations *From* Mother Tongue		Basic and Expanded Structures - Total		Basic and Expanded Structures in Translations *Into* Mother Tongue

As shown in the diagram, the percentage of basic and expanded structures in the translations *into* the mother tongue is about 7% higher than the percentage of these structures in the translations *from* the mother tongue. If one additionally takes into account the fact that the translations *into* the mother tongue

9 The minimal difference between the number of instances of translation problems (394) and the number of times a problem is addressed, which corresponds to the number of translation strategies (399), is neglected here.

contain an average of eight and the translations *from* the mother tongue an average of ten strategies, the assumption seems justified that the effort which the subjects must make to solve the problems of the translations *into* the mother tongue is slightly lower than for the problems in the translations *from* the mother tongue. Just as significant differences cannot be detected for translation strategies, they cannot be detected for translation problems.

Further-reaching conclusions about the translations from and into the mother tongue, *in general*, would be of a purely speculative kind.

The entire number of basic and expanded structures in the corpus (= 286) comprises both the successful structures, i.e. those which bring about a solution to a problem, and the unsuccessful ones. Further remarks on the success of translation strategies will be made in section 6.3.4. In this section, the distribution of the basic and expanded structures over the five structural types is considered. As these types are defined primarily with regard to their success, and since only a small percentage of these structures is unsuccessful[10], those cases will be discussed in the following part of this section in which the five structural types bring about a solution to the respective problem.

Type I : RP – (P)SP#; 18 times (= 4.51% of all the strategies)

In the translations *from* the mother tongue, this structural type occurs 6 times, corresponding to 2.42% of all the respective translation strategies. The pure form of this type can be found once, in the other five cases, bound elements are appended to the structure.

The translations *into* the mother tongue contain twelve type I basic structures which amount to 7.95% of all the respective strategies. The pure form of this type occurs 4 times, other forms with bound and/or embedded elements can be found eight times.

By means of type I strategies, the subjects solve 16 lexical, 1 lexico-syntactic, and 1 purely syntactic problem(s).

As the numbers and percentages reveal, translation strategies of this type occur rather infrequently. It can be assumed that the translation problems which are solved by means of these strategies are retrieval problems. The structural simplicity of type I is one reason for this assumption. Structures of this type do not contain elements which capture specific problem-solving activities of a subject. Rather, the assumption suggests itself that a TL text segment which the subject considers equivalent to a respective SL one is stored in the subject's memory but is temporarily not accessible to him or her. By putting the problematic SL item into the focus of cognitive attention, the subject succeeds in making the equivalent TL element accessible to him or her, possibly via a process of association.

10 Cf. sections 5.2.3 and 6.3.4.

This hypothetical assumption is also backed up by the fact that 16 of the 18 problems (= 88.89%) which are solved by using type I strategies are of a lexical kind. It can be expected, if not regarded an observational fact, that TL equivalents for SL lexemes are stored in memory and can be temporarily inaccessible to a subject.

The case that TL equivalents for SL syntactic structures are stored in memory and that a subject can retrieve these structures without any specific problem-solving activities is, however, much less probable and likely to occur more rarely.

As concerns the direction of the translations, it can be observed that type I structures occur about three times more frequently in the translations *into* the mother tongue (7.95%) than in the translations *from* the mother tongue (2.42%). If the hypothetical explanation given above is applied to this empirical fact, the assumption is justified that the subjects succeed better and more frequently in retrieving and making accessible to them items of their mother tongue than items of a foreign language. If this hypothesis can be corroborated by further empirical investigations, the assumption suggests itself that knowledge structures of the mother tongue and of a foreign language are stored in a (partially) different way, and/or that their accessing characteristics and conditions are (partially) different. Evidence for this assumption also comes from the network conceptions of human memory[11]. According to these, it is not single, unconnected elements of information which are stored in memory, but connected networks of information. For the knowledge structures of the mother tongue, the networks are more close-knit than for those of a foreign language.

In order to make information stored in memory accessible, the respective network within which the information is stored is activated. Closed-meshed networks have a much larger number of 'knots' from where activation can spread and reach the sought-for information in the end[12]. Thus, the chances of making a mother tongue item accessible to oneself within a very short period of time seem to be better, at least in principle, than is the case with foreign language items.

Type II : RP – –→SP – (P)SP#; 106 times (= 26.57% of all the strategies)

In the translations *from* the mother tongue, this type occurs 56 times, which amounts to 22.58% of all the respective strategies. The pure form of type II can be found 30 times; 22 cases contain bound and/or embedded elements, and expanded type II structures occur 4 times.

11 Cf. e.g. Dörner 1976: 31ff.; Jüttner 1979: 111ff., as well as the concepts of *script* (Schank/Abelson 1977), *frame* (Minsky 1975), and *schema* (Rumelhart 1975; 1980). Cf. also section 4.4.1.

12 Cf. Dörner 1976: 31ff. and section 4.4.1.

The translations *into* the mother tongue contain 50 structures of this type: 23 pure forms, 21 basic and 6 expanded structures with bound and/or embedded elements.

The 50 type II structures correspond to 33.11% of all the strategies in the translations into the mother tongue. By means of type II structures, 77 lexical problems (= 72.64%), 21 lexico-syntactic (= 19.81%), and 8 syntactic problems (= 7.55%) are solved.

Among the basic and expanded structures of the corpus, this type is most frequently to be found. More than a quarter of the translation strategies belong to it. It differs from type I by an additional phase of searching for a solution to the problem.

When a subject does not succeed in finding a TL equivalent to an SL item solely by putting the problematic item into his/her focus of attention, the subject can initiate a phase of searching as a specific problem-solving activity. It is indicated by a filled or unfilled pause. According to the definition in section 5.2.2, its minimum duration is three seconds. On average, phases of searching for a solution to a problem last eight seconds, although some can be found in the corpus which have a duration of a hundred and more seconds.

As pointed out above, the translation problems which are solved by using type I strategies are mainly retrieval problems. A target-language equivalent to a source-language lexeme is stored in memory and is made accessible. Translation problems which are addressed by type II strategies are only in part retrieval problems for lexeme equivalents. As the data suggest, subjects have often not stored lexeme equivalents. In order to be able to solve the respective problem, nonetheless, it can be necessary to work out an (approximative) paraphrase in the target-language. Especially in the 52 cases in which type II strategies with bound elements, embeddings, and/or expansions are used the subjects succeed in finding such paraphrases, and thus solutions to the respective problems.

In contrast to type I strategies, with which almost exclusively lexical problems are addressed, type II strategies are used to solve all kinds of problems. The percentages of the types of problems which are solved by type II strategies is almost the same as in the entire corpus: 77 (= 72.64%) lexical, 21 (= 19.81%) lexico-syntactic, and 8 (= 7.55%) syntactic problems. This empirical fact supports my assumption that type II strategies are not only used to solve retrieval problems but also problems for whose solution processes of construction or of syntactic or semantic paraphrasing are required.

As concerns the direction of the translations, type II strategies are preferred when addressing problems in translations *into* the mother tongue. Their percentage amounts to 33.11. In the translations *from* the mother tongue, 22.58% of all the strategies used belong to type II, which makes a difference of more than 10%. This fact as well as the considerations made above in connection with type I suggest that the subjects are generally more successful in solving problems of translations *into* the mother tongue by linguistically simpler strategies than problems of translations *from* the mother tongue. This assumption is also supported by what was pointed out at the beginning of this section, i.e. the fact that the strategies contained in the translations *into* the mother tongue realize basic and expanded, and thus linguistically simpler, structures more often than the strategies contained in the translations *from* the mother tongue.

Type III : (RP) – VP – (P)SP#; 15 times (= 3.76% of all the strategies)

In the translations *from* the mother tongue, this type occurs 10 times, which corresponds to 4.03%. The pure form of type III can be found 4 times and in 6 cases the structures contain bound elements or embeddings.

In the translations *into* the mother tongue, this type occurs 5 times (= 3.31%). Three of the structures are pure forms, one contains an embedded, and one a bound element. Type III strategies are employed to solve 12 (= 80%) lexical and 3 (= 20%) lexico-syntactic problems.

With a percentage of less than 4, this is the least frequently occurring type of structure. It differs from type I only by an additional verbalization of the respective problem. When a subject does not succeed in finding a TL equivalent to an SL item solely by putting the problematic item into his/her focus of attention, the subject can verbalize the SL item as a specific problem-solving activity. The verbalization results in a (further) mental focussing on the problem.

As will be discussed in detail in Chapter 7, verbalizations of problems can have various functions. As far as retrieval problems are concerned, one of them most probably coincides with what was pointed out by Dörner (1976: 53) in a different context.

> *Die Symbole der Sprache sind nicht nur ein zweites Signalsystem in dem Sinne, daß Inhalte durch Symbole aufgerufen werden können. Darüberhinaus stellt die Sprache ein zweites Übergangssystem von Gedächtnisinhalt zu Gedächtnisinhalt dar, und damit wird die Fähigkeit, Gedächtnisinhalte zu suchen, gewaltig gesteigert.*

Thus, according to Dörner, information stored in memory can be accessed efficiently by means of verbalizing other information which is, in some way, connected with the sought-for information.

A further function of verbalizations of a problem is to separate SL forms from their sense. On the basis of the sense constituted in this way, TL equivalents can then be searched for or worked out (cf. Chapter 7).

Both these functions of verbalizations mainly refer to lexical problems. Thus, it is not surprising that 80% of all the problems which are addressed by type III strategies are lexical problems. The remaining 20% are lexico-syntactic problems. Type III strategies are not used to solve syntactic problems. They obviously require different strategic measures, such as specific phases of searching, breaking a problem into parts and solving them successively.

In the translations *from* the mother tongue, type III structures have a percentage of 4.03 and in the translations *into* the mother tongue, their percentage is 3.31. This minimal difference, however, can hardly be interpreted as being an indicator of anything.

Type IV : ((RP) – (→SP)) – VP – (→SP) – (P)SP#; 61 times (= 15.29% of all the strategies)

In the translations *from* the mother tongue, this type occurs 38 times, which corresponds to 15.32%. The pure form of type IV can be found 10 times; 18 basic structures contain bound and/or embedded elements, and 10 expanded structures occur.

In the translations *into* the mother tongue, 23 type IV structures (= 15.23%) are contained. The pure form occurs 7 times, basic structures with bound and/or embedded elements 5 times, and expanded structures of type IV occur 11 times.

Type IV strategies are used to solve 53 lexical problems (= 86.89%), 4 lexico-syntactic (= 6.56%) and 4 syntactic problems (= 6.56%).

As the numerical values and percentages reveal, this is the type with the second highest frequency of occurrence in the data. Nearly every sixth translation strategy belongs to it. It differs from type I by an additional verbalization of the problem and one or two additional phases of searching for a solution.

When a subject does not succeed in finding a TL equivalent to an SL item solely by putting the problematic item into his/her focus of attention, specific problem-solving activities can follow. The subject can initiate a phase of searching for a solution (as in type II), or s/he can verbalize the problematic SL text segment. If both these strategic measures turn out to be unsuccessful, a further focussing on the problem can occur. In the case of type II, the phase of searching is followed by a verbalization of the problem and perhaps a further phase of searching for a solution. In the case of type III, the verbalization is followed by a phase of searching. Thus, type IV structures can be regarded as continuations of type II or type III structures. This is why they bring together the structural characteristics of these two types.

As with type III structures, the percentage of lexical problems which are addressed by type IV strategies is well above the average. It amounts to 86.89%, with the average being ca. 70%. Especially those lexical problems for which the subjects have no TL equivalents stored in memory and for whose solution paraphrasing and construction processes in the target-language are required, are solved by using type IV strategies.

In contrast to type III structures, the percentage of syntactic problems which are addressed by type IV strategies amounts to 6.56 and is thus hardly below the average (ca. 8%). The same applies to type II structures. Therefore, the assumption suggests itself that syntactic and other problems whose solution calls for mainly constructive procedures require strategies with specific phases of searching for a solution.

As concerns the direction of the translations, the percentages of type IV strategies in the translations *from* and *into* the mother tongue are nearly identical: 15.32 and 15.23 respectively.

Type V : a. **RP – (→SP) – (P)SPa – (→SP) – (P)SPb ...#; 41 times (= 10.28% of all strategies)**
b. **RP – (→SP) – VPa – (→SP) – (P)SPa – (→SP) – VPb (→SP) – (P)SPb ...#; 4 times (= 1.00% of all strategies)**
c. **RP – (→SP) – (VPa) – (→SP) – (P)SPa – (→SP) – (VPb) – (→SP) – (P)SPb ...#; 4 times (= 1.00% of all strategies)**

Types V occur 37 times (= 14.92%) in the translations *from* the mother tongue and 12 times (= 7.95%) in the translations *into* the mother tongue.

Strategies of the types V are used to address 14 lexical problems (= 28.57%), 28 lexico-syntactic (= 57.14%) and 7 syntactic problems (14.29%).

Type Va can be found 41 times, which corresponds to 83.67% of all type V structures. In the translations *from* the mother tongue, it occurs 32 times which amounts to 12.90% of all the strategies in the respective translations. The translations *into* the mother tongue contain 9 type Va structures, which corresponds to 5.96% of all the strategies in the translations into the mother tongue.

Type Va strategies are used to solve 10 lexical problems (= 24.39%), 24 lexico-syntactic (= 58.54%), and 7 syntactic problems (= 17.07%).

Type Vb occurs 4 times (= 8.16% of all type V structures). Both in the translations *from* and *into* the mother tongue it can be found 2 times. This corresponds to 0.81% of all the strategies in the translations *from* the mother tongue and to 1.32% of all the strategies in the translations *into* the mother tongue.

The 4 type Vb strategies are used to solve 2 lexical (= 50%) and 2 lexico-syntactic problems (= 50%).

Type Vc can also be found 4 times (= 8.16% of all type V structures). It occurs 3 times (= 1.21%) in the translations *from*, and once (= 0.66%) in the translations *into* the mother tongue.

Of the problems which are addressed by type Vc strategies, 3 (= 75%) are of a lexical, and 1 (= 25%) is of a lexico-syntactic kind.

As the numerical values and percentages reveal, nearly one eighth of the translation problems in the corpus are addressed by type V strategies. Among its subtypes (a, b, c), Va, with a percentage of 83.67, is by far the most frequently occurring.

Type V strategies are mainly used to solve complex problems if these can be split up into parts and solved successively. It is, therefore, not surprising that the percentage of the lexical problems which are solved by using type V strategies is only about 28, and thus 40% below average. The 14 lexical problems addressed are of a complex kind and mostly consist of several lexemes (e.g. *Eigenschaften und Merkmale* in T3, S13, Strategy 2) or compounds (e.g. *kommunikationsorientiert* in T3, S25, Strategy 17).

The numbers and percentages of lexico-syntactic and purely syntactic problems which are addressed by type V strategies are considerably above average. The lexico-syntactic problems amount to 57.14%, and thus 35% above average; the syntactic problems amount to 14.29%, and thus 9% above average.

Both the lexico-syntactic and the purely syntactic problems reveal a high degree of complexity and require mainly constructive procedures for their solution. Obviously, the problematic text segments do not function as units of translation. They are too large and/or too complex to be processed in one go. Rather, they are split into parts which can be handled by the processing system, successively transferred into TL and then joined together again. Type V strategies, therefore, seem to be very well suited for solving lexico-syntactic and syntactic problems.

This is especially true of the strategies of subtype Va. All the syntactic problems and nearly 86% of the lexico-syntactic problems which are split up into parts in order to be solved are addressed by means of strategies belonging to subtype V.

Subtypes Vb. and Vc. can only be found 4 times each in the corpus. They are used to solve 4 lexico-syntactic and 4 lexical problems. The verbalizations of problems (VP) which are contained in these structures bring about a further focussing on the parts of the problems and seem to favour the solution of lexical problems.

This may be an explanation of the fact that, as regards Vb. and Vc., the percentages of the lexical problems amount to 50% each, which is more than twice as high as with Va. (= 24.39%).

As concerns the direction of the translation, it is remarkable that the percentage of the type V strategies in the translations *from* the mother tongue amounts to 14.92, and is thus nearly twice as high as the respective percentage in the translations *into* the mother tongue (= 7.95%). The frequency of occurrence of the three types of problems in all the translations *from* and *into* the mother tongue is, however, almost equal. This suggests the assumption that the problems in the translations *into* the mother tongue require less and/or linguistically simpler strategies for their solution than the problems in the translations *from* the mother tongue. As pointed out above, the structurally simple types I and II do indeed occur with a considerably higher percentage in the translations *into* than *from* the mother tongue. This is especially true for the syntactic and lexico-syntactic problems of the translations *into* the mother tongue. Of the syntactic problems 50%, and of the lexico-syntactic ones 55% are solved by means of type I and type II structures, i.e. by strategies which seem to be almost exclusively (type I) or mostly (type II) suitable for addressing retrieval problems and not for addressing those problems whose solution requires the use of complex, constructive procedures.

The distribution of the types of problems addressed by type V strategies reveals further differences between the translations *from* and *into* the mother tongue. In the translations *from* the mother tongue, the syntactic problems which are solved by type V strategies amount to 16.22%, and thus more than 8% above the mean of all strategy types. In the translations *into* the mother tongue, the percentage of the syntactic problems solved by type V strategies amounts to 8.33, which largely corresponds to the mean. The mixed lexico-syntactic problems have a frequency of 58.33%, a percentage which is only slightly higher than the respective value in the translations *from* the mother tongue.

The percentage of the lexical problems in the translations *into* the mother is, however, more than 6% higher than in the translations *from* the mother tongue.

All these findings support my assumption that in the translations *into* the mother tongue, the subjects generally succceed better in solving their problems by means of structurally simple strategies than in the translations *from* the mother tongue. This applies especially to the syntactic problems. Their solution obviously requires fewer and/or linguistically less complex constructive procedures from the subjects than the syntactic problems in the translations *from* the mother tongue.

The assumption made above also seems plausible in view of the well-known observational fact that syntactic construction processes in the mother tongue are in general (psychologically) less complex than in a foreign language when the same information is to be verbalized.

The fact that type V strategies are used to solve 6% more lexical problems in the translation *into* than *from* the mother tongue may partly be explained by the higher frequency of lexical problems in the translations *into* the mother tongue. And as the percentage of the type V strategies employed for their solution is well above average, it can be hypothesized that the respective lexical problems are of a complex kind and can only be solved by the subjects by means of constructive procedures. The available data corroborate this hypothesis. Most of the lexical problems consist of two elements (e.g. *Sale* of *Honours*, *logic-chopping*) one or both of which is or are known to the subjects. But when translated into the target-language, these two elements do not combine to make an adequate TL text segment. In order to solve such problems, a process of formulating in the target-language is initiated in which the subjects try to construct an adequate text segment in their mother tongue (= target-language) by means of paraphrasing.

Summing up, it can be pointed out that 249 (successful) basic and expanded structures have been quantitatively analyzed in this section. This number corresponds to a percentage of 62.41 of all the translation strategies in the corpus. In the translations *from* the mother tongue, 147 (= 59.27%) basic and expanded structures occur. The translations *into* the mother tongue contain 102 of these structures, which amounts to 67.55% of all the strategies in the respective translations. The fact that the percentage of the basic and expanded structures in the translations *into* the mother tongue is more than 8% higher than in the translations *from* the mother tongue corroborates my hypothesis that the solution of the problems contained in the translations *into* the mother tongue generally requires linguistically less complex strategies than the solutions of the problems contained in the translations *from* the mother tongue.

6.3.3 Complex Structures

In addition to the 286 basic and expanded structures, 113 complex structures can be found in the corpus. They amount to 28% of all the translation strategies. Of the 113 complex structures, 77 (= 68%) occur in the translations *from* the mother tongue, and 36 (= 31%) in the translations *into* the mother tongue. For reasons of clarity, the exact numerical values and percentages are visualized in the following diagram.

Diagram 19: Complex Structures in the Translation from and into the Mother Tongue

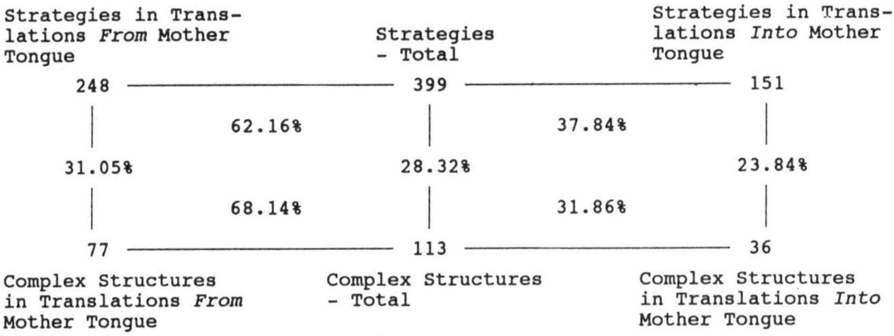

As shown in the diagram, complex structures occur 7% more frequently in the translations *from* than *into* the mother tongue. This finding supports the assumption made in the preceding section, that the subjects generally succeed better in solving their problems in the translations *into* than *from* the mother tongue. The numbers and percentages in diagram 19 can be differentiated according to the three types of problems. This yields the following insights:

In the translations *from* the mother tongue, 46 (= 68.66%) lexical problems, 16 (= 23.88%) lexico-syntactic, and 5 (= 7.46%) purely syntactic problems are solved by means of complex structures. The respective percentages of the types of problems are nearly identical with those of the distribution of the basic and expanded structures in the translations *from* the mother tongue, as well as with the distribution of the types of problems in the whole of the corpus. A preference in the use of complex structures for solving a certain type of problem in the translations *from* the mother tongue cannot be detected in the data.

The complex structures which occur in the translations *into* the mother tongue are used to solve 26 (= 83.87%) lexical problems, 2 (= 6.45%) lexico-syntactic, and 3 (= 9.68%) purely syntactic problems. Here, the distribution of the types of problems differs considerably from that in the basic and expanded structures. The frequency of the lexical problems is 13% higher among the complex structures; and it is 15% higher for the lexico-syntactic problems among the basic and expanded structures.

This finding also supports the hypothesis that in the translations *into* the mother tongue more lexical problems require complex strategies for their solution than in the translations *from* the mother tongue. The hypothesis can now be supplemented by a further hypothesis according to which considerably fewer lexico-syntactic problems are addressed by complex strategies in the translations *into* than *from* the mother tongue. This correlates with the fact that complex structures occur 7% more frequently in the translations *into* than *from* the mother tongue.

6.3.4 On the Success of Translation Strategies

In the two preceding sections, basic, expanded, and complex structures of translation strategies were quantitatively analyzed. The question of whether and to what extent the various structures were successful, i.e. brought about (preliminary/partial) solutions to a translation problem, remained open however. In the following subsections, the concept of 'success' which is used in this study will be discussed and critically commented upon, and the translation strategies in the data corpus will be quantitatively analyzed with regard to their success.

6.3.4.1 Preliminary Remarks on the Concept of 'Success'

In the preceding chapters, it has been pointed out several times that, because of the psycholinguistic orientation of this study, the analysis of translation performance is carried out from the perspective of the subjects as hypothetically reconstructed by the analyst. This also applies to the various concepts used. Accordingly, the observations on the success of translation strategies which will be made in the following section are based on a concept of success which is oriented towards what the *subjects* consider success. Thus, translation strategies are successful to the extent to which the subjects succeed in bringing about *what to them* are partial, preliminary or final solutions to translation problems.

It is evident that what the subjects consider to be successful and what the analyst does often do not coincide. It is just as evident and can be documented empirically that subjects more often than not find target-language text segments which they consider to be solutions to problems but which apparently are translation errors. Strategies which bring about such 'solutions' are to be considered successful, nonetheless, in view of the concept of success used here.

It would certainly be interesting and informative to compare what the subjects consider to be solutions to their translation problems with what professional translators and/or bilingual informants would consider to be solutions. Such a comparison, however, is beyond the scope of this investigation.

6.3.4.2 Successful and Unsuccessful Translation Strategies

Of the 399 translation strategies contained in the corpus, 346 are successful in so far as they result in a preliminary, partial or ultimate solution to a translation problem. This corresponds to a percentage of nearly 87. Thus, from the perspective of the subjects, it can be pointed out that the translation strategies they employed are extremely successful. Only one of ten translation problems remains unsolved in the end. The following diagram captures the numerical values and percentages of the successful basic, expanded and complex structures.

Diagram 20: Successful Basic, Expanded, and Complex Structures of Translation Strategies

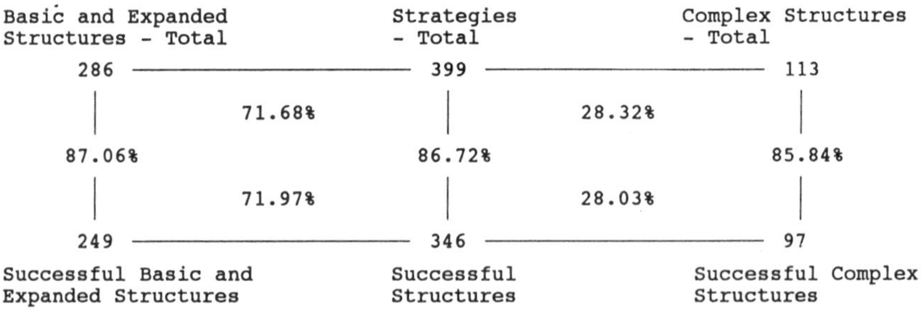

As the diagram shows, the basic and expanded structures (87.06%) are about as successful as the complex structures (85.84%). Furthermore, the percentage of the basic and expanded structures among the successful translation strategies amounts to 71.97 and is thus almost identical with the percentage of the basic and expanded structures total among the strategies total (71.68). The same applies to the complex structures. The relevant percentages are 28.03 and 28.32 respectively.

This finding is surprising when one takes into consideration the fact that complex structures consist of basic and expanded structures. When a subject, after having addressed a problem by a basic or expanded structure, cannot bring about a solution to the problem but continues with his/her strategic activities, the chances that s/he will find a solution by further addressing the problem are just as good as with the first addressing of the problem. This emphasizes the efficiency of the subjects' mental problem-solving system.

The success of the translation strategies, specified with regard to the direction of the translations, is documented in the following two diagrams:

Diagram 21: Successful Basic, Expanded, and Complex Structures in the Translations from the Mother Tongue

Basic and Expanded Structures - Total		Strategies - Total		Complex Structures - Total
171		248		77
	68.95%		31.05%	
85.96%		86.29%		87.01%
	68.69%		31.31%	
147		214		67
Successful Basic and Expanded Structures		Successful Structures		Successful Complex Structures

Diagram 22: Successful Basic, Expanded, and Complex Structures in the Translations into the Mother Tongue

Basic and Expanded Structures - Total		Strategies - Total		Complex Structures - Total
115		151		36
	76.16%		23.84%	
88.70%		88.08%		86.11%
	76.69%		23.31%	
102		133		31
Successful Basic and Expanded Structures		Successful Structures		Successful Complex Structures

As the diagrams show, the strategies in the translations *into* the mother tongue are a little more successful than the strategies in the translations *from* the mother tongue. In the former, the subjects succeed in solving 88% of the translation problems, in the latter the percentage of successful strategies amounts to 86. When specified with respect to basic, expanded, and complex structures, the differences between the translations *from* and *into* the mother tongue are more striking. The percentages reveal that in the translations *into* the mother tongue 7% more basic and expanded structures (and consequently 7% fewer complex structures) are employed by the subjects than in the translations *from* the mother tongue. This has already been pointed out in the previous section. Here, it is of special interest that the percentage of the successful basic and expanded structures in the translations *into* the mother tongue is even 8% higher (and consequently that of the complex structures 8% lower) than in the translations *from* the mother tongue.

This finding again confirms my hypothesis that in the translations *into* the mother tongue linguistically less complex strategies are used in general. The hypothesis must be supplemented here by an essential insight contained in the diagrams 20 and 21. Not only are the strategies in the translations *into* the mother tongue less complex, but they are also a little more successful than the more complex strategies in the translations *from* the mother tongue.

In the sections 6.3.2 and 6.3.3, the successful basic, expanded, and complex structures were discussed with respect to the types of problems solved by using these structures. In the following part of this section, the *un*successful translation strategies will be discussed.

In the translations *from* the mother tongue, 34 strategies remain unsuccessful, 24 of which were realized as basic or expanded structures. They can be differentiated according to the structural types as follows:

Type IV	(+ expanded element(s)/ + embedded element(s)/ + Bound element(s)):	22 =	91.67%
Type V	(+ expanded element(s)/ + embedded element(s)/ + bound element(s)):	1 =	4.17%
Type II	(+ expanded element(s)/ + embedded element(s)/ + bound element(s)):	1 =	4.17%

As can be seen, all the unsuccessful basic and expanded structures belong to the linguistically more complex types of structures. This shows that the subjects generally do not give up before they have dealt with a problem intensively and directed specific problem-solving activities towards it.

In the translations *into* the mother tongue, 18 strategies remain unsuccessful, 13 of which belong to the following types of basic and expanded structure:

Type IV	(+ expanded element(s)/ + embedded element(s)/ + bound element(s)):	7 =	53.85%
Type III	(+ expanded element(s)/ + embedded element(s)/ + bound element(s)):	3 =	23.08%
Type V	(+ expanded element(s)/ + embedded element(s)/ + bound element(s)):	2 =	15.38%
Type I	(+ embedded element(s)/ + bound element(s))[13]:	1 =	7.69%

This again shows what has been pointed out in connection with the translations *from* the mother tongue: The subjects generally do not give up before they have dealt with a problem intensively and directed specific problem-solving activities towards it. Such activities can be the intensive searching for a sol-

13 By definition, type I structures cannot contain expanded elements. Cf. section 5.2.3.

ution, (multiple) verbalizations of the problem, or the splitting of the problem into its parts in order to solve these successively.

The differentiation of the unsuccessful translation strategies according to the types of problems yields further interesting insights.

The unsuccessful strategies of the translations *from* the mother tongue are used to address 34 problems, which amounts to a percentage of 13.71 for all the respective strategies. Of the 34 problems which remained unsolved, 26 are lexical, 5 are lexico-syntactic, and 3 are purely syntactic problems. This means that 15.12% of the lexical problems, 8.92% of the lexico-syntactic, and 15.00% of the syntactic problems in the translations *from* the mother tongue remain unsolved. Thus, the percentages of the lexical and syntactic problems are slightly above the mean (13.71%), whereas the percentage of the lexico-syntactic problems is almost 5% below the mean.

Of the 34 unsolved problems, 24 were addressed by basic and expanded structures. In other words, 70% of the unsolved problems in the translations *from* the mother tongue result from unsuccessful basic or expanded structures, and 30% from unsuccessful complex structures. This ratio largely corresponds to that of all the basic and expanded structures to all the complex structures.

Among the problems addressed by the unsuccessful basic and expanded structures, the lexical represent the overwhelming majority (22 = 91.67%). Only 1 lexico-syntactic and 1 purely syntactic problem occurs, which amounts to a percentage of 4.17 each. The lexico-syntactic and syntactic problems which remain unsolved as a result of unsuccessful basic or expanded structures make a percentage of 2 and 5 respectively with regard to the total of lexico-syntactic and syntactic problems. The respective percentage of the lexical problems (12.79) is considerably higher but still below the percentage of *all* the unsolved problems in the translations *from* the mother tongue (13.71).

As regards the complex structures, 10 cases which do not bring about a solution can be found in the translations *from* the mother tongue. Among the complex structures, 13% are unsuccessful, which is a little below the respective percentage of the basic and expanded structures (14). Of the 10 problems which were addressed by complex structures but remained unsolved, 4 (= 40%) are lexical and lexico-syntactic, and 2 (= 20%) are purely syntactic.

In the translations *into* the mother tongue, 18 strategies are unsuccessful. The 18 problems which remain unsolved amount to a percentage of 11.92 of all the problems in the translations *into* the mother tongue. This percentage largely corresponds to the respective value for the translations *from* the mother tongue (13.71%). Differences become apparent, however, when the values are differentiated according to the types of problems. In the translations *into* the mother tongue, 12 lexical problems (= 10.91% of all the problems in the translations *into* the mother tongue) remain unsolved, 5 lexico-syntactic problems (= 17.24%), and 1 syntactic problem (= 8.33%).

The numbers and percentages above show that the frequency of the unsolved lexical and syntactic problems is a little below the mean, whilst that of the lexico-syntactic problems is 4% above the mean. The same deviations, but in reverse order (excess of lexical and syntactic problems), were previously found for the translations *from* the mother tongue.

Of the 18 unsolved problems in the translations *into* the mother tongue, 13 (= 72.22%) were addressed by basic and expanded structures, and 5 (= 27.78%) by complex structures. This ratio is nearly identical to that for the translations *from* the mother tongue and to that for the total of basic and expanded structures to complex structures.

The unsuccessful basic and expanded structures were used to address 9 lexical, 3 lexico-syntactic, and 1 syntactic problem(s). The respective percentages amount to 69.23, 23.08, and 7.69, and thus largely correspond to those of the problems in the entire corpus.

As concerns the use of unsuccessful complex structures in the translations *into* the mother tongue, 5 cases can be found. By means of complex structures, 3 lexical (= 60%) and 2 lexico-syntactic problems (= 40%) could not be solved. Thus 13% of complex structures are unsuccessful being a little above the percentage of unsuccessful basic and expanded structures (11%). The reverse was found in connection with the translations *from* the mother tongue. The differences, however, are so slight that any generalizing conclusions drawn from these findings would be purely speculative.

The considerations made above lead to the following main results: Basic, expanded, and complex structures have an almost identical success rate in the translations *from* and *into* the mother tongue. The most successfully addressed type of problem is the lexico-syntactic one in the translations *from* the mother tongue (91.07%), and the syntactic one in the translations *into* the mother tongue (91.67%). The least successfully addressed type of problem is the lexical one in the translations *from* the mother tongue (84.88%), and the lexico-syntactic one in the translations *into* the mother tongue (82.76%). The latter percentage must be seen in the light of what was pointed out in section 6.3.3, i.e. the fact that the basic and expanded structures are used with a 15% higher frequency in addressing the lexico-syntactic problems in the translations *into* the mother tongue than the complex structures. Possibly, the more frequent use of complex structures would have resulted in a higher success rate.

6.3.5 Elements of Translation Strategies

In the preceding sections, the translation strategies which can be detected in the corpus were analyzed quantitatively in various respects. The elements of the translation strategies and their function(s) in the respective structure, however, have not yet been considered. This will be done in the following sections. The elements of translation strategies which will be investigated in detail are Checking, Monitoring, Rephrasing, and Multiple Verbalizations of Problems. They can occur within and between basic, expanded, and complex structures, and can function as bound or free elements or as embeddings. One reason for investigating these particular elements in detail is the fact that they are the most frequently occurring ones; another reason is the fact that they have discernible functions within the problem-solving process. In addition to their frequency and distribution over the translations *from* and *into* the mother tongue, and over the types of problems, the elements of strategies selected will be analyzed according to the following criteria:

i. **their occurrence within the strategies;** this applies to Monitoring (MSL, MTL), Rephrasing (REPHR.SL, REPHR.TL), and to Multiple Verbalizations of translation problems;

ii. **the text segments which they embrace;** this applies to Monitoring (MSL, MTL) and Rephrasing (REPHR.SL, REPHR.TL);

iii. **their structure;** this applies to Multiple Verbalizations of translation problems;

iv. **their surroundings within the respective structure;** this applies to Monitoring (MSL, MTL) and Rephrasing (REPHR.SL, REPHR.TL);

v. **their types;** this applies to Rephrasing (REPHR.SL) and Checking;

vi. **their success;** this applies to Monitoring (MSL, MTL), Rephrasing (REPHR.SL, REPHR.TL), and to Multiple Verbalizations of translation problems.

6.3.5.1 CHECK

According to the definition given in section 5.2.2, CHECK means the testing of (preliminary) solutions to translation problems. When a subject tests the adequacy of a TL text segment which does *not* result from the use of a translation strategy but from a partly or fully automatized and unproblematic retrieval process, this is not a case of CHECK in the sense of the definition. Such kinds of testing, which sometimes occur in the data corpus, are not investigated here. As they are elements of non-strategic phases of translation, they are outside the aim and epistemological interest of this study.

In the corpus of investigation, 122 instances of CHECK occur. They are distributed over 104 translation strategies. In other words, in about a quarter (26.07%) of the strategies, an average of 1.17 instances of testing (preliminary) solutions are contained. As a result of the checking, the (preliminary) solution can be corroborated (CHECK+) or rejected (CHECK-). In the latter case, the subject either tries to work out another (preliminary) solution or the problem remains unsolved.

Checks which result in a corroboration of (preliminary) solution, i.e. CHECK+, represent the majority of the cases. They occur 67 times corresponding to a percentage of 54.92. If one considers the types of problems whose (preliminary) solutions are tested, it can be noticed that their percentage distribution largely corresponds to that of the types of problems in the entire corpus. CHECK+ occurs 47 times (= 70.15%) after lexical problems, 16 times (= 23.88%) after lexico-syntactic, and 4 times (= 5.97%) after syntactic problems. If, however, one differentiates according to the direction of the translations, considerable differences become apparent. In the translations *from* the mother tongue, CHECK+ is distributed as follows:

After (preliminary) solutions to lexical problems:	30 =	65.22%
After (preliminary) solutions to lexico-syntactic problems:	13 =	28.26%
After (preliminary) solutions to syntactic problems:	3 =	6.52%

This distribution is similar to that of the types of problems in the entire corpus. However, the lexico-syntactic problems are overrepresented by 6%, whereas the lexical and syntactic problems are underrepresented by 5% and 1% respectively.

This finding naturally corresponds to a high degree with the results yielded by the analysis of the successful strategies. As pointed out in subsection 6.3.4.2, the lexico-syntactic problems can be solved with the highest, and the lexical problems with the lowest success rate in the translations *from* the mother tongue. In the translations *into* the mother tongue, CHECK+ is distributed in a different way. It occurs:

After (preliminary) solutions to lexical problems:	17 =	80.95%
After (preliminary) solutions to lexico-syntactic problems:	3 =	14.29%
After (preliminary) solutions to syntactic problems:	1 =	4.76%

This percentage distribution differs considerably from that in the translations *from* the mother tongue. The percentage of the lexical problems is more than 15 above the respective value in the translations *from* the mother tongue and almost 11 above that in the entire corpus. The lexico-syntactic and the purely syntactic problems are accordingly underrepresented. The percentage of the former is only half as great as the respective percentage in the translations *from* the mother tongue, and about 8% below that in the entire corpus. The percentage of the latter is almost 2% below the respective one in the translations *from* the mother tongue, and more than 3% above that in the entire corpus.

If the findings above are compared with those on the success of the translation strategies, it becomes apparent that the lexico-syntactic problems in the translations *into* the mother tongue are not only the least successfully solved but also those which are the most underrepresented ones tested by CHECK+. The situation as regards syntactic problems is different. Although they are also underproportionally represented among those tested by CHECK+, they are the most successfully solved problems. As they are addressed by means of strategies which generally have a simpler structure than the respective strategies in the translations *from* the mother tongue, it can be assumed that the subjects also consider them relatively easy to solve. This might explain why the subjects, once they have found solutions to these problems, relatively seldom check them. The reverse may apply to many lexical problems. They require relatively complex strategies for their solution and are probably considered rather difficult to solve. As a result of this, solutions to lexical problems are frequently checked before the subjects acknowledge them to be solutions.

As concerns the structure of CHECK, the majority of instances belongs to the type CHECK SL/TL. In the translations *from* the mother tongue, 31 cases (= 67.39% of all instances of CHECK), and in the translations *into* the mother tongue, 34 cases (= 90.48%) occur. Obviously, this type of CHECK is considered to be especially appropriate for translation with its two languages involved.

CHECK TL/TL can be found 9 times (= 19.57%) in the translations *from* and 2 times (= 9.52%) in the translations *into* the mother tongue. This type of testing is mainly used when a subject has worked out two (preliminary) solutions and wants to find out which of the two is the most adequate.

Checks resulting in a rejection of a (preliminary) solution to a translation problem (= CHECK-) occur 55 times. This corresponds to a percentage of 45.08 of all instances of CHECK. When differentiated according to the types of problems whose (preliminary) solutions are checked, the following distribution occurs:

CHECK- in translations *from* the mother tongue	
After (preliminary) solutions to lexical problems:	28 = 65.12%
After (preliminary) solutions to lexico-syntactic problems:	12 = 27.91%
After (preliminary) solutions to syntactic problems:	3 = 6.98%

CHECK- in translations *into* the mother tongue	
After (preliminary) solutions to lexical problems:	10 = 83.33%
After (preliminary) solutions to lexico-syntactic problems:	2 = 16.67%
After (preliminary) solutions to syntactic problems:	0 = 0.00%

The distribution of the structural types of CHECK- shows similarities with that of CHECK+. The most frequently occurring type is CHECK SL/TL. It is used 34 times (= 79.07%) in the translations *from* and 11 times (= 91.67%) in the translations *into* the mother tongue. CHECK BSL/SL occurs 6 times in the translations *from* the mother tongue, which amounts to a percentage of 13.95. The other structural types of CHECK (TL/TL, TL/BSL, and CT) can only be found 1 or 2 times in the data corpus. As a consequence, their percentages are minimal and can be neglected here.

The similarities between CHECK+ and CHECK- with respect to their structure and the types of problems they capture are not surprising. Success or failure of a strategy is obviously the *result* of checking, and has thus no influence on the checking itself, as employed by the subjects.

As a result of the considerations made above it can be stated that CHECK occurs about 10% more frequently in the translations *from* than *into* the mother tongue. This may be explained by the fact that the effort the subjects must make to solve the problems in the translations *from* the mother tongue is slightly higher than in the reverse direction of translating, and that therefore the solutions to problems in the translations *from* the mother tongue are checked more frequently and more readily.

When a subject checks on the adequacy of a (preliminary) solution, s/he puts it into his/her focus of cognitive attention. As a result of this, the subject may either acknowledge the solution to be adequate, whereupon the strategy terminates successfully, or the subject realizes the inadequacy of the supposed solution, and may initiate a further problem-solving process. Its chances of bringing about a solution to the problem are relatively high. This can be interpreted from the fact that only in 6 cases (= 10.91%) did CHECK- lead to a definite zero solution to a problem (SPØ). In 49 cases (= 89.09%), however, an adequate solution could be found, nonetheless, after CHECK-.

Checks, therefore, can have two functions. They either corroborate solutions to translation problems, or they play a highly successful part in the process of working out new, adequate solutions.

6.3.5.2 MONITORING

The potential strategy element MONITORING was defined as exactly verbatim repetition of SL or TL text segments which a subject has already received in SL or verbalized in TL. As the instances of MONITORING of SL and TL text segments differ considerably with respect to their frequency of occurrence, their function and their distribution in the corpus, they will be investigated separately in the following subsections.

6.3.5.2.1 MONITORING of Source-Language Text Segments (MSL)

In the data corpus, 12 instances of MSL can be found. They are distributed over 11 strategies, which means that in fewer than 3% of the translation strategies, 1 instance of MSL occurs, on average. Thus, MSL is the least frequently occurring strategy element among those investigated here.

Monitorings of source-language text segments occur three times more frequently in the translations *into* (9) than *from* the mother tongue (3). This distribution can, above all, be explained by the fact that the source-language in the translations *into* the mother tongue is a foreign language (English) for the subjects. MSL is therefore mainly used when a subject is faced with a problem in the reception of a source- (= foreign) language text segment. By means of MONITORING, the subject concentrates on and verbalizes part of the context which precedes the problematic SL item. Thus, the respective stretch of SL discourse is put into the subject's focus of attention, as a result of which hints for a solution to the problem may be obtained.

MSL is used 9 times (= 75.00%) for addressing lexical, once (= 8.33%) for addressing lexico-syntactic, and twice (= 16.67%) for addressing syntactic problems. The excess of lexical and syntactic problems is even more striking in the translations *into* the mother tongue. Here, 7 of the 9 instances of MSL (= 77.78%) occur with lexical, and 2 (= 22.22%) with syntactic problems. This finding, as well as the hypothesis that MSL is mainly used when foreign language reception problems occur in the translations *into* the mother tongue, correlates highly with the thesis stated in section 6.3.2, according to which more complex strategies must be employed for the solution of more lexical problems in the translations *into* the mother tongue than in the translations *from* the mother tongue.

As concerns the *inter-* and *intra*strategic occurrence of MSL, a distinction is made between the process of the first addressing and the process of a further addressing of a translation problem. The first addressing of a problem is that strategic phase which ranges from the realization of a translation problem to its (partial/preliminary) solution or to the realization of its insolubility.

A further addressing of a problem is that strategic phase which follows a (preliminary/partial) solution or a zero-solution (SP∅).

By means of a further addressing of a problem, subjects attempt to find a solution to a problem or attempt to optimize a solution which they have already found.

MONITORING of SL text segments occurs 6 times in the process of the first and 6 times in the process of a further addressing of a translation problem.

If one differentiates according to the direction of the translation, it is noticeable that in the translations *into* the mother tongue, all the instances of MSL occur in the process of a further addressing of a problem. Probably, MSL is only used when a problem is considered difficult to solve and when a solution requires a great deal of effort. This assumption is supported by the fact that in the translations *into* the mother tongue, MSL is exclusively used in connection with lexical problems whose solutions often require relatively complex strategies.

The source-language text segments which the subjects repeat by MONITORING are either the entire sentence (2 cases) or the clause (10 cases) in which the respective problem to be solved is embedded. This is closely connected with the fact that the subjects primariliy take a sentence- or clause-oriented approach to translation[14].

MSL, like all other elements of translation strategies, occurs at specific points in the structures which envelop them. An investigation of their surroundings has shown that MSL can be found in the following abstract structure: (VP) – (→SP) – MSL – (→SP). The elements in brackets are optional, but at least one phase of searching must be realized in the structure. Its most important subtype: →SP – MSL – (→SP) contains 10 of the 12 cases of MSL alone. The fact that at least one phase of searching for a solution must be realized in

14 This was already pointed out in section 5.1.1, and can be observed in the exemplary translations analyzed in section 5.3. Cf. also Krings 1986a: 198.

the structure suggests the assumption that MSL plays a supporting role in the focussing of a problem.

A further aspect under which MSL has been investigated is its success within the respective strategy. In 3 cases (= 25.00%), MONITORING of SL text segments, possibly followed by a phase of searching, leads to a (preliminary/partial) solution and thus to a successful termination of the strategy; in 1 case (= 8.33%), MSL leads to a zero-solution (SPØ) and marks the unsuccessful termination of the strategy.

To sum up, it can be pointed out that in a quarter of the cases in which MSL is used, this structural element decisively contributes to finding a solution to a problem. In a third of the cases in which it is used, MSL contributes to finding a solution to a problem or to realizing its insolubility. In two thirds of the cases in which MSL occurs, its position is at the relative beginning of the respective structure. This means that it cannot be determined whether MSL plays a supporting role in bringing about a positive or negative termination to the respective strategy. On the whole, MONITORING of source-language text segments is only moderately successful in its contribution to the process of problem-solving.

6.3.5.2.2 MONITORING of Target-Language Text Segments (MTL)

Of the strategy elements which are analyzed quantitatively in this section, MTL is the most frequently occurring. The corpus of investigation contains 235 instances which are distributed over 130 translation strategies. In other words, in almost a third of all the strategies of the corpus, an average of 1.8 instances of MTL can be found.

MONITORING of TL text segments occurs 154 times (= 65.53%) in the translations *from* and 81 times (= 34.47%) in the translations *into* the mother tongue. If these values are related to the percentages of the strategies in the translations *from* and *into* the mother tongue, an excess of 3% in the occurrence of MTL in the translations *from* the mother tongue can be stated. This overrepresentation is, however, so insignificant that drawing any generalizing conclusions from it would be purely speculative.

MTL is used 158 times (= 67.23%) for solving lexical problems, 54 times (= 22.89%) for solving lexico-syntactic, and 23 times (= 9.79%) for solving purely syntactic problems. This distribution largely corresponds to that in the entire corpus. Differences become apparent, however, when the distribution is differentiated according to the direction of the translations. In the translations *into* the mother tongue, the percentages of the types of problems nearly coincide with those in the entire corpus of investigation. In the translations *from* the mother tongue, however, the lexical problems are underrepresented by 6%, whereas the lexico-syntactic and the syntactic problems are overrepresented by 3% each. If one also takes into consideration the fact that the lexical problems are those which are solved least successfully, and the lexico-syntactic problems are those which are solved most successfully, it can be assumed that MTL has a part in the success of the respective strategies. Further considerations about this assumption will be made towards the end of this subsection.

MONITORING of TL text segments occurs 217 times (= 92.34%) in the process of the first and 18 times (= 7.66%) in the process of a further addressing of a translation problem. The differences between the translations *from* and *into* the mother tongue are minimal and can be neglected here.

The finding stated above shows that even at the relative beginning of a strategy, subjects repeat verbatim parts of the translation in order to obtain hints for a solution to a translation problem. The phenomenon of repeating preceding text segments for the purpose of problem-solving probably occurs rather frequently in any type of oral text production which requires strategic activities. Thus, it is no wonder that the subjects use MTL even before a problem turns out to be difficult and/or laborious to solve.

Of the TL text segments which the subjects repeat by MONITORING, 45 (= 19.15%) are (preliminary/partial) solutions to translation problems and 190 (= 80.85%) are stretches of discourse from non-strategic parts of the translations. In the great majority of cases, the TL text segments are clauses or syntagmas which terminate immediately before the respective problems.

The fact that only relatively few text segments which are the result of the successful use of translation strategies are repeated by MTL can be explained hypothetically. As the translations of the corpus reveal, strategic and non-strategic phases generally alternate. Thus, a strategic phase is normally immediately preceded by a non-strategic phase.

As concerns its surroundings, 142 instances of MTL (= 60.43%) occur in the following abstract structure: (→SP) – MTL – (→SP), with one of the two phases of searching being obligatory. The remaining instances of MTL can be found in the following surroundings: MTL – MTL, 26 times (= 11.06%); (P)SP – MTL – ((P)SP), 17 times (= 7.23%); CHECK – MTL, 13 times (= 5.53%); SPa/SPb .. – MTL 10 times (= 4.26%); others 27 times (= 11.49%).

As a result of the above distribution, it can be assumed that MTL, like MSL, has a supporting function in the focussing of a problem, and that by means of MTL itself, a focussing of a problem or its context can be brought about. In how far this is successful, will be discussed in the following part of this section.

MONITORING of TL text segment, possibly followed by a phase of searching, results in a (preliminary/partial) solution, and thus in a successful termination of the respective strategy, in 123 cases (= 52.34%). Differences in the direction of the translations can hardly be observed.

MTL is used 75 times (= 60.98%) to address lexical problems, 34 times (= 27.64%) to address lexico-syntactic, and 14 times (= 11.38%) to address syntactic problems. Compared with the distribution of the types of problems in the entire corpus, the lexical problems are underrepresented by 10%; 8% in the translations *from* and 12% in the translations *into* the mother tongue. The lexico-syntactic and the syntactic problems, however, are overrepresented; the former by 5% (4% in the translations *from* and 7% in the translations *into* the mother tongue); the latter by 3% (3% in the translations *from* and 4% in the translations *into* the mother tongue).

Thus, in the translations *from* the mother tongue, MTL is used most successfully for solving lexico-syntactic problems and least successfully for solving lexical problems. This mainly coincides with what was pointed out about the success of basic and expanded structures in subsection 6.3.4.2.

As concerns the translations *into* the mother tongue, the percentage of the syntactic problems largely, even though they are overrepresented, corresponds to that of the successful basic and expanded structures (cf. subsection 6.3.4.2). The overrepresentation of the solved lexico-syntactic problems, however, may be decisively caused by MTL.

In 11 cases (= 4.68%), MONITORING of target-language text segments with a subsequent phase of searching and/or verbalization of the problem and/or continuation of the translation results in a (preliminary/partial) solution to the respective problem. These cases all occur in translations *into* the mother tongue and concern lexical problems.

The results of the investigation suggest that in 134 cases, MTL has a leading part, at least, in bringing about a (preliminary/partial) solution to the respective problem. This amounts to a success rate of 57.02%. A differentiation according to the direction of the translations yields the following values:

Translations *from* the mother tongue

MTL – total:	154	
MTL – successful:	82	(= 53.25%)

Translation *into* the mother tongue

MTL – total:	81	
MTL – successful:	52	(= 64.20%)

Thus, MONITORING of TL text segments is about 11% more successful in the translations *into* than *from* the mother tongue. As a result of this, it can be assumed that the problems in the translations *into* the mother tongue, in whose solutions MTL plays an important part, are production problems in the mother tongue. It is not surprising that these problems can be solved better when the subjects specifically repeat part of the verbal context which precedes them by means of MTL[15]. It is not surprising either that this does not apply to a foreign language to the same extent. Since the amount of information available in a foreign language is generally much smaller, the network in which the information is represented mentally is accordingly less close-knit with fewer

15 Cf. Chapter 7 for more details.

accessing points[16]. As a result of this, the chances of activating another network by a piece or a complex of information, e.g. parts of context captured by MTL, and of thus accessing the sought-for information, are accordingly worse.

In 16 cases (= 6.81%), MONITORING of TL text segments, possibly followed by a phase of searching and/or a verbalization of the problem, leads to the subjects' realization of the insolubility of a translation problem.

In sum, the following results of the investigation into the success of MTL should be emphasized: In almost two thirds of the cases in which MTL occurs, this element leads to the realization of a solution to or of the insolubility of a problem. In both these cases, a termination of the strategy used is reached under the decisive influence of MTL. Thus MONITORING of TL text segments has an important function as a catalyst within translation strategies. It focusses subjects' cognitive attention on the problems and/or their contexts and results in an early positive or negative (preliminary) termination to strategies.

The percentages given above may create the impression that MTL does not play a very successful part in the process of problem-solving. After all, its success rate amounts to 57% 'only'. This impression is, however, deceptive because the respective instances of MTL are the basis on which its frequency of occurrence has been calculated. As pointed out at the beginning of this subsection, MTL occurs almost twice on average in the respective strategies. In the calculation of the success rate, however, only those instances of MTL were taken into account which were used last and occur at the relative end of the strategies, i.e. which immediately precede the respective solutions. All other instances of MTL which precede the last were not taken into account even if they occur so close to the end of a strategy that they have probably played a supporting role in the problem-solving process.

The idea therefore suggests itself of calculating the success of MTL again, this time on the basis of the *strategies*, not of the instances of MTL. The calculation is carried out by relating the number of strategies which contain MTL to the number of strategies in which instances of MTL occur which play an important part in bringing about a solution to a problem. When differentiated according to the direction of the translations, the calculation yields the following values:

Translation *from* the mother tongue	
Strategies containing MTL – total:	96 = 100.00%
Strategies containing MTL with MTL playing an important part in the success of the strategy:	78 = 81.25%
Translation *into* the mother tongue	
Strategies containing MTL – total:	34 = 100.00%
Strategies containing MTL with MTL playing an important part in the success of the strategy:	30 = 88.24%

16 Cf. Dörner (1976: 31ff.) and section 6.3.2, type I.

As the above lists show, the success rate of MTL in the translations *from* the mother tongue is a little below and in the translations *into* the mother tongue it is a little above the success rate of all the strategies in the corpus (cf. section 6.3.4). It must be taken into account, however, that here the success of one strategy element only has been calculated, whereas the success rate stated in section 6.3.4 was calculated on the basis of all the elements of translation strategies. To this extent, the success rate of MTL which amounts to 83% must be considered rather high.

6.3.5.3 REPHRASING

REPHRASING as a potential element of translation strategies was defined in section 5.2.2 as taking up text segments and verbalizing them, not verbatim but in a different form from the original. REPHRASING can concern source- and target-language text segments. Both these cases will be analyzed in the following subsections.

6.3.5.3.1 REPHRASING of Source-Language Text Segments (REPHR.SL)

The translations constituting the corpus of investigation contain 41 instances of REPHRASING of SL text segments. They are distributed over 29 strategies. In other words, in 7% of the translation strategies, REPHR.SL occurs 1.4 times on average. Thus the frequency of this strategy element, similar to MSL, is rather low.

REPHRASING of SL text segments occurs about three times more frequently in the translations *from* than *into* the mother tongue. In the former 31, and in the latter 10 instances of REPHR.SL occur. This distribution can be explained mainly by the fact that in the translations *from* the mother tongue, the source-language is the subjects' native language. REPHRASING of SL text segments is mainly used when subjects are faced with production problems in the target (= foreign) language, i.e. when an adequate TL text segment cannot be found for an SL one. In these cases, subjects sometimes try to alter the respective SL text segment verbally in such a way that on the basis of this rephrasing a TL correspondence can either be found *ad hoc* or can be searched for with potentially greater chances of success.

REPHR.SL is used 31 times (= 75.61%) for solving lexical, and 10 times (= 24.39%) for solving lexico-syntactic problems. The strategy element is not used for solving purely syntactic problems. This is hardly surprising because, according to its definition, REPHRASING primarily refers to text segments as lexical items.

The instances of REPHR.SL can be found 32 times (= 78.05%) in the process of the first, and 9 times (= 21.95%) in the process of a further addressing of a problem. In the translations *into* the mother tongue, the ratio is as high as 90% to 10%. This finding shows that in most cases the subjects already use REPHR.SL at an early stage in the translation process when certain other strategic means have turned out to be unsuccessful[17].

In all cases, the text segments embraced by REPHR.SL are translation problems the subjects were faced with. The lexical items are predominant because, as stated above, they represent by far the most frequently occurring type of problem in the strategies in which REPHR.SL is used.

The instances of REPHRASING of SL text segments can, with one exception only, be assigned to two types:

Type 1 contains 21 cases, which corresponds to 51.22%. The respective SL text segments, single lexemes or syntagmas consisting of very few lexemes, are substituted by other lexemes of the same grammatical kind or by other syntagmas which the subjects consider synonymous or quasi-synonymous (e.g. ".. wie es in systematischer Variation *erscheint*" is substituted by ".. wie es ... *auftritt*" (T3, S25)).

Type 2 is constituted by 19 cases (= 46.34%), all of which are syntactic transformations. Most frequently (10 times), nouns are expressed by verbal constructions, e.g. "Entwicklung" is rephrased to "sich entwickeln" (T1, S8). Three times, adjectives are transformed into nouns, e.g. "sprachlich" becomes "Sprache" (T3, S25).

It can be justifiably assumed that rephrasings of type 1 open up a more direct, although not necessarily a more successful, route in the problem-solving process than type 2 rephrasings. The latter require, if the translation of the rephrasing is to succeed, a back-transformation of the respective TL text segment into the grammatical category or categories which the problematic lexeme(s) belonged to.

The results which the investigation of the surroundings of REPHR.SL has yielded are similar to those for MSL and MTL. Thirty-three instances of REPHR.SL (= 80.49%) occur in the following abstract structure: (VP) – (→SP) – REPHR.SL – (→SP). The elements in brackets are optional, although at least one of them must be realized in the structure. As can be seen, the great majority of the instances of REPHR.SL occur together with problem-focussing elements, e.g. VP or →SP. Their function of focussing on the translation problems and/or their surroundings is probably highly intensified by the rephrasing. As a result, subjects' cognitive attention to the problem culminates in their being able to verbally alter (= rephrase) the problematic SL text segments in specific ways on the basis of which the problem-solving process proceeds.

REPHRASING of TL text segments occurs 8 times (= 19.51%) in the process of a further addressing of a problem after a (preliminary) solution, a zero-solution, and after CHECK followed by a negative (preliminary) solution ((P)SP).

---

17 More details can be found later in this subsection when the results of the investigation into the surroundings of REPHR.SL are discussed.

To conclude this subsection, rephrasings of TL text segments will now be analyzed with regard to their success within the respective translation strategy in which they have a recognizable problem-solving function. The analysis of the success of REPHR.SL is based on those cases in which, as a result of the rephrasings, potentially together with up to three further strategy elements, (preliminary or partial) solutions are brought about. Between the rephrasing and the (potential) termination of the respective strategy, the following elements can be found: Verbalization of or Comment on the problem, Search for a solution, Monitoring of SL or TL text segments, Comment on a (preliminary) solution which is still to be found, (further) Rephrasing of an SL or TL text segment, as well as Continuation of the translation.

In 26 cases, REPHR.SL results in a successful termination of the translation strategy. This corresponds to a percentage of 63.42. The values for the translations *from* the mother tongue (20 = 64.52%) are only insignificantly higher than those for the translations *into* the mother tongue (6 = 60.00%).

If the calculation of the success of REPHR.SL is based on the strategies containing this element, not on the instances of its occurrence, the success rate amounts to more than 85%. This is very high indeed for a single strategy element when one takes into consideration what was said about the success of MTL in the preceding subsection.

In 6 cases (= 14.63%), the subjects realize the insolubility of a translation problem as a result of their using REPHR.SL, potentially followed by up to three more strategic elements.

In summary, it can be pointed out that in 32 cases (= 78.05%), REPHR.SL leads to the subjects' realization of a solution to or of the insolubility of a problem. Thus more than three fourths of all rephrasings have an important function as a catalyst within the respective translation strategies. As a result of their strong problem-focussing character, an early, even though potentially preliminary, but mostly positive termination of strategies can be brought about.

6.3.5.3.2 REPHRASING of Target-Language Text Segments (REPHR.TL)

In the corpus of investigation, target-language text segments are rephrased 78 times. The rephrasings are distributed over 64 strategies, which means that in about 16% of the translation strategies, 1.2 instances of REPHR.TL occur on average.

REPHRASING of TL text segments is used 41 times (= 52.56%) for addressing lexical problems, 27 times (= 34.62%) for addressing lexico-syntactic, and 10 times (= 12.82%) for addressing purely syntactic problems. When differentiated according to the direction of the translation, the calculation yields the following values:

Translations *from* the mother tongue	
REPHR.TL – total:	39 = 50.00%
REPHR.TL with lexical problems:	15 = 38.46%
REPHR.TL with lexico-syntactic problems:	17 = 43.59%
REPHR.TL with syntactic problems:	7 = 17.95%
Translation *into* the mother tongue	
REPHR.TL – total:	39 = 50.00%
REPHR.TL with lexical problems:	26 = 66.67%
REPHR.TL with lexico-syntactic problems:	10 = 25.64%
REPHR.TL with syntactic problems:	3 = 7.69%

The above list shows that half of the instances of REPHR.TL occur in the strategies of translations *from* and half in the strategies of the translations *into* the mother tongue. But since the latter amount to ca. 38% of all the translation strategies, REPHR.TL is overrepresented by 12% in the translations *into*, and underrepresented by 12% in the translations *from* the mother tongue. This finding can be hypothetically explained by the fact that the subjects' ability and willingness to rephrase text segments in their mother tongue, and thus to optimize or correct the TL text, is generally greater than in the foreign language.

As concerns the distribution of the types of problems, considerable differences can be noticed. In the translations *into* the mother tongue, the percentages largely correspond to those in the entire corpus. There is only a slight overrepresentation of lexico-syntactic, and a slight underrepresentation of lexical problems. In the translations *from* the mother tongue, however, the syntactic problems are overrepresented by 20% and the lexical problems are underrepresented by 30%. This finding shows that the subjects are more inclined to, and probably also more capable of, rephrasing, and thus correcting or optimizing, problematic syntactic or lexico-syntactic constructions than lexical elements in the foreign language. This correlates highly with the findings on the success of the translation strategies according to which the lexico-syntactic problems are the most successfully addressed and the lexical problems are the least successfully addressed in the translations *from* the mother tongue[18].

REPHRASING of TL text segments can be found 11 times (= 14.10%) in the process of the first addressing, and 67 times (= 85.90%) in the process of a further addressing of a translation problem. This finding is to be seen in close connection to the text segments embraced by REPHR.TL. The great majority of them (65 = 83.33%) are from strategic parts of a translation, i.e. (preliminary/partial) solutions to problems. By definition, rephrasings of these text segments constitute a process of a further addressing of a problem.

18 Cf. subsection 6.3.4.2.

The instances of REPHR.TL can be found within six different structures. The three most frequently occurring will be presented and analyzed.

Rephrasings of TL text segments occur 28 times after (preliminary/partial) solutions or their verbatim repetitions by means of MONITORING ((P)SP/-MTL – REPHR.TL). This corresponds to a percentage of almost 36. In two thirds of these cases, (preliminary/partial) solutions are optimized, and one third of the cases rerepresent corrections. Seventeen (= 43.59%) of the rephrasings in the translations *from* the mother tongue, and 11 (28.21%) of those in the translations *into* the mother tongue occur within the above structure.

In close connection to the cases mentioned above, must be seen the 12 (= 15.38%) instances of REPHR.TL which occur after CHECK. (Preliminary/partial) solutions whose adequacy is checked on are corrected or optimized by means of rephrasings.

In 20 cases (= 25.64%), REPHR.TL can be found in the following abstract structure: (→SP) – (MTL/VP/REPHR.SL) – REPHR.TL – (→SP). The bracketed elements are optional, but at least one of them must be realized in the structure. REPHRASING of TL text segments, together with the other elements which precede or follow it in the structure, has the function of focussing on the problem, and thus also of potentially furthering its solution.

The analysis of the rephrasings of TL text segments has yielded the surprising result that none of the strategies in which this element occurs terminates with a zero-solution. The success of REPHR.TL would be total, but 7 (= 8.97%) of its instances occur so far from the termination of the respective complex strategy that their function of supporting the problem-solving process cannot be definitely recognized. Nonetheless, the use of REPHR.TL leads to a (preliminary/partial) solution in 71 cases (= 91.03%) which makes this strategy element an extremely successful one.

Of the 41 lexical problems addressed by REPHR.TL, 36 (= 87.80%) are solved. The success rate for the purely syntactic (90.00%) and the lexico-syntactic problems (96.30%) is even higher.

REPHR.TL is extremely successful in both the translations *from* and *into* the mother tongue. In the former, 35 (= 89.74%), and in the latter, 36 (= 92.31%) of the problems were solved under the influence of REPHR.TL.

6.3.5.4 Multiple Verbalizations of Translation Problems

Within the translation process, multiple verbalizations of problems represent steps consisting of at least two single verbalizations (VP). Multiple verbalizations of problems occur within 25 translation strategies and contain 58 single verbalizations of problems. In other words, the 25 multiple verbalizations are distributed over 6.27% of the translation strategies in the corpus. Each of the multiple verbalizations consists of an average of 2.3 single ones.

Of the 25 multiple verbalizations, 12 (= 48%) occur in the translations *from*, and 13 (= 52%) in the translations *into* the mother tongue. Compared with the respective percentages of the strategies, the multiple verbalizations in the translations *from* the mother tongue are underrepresented and those in the translations *into* the mother tongue are overrepresented by 14% each. The situation as regards MONITORING of source-language text segments is very similar. Both these elements of translation strategies are employed mainly to address foreign language reception problems and put them into the focus of cognitive attention.

Multiple verbalizations are used 17 times (= 68%) for addressing lexical problems, 5 times (= 20%) for addressing lexico-syntactic, and 3 times (= 12%) for addressing purely syntactic problems. The differentiation according to the direction of the translations yields the following values:

Translation from the Mother Tongue	
Multiple Verbalizations of Lexical Problems:	8 = 66.67%
Multiple Verbalizations of Lexico-Syntactic Problems:	3 = 25.00%
Multiple Verbalizations of Syntactic Problems:	1 = 8.33%
Translations into the Mother Tongue	
Multiple Verbalizations of Lexical Problems:	9 = 69.23%
Multiple Verbalizations of Lexico-Syntactic Problems:	2 = 15.38%
Multiple Verbalizations of Syntactic Problems:	2 = 15.38%

Whilst the distribution of the types of problems in the translations *from* the mother tongue largely corresponds to that in the entire corpus, the translations *into* the mother tongue contain 7% more syntactic and 7% fewer lexico-syntactic problems. The subjects' difficulties as concerns the syntactic problems are not so much in the reception of source-language text segments but rather in the production of target-language equivalents. The respective SL text segments are verbalized several times in order to place them into the subject's focus of attention and thus to further the search for TL equivalents.

Multiple verbalizations of translation problems occur 22 times (= 88%) in the process of the first addressing of a problem. The differences as regards the translations *from* and *into* the mother tongue are insignificant and can be neglected here. Apparently, multiple verbalizations are problem-focussing means which the subjects employ in order to visualize a given translation problem in the exactest way possible. They most frequently occur after the realization of a problem and have a preparatory function in the problem-solving process. In the process of a further addressing of a translation problem, strategic means are generally required that realize specific problem-solving activities. Problem-focussing activities alone are generally not sufficient for bringing about solutions to problems at these stages of the translation process. As concerns the structure of multiple verbalizations, three types can be distinguished. In four cases (= 16%), the single verbalizations follow each other immediately, i.e. VP1 – VP2 – VP3 ... VPn. In 21 cases (= 84%), the single verbalizations are separated from each other by phases of searching for a solution, by comments on a problem, or by phases of continuation of the translation. In as many as nineteen cases (= 76%), phases of searching (→SP) occur between single verbalizations. One case (= 4%) represents a mixture of the two previously mentioned cases.

As can be seen, the great majority of multiple verbalizations occur together with specific phases of searching for a solution. Thus, the problem-focusssing potentials of these two strategic means mutually intensify each other.

In 13 cases (= 52%), multiple verbalizations strongly contribute to the success of the respective translation strategy. Nine lexical problems (= 69.23%) and two lexico-syntactic and purely syntactic problems (= 15.38% each) are solved under the decisive influence of multiple verbalizations. Eleven of the thirteen solutions immediately follow the multiple verbalizations. These findings can be interpreted as follows: The comparatively low success rate (52%) of this strategy element must be seen in the light of the fact that multiple verbalizations as problem-focussing means have a preparatory rather than a problem-solving function in the translation process. Further evidence for this interpretation is supplied by the fact that in 11 of the 13 cases, subjects find solutions to the respective problems immediately after the multiple verbalizations. The problems were of such kinds that their solutions neither required any special strategic nor any other complex means on the part of the subjects. Rather, the problems could be solved by solely placing them into the subjects' focus of cognitive attention.

A differentiation of the problems solved according to their types shows that the respective percentages are identical with those of the problems in the translations *into* the mother tongue which were addressed by multiple verbalizations. No explanation can be given so far for the overrepresentation of the syntactic and the underrepresentation of the lexico-syntactic problems. Individual factors may be responsible for this distribution.

To conclude this subsection, it remains to be mentioned that in 8 cases (= 32%), multiple verbalizations of translation problems led to zero-solutions and thus to a (preliminary) termination of the respective strategy. Thus, in 84% of all the cases in which multiple verbalizations are used, this strategy element strongly functions as a catalyst. Compared with the respective percentages of the other strategy elements, the value of 84% is extremely high.

6.3.6 Individually Caused Differences in Strategy Use

In section 6.3.4, it was investigated to what extent the subjects' translation *problems* are caused individually or supraindividually. The investigation yielded the result that about two thirds of all the translation problems are of an individual, and one third is of a supraindividual kind. In this section, it will be investigated whether the high degree of individuality of the translation *problems* also applies to the translation *strategies* employed for solving these problems.

The investigation is carried out on the basis of those translation problems of the corpus which were considered supraindividual with regard to the 25% boundary discussed in section 6.2.4. These problems together with the types of strategies which the subjects used for solving them are represented in the following diagram.

Diagram 23: Supraindividual Translation Problems and Strategies Used for Solving Them

TEXT 1

	Problems	**Number of Subjects**	**Types of Strategies Used**
1	In jüngerer Zeit	5	III, C*, C, IV, III (2xIII, 2xC, 1xIV)
2	Eigenschaften und Merkmale	9	C, II, IV, V, IV, C, II, IV, IV (4xIV, 2xII, 2xC, 1xV)
3	Merkmale	4	III, II, C, C (2xC, 1xII, 1xIII)
4	die sich ... ergeben	4	II, IV, IV, IV (3xIV, 1xII)
5	(auf unsere Zeit) verweisen	4	IV, IV, II, I (2xIV, 1xI, 1xII)
6	auf unsere Zeit verweisen	4	C, II, V, V (2xV, 1xII, 1xC)
7	dabei (scheint) ...	6	II, V, IV, II, II, C (3xII, 1xIV, 1xV, 1xC)
8	... scheint Übereinstimmung zu herrschen	5	II, V, V, C, C (2xV, 2xC, 1xII)
9	Erzählung	4	C, V, C, II (2xC, 1xII, 1xV)
10	Fähigkeiten	4	II, C, IV, IV (2xIV, 1xII, 1xC)
11	Erzählliteratur	9	II, II, C, I, C, V, V, V, IV (3xV, 2xII, 2xC, 1xI, 1xIV)

C* = Complex Structure

TEXT 1

Problems		Number of Subjects	Types of Strategies Used
12	literarischer Wirkung	5	IV, IV, IV, IV, V (4xIV, 1xV)
13	(...) ist dabei verhältnismäßig leicht zu beantworten	5	II, C, V, V (2xV, 1xII, 1xC)
14	(die Kurzgeschichte ist) einmal	4	C, IV, II, II (2xII, 1xIV, 1xC)
15	Reduktionen	4	IV, II, IV, II (2xII, 2xIV)
16	auf dem Gebiet	8	II, IV, IV, V, II, III, C, C (2xII, 2xIV, 2xC, 1xIII, 1xV)
17	Handlung	4	II, IV, IV, IV (3xIV, 1xII)
18	Charakterdarstellung und -ent-wicklung	5	IV, IV, C, V, V (2IV, 2xV, 1xC)

TEXT 2

Problems		Number of Subjects	Types of Strategies Used
1	Finden Sie's verändert?	2	II, II (2xII)
2	Dabei erwarten sie alles andere als die Antwort	2	V, C (1xV, 1xC)
3	Das finde ich aber	2	II, II (2xII)
4	in Verbindung mit	2	II, II (2xII)
5	nicht viel anders als uns	2	V, V (2xV)
6	Im Schwinden	2	C, II (1xII, 1xC)
7	Macht	2	IV, IV (2xIV)
8	erschreckt	2	C, IV (1xIV, 1xC)

TEXT 2

Problems		Number of Subjects	Types of Strategies Used
9	... die sie erschrecken	2	II, C (1xII, 1xC)
10	Zumindest	3	IV, II, IV (2xIV, 1xII)
11	... auch erfreulich sei	2	II, V (1xII, 1xV)

TEXT 3

Problems		Number of Subjects	Types of Strategies Used
1	sprachlich	2	IV, IV (2xIV)
2	beziehungsweise	2	C, C (2xC)
3	eigentlich	2	II, C (1xII, 1xC)
4	adäquate Verständigung	2	V, V (2xV)
5	Umgangssprache	3	V, V, V (3xV)
6	... mit einer mehrfachen Sprachbarriere	2	V, V (2xV)
7	zurechtkommen lernen	2	C, C (2xC)
8	wann welches Deutsch mit wem gesprochen wird	2	C, C (2xC)
9	setzt ... voraus	3	C, C, IV (2xC, 1xIV)
10	... beschäftigt	3	IV, II, C (1xII, 1xIV, 1xC)
11	kommunikationsorientiert	2	C, V (1xV, 1xC)
12	Unterricht	2	IV, C (1xIV, 1xC)

TEXT 3

Problems		Number of Subjects	Types of Strategies Used
13	(Unterricht), der vor allem ...	2	C, III (1xIII, 1xC)
14	Sprechstil	2	C, C (2xC)

TEXT 4

Problems		Number of Subjects	Types of Strategies Used
1	Sale of Honours	2	V, II (1xII, 1xV)
2	... on which the decision ...	2	II, II (2xII)
3	on which ...	2	IV, IV (2xIV)
4	congregation	6	II, C, C, IV, II, IV (2xII, 2xIV, 2xC)
5	... is worthy of respect	4	C, I, II, V (1xI, 1xII, 1xV, 1xC)
6	oscillated	3	IV, C, IV (2xIV, 1xC)
7	(political) spite	5	II, II, IV, C, II (3xII, 1xIV, 1xC)
8	logic-chopping	3	II, IV, C (1xII, 1xIV, 1xC)
9	graduate	3	I, IV, I (2xI, 1xIV)
10	... of whatever party	2	II, IV (1xII, 1xIV)
11	previously	3	II, II, II (3xII)
12	attained	3	C, II, II (2xII, 1xC)
13	dons	3	IV, I, C (1xI, 1xIV, 1xC)

TEXT 4

Problems		Number of Subjects	Types of Strategies Used
14	(dons) campaigning against her	2	IV, C (1xIV, 1xC)
15	concerned with	2	II, II (2xII)
16	award	3	IV, II, I (1xI, 1xII, 1xIV)

TEXT 5

Problems		Number of Subjects	Types of Strategies Used
1	(a cultural) subject	3	II, II, II (3xII)
2	chronicler	3	IV, I, C (1xI, 1xIV, 1xC)
3	(in these days) when	2	II, I (1xI, 1xII)
4	deficiencies	3	C, C, III (2xC, 1xIII)
5	the vehicle	2	IV, I (1xI, 1xIV)
6	the poetry of the race	2	C, II (1xII, 1xC)
7	race	4	II, C, II, C (2xII, 2xC)

TEXT 6

Problems		Number of Subjects	Types of Strategies Used
1	a drive	2	I, IV (1xI, 1xIV)
2	to encourage	2	III, II (1xII, 1xIII)
3	the Commons trade and industrial select committee	2	II, V (1xII, 1xV)

TEXT 6

Problems		Number of Subjects	Types of Strategies Used
4	dispersal	2	C, IV (1xIV, 1xC)
5	... is setting up	2	C, IV (1xIV, 1xC)

TEXT 7

Problems		Number of Subjects	Types of Strategies Used
1	evaluation	2	IV, IV (2xIV)

As with the investigation of the translation problems, the question of to what extent the translation strategies are of an individual or supraindividual kind implies many difficulties. They mainly result from the fact that the criteria according to which a strategy is to be considered individual or supraindividual are not given beforehand but must be developed and fixed by the analyst. The relevant data are included in the above diagram.

The quantitative analysis of the translation strategies is carried out in two different ways. One is based on a *strong*, the other on a *weak concept of supraindividuality.*

According to the former, supraindividuality only occurs when *identical types of strategies* are employed. According to the latter, supraindividuality is not bound to identical but to *similarly complex types of strategies*. The weak concept takes into account the fact that the basic structure types of the translation strategies can be of varying complexity, and that the more complex types, especially when they contain expansions, embedded and/or bound elements, can be just as complex as complex structures. Types IV and V are the more complex types of basic structures, whereas types I, II, and III can be considered to be the less complex types.

The analysis of the strategies as concerns their individuality or supraindividuality proceeds from the assumption that these two concepts are not discrete but have fluent boundaries, and that different degrees of supraindividuality exist. They can be calculated in percentages for every single strategy and differ from one another depending on what concept of supraindividuality is used.

I. The analysis is carried out using the *strong* concept of supraindividuality:

Example 1 (Text 3; 5)
Three instances (X1, X2, X3) of a problem (X) occur in the data. All of them are addressed by type V strategies. In this case, the degree or rate of supraindividuality (SI) amounts to 100%. As diagram 23 shows, however, not all the cases are that clear. A further example may elucidate this:

Example 2 (Text 5; 7)
Four instances (Y1, Y2, Y3, Y4) of a problem (Y) can be found. Two of them (Y1, Y3) are addressed by type II structures, the other two by complex structures (C). Thus, the supraindividuality rates amount to 50% for any of the two structural types. The difficulty that arises here is to calculate a supraindividuality rate which refers and is common to all the four translation strategies. On the one hand, the mere addition of the two rates of supraindividuality (SI (II) + SI (C)/50% + 50% = 100%) must certainly be ruled out because two different structural types are concerned. On the other hand, it is just as unsatisfactory to consider 50% the common rate of supraindividuality. This would not take into account the fact that *both* structural types each occur twice. It could be appropriate for a distribution such as 2xII, 1xI, 1xC.

Both for practical reasons and in order to ensure the consistency of the analysis, the following procedure is employed: In calculating the common rate of supraindividuality, the highest rate, or one among the highest rates of supraindividuality for the various structural types is added to half of the supraindividuality rate(s) for the other structural types. This procedure, when applied to example 2 above (Text 5; 7), leads to the following calculation:
SI (II) = 50%; SI (C) = 50%; SI (II,C) = 50% + $^1/_2$ x 50% = 75%
Another example may help to clarify the procedure.

Example 3 (Text 1; 5)
The following structural types were used for solving the respective translation problem:
3xV, 2xII, 2xC, 1xI, 1xIV; ⇒ SI (V) = 33.33%; SI (II) = 22.22%; SI (C) = 22.22%; SI (I) = 0%; SI (IV) = 0%;
SI (V,II,C) = 33,33% + $^1/_2$ x 22,22% + $^1/_2$ x 22.22% = 55.55%

II. The analysis is carried out using the *weak* concept of supraindividuality:

The percentages of the supraindividuality rates for any of the structural types is calculated in the same way as in the examples above. The common rate of supraindividuality is calculated by adding to the highest rate of supraindividuality for the various structural types half of the supraindividuality rate(s) for the other structural type(s). Furthermore, the supraindividuality rates for the less complex structural types (I, II, III) and for the more complex structural types (IV, V, C) are added and the respective sums are divided by 2.

The following example may illustrate this procedure:

***Example* 4** (Text 1; 5)
The following structural types were used for solving the respective translation problem: 3xV, 2xII, 2xC, 1xI, 1xV; ⇒ SI (V) = 33.33%; S(II,I) = $^1/_2$ x 33.33% = 16.67%; SI (IV,C) = $^1/_2$ x 33.33% = 16.67%:
S (V,II,I,IV,C) = 33.33% + 16.67% + 16.67% = 66.67%
When more than one highest supraindividuality rate occurs, the analyst starts his/her calculation from one of them and, at the same time, tries to add as many supraindividuality rates of the structural types as possible and divides them by 2. The procedure can be illustrated by the following example:

***Example* 5** (Text 1; 7)
Structural types used for solving the respective translation problem:
2xII, 2xIV, 2xC, 1xIII, 1xV; ⇒ SI (II) = 25%; SI (IV,C,V) = $^1/_2$ x 62.50% = 31.25%;
S (II,IV,C,V) = 25% + 31.25% = 56.25%

The quantitative analysis of the data according to the *strong* and the *weak* concept of supraindividuality yields the percentages represented in the following diagram:

Diagram 24: Supraindividuality Rates of Translation Strategies Calculated According to the Strong and the Weak Concept of Supraindividuality

		I. Analysis according to *Strong* Concept of Supraindividuality		II. Analysis according to *Weak* Concept of Supraindividuality	
Text 1:	1	40% + 20% =	60.00%	40% + 30% =	70.00%
	2	44.44% + 11.11% + 11.11% =	66.66%	44.44% + 11.11% + 16.67% =	72.22%
	3		50.00%	50% + 25% =	75.00%
	4		75.00%		75.00%
	5		50.00%	50% + 25% =	75.00%
	6		50.00%	50% + 12.50% =	62.50%
	7		50.00%	50% + 25% =	75.00%
	8	40% + 20% =	60.00%	40% + 20% =	60.00%
	9		50.00%	50% + 12.50% =	62.50%
	10		50.00%	50% + 12.50% =	62.50%

		I. Analysis according to *Strong* Concept of Supraindividuality		II. Analysis according to *Weak* Concept of Supraindividuality	
Text 1:	11	33.33% + 11.11% + 11.11% =	55.55%	33.33% + 16.67% + 16.67% =	66.67%
	12		80.00%	80% + 10% =	90.00%
	13		50.00%	50% + 12.50% =	62.50%
	14		50.00%	50% + 25% =	75.00%
	15	50% + 25% =	75.00%	50% + 25% =	75.00%
	16	25% + 12.50% + 12.50% =	50.00%	25% + 31.25% =	56.25%
	17		75.00%		75.00%
	18	40% + 20% =	60.00%	40% + 25% =	65.00%
MEAN :			58.73%	MEAN :	69.73%
Text 2:	1		100.00%		100.00%
	2		0.00%		50.00%
	3		100.00%		100.00%
	4		100.00%		100.00%
	5		100.00%		100.00%
	6		0.00%		0.00%
	7		100.00%		100.00%
	8		0.00%		50.00%
	9		0.00%		0.00%
	10		66.67%		66.67%
	11		0.00%		0.00%
MEAN :			51.52%	MEAN :	60.61%

		I. Analysis according to *Strong* Concept of Supraindividuality		II. Analysis according to *Weak* Concept of Supraindividuality	
Text 3:	1		100.00%		100.00%
	2		100.00%		100.00%
	3		0.00%		0.00%
	4		100.00%		100.00%
	5		100.00%		100.00%
	6		100.00%		100.00%
	7		100.00%		100.00%
	8		100.00%		100.00%
	9		66.67%	66.67% + 16.67% =	83.34%
	10		0.00%		33.33%
	11		0.00%		50.00%
	12		0.00%		50.00%
	13		0.00%		0.00%
	14		100.00%		100.00%
MEAN :			61.91%	Mean :	72.62%
Text 4:	1		0.00%		0.00%
	2		100.00%		100.00%
	3		100.00%		100.00%
	4	33.33% + 16,67% + 16.67% =	66.67%	33.33% + 33.33% =	66.66%
	5		0.00%	25% + 25% =	50.00%
	6		66.67%	66.67% + 16.67% =	83.34%
	7		60.00%	60% + 20% =	80.00%
	8		0.00%		33.33%
	9		66.67%		66.67%
	10		0.00%		0.00%
	11		100.00%		100.00%
	12		66.67%		66.67%
	13		0.00%		33.33%

I. Analysis according to *Strong* Concept of Supraindividuality				II. Analysis according to *Weak* Concept of Supraindividuality	
Text 4:	14		0.00%		50.00%
	15		100.00%		100.00%
	16		0.00%		0.00%
MEAN :			45.42%	MEAN :	60.21%
Text 5:	1		100.00%		100.00%
	2		0.00%		33.33%
	3		0.00%		50.00%
	4		66.67%		66.67%
	5		0.00%		0.00%
	6		0.00%		0.00%
	7	50% + 25% =	75.00%	50% + 25% =	75.00%
MEAN :			34.52%		46.43%
Text 6:	1		0.00%		0.00%
	2		0.00%		50.00%
	3		0.00%		0.00%
	4		0.00%		50.00%
	5		0.00%		50.00%
MEAN :			0.00%	MEAN :	30.00%
Text 7:	1		100.00%		100.00%
MEAN :			100.00%	MEAN :	100.00%

The means for the respective supraindividuality rates can be used to calculate the mean value common to all translation strategies in the seven texts. According to the *strong* concept of supraindividuality, an average of 50.30%, and thus almost exactly half of all the translation strategies in the corpus of investigation, are supraindividual. Calculated according to the *weak* concept of supraindividuality, the common mean value amounts to 62.80%, which is nearly two thirds of all the translation strategies. Both these means are considerably higher than the mean value calculated for the supraindividual translation *problems*, which amounts to 33.11%. Thus, when the calculation is carried out on the basis of the *weak* concept of supraindividuality, the values for the translation *strategies* (ca. one third individual and two thirds supraindividual) are in reverse relationship to those for the translation *problems* (ca. one third supraindividual and two thirds individual).

As a consequence of these findings, two assumptions suggest themselves. On the one hand, it must be assumed that the translation *problems* are caused individually to such a large extent because, apart from other factors, the subjects' competence in the respective source- and target-language, as well as their experience in translating, differ considerably. On the other hand, the high degree of supraindividuality of the translation *strategies* can probably be explained by the fact that the methods of operation of the human brain are largely similar, if not identical, as far as the processes of solving (translation) problems are concerned. This is in accord with the finding that mental processes reveal a high degree of economy (cf. Schönpflug/Schönpflug 1983). Factors on which the mental processes of translational problem-solving depend will be thematized in summary in Chapter 7.

As concerns the direction of the translations, the mean values calculated above also yield important insights. In the translations *from* the mother tongue, the supraindividuality rate is 12% or 8% above that for the translations *into* the mother tongue, depending on the concept of supraindividuality used. This difference may partly be caused by the structure of the data corpus. Above all, however, it may be caused by the fact that the subjects were far less experienced in translating *into* than *from* the mother tongue[19]. As a result of this, the procedures employed for problem-solving were less tried and tested, and thus more of an individual kind, in the translations *into* than *from* the mother tongue. That these procedures are, however, by no means less successful was pointed out in subsection 6.3.4.2.

6.3.7 Strategies for Translation into and from the Mother Tongue: A Summarizing Comparison

In the preceding (sub)sections, the results which the quantitative analysis has yielded have always been differentiated according to the direction of the translations. In spite of many differences, the abundance of individual results can be said to coalesce into quite a homogeneous picture. Some of its aspects have already been presented in the preceding (sub)sections. In this section, they will be summarized and the results on which the picture is based will be outlined.

i. The results of the respective analyses show that the subjects generally attempt to solve problems in the translations *into* the mother tongue by means of linguistically less complex strategies than problems in the translations *from*

19 In foreign language classrooms at the secondary schools and universities in the Federal Republic of Germany, translations *into* the mother tongue play quite a subordinate role.

the mother tongue. Possibly, they estimate the former problems to be less serious than the latter.

As the distribution of the basic and expanded structures (cf. section 6.3.2) reveals, their percentage in the translations *into* the mother tongue is about 7% above that in the translations *from* the mother tongue. Apparently, problems in the translations *into* the mother tongue are less difficult and laborious to solve than problems in the translations *from* the mother tongue. The reverse distribution is true for the complex structures (cf. section 6.3.3).

The assumption made above is also supported by the distribution of the types of basic structures (cf. section 6.3.2). The less complex types I and II occur more frequently in the translations *into* the mother tongue, whereas the more complex type V can be found twice more frequently in the translations *from* the mother tongue. The fact that the strategy element CHECK (cf. subsection 6.3.5.1) is overrepresented by ca. 10% in the translations *from* the mother tongue gives further support to the above assumption. Apparently, the subjects find problems in the translations *from* the mother tongue more difficult and their solutions more worthy of testing than problems in the translations *into* the mother tongue.

ii. The investigation of the success of translation strategies (cf. subsection 6.3.4.2) has shown that the linguistically less complex strategies in the translations *into* the mother tongue are generally a little more successful than the linguistically more complex strategies in the translations *from* the mother tongue.

The percentage of the successful basic and expanded structures in the translations *into* the mother tongue is about 8% above that in the translations *from* the mother tongue (cf. (sub)sections 6.3.2 and 6.3.4.2). The reverse distribution is true for the successful complex structures.

iii. As regards the types of problems, it was found that in the translations *into* the mother tongue slightly more lexical and slightly fewer lexico-syntactic problems were addressed by strategies (cf. section 6.3.2). Furthermore, in the translations *into* the mother tongue, more lexical problems require more complex strategies for solving them than in the translations *from* the mother tongue.

This finding is supported by the fact that in the strategies for solving lexical problems of the translations *into* the mother tongue, CHECK is overrepresented by about 15% (cf. subsection 6.3.5.1). Apparently, the subjects also found these problems rather difficult and their solutions especially worthy of testing. The above finding is also corroborated by another fact. The quantitative analysis of MONITORING of source-language text segments has shown that this potential element of translation strategies occurs overproportionally in strategies for solving lexical problems in the translations *into* the mother tongue (cf. subsection 6.3.5.2.1). Among the foreign language reception problems for whose solution strategies containing MSL are mainly used, lexical problems represent the great majority. These strategies are linguistically more complex than those employed for solving lexical problems in the translations *from* the mother tongue.

On balance, the result of this section can be summarized as follows: Although differences between the strategies of the translations *into* and *from* the mother tongue exist, these differences are of degree, and not of kind. They are partly caused by the different distributions of the types of problems and by the different degrees of difficulty of the respective problems.

7 Hypothetical Conclusions

Now that the qualitative and quantitative analyses of the translations have been completed, the aim of this investigation has already largely been achieved.

In this chapter, three hypothetical conclusions about aspects of the translation process which can be derived from the results of the preceding analyses will be outlined. The following considerations will also take into account to what extent the conclusions drawn from the qualitative and quantitative analysis are translation-specific. It will be shown that the degree of translation specificity increases from the first to the third hypothetical assumption discussed.

In the following section (7.1), the hypothesis is formed that translation can be modelled as a retrospective-prospective process. Section 7.2 shows that the translation process is largely controlled by an internalized expectation structure. The last section of this chapter (7.3) discusses the fact that the translation process proceeds both in a sense- and in a sign-oriented way and that different degrees of sense- and sign-orientation can predominate in it or in its phases.

7.1 Translation as a Retrospective-Prospective Process

As the data show, the translation process is characterized by phases in which the subjects transfer source-language text segments into target-language ones without any problems, and by phases in which the subjects are faced with problems and which thus call for strategic, i.e. problem-solving, procedures.

Within the strategic phases of the translations, the course of the translation process is neither exclusively linear nor continuous. In producing the translations, the subjects often use strategy elements of a retrospective kind, such as MONITORING and REPHRASING of SL or TL text segments. In addition to the prospective element, the (evident) progression towards the intended goal, there is a retrospective element, a going back to and taking up of antecedent information, which can be, but need not be, functional for reaching the goal.

Within the framework of problem-solving, the retrospective-prospective nature of the translation process can be described hypothetically as follows: After realizing and/or verbalizing a translation problem, the translator starts searching for a (possibly preliminary) solution to that problem. Focusing on the global aim of his/her activity, i.e. translation production, and striving to reach this aim (= *prospective element*), the translator often orients him- or herself backwards towards parts of the TL text which s/he has already produced [MTL, REPHR.TL] and/or towards parts of the SL text which s/he has already received [MSL, REPHR.SL] (= *retrospective element*). As the subjects' approach to the translations is almost exclusively sentence-, clause-, or even word-oriented, the retrospectives brought about by MONITORING or REPHRASING generally embrace the sentence or clause in which the respective problem is embedded. Very rarely, and only with lexical problems, can it be observed that subjects orient themselves back to the lexeme which immediately precedes the problematic text segment.

In connection with the modeling of text production as problem-solving, Antos (1982: 157) has shown that, in principle, the more exactly and unambiguously problems are realized, the more easily they can be solved. The process of realizing a problem need not necessarily be (fully) conscious to the text producer. If a problem is realized in a (fully) conscious way, it is thus placed into the text producer's focus of cognitive attention.

From the considerations made before, it can be concluded hypothetically that the subjects take up antecedent information in order to obtain hints for a (preliminary) solution to a problem by mere intuition, spontaneous association[1], or by activating a network of information in memory, or, and this is more likely, in order to obtain hints which serve as prerequisites for a solution. Such hints can emerge in at least three different ways:

1. In retrospect, diffuse problems can be localized and/or realized in their various dimensions more exactly, and can thus be better placed into the subjects' foci of cognitive attention. Towards the problems thus focussed upon specific problem-solving activities can be directed.

2. Problematic SL text segments are seen in their context, which allows the subjects to deduce additional information about their syntactic embeddedness, their range of meaning, and their use. This case mainly concerns the translations *into* the mother tongue.

3. By the subjects focussing (again) on the syntactic structure of the text segment which they have already produced in TL and in which the problematic SL text segment has to be embedded in the translation.

The retrospective element is especially important in the process of testing (preliminary) solutions to translation problems. The data clearly show that the subjects systematically relate (preliminary) solutions to antecedent SL and/or TL text segments. In doing so, they make use of their knowledge of or 'feeling' for, interlingual relations of equivalence and/or correctness and adequacy of TL text segments. When a (preliminary) solution turns out to be wrong or not optimal with regard to the subject's internalized expectation structure (cf. section 7.2) during the retrospective process of testing, the subject tries to work out a new (preliminary) solution. In doing so, s/he takes into consideration

---

1 Cf. Antos 1982: 133f.; Dörner 1976: 53f.; Kummer 1972: 29.

relevant insights which the process of testing has yielded. The (preliminary) solutions thus worked out will often be tested again.

As pointed out in subsection 6.3.5.1, the testing of (preliminary) solutions (CHECK), and thus also the retrospective element involved in it, plays a highly successful part in the process of working out new, potentially more adequate, (preliminary) solutions.

Retrospective-prospective procedures are not confined to the oral translation process. They have been documented and described in connection with language acquisition[2] and reading[3] processes, and probably occur in all processes (of language use) in which psycho-motor and conceptual skills integratively work together.

According to the nature of translation as interlingual language use (cf. Wilss 1977: 10; 1981), the translator's having recourse to both SL and TL text segments and his/her making use of both these sources of information in order to reach the goal, are specific for retrospective-prospective activities within the translation process. Parts of both the SL and the TL text which have already been received or produced are used and organized by the translator to achieve the aim (= translation production). So what to the outsider may look like a rather inefficient 'detour' towards the goal may well be optimal and economical for the translator. S/he may systematically collect antecedent information, process it, thus developing new information, and use this to achieve the aim.

When and under what circumstances a translator uses which retrospective strategies cannot be answered definitely at the present time. The data, however, clearly suggest the existence of a psycholinguistic minimax principle[4]. According to it, the subjects try to keep the cognitive load as light as possible during their translations. They generally do not proceed to a deeper level of cognitive processing, which is more abstract and implies a higher cognitive load, before the processing on the higher level has turned out to be successless or unsatisfactory. Accordingly, the subjects also generally use mentally less complex strategies and elements of strategies, such as MONITORING, first. Only if they do not succeed in solving the respective problem do they employ mentally more complex strategies and elements of strategies, such as REPHRASING. This finding is also corroborated by the results which the quantitative analysis of the distribution of MONITORING and REPHRASING has yielded (cf. subsections 6.3.5.2 and 6.3.5.3).

---

2 Cf. Selinker 1972: 215; Felix 1976; Ringbom 1985a;b; McDonough 1981: 97.

3 Cf. McDonuogh 1981: 49, 51ff.; Rigg 1976; Spiro et al. 1980; especially Smith 1971: 99.

4 The same phenomenon has also been observed by Krings (1986a: 105). Following Levý (1967: 1179), he speaks of a "psycholinguistische Minimax-Strategie".

7.2 Translation Process and Expectation Structure

In connection with the decoding phase of simultaneous interpretation Kade and Cartellieri (1971: 12) point out that

> *(...) the interpreter builds up within himself an expectation pattern which gets more and more unambiguous with every entity of the source language text he has received.*

The phenomenon of an expectation structure can also be assumed to exist within the translation process. This is suggested by several results which the qualitative and the quantitative analyses have yielded:

i. The results of the investigation into the basic and expanded structures suggest that it is not or not primarily the *type* of problem which is the decisive factor for the concrete realization of a translation strategy, but rather the complexity and difficulty of the problem as assessed by the subject.

When realizing and/or verbalizing a translation problem, the subjects often assess its complexity and difficulty. In doing so, they also develop expectations concerning the strategic effort to be made for solving the problem. These expectations represent *one* aspect of the subjects' expectation structure. That such expectations do exist is clearly suggested by the data. For example, when the subjects are faced with certain problems which they assess as difficult or laborious to solve, they frequently employ type V strategies, thus splitting up the problem into parts and trying to solve them successively. This mainly concerns syntactic problems in the translations *from* the mother tongue, lexical problems in the translations *into* the mother tongue, and lexico-syntactic problems in translations in both directions. For the solution of these three kinds of problems, type V strategies seem to be especially suitable (cf. section 6.3.2).

ii. The rephrasings of TL text segments, the instances of CHECK, and the cases in which further translation versions are conceived also presuppose the existence of subjects' expectations about the translation product.

When a subject rephrases a target-language text segment, s/he must already have certain ideas or expectations about another text segment which may serve as an equivalent and can thus function as a rephrasing.

When a (preliminary) solution is tested and corroborated, modified, or rejected, this is done against the background of expectations about what may serve as a possible or optimal solution and what may not.

The same applies to the conception of a second or further translation version. Here, the subjects' expectations about an optimal TL text play a crucial role, as pointed out in section 5.2.4.

Although expectation structures are of great importance for the translation process, they are by no means confined to this domain.

The quotation from Kade and Cartellieri concerning the decoding phase of simultaneous interpretation may well be generalized and is probably valid for any reception and production process of written and spoken language.

The observations made by the American conversation analysts Sacks, Schegloff, and Jefferson (1974) concerning *turn-taking* in conversations have shown that hearers generally anticipate speakers' utterances, i.e. develop an expectation structure with regard to their termination. In doing so, they have recourse to the syntactic and informational structure of utterances, to aspects of the speech situation, and to their metalinguistic knowledge, among other things.

For the domain of formulation, i.e. the production of oral or written text, Antos (1982: 133ff.) has shown that an anticipated, though often vague, final state in the sense of an expectation structure has a "magnetic attraction" on problem-solving attempts, i.e. controls them in a specific way.

Expectation structures are probably documented best for the reception and production of texts and stories within texts. Among others, de Beaugrande (1978) and de Beaugrande/Dressler (1981) describe expectation structures with regard to text types; Rihs-Middel (1982) and den Uyl/van Oostendorp (1980) for the reception, and Wintermantel/Christmann (1983) for the production of texts. Kintsch (1974), Kintsch/Greene (1978), Rumelhart (1975), Schank/Abelson (1977), and Thorndyke (1977) investigate expectation structures in the reception and production of stories within texts.

In some of the more recent psycholinguistic literature on the production and reception of texts as well as in the literature on artificial intelligence (AI), the concepts of *script*, (Schank/Abelson 1977), *frame* (Minsky 1975), and *schema* (Bartlett 1932; Rumelhart 1985; 1980) are used. These concepts represent one aspect of expectation structures and, with minor differences in their perspectives (cf. de Beaugrande 1980a: 163ff.), denote hierarchically organized systems of highly structured and conventionalized information networks of a segment of the real, or of a fictitious, constructed world (e.g. Schank and Abelson's *restaurant script* with the roles of the guest, the waiter, the cook, etc.). Scripts, frames, and schemata are conventionalized plans for problem-solving, in so far as they provide knowledge about recurring human problems and possible ways of coping with them (e.g. how to behave in the role of the guest in a restaurant).

Scripts, frames, and schemata do not only organize information about segments of reality but they also make information expectable. When individuals are in or negotiate real or fictitious situations, they generally expect that information conventionally or typically connected with the situational frame will potentially be dealt with in communication, and that certain courses of action and/or ways of behaving can thus be constituted.

Expectation structures in the reception and production of text can come into being by an activation of knowledge structures via an instantiation of scripts, frames, and schemata. Such an activation can be brought about in two different ways:

1. The text receiver or producer applies his/her goals as well as relevant parts of his/her knowledge to those text segments s/he has already received in SL or produced in TL and seeks to support his/her goals and knowledge by relevant information in the text. Thus, further knowledge structures can be activated. This type of processing is called *concept-driven* or *top-down processing* (cf. Bobrow/Norman 1975; Kurcz 1984).

2. The incoming information from those text segments which have already been received in SL or produced in TL start interacting with the text receiver's or text producer's relevant knowledge and goals. In this way, those knowledge structures stored in memory into which the incoming information from the text fits can be activated. This type of processing is referred to as *data-driven* or *bottom-up processing* (cf. Bobrow/Norman 1975; Kurcz 1984).

Human information processing always contains both top-down and bottom-up processing (cf. van Dijk/Kintsch 1983: 75, 400ff.; Wolff n.d. [1985]: 10ff.). Thus, on the one hand, experiential data can only be processed when an individual can relate them to his/her knowledge structures. On the other hand, concrete experiential data are required as incoming information so that internalized knowledge structures can be activated. Furthermore, a certain harmony of top-down and bottom-up processes seems to be necessary for human information processing to proceed in a successful and efficient way (cf. Wolff n.d. [1985]: 10ff.; 1987).

Expectation structures within processes of language use probably exist and develop both *ex positivo* and *ex negativo.*

In the first case, expectation structures contain the language user's knowledge of and assumptions about a possible or optimal goal state. In the domain of second language acquisition, for example, Kohn (1979: 83) assumes that learners have available an explicit and/or implicit knowledge of whether or which of their utterances fulfil certain requirements (e.g. grammatical correctness) or not. This knowledge is of a hypothetical kind and is constructed and continually elaborated during the processes of learning.

In the second case, language users have available knowledge and assumptions about what can*not* function as a possible or optimal linguistic goal state. The construction of expectation structures *ex negativo* probably does not occur very frequently. This is suggested, for example, by the study of Collins et al. (1975: 286ff.), according to which information not having any truth value, i.e. information *ex negativo,* is rarely stored in memory. Such a quantitative finding, however, does not say anything about the importance which information *ex negativo* can have in any individual case.

In the translation process, subjects' expectation structures are probably constructed by an interaction between the processes of SL text reception and TL text production. As can be interpreted from the data, the subjects develop certain vague ideas about the translation product during their first reception of the SL text. On the one hand, these ideas *ex positivo* refer to how a possible or optimal translation should be. On the other hand, they *ex negativo* refer to how a possible or optimal translation must not be. These ideas, which also depend highly on the subjects' competence in the languages involved, their experience in translating, and on those parts of their knowledge which are relevant for text comprehension, coalesce into an expectation structure during the production of the translation. It is continually developed, modified, and refined by the subjects. On the one hand, they systematically go back to the SL text, interpret it in its facets of meaning, and/or extract from it information of a formal kind[5], e.g. about syntactic constructions, sentence schemata or the text structure, and thus develop concrete ideas about an adequate translation. On the other hand, the subjects successively produce the TL text, work out interim results which have the status of (preliminary) solutions to problems, test them, possibly modify them, rephrase TL text segments and thus specify or change their expectation structures according to the interim results.

As regards the process of solving *dialectical problems* (cf. section 4.5.3), Dörner (1976: 95) points out

> *(...) daß die Kriterien für die Beurteilung, ob das Ziel erreicht ist, mit der Konstruktion des Zielzustandes zusammen entstehen. Zunächst ist oft nur ein Komparativkriterium vorhanden, z.B. von der Form 'schöner als', 'besser als' usw.*

Dörner's view that the criteria for deciding whether a goal has been reached come into being and develop during the process of construing the goal state is basically also valid for the process of translational problem solving. In it, Dörner's *Komparativkriterium* is realized in the form of any particular subject's expectation structure.

Expectation structures and the translation process bear a dialectical relationship to each other. On the one hand, the expectation structure develops mainly from the translation process, from the reception of the SL text and the production of the TL text, as has been shown before. On the other hand, the expectation structure also controls the translation process, because it is one basis, if not the decisive one, for rephrasing, for searching for, for producing, and for testing (preliminary) solutions to translation problems.

Characteristic of translational expectation structures seems to be the fact that both SL and TL text segments combine to produce such structures. Not only does the top-down processing of the SL and TL text and the bottom-up processing of the two texts interact, but the processing of the SL text, both top-down and bottom-up, and the processing of the TL text, both top-down and bottom-up, also interact. In other words, the processing of the two texts (SL and TL) as well as the direction of processing (top-down and bottom-up) mutually support each other and build up the expectation structures.

If one of the components of this complex information processing is disturbed, and if this disturbance cannot be compensated by other components, deficits in the translation production manifest themselves. As the corpus of investigation reveals, such deficits occur with many subjects. There is no harmony between the concept- and the data-driven processes. On the one hand, the bottom-up processing of the foreign language text (SL or TL) is insufficient because of a low competence in the foreign language. On the other hand,

5 Cf. van Dijk/Kintsch 1983: 91ff., 292; Rickheit/Strohner 1985b: 15.

the bottom-up processing of the target-language text is often rather unsatisfactory. Many subjects almost exclusively translate in a form-oriented way (cf. section 7.3). Although their SL text reception is both form- and sense-oriented (cf. section 7.3), their TL text production is generally form-oriented only. A sense-oriented production of the TL text hardly takes place, and, as a result of this deficit, the level of sense processing remains largely inactive.

7.3 Translation Between an Interlingual Exchange of Signs and a Mediation of Sense

As the elicited data show, text segments can be translated in basically two different ways: *sign-/form-oriented* or *sense-oriented.*

In sign- or form-oriented translating, subjects transfer source-language text segments by focussing on their forms (= succession of signs) and by replacing them by target-language forms. This transfer of forms/signs is brought about without recourse to the sense of the two text segments involved (cf. Seleskovitch 1976: 92; Goddard 1972: 19).

Substitutions of signs mainly occur in the lexical domain and result from vocabulary equations which the subjects have learned in foreign language lessons at school or at the university. Above all, decontextualized and purely sign-oriented vocabulary learning, which even today is rather widespread, forms and provides a large number of purely surface-structure lexeme equations, such as German “Entwicklung” is English “development”, or “country” in English means “Land” in German.

When a subject is faced with an SL text segment as part of a lexeme equation stored in memory, the TL text segment as the second part of the lexeme equation may become available to the subject through an automatic association process.

In the data corpus, a large number of indicators of sign-oriented translating can be detected, five of which will be discussed in the following paragraphs.

i. When a TL text segment is produced immediately after the reception of an SL one, the subject has probably translated in a sign-oriented way. By means of an automatic association process, the corresponding TL text segment becomes available within a very short period of time and can be verbalized. Sense-oriented translating is dependent on and controlled by mental processes which bring about a separation of SL forms/signs from their sense which is in turn combined with TL forms/signs. However, these processes of separation and combination require much longer periods of time than automatic association processes.

Sign-oriented translating by means of automatic association processes can frequently be found in the data corpus. It occurs primarily in non-strategic parts of translations, but is not confined to them, as will be shown in the following paragraphs.

ii. Sometimes, subjects verbalize TL text segments which represent a literal, if not a word-for-word, translation[6] of SL text segments but which either make no sense or make a sense which differs from that of the respective SL text segments. This phenomenon can be observed with metaphorical and idiomatic utterances. On the one hand, lack of foreign language competence may be one reason for this. On the other, it is also in the translations *into* the subjects' mother tongue that text segments are verbalized, which being literal or word-for-word translations, break grammatical rules or violate norms of usage of the target-language. Such deficient utterances in the subjects' mother tongue are by no means rare (cf. Krings 1986a: 470ff.; 503f.). They possibly result from the view held by many subjects that translation is basically an exchange of signs (words, syntagmas, clauses, and sentences) between two languages[7]. As a result of this view, the SL text is ascribed a dominant role. Being the "sacred original" (Hönig/Kußmaul 1982: 17ff.), it is to be translated as literally as possible into the target-language. Its succession of signs creates a syntagmatic pressure during a translation which the subjects often cannot resist during the TL text production, even though it results in apparently senseless or ungrammatical utterances. Often, the subjects are not aware of such deficient utterances because they are rarely checked for their sense, or the utterances are consciously accepted because they are not in opposition to the subjects' conception of translation, but rather considered legitimate because of it (cf. Krings 1986a: 504; Hönig/Kußmaul 1982: 120ff.).

iii. A further indicator of sign-oriented translating are the negative solutions to translation problems (SP = Ø). According to its definition (cf. section 5.2.2), this category of analysis captures text segments which can*not* function as solutions to translation problems although they suggest themselves as solutions.

---

6 According to Wilss (1981a: 87f.), "word-for-word translation (...) follows the syntactic structures of the SL, while preserving semantic TE [translation equivalence; W.L.] between the SL and TL segments; literal translation, on the other hand, follows the system of syntactic rules (on the level of system and norm) found in the TL, while again preserving TE between SL and TL textual segments (...). Rendering the English sentence
(1) I have read the book.
(2) Ich habe das Buch gelesen.
is a literal translation, since the translator, while retaining the SL clause construction, has changed the sequence of the individual words of the sentence in accordance with TL syntactic rules. The translation
(3) **Ich habe gelesen das Buch.*
on the other hand, would be a word-for-word translation, each word in the TL being the exact replica of the corresponding word in the SL clause." Cf. also Catford (1965: 25; Königs 1982: 149f.; Bassnet-McGuire 1980: 39).

7 This is also suggested by the fact that the subjects almost exclusively take a sentence-, clause-, or even word-oriented approach to translation and determine their units of translation accordingly (cf. section 5.3).

They often result from a literal translation of an SL text segment, such as English "cultivated" and German "kultiviert". But in contrast to what was described in the preceding paragraph, the users of SP = $\emptyset$ realize the inadequacy of the TL text segment. The problem-solving activities which follow negative solutions are always sense-oriented, probably because the subjects realize the limits and the problematic nature of sign-oriented translating.

iv. Multiple verbalizations of translation problems can function as potential indicators of sign-oriented translating. These strategy elements can indicate both sign- and sense-oriented translating. When subjects verbalize lexical translation problems several times, they can thus place them into their focus of cognitive attention. By means of an association process, for example, they may succeed in making available an equation of lexemes which they have learned before, and which they had previously no access to.

v. Rephrasings of source-language text segments can also indicate sign-oriented translating. The rephrasing itself is probably brought about in a sense-oriented way. The text segment being the result of the rephrasing, however, can activate an equation of lexemes stored in memory and recall the second part of the equation, again by means of an association process, for example.

As pointed out before, sign-oriented translating is characterized by a recall from memory and a verbalization of TL forms which correspond to the respective SL forms. Sign-oriented translations are brought about by automatic association processes, for example, and employ an inventory of stored surface-structure equations of lexemes. This can be diagrammatically represented as follows:

Diagram 25: Sign-Oriented Translating

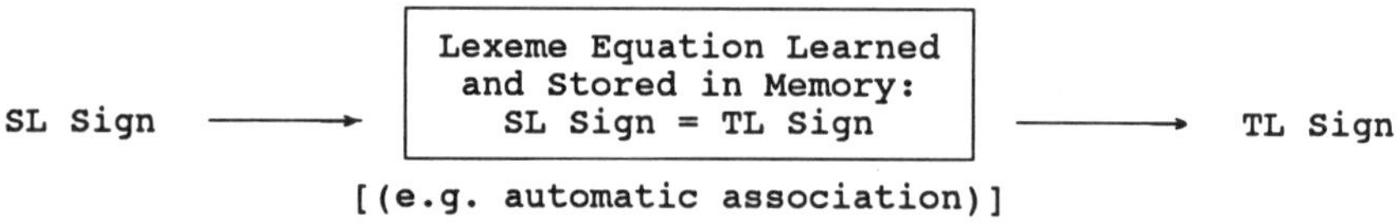

A further possibility of finding target-language text segments which correspond to source-language ones is sense-oriented translating. The sense combined with an SL text segment is made explicit by the translator and thus "separated" from it. On the basis of the sense thus constituted, the translator searches for adequate TL signs. The process of sense-oriented translating is represented in the following diagram:

Diagram 26: Sense-Oriented Translating

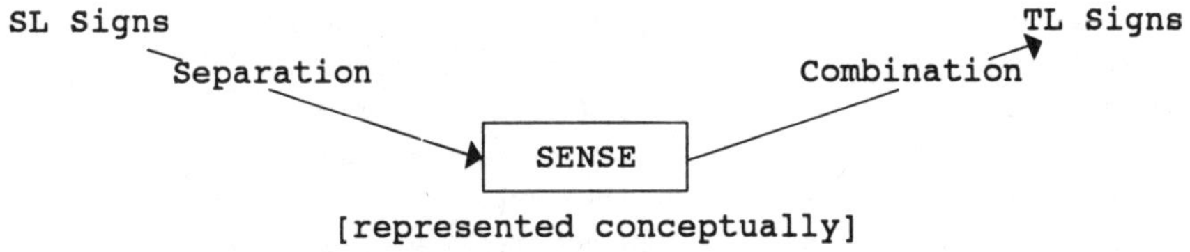

The process of separating SL signs from their sense has been described by Seleskovitch (1976: 103; 1978: 336) in connection with the process of interpreting and is also assumed to be operating in the translation process.

As the data show, the separation of forms from their sense can be realized in two different ways:

1. As described in iv., subjects sometimes have recourse to antecedent, problematic SL text segments and repeat them several times. By means of this monitoring, which mostly occurs on the level of lexemes and syntagmas (cf. subsection 6.3.5.4), the subjects can determine the sense combined with the SL signs, or, when reception problems occur, can successively approach it. In this way, the sense is separated from the SL signs and is placed into the subjects' foci of attention.

2. As described in v., subjects sometimes have recourse to antecedent, problematic SL text segments and rephrase them, i.e. try to find SL text segments which are different in form but have (approximately) the same sense (cf. Butterworth 1980b: 172). On the one hand, such rephrasings require from the translator (partially unreflected) knowledge or expectations about elements which have (approximately) the same sense in SL, and which can therefore serve as rephrasings. On the other, it is mainly by developing rephrasings that subjects become aware of the sense of an SL text segment and of those components of sense in which two SL text segments may differ.

During or after the separation of SL forms from their sense, the subjects try to combine the sense, to the extent to which they have interpreted it, with (a sequence of) TL forms (cf. Butterworth 1980b: 172). This requires a process of searching in which situational and contextual factors that determine the range of sense of an SL text segment are taken into account. This again depends on the translator's competence and experience in translating and in the two languages involved. As discussed in section 7.2, the process of searching is probably highly controlled by the subjects' expectation structures.

The two approaches to translation which have been outlined are like two extremes, between which the concrete translational activities of the subjects range. Neither exclusively sense-oriented nor exclusively sign-oriented translating can be found in the corpus and probably does not occur with professional translators either[8].

Nonetheless, the data clearly show that the subjects tend to produce the translations primarily in a sign-oriented way. This does not at all exclude the sense-oriented translation of certain text segments. But on the whole, it can be assumed that non-professional translators take a mainly sign-oriented and professional translators a mainly sense-oriented approach to translation.

In order to obtain hints about whether and to what extent the subjects had the sense of the SL text mentally available, thus meeting a basic requirement for performing sense-oriented translations, 18 subjects were asked to retell the SL text in the target-language in as precise and detailed a way as possible. In spite of the manifold problems connected with this experiment, the reproductions produced, nonetheless showed that the subjects had mentally processed the texts for the translations to a high degree and that they largely had the sense of the texts conceptually represented and mentally available. Although individual differences can be detected, it is quite obvious that the subjects have interpreted the SL texts and thus constituted their sense. But although they met this requirement, they nonetheless produced their translations in a basically sign-oriented way. One reason for this may be the subjects' experiences in translating gained in foreign language lessons at school and at the university and, as a result of these, their conception of translation.

A further explanation of the apparent dominance of sign-oriented translation is provided by the psycholinguistic minimax strategy discussed by Krings (1986a: 507ff.). As pointed out in section 7.1, the data clearly suggest that the subjects try to keep the cognitive load as light as possible during their translations. This is in accordance with the principle of economy which applies to mental processes. The subjects generally do not proceed to a deeper level of cognitive processing, which is more abstract and implies a higher cognitive load, before the processing on the higher level has turned out to be unsuccessful or unsatisfactory[9]. But as sign-oriented translating probably goes along with information processing which is, in principle, less complex and/or laborious, it can be expected that the subjects do not proceed to sense-oriented translating before sign-oriented procedures have turned out to be unsuccessful or unsatisfactory. This assumption is supported by the results which the quantitative analysis in the preceding chapter yielded. Normally, the subjects do not bring about separations of SL forms from their sense by means of rephrasings

---

8 Among others, Seleskovitch (1976: 94) and Goddard (1972: 19) have pointed out that translation always represents a mixture of sign- and sense-oriented procedures. Cf. also Krings 1986a: 507ff.

9 This is largely in accordance with the levels-of-processing approach (cf. Craik/Lockhart 1972; Shiffrin/Schneider 1977; Schneider/Shiffrin 1977; Obliers 1985: 9ff.) according to which information is processed on levels of differing depth in a (potentially) successive way. The depth of the level on which an item is processed corresponds highly to the degree to which it is fixed in memory.

or multiple verbalizations of translation problems, and thus create the basis for sense-oriented translating, when translation problems can be solved by employing less complex and/or laborious sign-oriented procedures.

8 Concluding Remarks

In the preceding chapters, an attempt was made to achieve the aim of this investigation in four steps. In the first step, specific methods for investigating the translation process by analyzing translation performance were constructed or elaborated. The application of these methods to the corpus of investigation represented the second step. Thus translation strategies, their elements, and translation versions were isolated and categorized to make types. In the third step, the types of strategies and their essential elements were analyzed quantitatively. On the basis of the results which the investigation carried out in the second and third step yielded, three hypotheses about the translation process were constructed in the fourth and last step.

In this concluding chapter, three facts will be outlined which refer to one or several of the steps just mentioned and which have consequences for future research into the translation process.

I. The methods employed in this investigation have, on the whole, turned out to be fruitful and reliable. This applies to both the methods for *eliciting* and for *analyzing* the data. The latter methods are basically those of interpretive reconstruction and of employing strategy indicators. It has become clear that an interpretive, sense-constituting approach to performance data need not necessarily have a subjectivist character. Rather, the analysis can well yield supra-individually valid and accepted results when the analyst uses his/her interpretive knowledge in a methodologically controlled way and makes the process of sense-constitution argumentatively explicit and thus comprehensible. However, this does not exclude cases in which different analysts may interpret performance data in different ways.

Among the methods for *eliciting* data, the thinking-aloud technique plays the most important role. When the target-language texts as the end products of the translation processes are compared with the thinking-aloud protocols, it is easy to recognize what an abundance of data on the steps in the processes of TL text production is yielded by the thinking-aloud technique. Nonetheless, there are considerable differences as regards the quantity and kind of data externalized by the various subjects. Possibly, phases in which the subjects could have practised thinking-aloud before the elicitation of the data would have been helpful. But certainly, the subjects' willingness and ability to "reveal" themselves by thinking-aloud are largely personality-specific and individually caused. In future investigations, it might therefore be worth considering whether a combination of introspective, i.e. thinking-aloud, and retrospective procedures should be used. Especially when thinking-aloud only yields few data or data which are not indicative of elements of translation strategies, retrospective procedures might be helpful. Such a combined introspective-retrospective approach is also propagated by Ericsson and Simon (1984).

II. Both the qualitative and the quantitative analysis of the translation strategies and their elements has shown that in addition to the manifold individual differences there is a large number of supraindividual rules and regularities in the data. Translation strategies have a high degree of inherent variability. Discrete "when -- then" statements of the kind: "When faced with problem X, the subjects employ strategy Y" are obviously not possible. Such statements are based on an erroneous concept of performance. As diagram 11 (page 118), which graphically represents strategic translating, shows, the subjects/translators have different procedures for solving translation problems available. Furthermore, the quantitative analysis of the data has yielded the result that one and the same problem can be successfully addressed by different strategies, and that one and the same strategy can be used to solve different problems. On the basis of the investigation of individual and supraindividual translation problems and strategies it must be assumed that although translation strategies are procedures of a "when -- then" kind, they are by their very nature not nomological hypotheses. They take into account variability as a characteristic feature of performance. In their most general form, they can be modelled as follows: "When several subjects are faced with a problem X, many or most of them employ similar or the same *types* of strategy."

III. As pointed out in Chapter 7, the analysis of the translations has hardly yielded any strategies which exclusively occur within the *translation* process, and are thus translation-specific. Rather, the analysis has shown that general strategies for processing texts, and especially sentences, clauses, and words (cf. Bock 1978) have a characteristic shape when employed in the translation process: The information contained in the SL text(segment) received and in the TL text(segment) already produced is processed separately from or in combination with the various pieces of information supporting and completing each other. Top-down and bottom-up processing has three sources: the subjects' factual, linguistic, and processing knowledge, the information contained in the SL text, and the information contained in the TL text. The last two types of information mentioned do not only interact with each other but also, singly or in combination, with the knowledge structures stored in the subjects' episodic and/or semantic memory. In this way, information networks whose "architecture" is basically determined by the subjects' expectation structures are constructed. According to this conception, solutions to problems can be brought about by the subjects selecting the available information in a goal-oriented way and by processing it. How this is done in detail is still largely unknown. But it is hoped that this study has shed some light on certain aspects of language processing in translation.

9 Bibliography

Aebli, H. (1973): "Einführung." In: Miller et al. (1973), 7–9.

Albrecht, J. (1973): *Linguistik und Übersetzung*. Tübingen.

Alderson, C.J./Urquhart, A.H. (eds.) (1984): *Reading in a Foreign Language*. London.

Anderson, J.R. (1976): *Language, Memory, and Thought*. Hillsdale/N.J.

Anderson, J.R. (1980): *Cognitive Psychology and its Implications*. San Francisco.

Antos, G. (1981): "Zum Problem der Zeichenproduktion am Beispiel der gesprochenen Sprache." In: Lange-Seidl (1981), Volume 1, 181–188.

Antos, G. (1982): *Grundlagen einer Theorie des Formulierens*. Textherstellung in geschriebener und gesprochener Sprache. Tübingen.

Arbeitsgruppe Bielefelder Soziologen (ed.) (1973): *Alltagswissen, Interaktion und gesellschaftliche Wirklichkeit*. Reinbek. 2 Volumes.

Arbeitsgruppe Fremdsprachenerwerb Bielefeld (1987): "Welcher Typ von Forschung in der Fremdsprachendidaktik? Zum Verhältnis von qualitativer und quantitativer Forschung. In: Lörscher/Schulze (1987), 943–975.

Arrowsmith, W./Shattuck, R. (eds.) ^{2}1964): *The Craft and Context of Translation. A Symposium*. Austin, TX.

Baars, B.J. (1980): "The competing plans hypothesis: an heuristic viewpoint on the causes of errors in speech." In: Dechert/Raupach (1980), 39–49.

Ballmer, T.T. (1976): "Inwiefern ist Linguistik empirisch? Eine allgemeine Explikation des Empiriebegriffs mit spezieller Berücksichtigung der sich für die Linguistik ergebenden Konsequenzen." In: Wunderlich (1976), 6–53.

Ballmer, T.T. (1980): "The role of pauses and suprasegmentals in a grammar." In: Dechert/ Raupach (1980), 211–220.

Ballstaedt, S.P. et al. (1981): *Texte verstehen, Texte gestalten*. München.

Bar-Hillel, J. (1954): "Indexical expressions." *Mind* 63, 359–379.

Barik, H.C. (1975): "Simultaneous interpretation: qualitative and linguistic data." *Language and Speech* 18, 272–297.

Bartlett, F.C. (1932): *Remembering: A Study in Experimental and Social Psychology*. Cambridge.

Bassnet-McGuire, S. (1980): *Translation Studies*. London.

Bathgate, R.H. (1980): "Studies of translation models, 1: An operational model of the translation process." *The Incorporated Linguist* 19, 113f.

Bäuerle, R. et al. (eds.) (1983): *Meaning, Use, and Interpretation of Language*. Berlin.

Baumgärtner, K. (ed.) (1977): *Sprachliches Handeln*. Heidelberg.

Baur, R.S et al. (1980): *Resümierende Auswahlbibliographie der neueren sowjetischen Sprachlehrforschung (gesteuerter Fremdsprachenerwerb)*. Amsterdam.

Baur, R.S./Grzybek, P. (1985): "Neuropsychologische Grundlagen des Fremdsprachenerwerbs." In: Donnerstag/Knapp-Potthoff (1985), 173–182.

Bausch, K.-R. (1977a): "Hilft das Konstrukt der latenten Psychostruktur die Krise der angewandt-kontrastiven Linguistik überwinden?" In: Christ/Piepho (1977), 266–269.

Bausch, K.-R. (1977b): "Zur Übertragbarkeit der 'Übersetzung als Fertigkeit' auf die 'Übersetzung als Übungsform'." *Die Neueren Sprachen* 76, 517–535.

Bausch, K.-R./Raabe, H. (1978): "Zur Frage der Relevanz von kontrastiver Analyse, Fehleranalyse und Interimsprachenanalyse für den Fremdsprachenunterricht." In: Wierlacher (1978), 56–75.

Bausch, K.-R. et al. (1970/1972): *The Science of Translation: An Analytical Bibliography.* Tübingen. 2 Volumes.
Bausch, K.-R./Weller, F.-R. (eds.) (1981): *Übersetzen im Fremdsprachenunterricht.* Frankfurt/M.
de Beaugrande, R.A. (1976): *Linguistik und Poetisches Übersetzen am Beispiel von Rilkes Duineser Elegien.* Ph.D. dissertation, University of California, Irvine. Xerox University Microfilms.
de Beaugrande, R.A. (1978a): *Factors in a Theory of Poetic Translating.* Assen.
de Beaugrande, R.A. (1978b): "Information, expectation, and processing: On classifying poetic texts." *Poetics* 7, 3–44.
de Beaugrande, R.A. (1980a): *Text, Discourse, and Process.* Norwood/NJ.
de Beaugrande, R.A. (1980b): "Toward a semiotic theory of literary translating." In: Wilss (1980), 23–42.
de Beaugrande, R.A. (1984): *Text Production.* Toward a Science of Composition. Norwood/NJ.
de Beaugrande, R.A./Dressler, W. (1981): *Introduction to Text Linguistics.* London.
Bellezza, F.S./Bower, G.H. (1981): "The representational and processing characteristics of scripts." *Bulletin of the Psychonomic Society* 18, 1–4.
Bellezza, F.S./Bower, G.H. (1982): "Remembering script-based text." *Poetics* 11, 1–23.
Bender, K.-H. et al. (eds.) (1977): *Imago Linguae. Beiträge zu Sprache, Deutung und Übersetzen.* Festschrift zum 60. Geburtstag von Fritz Paepcke. München.
Benediktov, B.A. (1974): *Psichologija ovladenija inostrannym jazykom. (Psychologie des Fremdsprachenerwerbs.)* Minsk. (German summary in Baur (1980), 22–27.)
Bense, E. (1973): *Mentalismus in der Sprachtheorie Noam Chomskys.* Kronberg/Ts.
Bereiter, C. (1980): "Development in writing." In: Gregg/Steinberg (1980), 73–93.
Berger, P.L./Luckmann, T. (1966): *The Social Construction of Reality.* Treatise in the Sociology of Knowledge. Garden City/NY.
Bergmann, J.R. (1981): "Ethnomethodologische Konversationsanalyse." In: Schröder/Steger (1981), 9–52.
Bialystok, E. (1983): "Some factors in the selection and implementation of communication strategies." In: Færch/Kasper (1983a), 100–118.
Bialystok, E. (1984): "Strategies in interlanguage learning and performance." In: Davies et al. (1984), 37–48.
Black, J.B. (1982): "Psycholinguistic processes in writing." In: Rosenberg (1982), 199–216.
Black, J.B./Bower, G.H. (1980): "Story understanding as problem-solving." *Poetics* 9, 223–250.
Bobrow, D.C./Collins, A.M.(eds.) (1975): *Representation and Understanding: Studies in Cognitive Science.* New York.
Bobrow, D.C./Norman, D. A. (1975): "Some principles of memory schemata." In: Bobrow/Collins (1975), 131–149.
Bock, M. (1978): *Wort-, Satz-, Textverarbeitung.* Stuttgart.
Börner, W. (1987): "Schreiben im Fremdsprachenunterricht: Überlegungen zu einem Modell." In: Lörscher/Schulze (1987), 1336–1349.
Börsch, S. (ed.) (1986): *Die Rolle der Psychologie in der Sprachlehrforschung.* Tübingen.
Bosshardt, H.-G./Meyer, A. (1985): "Experimentelle Untersuchung des Simultandolmetschens: Einheitenbildung und zeitliche Koordination." *Archiv für Psychologie* 137, 137–157.
Bransford, J.D./Johnson, M.K. (1972): "Conceptual prerequisites for understanding: some investigations of comprehension and recall." *Journal of Verbal Learning and Verbal Behaviour* 11, 717–726.
Breen, M.M./Candlin, C.N. (eds.) (1983): *Interpretive Strategies in Language Learning.* Oxford.
Brislin, R.W. (ed.) (1976): *Translation: Applications and Research.* New York.
Brockhaus Wahrig (1984): *Deutsches Wörterbuch.* In sechs Bänden. Volume 6, Wiesbaden.

van den Broeck, R. (1978): "The concept of equivalence in translation theory: some critical reflections." In: Holmes et al. (1978), 29–47.

van den Broeck, R. (1980): "Toward a text-type-oriented theory of translation." In: Poulsen/Wilss (1980), 82–96.

van den Broeck, R./Lefevere, A. ²(1984): *Uitnodiging tot de vertaalwetenschap*. Muiderberg.

Brown, P./Levinson, S. (1978): "Universals in language usage: Politeness phenomena." In: Goody (1978), 56–289.

Brunner, E.-J. (1982): "Interpretative Auswertung." In: Huber/Mandl (1982), 197–219.

Bublitz, W. (1988): *Supportive Fellow-Speakers and Cooperative Conversations: Discourse Topics and Topical Actions, Participant Roles and 'Recipient Action' in a Particular Type of Everyday Conversation*. Amsterdam.

Büchel, F.P. (1982): "Metacognitive variables in the learning of written text." In: Flammer/Kintsch (1982), 352359.

Bühl, W.L. (ed.) (1972): *Verstehende Soziologie – Grundzüge und Entwicklungstendenzen*. München.

Bühler, K. (1907/1971): "Tatsachen und Probleme zu einer Psychologie der Denkvorgänge: I. Über Gedanken." *Archiv für die gesamte Psychologie* IX, 297–365. Shortened version entitled "Über Gedanken" In: Graumann (1971), 60–74.

Butterworth, B. (ed.) (1980a): *Language Production*. Volume 1: Speech and Talk. London.

Butterworth, B. (1980b): "Evidence from pauses in speech." In: Butterworth (1980a), 155–176.

Butterworth, B. (1980c): "Introduction: a brief review of methods of studying language production." In: Butterworth (1980a), 1–17.

Campbell, R.N./Smith, P.T. (1978): *Recent Advances in the Psychology of Languages – Formal and Experimental Approaches*. New York.

Carterette, E.C./Friedman, M.P. (eds.) (1976): *Handbook of Perception*. Volume VII: Language and Speech. New York.

Catford, J.C. (1965): *A Linguistic Theory of Translation*. London.

Chao, Y.R. (1962): "Models in linguistics and models in general." In: Nagel et al. (1962), 558–566.

Chlenov, L. (1948): "Ob afazii u poliglotov." *Izvestiia Akademii Pedagogicheskich nauk RSFSR* 15, 783–790.

Chomsky, N. (1957): *Syntactic Structures*. Den Haag.

Chomsky, N. (1959): "Review of B.F. Skinner: *Verbal Behavior*." *Language* 35, 26–58.

Chomsky, N. (1965): Aspects of the Theory of Syntax. Cambridge/MA.

Christ, H./Piepho, E. (eds.) (1977): *Kongreßdokumentation der 7. Arbeitstagung der Fremdsprachendidaktiker in Gießen 1976*. Limburg.

Cicourel, A.V. (1964): *Method and Measurement in Sociology*. New York.

Cicourel, A.V. (1973a): *Cognitive Sociology*. London.

Cicourel, A.V. (1973b): "Basisregeln und normative Regeln im Prozeß des Aushandelns von Status und Rolle." In: Arbeitsgruppe Bielefelder Soziologen (1973), 147–188.

Claparède, E. (1932/1971): *"La découverte de l'hypothèse." Journal de Psychologie Normale et Pathologique* 29, 648–656. German version: "Die Entdeckung der Hypothese." In: Graumann (1971), 109–115.

Claparède, E. (1933): "L'origine de l'hypothèse. Etude expérimentale." *Archives de Psychologie* 24), 155.

Claparède, E. (1934): *La genèse de l'hypothèse*. Genève.

Clark, H.H./Clark, E.V. (1977): *Psychology and Language*. An Introduction to Psycholinguistics. New York.

Cogen, C. et al. (eds.) (1975): *Proceedings of the First Annual Meeting of the Berkeley Linguistics Society*. February 15–17, 1975. Berkeley/CA.

Cohen, A.D. (1982): "Introspecting about second language learning." *Studia Anglia Posnaniensia* 15, 139–146.
Cohen, A.D. (1984): "Studying second-language learning strategies: how do we get the information?" *Applied Linguistics* 5, 101–112.
Cohen, A.D./Hosenfeld, C. (1981): "Some uses of mentalistic data in second language research." *Language Learning* 31, 285–313.
Collins, A.M./Loftus, E.F. (1975): "A spreading-activation theory of semantic processing." *Psychological Review* 82, 407–428.
Collins, A.M. et al. (1975): "Reasoning from incomplete knowledge." In: Bobrow/Collins (1975), 383–415.
Collins, A.M./Gentner, D. (1980): "A framework for a cognitive theory of writing." In: Gregg/Steinberg (1980), 51–72.
Cook, V. (ed.) (1986): *Experimental Approaches to Second Language Learning*. Oxford.
Corder, S.P. (1983): "Strategies of communication." In: Færch/Kasper (1983a), 15–19.
Coseriu, E. (1978): "Falsche und richtige Fragestellungen in der Übersetzungstheorie." In: Grähs et al. (1978), 17–32.
Coseriu, E. (1980): *Textlinguistik*. Eine Einführung. Tübingen.
Craik, F.I.M./Lockhart, R.S. (1972): "Levels of processing: a framework for memory research." *Journal of Verbal Learning and Verbal Behaviour* 11, 671–684.
Crystal, D. (1974): "Paralinguistics." In: Sebeok (1974), 265–295.
Crystal, D. (1976): *Child Language, Learning, and Linguistics*. London.
Crystal, D./Davy, D. (1969): *Investigating English Style*. London.
Danks, J.H. (1977): "Producing ideas and sentences." In: Rosenberg (1977), 229258.
Dascal, M. (1983): *Pragmatics and the Philosophy of Mind I; Thought in Language*. Amsterdam.
Davies, A. et al. (eds.) (1984): *Interlanguage*. Edinburgh.
Dechert, H.W. (1983): "How a story is done in a second language." In: Færch/Kasper (1983a), 175–195.
Dechert, H.W. (1987): "Analyzing language processing through verbal protocols." In: Færch/Kasper (1987), 96–112.
Dechert, H.W./Raupach, M. (eds.) (1980): *Temporal Variables in Speech*. Studies in Honour of Frieda Goldman–Eisler. Den Haag.
Dechert, H.W. et al. (eds.) (1984): *Second Language Productions*. Tübingen.
Dechert, H.W./Sandrock, U. (1986): "Thinking-aloud protocols: the decomposition of language processing." In: Cook (1986), 111–126.
Deffner, G. (1984): *Lautes Denken – Untersuchung zur Qualität eines Datenerhebungsverfahrens*. Frankfurt/M.
Delisle, J. (1981): *L'analyse du discours comme méthode de traduction. Initiation à la traduction de textes pragmatiques anglais: théorie et pratique*. [Cahiers de traductologie 2.] (Ed. de l'université d'Ottawa).
van Dijk, T.A./Kintsch, W. (1983): *Strategies of Discourse Comprehension*. New York.
Diller, H.-J./Kornelius, J. (1978): *Linguistische Probleme der Übersetzung*. Tübingen.
Dirven, R. (1981): "Language as a symbiosis of form and meaning." In: Esser/Hübler (1981), 33–42.
Dittmann, J. (ed.) (1979a): *Arbeiten zur Konversationsanalyse*. Tübingen.
Dittmann, J. (1979b): "Einleitung – Was ist, zu welchen Zwecken und wie betreiben wir Konversationsanalyse?" In: Dittmann (1979a), 1–43.
Donnerstag, J./Knapp-Potthoff, A. (eds.) (1985): *Kongreßdokumentation der 10. Arbeitstagung der Fremdsprachendidaktiker*. Tübingen.
Dörner, D. (1974): *Die kognitive Organisation beim Problemlösen*. Bern.
Dörner, D. (1976): *Problemlösen als Informationsverarbeitung*. Stuttgart.

Dorsch, F. (1976): *Psychologisches Wörterbuch*. Bern.

Drescher, H.W./Scheffzek, S. (eds.) (1976): *Theorie und Praxis des Übersetzens und Dolmetschens*. Referate und Diskussionsbeiträge des Internationalen Kolloquiums am Fachbereich Angewandte Sprachwissenschaft der Johannes-Gutenberg-Universität Mainz in Germersheim (2.–4. Mai 1975). Bern.

Dressler, W. (1972): "Textgrammatische Invarianz in Übersetzungen?" In: Gülich/Raible (1972), 98–106.

Dressler, W. (1974): "Der Beitrag der Textlinguistik zur Übersetzungswissenschaft." In: Kapp (1974), 61–71.

Duden. Das Fremdwörterbuch (1974): Mannheim.

Durkheim, E. (1895/1938): *The Rules of Sociological Method*. Chicago. French Original Edition 1895.

Ehlich, K. (ed.) (1980a): *Erzählen im Alltag*. Frankfurt/M.

Ehlich, K. (1980b): "Der Alltag des Erzählens." In Ehlich (1980a), 11–27.

Ehlich, K./Switalla, B. (1976): "Transkriptionssysteme – Eine exemplarische Übersicht." *Studium Linguistik* 1, 78–105.

Eigler, G. (1985): "Textverarbeiten und Textproduzieren. Entwicklungstendenzen angewandter kognitiver Wissenschaft." *Unterrichtswissenschaft* 13, 301–318.

Eigler, G./Nenninger, P. (1985): "Zusammenfassung von Lehrtexten – mündlich/schriftlich." *Unterrichtswissenschaft* 13, 346–361.

Enkvist, N.E. (ed.) (1982): *Impromptu Speech*: A Symposium. Åbo.

Ericsson, K.A./Simon, H.A. (1980): "Verbal reports as data." *Psychological Review* 87, 215 - 251.

Ericsson, K.A./Simon, H.A. (1984): *Protocol Analysis*. Verbal Reports as Data. Cambridge/ MA.

Ericsson, K.A./Simon, H.A. (1987): "Verbal reports on thinking." In: Færch/Kasper (1987), 24–53.

Esper, E.A. (1968): *Mentalism and Objectivism in Linguistics*. New York.

Esser, J./Hübler, A. (eds.) (1981): *Forms and Functions*. Papers in General, English, and Applied Linguistics Presented to Vilém Fried on the Occasion of His Sixty-fifth Birthday. Tübingen.

Færch, C. (1984): "Strategies in production and reception – some empirical evidence." In: Davies et al. (1984), 49–70.

Færch, C./Kasper, G. (1980): "Processes and strategies in foreign language learning and communication." *Interlanguage Studies Bulletin* 5, 47–118.

Færch, C./Kasper, G. (eds.) (1983a): Strategies in *Interlanguage Communication*. London.

Færch, C./Kasper, G. (1983b): "On identifying communication strategies in interlanguage production." In: Færch/Kasper (1983a), 210–238.

Færch, C./Kasper, G. (1983c): "Plans and strategies in foreign language communication." In: Færch/Kasper (1983a), 20–60.

Færch, C./Kasper, G. (1984a): "Two ways of defining communication strategies." *Language Learning* 34, 45–63.

Færch, C./Kasper, G. (1984b): "Pragmatic knowledge: rules and procedures." *Applied Linguistics* 5, 214–225.

Færch, C./Kasper, G. (1986a): "The role of comprehension in second-language learning." *Applied Linguistics* 7, 257–274.

Færch, C./Kasper, G. (1986b): "Introspektive Methoden in der Lernersprachenanalyse." In: Börsch (1986), 296–303.

Færch, C./Kasper, G. (1987): *Introspection in Second Language Research*. Clevedon.

Faiß, K. (1972): "Übersetzung und Sprachwissenschaft – Eine Orientierung." *International Review of Applied Linguistics in Language Teaching* X, 1–20.

Fanselow, J.F./Crymes, R. (eds.) (1976): *On TESOL '76*. Washington DC.
Feldmann, U./Stemmer, B. (1987): "Thin__ aloud a__ retrospective da__ in te__ taking: diffe__ languages – diff__ learners – sa__ approaches?" In: Færch/Kasper (1987), 251–266.
Felix, S.W. (1976): "Interference, interlanguage, and related issues." In: Molony/Zobl (1976), 237–258.
Fillmore, C. (1975): "An alternative to checklist theories of meaning." In: *Proceedings of the First Annual Meeting of the Berkeley Linguistics Society*, 123–131.
Fillmore, C. (1976): "Frame semantics and the nature of language." In: Harnad et al. (1976), 20–32.
Fillmore, C. (1977): "Scenes and frames semantics." In: Zampolli (1977), 55–81.
Flammer, A./Kintsch, W. (eds.) (1982): *Discourse Processing*. Amsterdam.
Flanders, N.A. (1970) Analyzing Teaching Behavior. Reading/MA.
Flower, L.S./Hayes, J.R. (1980): "The dynamics of composing: making plans and juggling constraints." In: Gregg/Steinberg (1980), 31–50.
Fodor, J.A. (1983): *The Modularity of Mind.* An essay on faculty psychology. Cambridge/Mass.
Fodor, J.A./Katz, J.J. (eds.) (1964): *The Structure of Language*. Englewood Cliffs/NJ.
Foss, D.J./Hakes, D.T. (1978): *Psycholinguistics*. An Introduction to the Psychology of Language. Englewood Cliffs/NJ.
Frege, G. (³1969a): *Funktion, Begriff, Bedeutung*. Fünf logische Studien. Göttingen.
Frege, G. (1969b): "Über Sinn und Bedeutung." In: Frege (1969a), 40–65.
Fritz, G. (1977): "Strategische Maximen für sprachliche Interaktion." In: Baumgärtner (1977), 47–68.
Fromkin, V.A. (1971): "The non-anomalous nature of anomalous utterances." *Language* 47, 27–52.
Funk-Kolleg Sprache (1973): Volume 1. Eine Einführung in die moderne Linguistik. Stuttgart.
Gadamer, H.-G. ²1965): *Wahrheit und Methode*. Grundzüge einer philosophischen Hermeneutik. Tübingen.
Gadamer, H.-G. (1974): "Hermeneutik." In: Ritter (1974), Volume 3, 1061–1073.
Garfinkel, H. (1967): *Studies in Ethnomethodology*. New York.
Garfinkel, H. (1973): "Das Alltagswissen über soziale und innerhalb sozialer Strukturen." In: Arbeitsgruppe Bielefelder Soziologen (1973), 189–262.
Garnham, A. (1985): *Psycholinguistics*. Central Topics. London.
Garretson, D.A. (1981): "A psychological approach to consecutive interpretation." *Meta* 26, 244–254.
Garrett, M.F. (1980): "Levels of processing in sentence production." In: Butterworth (1980a), 177–220.
Gerloff, P.: (1986): "Second language learners' reports on the interpretive process: talk-aloud protocols of translation." In: House/BlumKulka (1986), 243–262.
Gerloff, P. (1987): "Identifying the unit of analysis in translation: some uses of think-aloud protocol data." In: Færch/Kasper (1987), 135–158.
Gerver, D. (1976): "Empirical studies of simultaneous interpretation: A review and a model." In: Brislin (1976), 165–207.
Gerver, D./Sinaiko, H.W. (eds.) (1978): *Language Interpretation and Communication*. New York.
Giglioli, P.P. (ed.) (1973a): *Language and Social Context*. Harmondsworth.
Giglioli, P.P. (1973b): "Introduction." In: Giglioli (1973a), 7–17.
Goddard, K.A. (1972): "Translation and bilingualism." *Babel* XVIII, 18–23.
Goeppert, H.C. (ed.) (1977): *Sprachverhalten im Unterricht*. Zur Kommunikation von Lehrer und Schüler in der Unterrichtssituation. München.

Goldman-Eisler, F. (1980): "Psychological mechanisms of speech production as studied through the analysis of simultaneous translation." In: Butterworth (1980a), 143–153.

Goody, E.N. (ed.) (1978): *Questions and Politeness*. Strategies in Social Interaction. Cambridge.

Gottschaldt, K. et al. (eds.) (1964): *Handbuch der Psychologie in 12 Bänden*. Volume 1.2: Lernen und Denken. (ed. R. Bergius) Göttingen.

Gottwald, J. (1982a): *Übersetzung Englisch-Deutsch*. Texte – Fehlerquellen – Übungen. München.

Gottwald, J. (1982b): "Äquivalenzkriterien im Übersetzen an der Hochschule." In: Welte (1982), 187–200.

Grähs, L. et al. (eds.) (1978): *Theory and Practice of Translation*. Nobel Symposium 39, Stockholm, September 6–10, 1976. Bern.

Graumann, C.F. (ed.) ([5]1971): *Denken*. Köln.

Gregg, L./Steinberg, E.R. (eds.) (1980): *Cognitive Processes in Writing*. Hillsdale/NJ.

Grotjahn, R. (1987): "On the methodological basis of introspective methods." In: Færch/Kasper (1987), 54–81.

Grünbeck, B. (1976): *Moderne deutsch-französische Stilistik auf der Basis des Übersetzungsvergleichs*. Teil 1: Ordnungsliebe und logisierende Präzision als Übersetzungsdominanten. Heidelberg.

Grünbeck, B. (1983): *Moderne deutsch-französische Stilistik auf der Basis des Übersetzungsvergleichs*. Teil 2: Konzision als Übersetzungsdominante; Teil 3): Harmonie als Übersetzungsdominante. Heidelberg.

Gülich, E./Raible, W. (eds.) (1972): *Textsorten*. Differenzierungskriterien aus linguistischer Sicht. Frankfurt/M.

Gumperz, J.J. (1982a): *Discourse Strategies*. Cambridge.

Gumperz, J.J. (1982b): "Conversational code switching." In: Gumperz (1982a), 59–99.

Gumperz, J.J. (1982c): "Postscript." In: Gumperz (1982a), 204–210.

Gumperz, J.J./Hymes, D.H. (eds.) (1972): *Directions in Sociolinguistics: The Ethnography of Communication*. New York.

Günther, S. et al. (1983): "Ereignisnetze: Zeitnetze und referentielle Netze." *Linguistische Berichte* 88, 37–55.

Habel, C. (1985): "Künstliche Intelligenz und einige Folgen (für die Linguistik ?)." *Osnabrükker Beiträge zur Sprachtheorie* 29, 19–36.

Haberlandt, K./Bingham, G. (1982): "The role of scripts in the comprehension and retention of texts." *Text* 2, 29–46.

Habermas, J. (1969): *Erkenntnis und Interesse*. Frankfurt/M.

Halle, M./Stevens, K. (1964): "Speech recognition. A model and a program for research." In: Fodor/Katz (1964), 604–612.

Halliday, M.A.K. (1962): "Linguistics and machine translation." *Zeitschrift für Phonetik, Sprachwissenschaft und Kommunikationsforschung* XV, 145–158.

Harnad, S.R. et al. (1976): *Origins and Evolution of Language and Speech*. Annals of the New York Academy of Science. Volume 250. New York.

Harris, B. (1977): "The importance of natural translation." *Working Papers on Bilingualism* 12, 96–114.

Harris, B. (1978): "The difference between natural and professional translation." *Canadian Modern Language Review* 34, 417–427.

Harris, B./Sherwood, B. (1978): "Translation as an innate skill." In: Gerver/Sinaiko (1978), 155–170.

Hartfiel, G. (1972): *Wörterbuch der Soziologie*. Stuttgart.

Hartmann, P. (1970): "Übersetzen als Thema im linguistischen Aufgabenbereich." In: Hartmann/Vernay (1970), 12–32.

Hartmann, P./Vernay, H. (eds.) (1970): *Sprachwissenschaft und Übersetzung*. Symposium an der Universität Heidelberg 24.2. – 26.2.1969. München.

Hartmann, R.R.K. (1980): *Contrastive Textology – Comparative Discourse Analysis in Applied Linguistics*. Heidelberg.

Hartmann, R.R.K. (1982): "Betrachtungen zur arabischen Version von ASTERIX. Ein Übersetzungsvergleich." *Linguistische Berichte* 81, 1–31.

Hayes, J.R./Flower, L.S. (1980): "Identifying the organization of writing processes." In: Gregg/Steinberg (1980), 3–30.

Heger, K. (1971): *Monem, Wort und Satz*. Tübingen.

Heinemann, P. (1976): *Grundriß einer Pädagogik der nonverbalen Kommunikation*. Saarbrücken.

Herdan, G. (1956): *Language as Choice and Chance*. Groningen.

Herdan, G. (1960): *Type Token Mathematics*. Den Haag.

Herdan, G. (1966): *The Advanced Theory of Language as Choice and Chance*. Berlin.

Herrmann, T. et al. (eds.) (1977): *Handbuch psychologischer Grundbegriffe*. München.

Hoffmann-Riem, C. (1980): "Die Sozialforschung einer interpretativen Soziologie – Der Datengewinn." *Kölner Zeitschrift für Soziologie und Sozialpsychologie* 32, 339–372.

Holly, W. et al. (1984): "Für einen 'sinnvollen' Handlungsbegriff in der linguistischen Pragmatik." *Zeitschrift für germanistische Linguistik* 12, 275–312.

Holmes, J. S et al. (eds.) (1978): *Literature and Translation*. New Perspectives in Literary Studies. With a basic bibliography of books on translation studies. Leuven.

Hölscher, A./Möhle, D. (1987): "Cognitive plans in translation." In: Færch/Kasper (1987), 113–134.

Holz-Mänttäri, J. (1984): *Translatorisches Handeln*. Theorie und Methode. Helsinki.

Hönig, H.G. (1976): "Zur Analysephase beim Übersetzen aus der Fremdsprache." In: Drescher/Scheffzek (1976), 48–57.

Hönig, H.G. (1988): "Wissen Übersetzer eigentlich, was sie tun?" *Lebende Sprachen* 1/88, 10–14.

Hönig, H.G./Kußmaul, P. (1982): *Strategie der Übersetzung*. Ein Lehr- und Arbeitbuch. Tübingen.

Hoppe-Graff, S. (1984): "Verstehen als kognitiver Prozeß. Psychologische Ansätze und Beiträge zum Textverstehen." *Zeitschrift für Literaturwissenschaft und Linguistik* 55, 10–37.

Hörmann, H. ²1977): *Psychologie der Sprache*. Berlin.

Horton, D.L./Bergfeld Mills, C. (1984): "Human learning and memory." *Annual Review of Psychology* 35, 361–394.

House, J. (1980): "Übersetzen im Fremdsprachenunterricht: Zur Konzeption eines kommunikativen Übersetzungskurses im Rahmen der sprachpraktischen Ausbildung von Lehrerstudenten des Englischen." In: Poulsen/Wilss (1980), 7–17.

House, J. (²1981): *A Model for Translation Quality Assessment*. Tübingen.

House, J./Blum-Kulka, S. (eds.) (1986): *Interlingual and Intercultural Communication*. Discourse and Cognition in Translation and Second Language Acquisition Studies. Tübingen.

Huber, G.L./Mandl, H. (eds.) (1982): *Verbale Daten*. Eine Einführung in die Grundlagen und Methoden der Erhebung und Auswertung. Weinheim.

Hüllen, W. (ed.) (1980a): *Understanding Bilingualism*. Frankfurt/M.

Hüllen, W. (1980b): "Introduction, or: our interest in bilingualism." In: Hüllen (1980a), 3–12.

Hüllen, W. (1987): *Englisch als Fremdsprache*. Tübingen.

Hüllen, W. (1976): "Fremdsprachendidaktik und linguistische Pragmatik." *Die Neueren Sprachen* 75, 217–229.

Hüllen, W./Jung, L. (1979): *Sprachstruktur und Spracherwerb*. Düsseldorf.

Hüllen, W./Lörscher, W. (1987): "Ein Modell zur Beschreibung und Analyse des Lehrer-Schüler-Diskurses im Fremdsprachenunterricht." In: Hüllen (1987), 172–193.

Hüllen, W./Lörscher, W. (1989): "On describing and analyzing foreign language classroom discourse." In: Oleksy (1989), 169188.
Hussy, W. (1984): *Denkpsychologie.* Ein Lehrbuch. Volume 1: Geschichte, Begriffs- und Problemlöseforschung, Intelligenz. Stuttgart.
Hymes, D.H. (1972): "Models of the interaction of language and social life." In: Gumperz/ Hymes (1972), 35–71.
Imhasly, B. et al. ([2]1982): *Konzepte der Linguistik.* Eine Einführung. Wiesbaden.
Jäger, G. (1973a): "Studien zur Translation und zur Translationslinguistik." Diss. B. Karl-Marx-Universität Leipzig.
Jäger, G. (1973b): "Kommunikative und funktionelle Äquivalenz." *Linguistische Arbeitsberichte,* Leipzig, 60–74.
Jäger, G. (1975): *Translation und Translationslinguistik.* Halle/Saale.
Jäger, G. (1977): "Nochmals zur Frage der sogenannten Übersetzungseinheit." *Linguistische Arbeitsberichte,* Leipzig, 9–14.
Jakobson, R. (1971a): *Selected Writings* II. Den Haag.
Jakobson, R. (1971b): "On linguistic aspects of translation." In: Jakobson (1971a), 260–266.
Jefferson, G. (1972): "Side sequences." In: Sudnow (1972), 294–338.
Johnson-Laird, P.N./Wason, P.C. (eds.) (1977): *Thinking: Readings in Cognitive Science.* Cambridge.
Just, M.A./Carpenter, P.A. (eds.) (1977): *Cognitive Processes in Comprehension.* Hillsdale/NJ.
Jüttner, C. (1979): *Gedächtnis.* Grundlagen der psychologischen Gedächtnisforschung. München.
Kade, O. (1968a): "Zufall und Gesetzmäßigkeit in der Übersetzung." *Beihefte zur Zeitschrift 'Fremdsprachen'* I. Leipzig.
Kade, O. (1968b): "Kommunikationswissenschaftliche Probleme der Translation." *Beihefte zur Zeitschrift 'Fremdsprachen'* II. Leipzig, 3–19.
Kade, O. (1971): "Das Problem der Übersetzbarkeit aus der Sicht der marxistisch-leninistischen Erkenntnistheorie." *Linguistische Arbeitsberichte,* Leipzig, 13–28.
Kade, O. (1973): "Zur Anwendung verschiedener Realisationsformen der Translation (Bemerkungen zur Bestimmung des Gegenstandes der Übersetzungswissenschaft)." *Linguistische Arbeitsberichte,* Leipzig, 75–119.
Kade, O./Cartellieri, C. (1971): "Some methodological aspects of simultaneous interpreting." *Babel* XVII, 12–16.
Kallmeyer, W./Schütze, F. (1976): "Konversationsanalyse." *Studium Linguistik* 1, 1–28.
Kämmerer, A. (1983): *Die therapeutische Strategie 'Problemlösen'.* Theoretische und empirische Perspektiven ihrer Anwendung in der kognitiven Psychotherapie. Münster.
Kapp, V. (ed.) (1974/[2]1984): *Übersetzer und Dolmetscher.* Theoretische Grundlagen, Ausbildung, Berufspraxis. München.
Kasper, G. (1984): "Pragmatic comprehension in learner-native speaker discourse." *Language Learning* 34, 1–20.
Katz, J.J. (1964): "Mentalism in linguistics." *Language* 40, 124–137.
Keller, H.-J. (1978): "Rephrasieren im Schulunterricht." Unpublished M.A. thesis. Universität Düsseldorf: Philosophische Fakultät.
Kelly, L.G. (1979): *The True Interpreter.* Oxford.
Kempen, G. (1977): "Conceptualizing and formulating in sentence production." In: Rosenberg (1977), 259–274.
Kenny, A.J. (1966): "Practical Inference." *Analysis* 26, 65–75.
Kintsch, W. (1974): *The Representation of Meaning in Memory.* Hillsdale/NJ.
Kintsch, W./van Dijk, T. (1978): "Towards a model of text comprehension and production." *Psychological Review* 85, 363–394.

Kintsch, W./Greene, E. (1978): "The role of culture-specific schemata in the comprehension and recall of stories." *Discourse Processes* 1, 1–13.

Kirchhoff, H. (1976): "Das Simultandolmetschen: Interdependenz der Variablen im Dolmetschprozeß, Dolmetschmodelle und Dolmetschstrategien." In: Drescher/Scheffzek (1976), 59–71.

Klaus, G./Buhr, M. (eds.) (1976): *Philosophisches Wörterbuch.* Leipzig.

Klix, F. (1971): *Information und Verhalten.* Bern.

Knapp-Potthoff, A./Knapp, K. (1982): *Fremdsprachenlernen und -lehren.* Eine Einführung in die Didaktik der Fremdsprachen vom Standpunkt der Zweitsprachenerwerbsforschung. Stuttgart.

Knapp-Potthoff, A./Knapp, K. (1986): "Interweaving two discourses – The difficult task of the non-professional interpreter." In: House/Blum-Kulka (1986), 151–168.

Knapp-Potthoff, A./Knapp, K. n.d.: "The man (or woman) in the middle. – Discoursal aspects of non-professional interpreting." MS.

Koch, M. (1964): "Gedanken und Gedankenerinnerungen." In: Gottschaldt (1964), 51–75.

Kohn, K. (1979): "Was der Lerner nicht weiß, macht ihn nicht heiß." *Linguistische Berichte* 64, 82–94.

Kolb, E./Hasler, J. (eds.) (1969): *Festschrift für Rudolf Stamm.* Bern.

Koller, W. (1978): "Äquivalenz in kontrastiver Linguistik und Übersetzungswissenschaft." In: Grähs et al. (1978), 69–92.

Koller, W. (1981): "Anmerkungen zu Definitionen des Übersetzungs,vorgangs' und zur Übersetzungskritik." In: Wilss (1981b), 263–274.

Koller, W. (^{2}1983): *Einführung in die Übersetzungswissenschaft.* Heidelberg.

Kommissarov, V.N. (1981): "Linguistische Modelle des Übersetzungsprozesses." In: Wilss (1981b), 171–185.

Königs, F.G. (1979): *Übersetzung in Theorie und Praxis: Ansatzpunkte für die Konzeption einer Didaktik des Übersetzens.* Heidelberg.

Königs, F.G. (1981): "Zur Frage der Übersetzungseinheit und ihre Relevanz für den Fremdsprachenunterricht." *Linguistische Berichte* 74, 82–103.

Königs, F.G. (1982): "Zentrale Begriffe aus der wissenschaftlichen Beschäftigung mit Übersetzen." *Lebende Sprachen* XXVII, 145–150. (Part 1).

Königs, F.G. (1983): "Zentrale Begriffe aus der wissenschaftlichen Beschäftigung mit Übersetzen." *Lebende Sprachen* XXVIII, 154–156. (Part 3).

Königs, F.G. (1986): "Der Vorgang des Übersetzens: Theoretische Befunde und praktischer Vollzug. Zum Verhältnis von Theorie und Praxis in der Übersetzungswissenschaft." *Lebende Sprachen* XXXI, 5–12.

Königs, F.G. (1987): "Was beim Übersetzen passiert. Theoretische Aspekte, empirische Befunde und praktische Konsequenzen." *Die Neueren Sprachen* 86, 162–185.

Kopczyński, A. (1982): "Effects of some characteristics of impromptu speech on conference interpreting." In: Enkvist (1982), 255–266.

Kornelius, J. (1982): "Übersetzungsübungen als Reduktion von Komplexität." *Neusprachliche Mitteilungen aus Wissenschaft und Praxis* 35, 88–94.

Koschmieder, E.K. (1965a): "Das Gemeinte." In: Koschmieder (1965c), 101–106.

Koschmieder, E.K. (1965b): "Das Problem der Übersetzung." In: Koschmieder (1965c), 107–115.

Koschmieder, E.K. (1965c): *Beiträge zur allgemeinen Syntax.* Heidelberg.

Krings, H.P. (1986a): *Was in den Köpfen von Übersetzern vorgeht.* Eine empirische Untersuchung der Struktur des Übersetzungsprozesses an fortgeschrittenen Französischlernern. Tübingen.

Krings, H.P. (1986b): "Translation problems and translation strategies of advanced German learners of French." In: House/Blum-Kulka (1986), 263–276.

Krings, H.P. (1987): "The use of introspective data in translation." In: Færch/Kasper (1987), 159–176.

Krzeszowski, T.P. (1982): "Thc problem of equivalence revisited." *International Review of Applied Linguistics in Language Teaching* XIX, 113–128.

Kühlwein, W. et al. (eds.) (1981): *Kontrastive Linguistik und Übersetzungswissenschaft*. Akten des Internationalen Kolloquiums Trier/Saarbrücken 25.–30.9.1978, München.

Kummer, W. (1972): "Aspects of a theory of argumentation." In: Gülich/Raible (1972), 25–49.

Kummer, W. (1975): *Grundlagen der Texttheorie*. Zur handlungstheoretischen Begründung einer materialistischen Sprachwissenschaft. Reinbek.

Kurcz, I. (1984): "A model of language knowledge as related to knowledge of the world." In: Lagerspetz/Niemi (1984), 133–161.

Kußmaul, P. (1978): "Kommunikationskonventionen in Textsorten am Beispiel deutscher und englischer geisteswissenschaftlicher Abhandlungen. Ein Beitrag zur deutsch-englischen Übersetzungstechnik." *Lebende Sprachen* II, 54–58.

La Berge, D. (1977): *Basic Processes in Reading*: Perception and Comprehension. New York.

La Berge, D./Samuels, S. (1974): "Toward a theory of automatic information processing in reading." *Cognitive Psychology* 6, 293–323.

Ladmiral, J.R. (1981): "La traduction comme linguistique d'intervention." In: Pöckl (1981), 375–400.

Lagerspetz, K.M.J./Niemi, P. (eds.) (1984): *Psychology in the 1990's*. Amsterdam.

Lange-Seidl, A. (ed.) (1981): *Zeichenkonstitution*. Akten des 2. Semiotischen Kolloquiums, Regensburg (1978). 2 Volumes. Berlin.

Leathers, D.G. (1976): *Nonverbal Communication Systems*. Boston.

Lee, W. (1977): *Psychologische Entscheidungstheorie*. Eine Einführung. Weinheim.

Leech, G.N. (1983): *Principles of Pragmatics*. London.

Lehmann, D. (1982): "Arbeitsbibliographie Übersetzen: Interdisziplinäre Aspekte der Sprach- und Übersetzungswissenschaft sowie der Übersetzungspraxis. LAUT-Paper No. 83, Series B; Trier.

Leontev, A.A. (1971): *Sprache-Sprechen-Sprechtätigkeit*. Stuttgart.

Leontev, A.A. (1975): *Psycholinguistische Einheiten und die Erzeugung sprachlicher Äußerungen*. Berlin.

Lesser, V.R./Erman, L.D. (1977): "A retrospective view of the Hearsay-II architecture." In: *Proceedings of the 5th International Joint Conference on Artificial Intelligence*. Volume 2. Cambridge/Mass., 790–800.

Levelt, W.J.M. (1978): "A survey of studies in sentence perception: 1970–1976. In: Levelt/ Flores d'Arcais (1978), 1–74.

Levelt, W.J.M./Flores d'Archais, G.B. (eds.) (1978): *Studies in the Perception of Language*. Chichester.

Levinson, S. (1983): *Pragmatics*. London.

Levý, J. (1967): "Translation as a decision process." In: *To Honor Roman Jakobson*. Volume II. Den Haag, 1171–1182.

Lewandowski, T. (1976): "Sowjetische Psycholinguistik." *Die Neueren Sprachen* 75, 188–216.

Liberman, A.M. et al. (1963): "A motor theory of speech perception." In: *Proceedings of the Speech Communication Seminar*. Volume II. Stockholm.

Liberman, A.M. et al. (1967): "Perception of the speech code." *Psychological Review* 74, 431–459.

Lindemann, B. (1984): "Text as system and process: On reading Joyce Carol Oates' Notes on Contributors." *anglistik & englischunterricht* 23, 95–109.

Loftus, E. (1980): *Memory*. Reading/Mass.

Lörscher, W. (1983): *Linguistische Beschreibung und Analyse von Fremdsprachenunterricht als Diskurs*. Tübingen.

Lörscher, W. (1981): "Aspekte nonverbaler und parasprachlicher Verhaltensweisen im Diskurs." Unpublished MS.

Lörscher, W. (1986): "Linguistic aspects of translation processes: Towards an analysis of translation performance." In: House/Blum-Kulka (1986), 277–292.

Lörscher, W. (1987): "On analysing translation performance." In: Lörscher/Schulze (1987), 424–440.

Lörscher, W. (1989): "Strategien des Übersetzungsprozesses." *Linguistische Berichte* 119, 53–84.

Lörscher, W. n.d. [1987]: "Übersetzungsperformanz, Übersetzungsprozeß und Übersetzungsstrategien. Eine psycholinguistische Untersuchung." Habilitationsschrift, University of Essen. Mimeo.

Lörscher, W./Schulze, R. (eds.) (1987): *Perspectives on Language in Performance.* Studies in Linguistics, Literary Criticism, and Language Learning and Teaching. To Honour Werner Hüllen on the Occasion of His Sixtieth Birthday, 17. October 1987. Tübingen.

Lörscher, W./Schulze, R. (1988): "On polite speaking and foreign language classroom discourse." *International Review of Applied Linguistics in Language Teaching* XXVI, 183–199.

Lüer, G. (1973): *Gesetzmäßige Denkabläufe beim Problemlösen.* Weinheim.

Lüer, G. (1977): "Denken und Problemlösen." In: Herrmann et al. (1977), 92–102.

Lyons, J. (1977): *Semantics.* Volume 1. Cambridge.

Lytinen, S.L./Schank, R.C. (1982): "Representation and Translation." *Text* 2, 83–111.

Malone, J.L. (1982): "False friendship." *Babel* XXVIII, 21–25.

McCarthy, J. (1956): "The inversion of functions defined by turing machines." In: Shannon/ McCarthy (1956), 177188.

McDonough, S.H. (1981): *Psychology in Foreign Language Teaching.* London.

McQuown, N.A. (ed.) (1971): *The Natural History of an Interview.* Chicago (University of Chicago Microfilms).

Mehan, H./Wood, H. (1975): *The Reality of Ethnomethodology.* New York.

Merritt, M. (1976): "On questions following questions in service encounters." *Language in Society* 5, 315–357.

Metzing, D. (ed.) (1980): *Frame Conceptions and Text Understanding.* Berlin.

Meyer, E. (1974): "Die Übersetzung im neusprachlichen Unterricht." Ph.D. dissertation. Universität Frankfurt.

Meyer, P.G. (1983): *Sprachliches Handels ohne Sprechsituation.* Tübingen.

Miller, G.A. (1956): "The magical number seven, plus or minus two. Some limits on our capacity for processing information." *Psychological Review* 63, 81–97.

Miller, G.A. et al. (1960): *Plans and the Structure of Behavior.* New York. [German edition 1973].

Miller, J.G. (1964): "Adjusting to overloads of information." *Research on Public Assistance for Nervous and Mental Disease* 42, 87–110.

Mininni, G. (1981): "On the need of psycholinguistic research on translation." *International Journal of Psycholinguistics* 8, 79–107.

Minsky, M. (1975): "A framework for representing knowledge." In: Winston (1975), 211–277.

Möhle, D./Raupach, M. (1983): *Planen in der Fremdsprache.* Frankfurt/M.

Molony, C./Zobl, H. (1976): *German in Contact with Other Languages.* Kronberg/Ts.

Muller, Ch. (1972): *Einführung in die Sprachstatistik.* München. [Original French edition 1968].

Müller, J.E. (1981): "Alltagswissen über Face-to-Face Situationen und Notationssysteme." In: Lange-Seidl (1981. Volume II, 80–92.

Müller, K. (1984): *Rahmenanalyse des Dialogs.* Aspekte des Sprachverstehens in Alltagssituationen. Tübingen.

Nagel, E. et al. (eds.) (1962): *Logic, Methodology, and Philosophy of Science*. Proceedings of the 1960 International Congress. Stanford/CA.
Neubert, A. (ed.) (1968): "Grundfragen der Übersetzungswissenschaft." *Beihefte zur Zeitschrift 'Fremdsprachen'* II, Leipzig.
Neubert, A. (1974): "Theorie und Praxis für die Übersetzungswissenschaft." In: Qvistgaard et al. (1974), 38–60.
Neubert, A. (1981): "Translation, interpreting, and text linguistics." *Studia Linguistica* 35, 1–2; 130–145.
Neubert, A. (1983): "Discourse analysis of translation." *Zeitschrift für Anglistik und Amerikanistik* 31, 160–162.
Newman, A. (1980): *Mapping Translation Equivalence*. Leuven.
Newmark, P. (1981): *Approaches to Translation*. Oxford.
Newmark, P. (1977): "Communicative and semantic translation." *Babel* XXIII, 163–180.
Newmark, P. (1978): "Thought, Speech and Translation." *Babel* XXIV, 127–129.
Newmark, P. (1982): "A further note on communicative and semantic translation." *Babel* XXVIII, 18–20.
Nickel, G. (ed.) (1976): *Proceedings of the Fourth International Congress of Applied Linguistics*. Volume 2. Stuttgart.
Nida, E.A. (1969): "Science of translation." *Language* 45, 483–498.
Nida, E.A. (1976): "Translation as communication." In: Nickel (1976), 61–82.
Nida, E.A./Taber, C.R. (1969): *The Theory and Practice of Translation*. Leiden.
Nisbett, R.E./Wilson, T.D. (1977): "Telling more than we know: verbal reports on mental processes." *Psychological Review* 84, 231–259.
Norman, D.A. et al. (1975): Explorations in Cognition. San Francisco.
Obliers, R. (1985): *Semantische Grundfiguren*. Die Bedeutung der propositionalen Binnengliederung für die semantische Satzverarbeitung. Pfaffenweiler.
Oerter, R. (^{6}1980): *Psychologie des Denkens*. Donauwörth.
Oleksy, W. (ed.) (1989): *Contrastive Pragmatics*. Amsterdam.
Oller, J.W. (1976): "Evidence for a general language proficiency factor: an expectancy grammar." *Die Neueren Sprachen* 75, 165–174.
Olson, G.M./Clark, H.H. (1976): "Research methods in psycholinguistics." In: Carterette/ Friedman (1976), 25–74.
Paepcke, F./Forget, P. (1981): *Textverstehen und Übersetzen*. Ouvertures sur la traduction. Heidelberg.
Palmer, S.E. (1975): "Visual perception and world knowledge: notes on a model of sensory-cognitive interaction." In: Norman et al. (1975), 279–307.
Parret, H. (1985): "Regularities, rules and strategies." *Journal of Pragmatics* 8, 569–592.
Pasierbsky, F. (1976): "Textherstellung und Optimierung. Eine Anwendung der Operations Research in der Linguistik." In: Weber/Weydt (1976), 269–278.
Pause, E. (1983): "Context and translation." In: Bäuerle et al. (1983), 384–399.
Peirce, C.S. (^{5}1980): *Collected Papers*. Volume IV: The Simplest Mathematics. Cambridge/ Mass.
Picken, C. (1983): *The Translator's Handbook*. London.
Pittenger, R.E. et al. (1960): *The First Five Minutes: A Sample of Microscopic Interview Analysis*. New York.
Pöckl, W. (ed.) (1981): *Europäische Mehrsprachigkeit*. Festschrift zum 70. Geburtstag von Mario Wandruszka. Tübingen.
Posner, M.I./Snyder, C.R. (1975): "Attention and cognitive control." In: Solso (1975), 55–86.
Poulsen, S.-O./Wilss, W. (eds.) (1980): *Angewandte Übersetzungswissenschaft*. Internationales übersetzungswissenschaftliches Kolloquium an der Wirtschaftsuniversität Århus/Dänemark, 19.–21. Juni 1980. Århus.

Prideaux, G.D. (1984): *Psycholinguistics*: The Experimental Study of Language. London.
Průcha, J. (1974): *Sowjetische Psycholinguistik*. Düsseldorf.
Psathas, G. (1972): "Verstehen, Ethnomethodologie und Phänomenologie." In: Bühl (1972), 284–303.
Qvistgaard, J. et al. (eds.) (1974): *Applied Linguistics: Problems and Solutions*. Proceedings of the Third International Congress of Applied Linguistics, Copenhagen 1972. Volume 3. Heidelberg.
Ramge, H. (1978): *Alltagsgespräche*. Frankfurt/M.
Ramge, H. (1977): "Zur sprachwissenschaftlichen Analyse von Alltagsgesprächen." In: Baumgärtner (1977), 109–128.
Raupach, M. (1983): "Analysis and evaluation of communication strategies." In: Færch/Kasper (1983a), 199–209.
Rehbein, J. (1976a): "Planen I: Elemente des Handlungsplans." LAUT-Paper No. 38 Series A; Trier.
Rehbein, J. (1976b): "Planen II: Planbildung in Sprechhandlungssequenzen." LAUT-Paper No. 39, Series A. Trier.
Rehbein, J. (1977): *Komplexes Handeln*. Elemente zur Handlungstheorie der Sprache. Stuttgart.
Reiß, K. (1971): *Möglichkeiten und Grenzen der Übersetzungskritik*. München.
Reiß, K. (1976): *Texttyp und Übersetzungsmethode*. Der operative Text. Kronberg/Ts.
Reiß, K. (1983): "Quality in translation oder Wann ist eine Übersetzung gut?" *Babel* XXIX, 198–208.
Reiß, K. (1984): "Adäquatheit und Äquivalenz." In: Wilss/Thome (1984), 80–89.
Reiß, K. (1986): "Übersetzungstheorien und ihre Relevanz für die Praxis." *Lebende Sprachen* XXXI, 1–5.
Reiß, K./Vermeer, H.J. (1984): *Grundlegung einer allgemeinen Translationstheorie*. Tübingen.
Richards, I.A. (1953): "Toward a theory of translating." In: Wright (1953), 247–262.
Rickheit, G./Bock, M. (eds.) (1983): *Psycholinguistic Studies in Language Processing*. Berlin.
Rickheit, G./Strohner, H. (eds.) (1985a): *Inferences in Text Processing*.
Rickheit, G./Strohner, H. (eds.) (1985b): "Psycholinguistik der Textverarbeitung." *Studium Linguistik* 17/18, 1–78.
Rigg, P. (1976): "Reading in ESL." In: Fanselow/Crymes (1976), 203–210.
Rihs-Middel, M. (1982): "Expectancy structures in prose reading." In: Flammer/Kintsch (1982), 76–86.
Ringbom, H. (ed.) (1985a): *Foreign Language Learning and Bilingualism*. Åbo.
Ringbom, H. (1985b): "Transfer in relation to some other variables in L2-learning." In: Ringbom (1985a), 9–21.
Ringbom, H. n.d. [1985]: "L3-influence on L2-vocabulary." MS.
Ritter, J. (ed.) (1974): *Historisches Wörterbuch der Philosophie*. 3 Volumes. Darmstadt.
Robberecht, P. (1982): "Linguistics and translation." *International Review of Applied Linguistics in Language Teaching* XX, 217–227.
Rollinger, C.-R. (ed.) (1984): *Probleme des (Text-)Verstehens*. Ansätze der Künstlichen Intelligenz. Tübingen.
Rosch, E. (1977a): "Human categorization." In: Warren (1977), 1–49.
Rosch, E. (1977b): "Classifications of real-world objects: origins and representations in cognition." In: Johnson-Laird/Wason (1977), 212–222.
Rosch, E. (1978): "Principles of Categorization." In: Rosch/Lloyd (1978), 27–48.
Rosch, E./Lloyd, B.B. (eds.) (1978): *Cognition and Categorization*. Hillsdale/NJ.
Rosenberg, S. (ed.) (1977): *Sentence Production: Developments in Research and Theory*. Hillsdale/NJ.
Rosenberg, S. (1982): *Handbook of Applied Psycholinguistics*. Major Thrusts of Research and Theory. Hillsdale/NJ.

Rühl, P.G. (1983): *Tätigkeit- Einstellung- Fremdsprachenunterricht.* Zum Verhältnis Psychologie, Psycholinguistik und gesteuerter Fremdsprachenerwerb in der Sowjetunion. Tübingen.

Rumelhart, D. (1975): "Notes on a schema for stories." In: Bobrow/Collins (1975), 211–236.

Rumelhart, D. (1980): "Schemata: the building blocks of cognition." In: Spiro et al. (1980), 33–58.

Ryle, G. (1946): "Knowing how and knowing that." In: Proceedings of the Aristotelian Society. Volume XLVI. [reprinted in Ryle (1971), 212–225.]

Ryle, G. (1949): *The Concept of Mind.* London.

Ryle, G. (1971): *Collected Papers.* Volume II: Collected Essays 1929–1968. London.

Sacks, H. et al. (1974): "A simplest systematics for the organization of turn-taking for conversation." *Language* 50, 696–735.

Sager, S.F. (1981): *Sprache und Beziehung.* Linguistische Untersuchungen zum Zusammenhang von sprachlicher Kommunikation und zwischenmenschlicher Beziehung. Tübingen.

Sandrock, U. (1982): "Thinking-Aloud Protocols (TAPs) – Ein Instrument zur Dekomposition des komplexen Prozesses 'Übersetzen'." Unpublished thesis. Universität Kassel.

Sebeok, T.A. (ed.) (1974): *Current Trends in Linguistics.* Den Haag.

Sebeok, T.A. (ed.) (1986): *Encyclopedic Dictionary of Semiotics.* Tome 2. Berlin.

Secord, P.F./Backman, C.W. (^{2}1974): *Social Psychology.* New York.

Seleskovitch, D. (1968): *L'interprète dans les conférences internationales.* Problèmes de langage et de la communication. Paris.

Seleskovitch, D. (1975): *Langage, langues et mémoire.* Etude de la prise de notes en interprétation consécutive. Paris.

Seleskovitch, D. (1974): "Zur Theorie des Dolmetschens." In: Kapp (1974), 37–50.

Seleskovitch, D. (1976): "Interpretation, a psychological approach to translating." In: Brislin (1976), 92–116.

Seleskovitch, D. (1978): "Language and cognition." In: Gerver/Sinaiko (1978), 333–341.

Seleskovitch, D. (1982): "Impromptu speech and oral translation." In: Enkvist (1982), 241–253.

Seleskovitch, D. (1987): "Context-free language and sense in translation." In: Lörscher/Schulze (1987), 441–446.

Seleskovitch, D./Lederer, M. (1984): *Interpréter Pour Traduire.* Publications de la Sorbonne. Littératures/10. Paris.

Selinker, L. (1972): "Interlanguage." *International Review of Applied Linguistics in Language Teaching* 10, 219–231.

Shannon, D.E./McCarthy, J. (eds.) (1956): *Automata Studies.* Annals of Mathematical Studies 34. Princeton/Mass.

Sharwood-Smith, M. (1979): "Strategies, language transfer, and simulation of second language learner's mental operations." *Interlanguage Studies Bulletin* 4, 66–83.

Shiffrin, R.M./Schneider, W. (1977): "Controlled and automatic processing: II. Perceptual learning, automatic attending and a general theory." *Psychological Review* 84, 127–189.

Siegman, A.W./Feldstein, S. (eds.) (1978): *Nonverbal Behavior and Communication.* New York.

Simon, H.A. (1979): *Models of Thought.* New Haven.

Smelcer, P. et al. (1980): "Linguistic awareness of the translation process." *System* 8, 59–70.

Smith, F. (1971): *Understanding Reading.* A Psycholinguistic Analysis of Reading and Learning to Read. New York.

Snell, B./Crampton, P. (1983): "Types of translation." In: Picken (1983), 109–120.

Snell-Hornby, M. (1984): "Dimension and perspective in literary translation." In: Wilss/Thome (1984), 105–113.

Soeffner, H.G. (ed.) (1982a): *Beiträge zu einer empirischen Sprachsoziologie.* Tübingen.

Soeffner, H.G. (1982b): "Statt einer Einleitung: Prämissen einer sozialwissenschaftlichen Hermeneutik." In: Soeffner (1982a), 9–48.

Solso, R.L. (ed.) (1975): *Information Processing and Cognition.* The Loyola Symposium. Hillsdale/NJ.

Spillner, B. (1981): "Textsorten im Sprachvergleich. Ansätze zu einer kontrastiven Textologie." In: Kühlwein et al. (1981), 239–250.

Spiro, R.J. et al. (eds.) (1980): *Theoretical Issues in Reading Comprehension.* Hillsdale/NJ.

Sudnow, D. (ed.) (1972): *Studies in Social Interaction.* New York.

Suerbaum, U. (1969): "Der deutsche Shakespeare: Übersetzungsgeschichte und Übersetzungstheorie." In: Kolb/Hasler (1969), 61–80.

Swain, M. et al. (1974): "Alternatives to spontaneous speech: elicited translation and imitation as indicators of second language competence." *Working Papers on Bilingualism* 3, 68–79.

Switalla, B. (1977): "Verständigungskritik im Unterricht. Zur methodischen Rekonstruktion unterrichtlicher Argumentation." In: Goeppert (1977), 158–223.

Schank, R.C. (1978): "Predictive understanding." In: Campbell/Smith (1978), 91–101.

Schank, R.C./Abelson, R.P. (1977): *Scripts, Plans, Goals, and Understanding.* An Inquiry into Human Knowledge Structures. Hillsdale/NJ.

Scherer, K.R. ([3]1973): *Nonverbale Kommunikation.* Hamburg.

Scherer, K.R. (1980): "The functions of nonverbal signs in conversation." In: St. Clair/Giles (1980), 225–244.

Schmidt, S.J. (1973): *Texttheorie.* Probleme einer Linguistik der sprachlichen Kommunikation. München.

Schmidt, S.J. (ed.) (1974a): *Pragmatik* I. München.

Schmidt, S.J. (1974b): "Das 'kommunikative Handlungsspiel' als Kategorie der Wirklichkeitskonstitution." In: Schmidt (1974a), 103–118.

Schneider, W./Shiffrin, R.M. (1977): "Controlled and automatic human information processing I: Detection, search, and attention." *Psychological Review* 84, 1–66.

Schnotz, W. (1985): "Selectivity in drawing inferences." In: Rickheit/Strohner (1985a), 287–326.

Schönpflug, W./Schönpflug, U. (1983): *Psychologie.* Allgemeine Psychologie und ihre Verzweigungen in die Entwicklungs-, Persönlichkeits- und Sozialpsychologie. München.

Schröder, P./Steger, H. (eds.) (1981): *Dialogforschung.* Jahrbuch 1980 des Instituts für deutsche Sprache. Düsseldorf.

Schulze, R. (1985): *Höflichkeit im Englischen.* Zur linguistischen Beschreibung und Analyse von Alltagsgesprächen. Tübingen.

Schulze, R. (1986): "Some methodological remarks on the reconstructive description and analysis of impromptu speech." *Grazer Linguistische Studien* 26, 117–129.

Schütz, A. (1932): *Der sinnhafte Aufbau der sozialen Welt.* Eine Einleitung in die verstehende Soziologie. Wien.

St. Clair, R.N./Giles, H. (eds.) (1980): *The Social and Psychological Contexts of Language.* Hillsdale/NJ.

Stachowiak, H. (1965): "Gedanken zu einer allgemeinen Theorie der Modelle." *Studium Generale* 18, 432–463.

Stachowiak, H. (1973): *Allgemeine Modelltheorie.* Wien.

Stammerjohann, H. (1975): *Handbuch der Linguistik.* München.

Stein, D. (1980): *Theoretische Grundlagen der Übersetzungswissenschaft.* Tübingen.

Stein, D. (1982): "Zur Dialektik von linguistischer Theoriebildung und angewandter Disziplin: Bemerkungen zu den Schwierigkeiten einer Wissenschaft vom Übersetzen." *International Review of Applied Linguistics in Language Teaching* XX, 233–240.

Steinbach, H.-R. (1981): "On the classification of errors in translation papers with some considerations of interference phenomena." *Papers and Studies in Contrastive Linguistics* XIII, 249–259.

Steinberg, D.D. (1982): *Psycholinguistics*. Language, Mind and World. London.

Stolze, R. (1982): *Grundlagen der Textübersetzung*. Heidelberg.

Tarone, E. (1981): "Decoding a nonprimary language: the crucial role of strategic competence." Paper read at the BAAL-Seminar on Interpretive Strategies, University of Lancaster. MS.

Tarone, E. (1983): "Some thoughts on the notion of 'communication strategy'." *TESOL Quarterly* 15 (1981), 285–295; reprinted in Færch/Kasper (1983a), 61–74.

Tarone, E. et al. (1976): "A closer look at some interlanguage terminology." *Working Papers on Bilingualism* 9, 76–90.

Thiel, G. (1974): "Ansätze zu einer Methodologie der übersetzungsrelevanten Textanalyse." In: Kapp (1974), 174–185.

Thiel, G. (1980): "Vergleichende Textanalyse als Basis für die Entwicklung einer Übersetzungsmethodik, dargestellt anhand der Textsorte Resolution." In: Wilss (1980a), 87–98.

Thiel, G. (1981): "Überlegungen zur übersetzungsrelevanten Textanalyse." In: Wilss (1981b), 367–383.

Thorndyke, P. (1977): "Cognitive structures in comprehension and memory of narrative discourse." *Cognitive Psychology* 9, 77–110.

Titford, C./Hieke, A.E. (eds.) (1985): *Translation in Foreign Language Teaching and Testing*. Tübingen.

Tollefson, J.W. et al. (1983): "The monitor model and neurofunctional theory: an integrated view." *Studies in Second Language Acquisition* 6, 1–16.

Toury, G. (1978): "The nature and role of norms in literary translation." In: Holmes et al. (1978), 83–100.

Toury, G. (1979): "Interlanguage and its manifestations in translation." *Meta* 24, 223–231.

Toury, G. (1980a): *In Search of a Theory of Translation*. Tel Aviv.

Toury, G. (1980b): "Communication in translated texts: a semiotic approach." In: Wilss (1980a), 99–109.

Toury, G. (1981): "Contrastive linguistics and translation studies. Towards a tripartite model." In: Kühlwein et al. (1981), 251–261.

Toury, G. (1984): "The notion of 'native translator' and translation teaching." In: Wilss/Thome (1984), 186–195.

Toury, G. (1986a): "Monitoring discourse transfer: A testcase for a developmental model of translation." In: House/Blum-Kulka (1986), 79–94.

Toury, G. (1986b): "Natural translation and the making of a native translator." *TEXTconTEXT* 1, 11–29.

Toury, G. (1986c): "Translation: A cultural-semiotic perspective" In: Sebeok (1986), 1111–1124.

Ungeheuer, G. (1974): "Kommunikationssemantik. Skizze eines Problemfeldes." *Zeitschrift für germanistische Linguistik* 2, 1–24.

den Uyl, M./van Oostendorp, H. (1980): "The use of scripts in text comprehension." *Poetics* 9, 275–294.

van Hoof, H. (1973): *Internationale Bibliographie der Übersetzung*. Pullach.

Vermeer, H.J. (1978): "Ein Rahmen für eine allgemeine Translationstheorie." *Lebende Sprachen* XIII, 99–102.

Vermeer, H.J. (1979): "Vom 'richtigen' Übersetzen." *Mitteilungsblatt für Dolmetscher und Übersetzer* 4, 2–8.

Vermeer, H.J. (1981): "Zur Beschreibung des Übersetzungsvorgangs." In: Wilss (1981b), 250–262.

Vermeer, H.J. (1982): "Translation als 'Informationsangebot'." *Lebende Sprachen* XXVII, 97–101.

Vermeer, H.J. (1984): "Textkohärenz in Übersetzungstheorie und -didaktik." In: Wilss/Thome (1984), 46–51.

Vernay, H. (1974): "Elemente einer Übersetzungswissenschaft." In: Kapp (1974), 26–37.
Verschuren, J. (1981): "Problems of lexical semantics." *Lingua* 53, 317–351.
Vollmer, H.J. (1982): *Spracherwerb und Sprachbeherrschung: Untersuchungen zur Struktur von Fremdsprachenfähigkeit.* Ein empirischer Beitrag zu einer psycholinguistisch orientierten Sprachlehr-/lernforschung. Tübingen.
Vygotski, L.S. (1962): *Thought and Language.* Cambridge/Mass. [Russian Original Editions 1934 and 1956].
Wagner, A.C. et al. (1977): "Die Analyse von Unterrichtsstrategien mit der Methode des 'Nachträglichen Lauten Denkens' von Lehrern und Schülern zu ihrem unterrichtlichen Handeln." *Unterrichtswissenschaft* 5, 244–250.
Wahmhoff, S. (1980): *Inneres Sprechen.* Psycholinguistische Untersuchungen an aphasischen Patienten. Weinheim.
Wald, I. (1961): "Problema afazii u poliglotov." *Voprosy kliniki i patofiziologii afazii.* Moskva, 140–176.
Warren, N. (ed.) (1977): *Studies in Cross-Cultural Psychology.* New York.
Watson, J.B. (1913): "Psychology as the bahaviorist views it." *Psychological Review* 20, 158–177.
Weber, H./Weydt, H. (eds.) (1976): *Sprachtheorie und Pragmatik.* Akten des 10. Linguistischen Kolloquiums. Tübingen.
Weber, M. ([2]1966): *Soziologische Grundbegriffe.* Tübingen.
Weidle, R./Wagner, A.C. (1982): "Die Methode des Lauten Denkens." In: Huber/Mandl (1982), 81–103.
Weingarten, R. et al. (1983): "Strategies of repeated text processing." In: Rickheit/Bock (1983), 207–217.
Weinrich, H. (1966): *Linguistik der Lüge.* Heidelberg.
Welte, W. (ed.) (1982): *Sprachtheorie und Angewandte Linguistik.* Festschrift zum 60. Geburtstag von Alfred Wollmann. Tübingen.
White, P. (1980): "Limitations on verbal reports of internal events: a refutation of Nisbett and Wilson and of Bem." *Psychological Review* 87, 105–112.
Wierlacher, A. (ed.) (1978): *Jahrbuch Deutsch als Fremdsprache.* Volume 4. Heidelberg.
Wiese, R. (1984): "Language production in foreign and native languages: same or different?" In: Dechert et al. (1984), 11–25.
Wilson, T.D. et al. (1981): "Awareness and self-perception: verbal reports on internal states." *Journal of Personality and Social Psychology* 43, 53–71.
Wilss, W. (1977a): *Übersetzungswissenschaft.* Probleme und Methoden. Stuttgart.
Wilss, W. (1977b): "Analytische und hermeneutische Tendenzen in der Übersetzungswissenschaft." *Lebende Sprachen* XXII, 51–58.
Wilss, W. (1977c): "Textanalyse und Übersetzen. Terminologie als angewandte Sprachwissenschaft." In: Bender et al. (1977), 625–651.
Wilss, W. (1978): "Nato-Symposium 'Language Interpretation and Communication'." *Lebende Sprachen* XXIII, 138–140.
Wilss, W. (ed.) (1980a): *Semiotik und Übersetzen.* Tübingen.
Wilss, W. (1980b): "Semiotik und Übersetzungswissenschaft." In: Wilss (1980a), 9–22.
Wilss, W. (1981a): *The Science of Translation.* Tübingen.
Wilss, W. (ed.) (1981b): *Übersetzungswissenschaft.* Darmstadt.
Wilss, W. (1981c): "Das didaktische Potential der Herübersetzung." In: Bausch/Weller (1981), 297–313.
Wilss, W. (1981d:) "Handlungstheoretische Aspekte des Übersetzungsprozesses." In: Pöckl (1981), 455–468.

Wilss, W. (1983): "Translation strategy, translation method and translation technique: a clarification of three translational concepts." *Revue de Phonétique Appliquée* 66/68, 143–152.

Wilss, W. (1985): "Menschliche Übersetzung und maschinelle Übersetzung." *Lebende Sprachen* XXX, 10–15.

Wilss, W./Thome, G. (eds.) (1984): *Die Theorie des Übersetzens und ihr Aufschlußwert für die Übersetzungs- und Dolmetschdidaktik:* Akten des Internationalen Kolloquiums der Association Internationale de Linguistique Appliquée (AILA), Saarbrücken, 25.–30. Juli 1983. Tübingen.

Winograd, T. (1977): "A framework for understanding discourse." In: Just/Carpenter (1977), 63–88.

Winston, P. (ed.) (1975): *The Psychology of Computer Vision.* New York.

Winter, W. (1964): "Impossibilities of translation." In: Arrowsmith/Shattuck (1964), 68–82.

Wintermantel, M./Christmann, U. (1983): "Person description: some empirical findings concerning the production and reproduction of a specific text type." In: Rickheit/Bock (1983), 137–151.

Wolff, D. (1985): "Verstehensprozesse in einer zweiten Sprache." *Studium Linguistik* 17/18, 162–174.

Wolff, D. n.d. [1985]: "Unterschiede beim muttersprachlichen und zweitsprachlichen Verstehen." MS.

Wolff, D. (1987): "Auf- und absteigende Verarbeitungsprozesse bei der Textverarbeitung in einer zweiten Sprache." In: Lörscher/Schulze (1987), 1310–1323.

Wright, A.F. (ed.) (1953): *Studies in Chinese Thought.* Chicago.

Wulz, H. (1979): *Formalismen einer Übersetzungsgrammatik.* Tübingen.

Wunderlich, D. (1974): *Grundlagen der Linguistik.* Reinbek.

Wunderlich, D. (ed.) (1976): *Wissenschaftstheorie der Linguistik.* Kronberg/Ts.

Zammuner, V.L. (1981): *Speech Production.* Strategies in Discourse Planning: A Theoretical and Empirical Enquiry. Hamburg.

Zampolli, A. (ed.) (1977): *Linguistic Structures Processing.* Amsterdam.

Zydatiß, W. (1982): "Text type oriented contrastive linguistics and its implications for translation pedagogy at university level." *International Review of Applied Linguistics in Language Teaching* XX, 175–191.

Subject Index

Author Index